PAUL AND THE CORINTHIANS

SUPPLEMENTS TO
NOVUM TESTAMENTUM

VOLUME CIX

PAUL AND THE CORINTHIANS

Studies on a Community in Conflict.
Essays in Honour of Margaret Thrall

EDITED BY

TREVOR J. BURKE
J. KEITH ELLIOTT

BRILL
LEIDEN · BOSTON
2003

This book is printed on acid-free paper.

Library of Congress Cataloging-in-Publication Data

Paul and the Corinthians : studies on a community in conflict : essays in honour of
  Margaret Thrall / edited by Trevor J. Burke, J. Keith Elliott.
      p. cm. -- (Supplements to Novum Testamentum, ISSN 0167-9732 ; v. 109)
  Includes bibliographical references and index.
  ISBN 90-04-12920-0 (alk. paper)
    1. Bible, N.T. Corinthians--Criticism, interpretation, etc. I. Thrall, Margaret E.
  (Margaret Eleanor) II. Burke, Trevor J. III. Elliott, J. K. (James Keith) IV. Series.

BS2675.52.P38 2003
227'.206--dc21
                                                                    2002033029

BS
2675.52
.P38
2003

ISSN   0167-9732
ISBN   90 04 12920 0

PRINTED IN THE NETHERLANDS

CONTENTS

PART THREE

THEOLOGY IN THE LETTERS

PART FOUR

SECTS, POLEMIC AND THE APOLOGETICS OF PAUL

CONTRIBUTORS

Paul Barnett, Lecturer, Moore Theological College, Sydney and Visiting fellow at Macquarie University, Sydney, Australia

C.K. Barrett, Emeritus Professor of Divinity, University of Durham, UK

Linda Belleville, Professor of New Testament, Northpark Theological Seminary, Chicago, USA

Trevor J. Burke, Head of Department of Biblical Studies and Lecturer in New Testament, Pacific Theological College, Suva, Fiji [Postgraduate, University of Wales, Bangor 1991-1994]

Nina L. Collins, Lecturer in Jewish Studies, School of Theology and Religious Studies, University of Leeds, UK

J.K. Elliott, Professor of New Testament Textual Criticism, School of Theology and Religious Studies, University of Leeds, UK [Undergraduate, University College of North Wales, Bangor 1961-1964]

Gordon D. Fee, Professor of New Testament, Regent College, Vancouver, Canada

Michael Goulder, Emeritus Professor, Department of Adult Education, University of Birmingham, UK

Morna D. Hooker, Former Lady Margaret's Professor of Divinity, University of Cambridge, UK

Jan Lambrecht SJ, Professor Emeritus, Faculty of Divinity, Catholic University of Leuven, Belgium

Clive Marsh, Secretary of the Faith and Order Committee of the Methodist Church of Great Britain, UK [Undergraduate, University College of North Wales, Bangor, 1978-1981]

Margaret Mitchell, Professor of New Testament, University of Chicago Divinity School, USA

Julie Renshaw, M.A. graduate, School of Theology and Religious Studies, University of Leeds, UK

Vernon Robbins, Professor of New Testament, Candler School of Theology, Emory University, Atlanta, Georgia, USA

Christopher M. Tuckett, Professor of New Testament Studies, Faculty of Theology, University of Oxford, UK

Charles Wanamaker, Professor of Religious Studies, University of Cape Town, South Africa

A.J.M. Wedderburn, Professor of New Testament, Institute for New Testament Theology, Evangelical Faculty of Theology, University of Munich, Germany

Bruce Winter, Warden, Tyndale House, Cambridge, UK

Paul Woodbridge, Academic Dean and Tutor in Biblical Studies, Oak Hill College, London, UK [Undergraduate, University College of North Wales, Bangor 1971-1974; post-graduate 1974-1978]

MARGARET E. THRALL

The publication of Margaret Thrall's two-volume commentary on 2 Corinthians in the ICC series marked the culmination of a lifetime's study of Pauline theology. Reviewers have been unanimous in their praise for this achievement; they have recognised the high standard of its scholarship and exegesis, and have placed it in the forefront of commentaries on this epistle. With Horace we may say: Principibus placuisse viris non ultima laus est. Non cuivis homini contingit adire Corinthum.

It is in recognition of that scholarship and her interest in the Corinthian correspondence that this *Festschrift* is presented in honour of Margaret in her seventy-fifth year.

Margaret Eleanor Thrall was born in 1928 in the Nottingham-shire town of Mansfield. She attended the Queen Elizabeth Grammar School there before going up to Cambridge in 1947 to read Classics and Theology at Girton College. After a period of school teaching she returned to Cambridge to study under Professor C.F.D. Moule. Her PhD was conferred in 1960 for her work on the Greek particles in the New Testament. The thesis was subsequently published in 1962; since then it has established itself as a key reference tool regularly to be found cited in many a learned footnote.

In 1962 she was appointed as an assistant lecturer in New Testament in the Department of Hebrew and Biblical Studies under Professor Bleddyn Jones Roberts at the University College of North Wales, Bangor (Coleg Prifysgol Gogledd Cymru). She served as a member of the full-time teaching staff of the Department (later renamed the School of Theology and Religious Studies in the University of Wales, Bangor) until 1983, rising to Reader, an appointment made in 1974. From 1983-1996 she remained as a part time tutor; since 1999 she has been Senior Fellow. In 1997 Margaret was honoured with the award of the prestige Burkitt Medal for services to Biblical Studies by the British Academy.

For many years during her teaching career the Greek text of Paul's letters, especially 1 and 2 Corinthians, was on the syllabus. Students who attended those courses readily recognised that they were being taught by an acknowledged expert and world-class leader in the

subject and their understanding of the complexities of Paul's language and theology were aided by Margaret's enviably lucid lectures
as each problem was teased out and explained in a logical presentation that was a boon to note-takers.

Margaret had long had an interest in ordination and in 1958 wrote
a monograph *The Ordination of Women to the Priesthood*. At that time
the constitution of the Church of England made any ambitions in
that direction impossible for her. However, the disestablished Anglican church in Wales was more congenial and it was as a Deacon
of the Church in Wales that Margaret entered Holy Orders in 1982.
She was ordained Priest in 1997. From 1994-7 she served as Canon Theologian at Bangor Cathedral.

The two editors of this *Festschrift*, Keith Elliott and Trevor Burke,
span both ends of Margaret's academic career in Bangor. The former
was among the first cohort of students awaiting her on her arrival
in 1962; the latter was one of the last students to be supervised by
her shortly before her retirement.

As will be seen in the list of contributors four are former Bangor
students. In addition to the two editors, Paul Woodbridge and Clive
Marsh were students during Margaret's time. Among other contributors are some who were her regular colleagues at specialised learned
conferences, usually on matters Pauline; others shared the Pauline
seminar with her at the annual meetings of Studiorum Novi Testamenti Societas (SNTS). Margaret's visits to study and work in the
United States and at the Catholic University in Leuven, Belgium
made her many friends in both those countries. It is therefore also
appropriate that we have articles too by scholars from America and
Belgium. As an example of how the Corinthian torch is passed on,
two members of the New Testament seminar in Leeds kindly agreed
to contribute a paper.

The committee and membership of SNTS, recognising Margaret's scrupulous and fair-minded scholarship, elected her as the editor
of its Monograph Series, associated with the journal *New Testament
Studies*. She served in this capacity for five years from 1991, which
happened to be a period when a huge number of proposals were
submitted. Margaret's assiduous reading of these many typescripts
resulted in detailed reports. Those manuscripts submitted that were
eventually accepted and published in the Monograph Series with her
imprimatur often carry an appreciation by their authors, in which they
acknowledge in their prefatory words the immense help and guidance they were given by Margaret. We are happy that two of

Margaret's successors on the Board of *New Testament Studies* (Professors Wedderburn and Tuckett) are contributors to this *Festschrift*.

Like those submitting typescripts for publication in the Monograph Series, students taught by Margaret in Bangor also received much written guidance on their work. Her copious annotations on their returned work, unmistakably written with her fountain pen in its characteristically bold jet-black ink, often disconcerted the average undergraduate—initially interested in marks rather than remarks—until they worked through her comments and came to appreciate her kind help and rigorous criticism of their efforts.

In her early years in Bangor Margaret lived as a tutor in the women's hall of residence. There and in her department she was a ready guide, friend and counsellor to generations of undergraduates. Among her academic colleagues she was a popular and respected member of the college staff. In retirement, Margaret continues to live in her adopted country, Wales and has her home in Penrhosgarnedd, not far from the University. She is thus able to maintain contact with the College, her former colleagues and the library.

The following is a select list of Margaret's publications:

BOOKS

The Ordination of Women to the Priesthood (London: SCM, 1958)

Greek Particles in the New Testament: Linguistic and Exegetical Studies (Leiden: Brill, 1962) (*New Testament Tools and Studies* 3)

I and II Corinthians (Cambridge: Cambridge University Press, 1965) (*Cambridge Bible Commentary*)

The Second Epistle to the Corinthians 2 volumes (Edinburgh: T&T Clark, Vol. 1, 1994; vol. 2, 2000) (*International Critical Commentaries*)

ARTICLES

"Ordination of Women to the Priesthood," *Theology* 57 (1954) 330-5

"The Suffering Servant and the Mission of Jesus," *Church Quarterly Review* 164 (1963) 281-8

"Christian Approaches?," *Theology* 69 (1966) 339-45

"The Pauline Use of συνείδησις," *New Testament Studies* 14 (1967-8) 118-25

"The Meaning of οἰκοδομέω in Relation to the Concept of συνείδησις (1 Cor 8,10)," in F.L Cross (ed.), *Studia Evangelia* IV (Berlin: Akademie Verlag, 1968) 468-72 (*Texte und Untersuchungen* 102)

"Elijah and Moses in Mark's Account of the Transfiguration," *New Testament Studies* 16 (1969-70) 305-17

"The Origin of Pauline Christology," in W. Ward Gasque and Ralph Martin (eds.), *Apostolic History and the Gospel* (Exeter: Paternoster Press, 1970) 304-16

"The Bishops and the Nuclear Deterrent," *Theology* 75 (1972) 416-23

"Christ Crucified or Second Adam? A Christological Debate between Paul and the Corinthians," in B. Lindars and S.S. Smalley (eds.), *Christ and Spirit in the New Testament* (Cambridge: Cambridge University Press, 1974) 143-56

"2 Corinthians 1:12: ἁγιότητι or ἁπλότητι," in J.K. Elliott (ed.), *Studies in New Testament Language and Text* (Leiden: Brill, 1976) 366-72 (*Supplements* to *Novum Testamentum* 44)

"Alternative Versions of Christian Faith," *Expository Times* 88 (1976-7) 115-9

"The Problem of 2 Corinthians 6:14-7:1 in some Recent Discussion," *New Testament Studies* 24 (1977) 132-48

"Super-Apostles, Servants of Christ, and Servants of Satan," *Journal for the Study of the New Testament* 6 (1980) 42-57

"'Putting on,' or 'Stripping off,' in 2 Corinthians 5:3," in E.J. Epp and G.D. Fee (eds.), *New Testament Textual Criticism: Its Significance for Exegesis* (Oxford: Clarendon Press, 1981) 221-37

"A Second Thanksgiving Period in 2 Corinthians," *Journal for the Study of the New Testament* 16 (1982) 101-24

"Salvation Proclaimed V; 2 Corinthians 5:18-21," *Expository Times* 93 (1981-2) 227-32

"Conversion to the Lord: The Interpretation of Exodus 34 in 2 Corinthians 3: 14b-18," in L. de Lorenzo (ed.), *Paolo Ministro del Nuovo Testamento (2 Cor. 2:14-4:6)* (Rome: Benedictina, 1987) (*Serie Monografica di 'Benedictina': Sezione Biblico Ecumenico* 9) 197-234

"The Offender and the Offence: A Problem of Detection in 2 Corinthians," in B.P. Thompson (ed.) *Scripture: Meaning and Method* (Hull: Hull University Press, 1987) 65-78

"Paul's Journey to Paradise: Some Exegetical Issues in 2 Corinthians 12:2-4," in R. Bieringer (ed.), *The Corinthian Correspondence* (Leuven: Leuven University Press, 1996) 347-63 (*Bibliotheca Ephemeridum Theologicarum Lovaniensium* 125)

"Paul's Understanding of Personal Continuity between the Present Life and the Life of the Resurrection," in R. Bieringer, V. Koperski and B. Lataire (eds.), *Resurrection in the New Testament: Festschrift J. Lambrecht* (Leuven: Leuven University Press and Peeters, 2002) 283-300 (*Biblioteca Ephemeridum Theologicarum Lovaniensium* 165)

"The Initial Attraction of Paul's Mission in Corinth and of the Church he founded there," in Alf Christopherson, Carsten Claussen, Jürg Frey and Bruce Longenecker (eds.), *Paul, Luke and the Graeco-Roman World. Essays in Honour of Alexander J.M. Wedderburn* (Sheffield: Sheffield Academic Press, 2002) 59-73 (= *Journal for the Study of the New Testament Supplement Series* 217)

INTRODUCTION

Within the last twenty-five years, and in the light of Sanders' epoch-making 'new perspective,' the subject of Paul and the corpus Paulinum have become a storm centre in the scholarly study of the New Testament. Old questions long associated with literary form and historical-criticism have today been replaced by a multi-disciplinary approach to the study of the Pauline letters, including textual and rhetorical criticism, socio-historical background and classics, anthropology and linguistics, to name but a few. This volume brings together these different disciplines in a unique and authoritative collection of essays in the study of two of Paul's letters—1 and 2 Corinthians.

Paul's letters to the Corinthians merit consideration for two main reasons at least. First, 1 and 2 Corinthians is Paul's longest and arguably most important correspondence—he wrote more letters (two out of a possible four are extant) to this church than to any other. Second, and perhaps more importantly, the church at Corinth proved the most troublesome to Paul. Thus, in 1 Corinthians Paul grapples with a range of problems (e.g., factionalism, and sexual immorality) whereas in 2 Corinthians Paul is portrayed at his most personal. In short, 1 and 2 Corinthians provide a fascinating and valuable case study of Paul and life in one of the earliest Christian communities.

This collection of essays on the Corinthian correspondence comprises four sections. In the first section, the four essays are centred around the twin themes of the text and traditions in the Corinthian correspondence. *Keith Elliott* examines a number of key textual variants in 1 and 2 Corinthians with a view to resolving the text critical problems from the standpoint of thoroughgoing textual criticism and to explaining the history of the variation. His focus is on the four contracted forms of the divine names—IC, XC, KC and ΘC—which scribes have carelessly reproduced on many occasions. Whilst some variants are deliberate and arise when a scribe sought to provide an explanation or to avoid apparent ambiguity, others are a result of an expansion due to piety and the influence of liturgical formulae. In general it is the sheer interchangeability and flexibility of these names that is striking, and it seems to have been there from the beginning of the textual transmission.

Margaret Mitchell takes up the subject of the Corinthian correspondence and the birth of Pauline hermeneutics, arguing that it is here that with others (i.e. Paul's opponents) and remarkably with Paul himself the process of interpretation begins. In the first part of the essay Mitchell focuses on the place of 2 Cor. 8 within the Corinthian correspondence, contending that this chapter was the first portion of 2 Corinthians which Paul sent and is best situated between 1 Corinthians and 2 Cor. 2:14-7:4. Having established the sequence of the letters to the Corinthians, she then considers three stages of the interpretative process: first, there is the question of Paul as self-interpreter in the writing of his letters; second, his readers' responses to them; and, finally, Paul's retrospective hermeneutics in dialogue with his readers. In the light of this dialogue, one can easily see how misunderstandings could easily arise.

Christopher Tuckett, in keeping with the recent trend in studies regarding the Paul-Jesus debate, considers the importance of non-canonical evidence. In particular, Tuckett reflects on the apparent 'quotation' of Paul in 1 Cor. 2:9 and the parallel in the Gospel of Thomas 17. He argues that 1 Cor. 2:9 may have been known and employed by the Corinthians but there is no evidence to suggest it was known as a saying of Jesus or that the apostle Paul knew it as such. Moreover, there is no indication that Paul has altered the saying in order to fit the Corinthian context as a means of 'improving' the behaviour of the Corinthians. He concludes that the saying in GTh 17 may be due to Thomas' own redaction and that any development between Paul and the synoptic gospels may run *from* Paul *to* the gospel tradition rather than vice versa.

Nina Collins argues that the structure of a rabbinic statement *a fortiori* indicates that Paul's statements at 2 Cor. 3:9; 3:7-8 and 3:11 were composed in this order, rather than the order they now appear in his text. This analysis also discusses the main theme of Paul's statements and suggests why the reading τῇ διακονίᾳ is probably the preferred variant for 2 Cor. 3:9.

The second section is concerned with the application of new research methodologies, which blend together sociological and rhetorical scholarship on Paul in order to provide new insights into the text. *Trevor Burke* uses insights from linguistics and the classics to discuss

Paul's paternal relations with his Corinthian children (1 Cor 4:14-21). First, he shows how Paul is drawing on the biological family in antiquity in order to understand Christian relations as a family. He then identifies a number of stock meanings of the father-child relationship in antiquity before turning to the text. Burke argues that one of the problems in the Corinth community was that of competing households, a problem compounded by the fact that others (e.g., Apollos) had followed Paul's founding of the church. In response, Paul stresses his pre-eminent role as *paterfamilias* and the need for his convert-children to behave in accordance with the normal social conventions of the ancient world. While Paul's main goal is to unite the contentious household churches under his common paternity, the point is also made that the Corinthian community—one of the earliest—could be more hierarchical in structure than is usually thought.

Charles Wanamaker argues that Paul confronts the factionalism at Corinth (1 Cor.1-4) by the only means available to him—a rhetoric of power. After laying the necessary theoretical basis, that of the theory of ideology, the author moves on to define key concepts such as power, domination, and the social and political strategies of those who use them. Wanamaker demonstrates how these are embedded in Paul's discourse, especially the first four chapters of Corinthians which are marked by one of the most sustained uses of the language of power in any of Paul's extant letters. Paul's apostolic status and privileged position, his carefully chosen metaphorical language (i.e., agricultural, architectural, and familial) all serve the purpose of re-affirming or reestablishing Paul's own power while disempowering others (e.g., Apollos).

Bruce Winter carries out a statistical analysis of the number of words compared with the number of lines used by Paul in writing 1 Corinthians. This examination reveals that forty-five per cent is devoted to a cluster of issues concerning conflicts and forty-eight per cent to the problems of compromise by Corinthian Christians. Their origins can be traced to the heart of first-century culture where conflicts were endemic and conformity to agreed norms epitomised the relationship in this class-ridden Roman colony. Part of Paul's letter writing strategy is uncovered by an examination of cluster issues. His 'final' solution to the impact of these two social 'underlays' are not to be found at the end of each of those individual discussions but in his assaults on them in chapters 12-15 of 1 Corinthians.

Clive Marsh takes a key text, 1 Cor.1:10-17, and adopts a reader-response approach to uncover the dynamic between the text and its receivers. By the use of a contemporary case-study, Marsh argues that 1 Corinthians 1 invites the reader to enter imaginatively into a likely scenario within which Paul's meaning can be understood. This does not mean overlooking the communal context of such a reading or the historical-critical concerns of the text which are important in order to be 'true to Paul'. Such loyalty is located in the text's theological meaning within the context of Paul's thought as a whole. In this passage, Paul's christological concerns remain uppermost and throughout his theology and here Paul underplays aspects of human disunity in his desire to assert oneness in Christ. The case-study underscores the complexity of disunity and that Christians read 1 Corinthians as scripture within the context of community, but always from a variety of other communal contexts in which Christ seeks to become present.

Julie Renshaw makes connections between Boolean Logic and the theological arguments that Paul employs in his epistles. She begins by explaining three specific Boolean Logic conditions after which a number of examples from the Corinthian correspondence of each condition are given consideration. Boolean Logic is used in computer circuitry today and the author suggests that it may have its roots in the rhetorical education of the Graeco-Roman world, which was so popular in the days of the apostle Paul.

The third section has to do with the fact that the Corinthian correspondence is sometimes regarded as lacking in theological content. However, as the following essays make clear, Paul is here concerned with *doing* theology in the sense that it is applied.

Gordon Fee responds to a recent study by C.C. Caragounis, who has taken exception to the growing consensus that in 1 Corinthians 7:1-7 Paul is citing from, but sharply qualifying, the position of the Corinthian believers that "it is good for a man not to have sexual relations with a woman." Caragounis objects that both the traditional view (that Paul was conceding marriage) and the new consensus (that Paul is urging continued sexual relations within marriage) are predicated on a false attribution that the Corinthians were "uniquely lascivious". He thus offers a new meaning for πορνεία in verse 2 (a metonymy for marriage, as also, he argues, is the idiom "to touch a woman" in verse 1) and a more common meaning for συγγνώμη in verse 6 (Paul is begging their "pardon" for intruding like this into their private lives). This paper offers another look at the data regarding the idiom "to touch a woman" pointing out again that it consistently serves as a euphemism for sexual relations. Caragounis's suggested new meanings for the two words in question are then examined and found wanting. Thus, it is concluded, the emerging consensus has good reason for having become so.

Linda Belleville discusses the issue of head-coverings in 1 Cor. 11:2-16 and argues that far too little attention has been paid to vv. 3 and 11 within the context of the pericope. All too often, Paul's overriding concern has been reduced to that of flaunting social conventions regarding head-coverings where the specifics of the passage have been dismissed on the basis of cultural ignorance *vis-à-vis* first century Graeco-Roman customs. Drawing on recent social scientific research, Belleville argues that the problem is not a breach of etiquette but is more to do with theology, the worship of God, and in particular appropriate gender-based forms of worship.

Morna Hooker takes another look at 2 Cor. 1:17-24 where Paul bases his answer to the charge that he is guilty of vacillation on the faithfulness of God himself. Here, as elsewhere, he links the statement that 'God is faithful' with the belief that God's people will also be faithful. Paul shares in God's faithfulness by his incorporation into Christ, who is himself the embodiment of God's faithfulness, the 'Yes' to all his promises. Since in Christ there is always a 'Yes', not 'Yes and No', the same is true of Paul's own word to the Corinthians. He reminds them of the word he and his companions had originally proclaimed to them, namely, the gospel about Jesus Christ the Son of God: their preaching was the 'Amen' to the divine 'Yes' spoken in Christ. Since Paul, together with the Corinthians, is being 'confirmed in Christ', everything he does and says is reliable. The Corinthians, together with Paul, 'stand firm in faith'. This passage supports the view that the faithfulness of Christ the Son of God who was like God was the basis of believers' own faith and faithfulness.

Paul Woodbridge grapples with the eschatological problem of when Paul believed Christians would receive their resurrection body. Two key passages (1 Cor. 15 and 2 Cor. 5) are said to give inconsistent teaching on this subject: the former teaches that this will happen at the *parousia*, whereas 2 Cor. 5 appears to teach this will occur at the moment of death when the heavenly body is received. In response to the apparent development in Paul's thinking, Woodbridge shows that it is possible to understand 2 Cor. 5 not in terms of a change or development but rather in terms of fitting in with Paul's overall teaching on the time a believer receives the resurrection body, which was at the parousia.

In his exegesis of 2 Cor. 4:7-5:10 *Jan Lambrecht* compares the differing nuances between Margaret Thrall and Hans Betz regarding Paul's use of the term 'body'. At issue is Paul's understanding of the relationship between the outer and inner self. Lambrecht argues that for Paul the term 'body' is not just an aspect of the person. In 2 Cor. 5:1-10, as in 4:17-8, there is no radically holistic use of the term sôma. Because the human being constitutes a living unity, the "body" (as e.g., the "heart") is representative of the whole. Of course, in order to stress the unity of this dually composed human being, one can say that Paul is his body, but he is more than his body. Therefore, one can also say that Paul has an earthly body. Moreover, in the eschaton Paul and all Christians expect a glorified, "spiritual" body, which implies a somatic existence.

Sandy Wedderburn takes up what is arguably one of Paul's most curious statements in 2 Cor. 5:14. The understanding of the relationship between Christ and the 'all' presupposed in this text and the logic of Paul's statements there have led to a wide range of suggestions, and raise the question how Paul's readers would have followed his line of argument. Both the Graeco-Roman world and Jewish traditions offer points of contact, but no complete parallels. The relationship between the one and the many, either synchronically or diachronically, whether for good or ill, the idea of dying for or instead of others, but not the idea that the one dies for others and saves them by drawing them into his death so as to share it is novel and remarkable. This death of the one can at the same time be viewed as a 'speech-act' in which the many pass with the one under the judgement of God declared in that death.

The final section concerns the subjects of Paul's opponents, apologetics and visions in the Corinthian letters, which have long been contentious issues among commentators. *Kingsley Barrett* addresses the many questions and disagreements which the Corinthians had to raise with Paul and argues that it is unlikely that all came from the same group of dissidents. In addition to the Paul, Cephas and Apollos groups, Barrett posits many others besides (e.g., celibate, Gnostic, anti-resurrection groups) and Paul moves from one practical issue to another in addressing these needs. The situation in 1 Corinthians, appears different to the one confronting the apostle in 2 Corinthians, or is it? Barrett argues that the old problems encountered by Paul in 1 Corinthians have not gone away but have been eclipsed by a new, hazardous problem which took the form of a personal attack on Paul by an anti-Paul party with whom Paul now has to deal.

Michael Goulder acknowledges Margaret Thrall's helpful critique of his earlier exegesis of 2 Cor. 12:1-5 but still contends Paul is critical of visionary claims. Paul's opponents have been accusing him of lack of visions and Goulder argues that the 'man in Christ' is not Paul's own personal experience of having seen a vision but instead he is relating someone else's experience. There is no description of the Merkabah and it is strongly stressed that the man said nothing of what he had seen. Moreover, the "in/out of the body" language passage suggests Paul's impatience with visionary claims. To Paul's mind the gospel is not about having experienced the glory of God; rather it is about the coming of the glory of Christ into the world and Christ himself is the image of God. Paul's resistance to visionary claims here is consistent with what he says elsewhere in the Corinthian correspondence and the rest of the New Testament.

Paul Barnett considers Paul's apologetic language in 1 Cor. 9:3 and 2 Cor. 12:19a which signals significant but varying attacks on Paul— his style, apostolic qualifications, integrity, and grasp of the gospel. Paul's mission strategy of 'foundation laying' then moving on invited problems in the fledging assemblies in their interface with the dominant Graeco-Roman and Jewish cultures from which the converts had come. In Corinth, however, Paul faced special additional problems. Apollos and Cephas, each of whom possessed qualities quite different to Paul's, had visited the church and many of the issues Paul faced in Corinth appear to have arisen from their visits, though not necessarily at their instigation. Much of 1 and 2 Corinthians is in the nature of a 'defence' or 'apologia' arising from the ministry of these men.

Vernon Robbins draws attention to the paucity of references by commentators on 2 Corinthians to the third/fourth century work the *Apocalypse of Paul*. Robbins redresses this imbalance by examining how the writer of the *Apocalypse of Paul* constructed a complete work from 2 Cor.12:2-4. Although he does not directly address 2 Cor.12:2-4, Robbins gives due attention to the phrases 'visions and revelations of the Lord' (2 Cor. 12:1) and 'hearing unutterable words' (2 Cor.

12:4) before discussing Paul's body and the journey of souls when the bodily existence is vacated. This essay is important for it not only sets a context for interpreting New Testament texts, which take us through to the stages of later antiquity but also shows how early Christians developed a first century rhetorolect into multiple apocalypses through to the third and fourth centuries. In particular, we see the resources of invention at work as early Christians sought to elaborate apocalyptic *topoi* through amplificatory description.

PART ONE

TEXT AND TRADITIONS

THE DIVINE NAMES IN THE CORINTHIAN LETTERS

J.K. Elliott

Many text-critical variants concern the *nomina sacra*. Editors of the Greek New Testament need to resolve these variants when printing a critically established text. Commentators must also heed such matters.

We shall concentrate in this essay on the four names that are invariably contracted in the manuscripts, namely $\overline{\text{IC}}$ $\overline{\text{XC}}$ $\overline{\text{KC}}$ and $\overline{\Theta\text{C}}$. In this context conventional wisdom often informs us that scribes were prone to expand divine names out of piety or under the influence of liturgical practice or the lectionary text, and that therefore the original text of the New Testament authors should be the variant with the simplest form. Conversely, we are told that scribes would be disinclined to omit the *nomina sacra* deliberately from the texts. Another commonly expressed opinion concerns the many variants where the mss. are divided over $\overline{\text{KC}}$ and $\overline{\text{IC}}$ (or $\overline{\text{XC}}$) and $\overline{\text{KC}}$ and $\overline{\Theta\text{C}}$; it is said that the apparent ambiguity of $\overline{\text{KC}}$, which may mean either Jesus or God, encouraged scribes to opt for a more precise name in preference to the original $\overline{\text{KC}}$, and that therefore *v.l.* (= *varia lectio*) $\overline{\text{KC}}$ is to be preferred as the original reading.

It is also pointed out in some introductory guides that the large number of variants involving the exchange of the abbreviated *nomina sacra* especially $\overline{\text{IC}}$ $\overline{\text{KC}}$ $\overline{\text{XC}}$ and $\overline{\Theta\text{C}}$ was precisely because these contracted forms (typically the initial letter and the last letter) looked alike and one *nomen sacrum* could be accidentally misread as another and therefore be mis-copied. (Such an observation, even if true, would not of course help us to solve the direction of change in textual variants involving the substitution of the one for the other.)

All of those guidelines may be correct in some instances, but none must be applied mechanically without regard to the contexts and the author's discernible preferences. It is Paul's established practice and the context of the variants that will concern us in this essay.

Many variants also concern the sequence of the combined names $\overline{\text{IC}}$ and $\overline{\text{XC}}$. Logic may suggest that the sequence should have $\overline{\text{IC}}$ first with $\overline{\text{XC}}$ as the designation following. Obviously once $\overline{\text{XC}}$ was being seen less as a title and increasingly as a proper name then scribes would have less compunction in reversing the names. We shall examine that argument too.

To establish our author's preferences and usage we need to look to firm examples (that is, examples where the recorded manuscript evidence is united and for which no deviation has been reported as yet). Restricting ourselves to examples in the Corinthian correspondence for the purpose of this study, we shall separate the title in which $\overline{\text{KC}}$ is present, preceding or following $\overline{\text{IC}}$ $\overline{\text{XC}}$/ $\overline{\text{XC}}$ $\overline{\text{IC}}$, from those instances where $\overline{\text{KC}}$ is either not present or where its presence is not firm. (Later we examine variants involving other instances of *v.ll.* concerning $\overline{\text{KC}}$ and also variants involving $\overline{\text{ΘC}}$.)

A.
Where $\overline{\text{KC}}$ is present and firm.
1) When '[Our] Lord' precedes 'Jesus Christ' or 'Christ Jesus':
   i) In the formula του $\overline{\text{KY}}$ ημων[1] $\overline{\text{IY}}$ $\overline{\text{XY}}$ (genitive). An asterisk denotes that there are variants involving the presence of 'Jesus' and/ or 'Christ' (see below A3):[2]
1 Cor. 1:2, 7, 8*, 10 (but D reads $\overline{\text{XY}}$ $\overline{\text{IY}}$ του $\overline{\text{KU}}$ ημων); 5:4pr. * (and note word-order variant *4-5, 1-3* $\overline{\text{IY}}$ $\overline{\text{XY}}$ του $\overline{\text{KY}}$ ημων in minuscule 81), 5:4sec.*, 5:5* ; 6:11*; 15:57 (again, note word order *4-5, 1-3* in majuscules 0121 0243 and cf. 1 Cor. 15:31); 16: 23*; 2 Cor. 1:3, 14*; 8:9*; 11:31* (a reading not given in the apparatus of NA = Nestle-Aland 27th ed.). [The word order in 81 and in 0121 0243 noted here is unlikely to be original, given the prevalence of the order with $\overline{\text{KC}}$ preceding, but see 2 below.]
The phrase in the accusative occurs at 1 Cor. 16:22*.
   ii) In the formula 'Lord Jesus Christ' (nominative or genitive):
1 Cor. 1:3 (grace, cf. 1 Cor. 16:23; 2 Cor. 1:2; 13:13); 8:6; 11:23*; 2 Cor. 1:2*; 13:13*

2) Where '[Our] Lord' follows 'Jesus Christ':
1 Cor. 1:9 (a sequence demanded in the context)

---

[1] ημων is not firm at 1 Cor. 5:4*bis*, 5; 6:11; 16:22, 23; 2 Cor. 1:14; 11:31. These are discussed below pp. 7-8.
[2] The apparatus here has been assembled from NA[27], UBS[4], von Soden, Tischendorf[8], *Text und Textwert* II,2 (*ANTF* 17), and *Das Neue Testament auf Papyrus* (hereafter *NTAP*) II,2 (*ANTF* 12)—only a sample of the witnesses appears in this article.

1 Cor. 9:1 where the inversion may be explained by the unusual word order of the whole sentence. (*v.l.* om. $\overline{XV}$ P[46] ℵ A B 0150 and cf. $\overline{XV}$ $\overline{IV}$ FG).

1 Cor. 15:31 εν $\overline{XW}$ $\overline{IY}$ τω $\overline{KW}$ ημων: εν $\overline{KW}$ D*. In view of the fact that the understandable sequence in 1 Cor. 1:9 (and possibly also at 1 Cor. 9:1) are the only exceptions we must consider that here the reading by D* alone could be original.

3) Where $\overline{XC}$ and/ or $\overline{IC}$ is disputed (i.e. those places asterisked above A 1 i and ii):

1 Cor.

1:8 om. $\overline{XY}$ P[46] B, a reading that has influenced NA which brackets the name. As $\overline{IY}$ $\overline{XY}$ occurs in vv. 7 and 9 the longer reading could have been due to assimilation to these neighbouring verses but the title 'Our Lord Jesus' is less common than 'Our Lord Jesus Christ.'

5:4pr. om. $\overline{XY}$ A B D* Ψ. 'Our Lord Jesus' follows in the verse in these mss. The shortening of the title could therefore be due to assimilation in order to create an exact parallel. Other mss. read the fuller title '(Our) Lord Jesus Christ' (P[46] D[2] F G L P maj). These are mss. that show a tendency to read the full title elsewhere. Fee (*Commentary*[3] p. 198) says that the later scribal addition of $\overline{XY}$ relates to the syntactical problem of finding which verb the prepositional phrase modifies.

5:4sec. The readings here are a) του $\overline{KY}$ 630 1739 *pc.*; b) του $\overline{KY}$ ημων $\overline{IY}$ $\overline{XY}$ P[11] D[2] F G L; c) του $\overline{KY}$ ημων $\overline{IY}$ *cett*. Only (a) and (b) fit Paul's style. Maybe (a) is correct, the others being expanded forms based on 5:4pr. Zuntz[4] favours (a). Fee says that if $\overline{IY}$ were original, its omission could only have been accidental through homoioteleuton.

5:5 $\overline{KY}$: + $\overline{IY}$ P[61] ℵ L Ψ maj.; + $\overline{IY}$ $\overline{XY}$ A D F G P (some of these mss. add ημων—see below, under 'Possessive'). Fee, *Commentary*, thinks that the shorter reading is the likeliest and states that the expression 'The Day of the Lord' is decisive, drawing attention to that term in 1 Thess. 5:2; 2 Thess. 2:2, although in the latter *v.l.* $\overline{XY}$ is read by D[2] maj. Fee also ignores 1 Cor. 1:8 (see above). Also see 2 Cor. 1:14 following.

---

[3] G.D. Fee, *The New International Commentary on the New Testament: The First Epistle to the Corinthians* (Grand Rapids: Eerdmans, 1987).

[4] G. Zuntz, *The Text of the Epistles* (London: Oxford University Press, 1953), 235

6:11 om. $\overline{XY}$ A D² L Ψ etc. Metzger, *Textual Commentary*,[5] in a signed dissentient note in his *Textual Commentary*, argues that the shorter reading is original, given the general scribal tendency to expand divine names. This is a constant thesis in his notes and commentary but we need to treat that advice with caution because in certain contexts (such as a formal grace) our author himself may favour a fuller title. Fee (*Commentary*) says $\overline{XY}$ was added for liturgical reasons, then the possessive was added at an even later stage of development. (On the presence or absence of the possessive see further below.)

11:23 $\overline{IC}$ $\overline{XC}$ 2 221 257 314 319ᶜ 378 823; om. $\overline{IC}$ $\overline{XC}$ B 328 383; $\overline{IC}$ *cett.* $\overline{XC}$ here in this narrative looks like a scribal expansion but $\overline{KC}$ $\overline{IC}$ is unusual (see below). The omission of $\overline{IC}$ ($\overline{XC}$) has probably been encouraged by $\overline{KC}$ alone earlier in the sentence.

16:22 $\overline{KV}$: + (ημων) $\overline{IY}$ $\overline{XY}$ ℵ² C³ D F G K L P Ψ etc. This seems to be a good example of a scribal expansion of a title, especially in this context.

16:23 (grace) om. $\overline{XY}$ ℵ* B 33. Here the longer form seems plausible, appearing as it does in a formal grace (see 1 Cor. 1:3). Metzger, *Textual Commentary*, argues in favour of $\overline{IY}$, despite the fact that the longer reading is characteristic of the benedictions at Rom. 16:24; 2 Cor. 13: 13 *q.v.*; Gal. 6:18; Phil. 4:23; 1 Thess. 5:28; 2 Thess. 3:18; Philm. 25. Again, he emphasises the tendency of scribes only to increase the divine names.

2 Cor

1:2 om. $\overline{XY}$ 075. The grace (with $\overline{XY}$) is firm at 1 Cor. 1:3: this suggests that the same formula should occur here too.

1:14 om. $\overline{XY}$ all except ℵ² D* F G P 0121 0242. 'The Day of the Lord Jesus' may be said to have attracted a growing tradition: first + $\overline{XY}$ then + the possessive, but, as we see below, the combination 'Lord Jesus' is not firm in these letters.

8:9 om. $\overline{XY}$ B*. See below on 'Lord Jesus'.

11:31 $\overline{KY}$ $\overline{IY}$: + $\overline{XY}$ Hᶜ K L 049 0150 0151; om. $\overline{IY}$ 216. The context, stating the relationship of God the Father to Jesus, suggests that Paul would have written 'the Lord Jesus Christ' here. For *v.l.* +/- ημων see below, under 'Possessive'.

---

[5] B.M. Metzger, *A Textual Commentary on the* Greek *New Testament (*Stuttgart: Deutsche Bibelgesellschaft and the United Bible Societies, 2nd ed. 1994).

13:13 om. $\overline{XY}$ B Ψ. Again, the firm example of a grace at 1 Cor. 1:3 may be decisive in favour of the full title here as at the *v.ll.*. at 1 Cor. 16:23; 2 Cor. 1:2. Thrall, *Commentary*,[6] says that B Ψ have the shorter form at 1 Cor. 16: 23 but, according to the apparatus in *NTAP*, Ψ has + $\overline{KY}$. If it were correct, that would show this scribe's inconsistency of practice at the endings of 1 and 2 Cor.

Were we to accept $\overline{KC}$ $\overline{IC}$ (i.e. without 'Christ') at 1 Cor. 5: 4pr.; 11:23; 16:23; 2 Cor. 1: 14; 8:9; 13:13 this would result in a title of which there are no firm examples in these letters.[7] So, in none of these places do I advocate reading $\overline{KC}$ $\overline{IC}$.

Possessive

The possessive is firm at 1 Cor. 1:8; 2 Cor. 8:9; it is disputed at 1 Cor. 5:4pr. om. ℵ A Ψ a (and, as a consequence, is bracketed in NA); 5:4sec. om. P46 P Ψ 629 (but see above, where we accept *v.l.* om. ημων $\overline{IY}$); 5:5 + ημων A F G P 0150; 6:11 possessive in only B Cvid P and, according to Metzger, *Textual Commentary*, is due to assimilation to the possessive following; 16:22 + ημων K P; 16:23 + ημων A L P 056 075 0142; 2 Cor. 1:14 om. P46 A C maj. (and bracketed in NA) ; 11:31 + ημων D P 056 075 *pc*.

On the basis of those places where the possessive is firm (1 Cor. 1:8; 2 Cor. 8:9) I am inclined to accept as original the full title 'Our Lord Jesus Christ' elsewhere. Where the possessive is not firm, the issue is more complex and may suggest an evolution from a simple title to the addition of another name and later the further adding of the possessive. There the original would have been expanded out of piety to conform to the full, firm title. If, however, we think our author would have shown consistency in such matters then we should accept the variant giving the full title including the possessive at 1 Cor. 5:4pr., 5; 6:11; 16:22, 23; 2 Cor. 1:14; 11:31.

In all the instances above (even where the names 'Jesus Christ' occur only in disputed readings as at 1 Cor. 5:5; 11:23) the sequence is always 'Jesus' followed by 'Christ'. There is no instance of the reverse. If we argue that the presence of $\overline{KC}$ preceding $\overline{IC}$ $\overline{XC}$ in the formula in the genitive is decisive because it determines

---

[6] Margaret E. Thrall, *The Second Epistle to the Corinthians* 2 vols. (Edinburgh: T. & T. Clark, 1994, 2000) (= *International Critical Commentary*).

[7] 1 Cor.12: 3 is clearly different.

unambiguously the case and that is why $\overline{\text{IC}}$ can precede $\overline{\text{XC}}$, such an argument is of minimal importance. (As Thrall, *Commentary* p. 81, says, both names would as it were have been read and pronounced in one breath and 'Jesus', whatever the case, would not have been understood in isolation.) Also we see that $\overline{\text{IC}}$ $\overline{\text{XC}}$ is the natural order even in those rare instances where $\overline{\text{KC}}$ follows.

B.

i) Where $\overline{\text{KC}}$ occurs as a variant (see also G below):

1 Cor.

1:30 + τω $\overline{\text{KW}}$ $\overline{\text{IY}}$ (*sic*) 056; + τω $\overline{\text{KW}}$ ημων 0142. These readings look like expansions.

4:17 om. $\overline{\text{IY}}$ A B D² L P Ψ ($\overline{\text{IY}}$ is bracketed in NA); $\overline{\text{KW}}$ $\overline{\text{IY}}$ D* F G; $\overline{\text{XW}}$ $\overline{\text{IY}}$ *cett.* Again, we may we witnessing an expansion from an original $\overline{\text{XW}}$ to + $\overline{\text{IY}}$ and then $\overline{\text{XW}}$ misread as $\overline{\text{KW}}$ later. (On the improbability of 'Lord Jesus' being original see above.)

16:24 + τω $\overline{\text{KW}}$ ημων lect. 592; om. εν $\overline{\text{XW}}$ $\overline{\text{IU}}$ 075 81 and lectt. 597, 598, 895, 1356, 1977. These are interesting readings to find in lectionary texts.

2 Cor

4:5pr. om. $\overline{\text{KV}}$ P; om. $\overline{\text{IV}}$ 913 1610. $\overline{\text{KY}}$ could have been omitted through hom. There is no obvious reason why $\overline{\text{IY}}$ was omitted.

4:10pr. $\overline{\text{IY}}^1$: $\overline{\text{XY}}$ D* F G ; $\overline{\text{XY}}$ $\overline{\text{IY}}$ D¹; $\overline{\text{KY}}$ $\overline{\text{IY}}$ K L Ψ; $\overline{\text{KY}}$ ημων $\overline{\text{IY}}$ 0142. The reference here is to the death of Jesus which leads us to favour Jesus *simpliciter* as in the Gospels. Cf. v.14 following.

4:14 τον $\overline{\text{KV}}$ $\overline{\text{IV}}$: om. $\overline{\text{KV}}$ P⁴⁶ B 33 (an attestation that results in the word being bracketed in NA); om. τον $\overline{\text{KV}}$ 0243 33 640 1739; τον $\overline{\text{KV}}$ $\overline{\text{IV}}$ $\overline{\text{XV}}$ 056 0142 1845.

Thrall, *Commentary* note 1055, accepts that the shorter reading is an assimilation to Rom. 8:11, referring to Jesus' being raised from the dead. Simple $\overline{\text{IC}}$ has preceded in vv. 10-11 as befits the context.[8] But Metzger, *Textual Commentary*, argues that assimilation to Rom. 8:11 is not nearly as strong as the ever-present tendency to expand the divine titles.

---

[8] See J. Lambrecht, "The nekrosis of Jesus: Ministry and Suffering in 2 Cor. 4: 7-15" in A. Vanhoye (ed.), *L'apôtre Paul: Personnalité, style et conception du ministère* (*BETL* 73, Leuven: Leuven University Press, 1986), 120-43 here 128 note 26.

8:23 $\overline{XY}$: $\overline{KY}$ C F ; + $\overline{IY}$ 048. δοξα + $\overline{KY}$ occurs at 2 Cor. 3:18; 8:19. There is no example of δοξα + $\overline{IY}$ in the NT. (At 2 Cor. 4:6 δοξα is followed by $\overline{\Theta Y}$.) Therefore read $\overline{XY}$.

ii) places without $\overline{KC}$ but where there are *v.ll.* concerning the presence or absence of $\overline{IC}$ and/or $\overline{XC}$:

1 Cor.

1:2pr. om. $\overline{IY}$ 056 0142 . The shortening may have been influenced by εν $\overline{XW}$ earlier in this verse.

4:15 εν...$\overline{XW}$ $\overline{IY}$: om. $\overline{IY}$ B. εν $\overline{XW}$ stands alone without $\overline{IY}$ at 1 Cor. 3:1; 4:10 (*v.l.* εν $\overline{KW}$ P[11]); 4:15; 15:18, 22; 2 Cor. 3: 14; 5:17, 19; 12:2, 19sec. (*v.l.* om. P[46] 075).

2 Cor.

2:10 $\overline{XU}$: $\overline{\Theta Y}$ 33; + $\overline{IY}$ 1149 1872 (cf. 2 Cor. 4:6 under C below).

2:14 $\overline{XW}$: + $\overline{IY}$ P[46] and cf. 3:14 *v.l.* $\overline{IY}$ $\overline{XY}$ 69.

4:5 $\overline{IV}$[2]: $\overline{XY}$ א[1]; $\overline{IY}$ $\overline{XY}$ 0186; $\overline{IV}$ $\overline{XV}$ 629 630; $\overline{XV}$ 056 0142 (cf. the reading of these two mss. at 1 Cor. 1:2 above). Metzger, *Textual Commentary* prefers $\overline{IV}$ or possibly $\overline{IY}$ but views the longer readings with 'Christ' as pious expansions.

4:10sec. + $\overline{XY}$ P[46] D* F G 0186. ζωη του $\overline{IY}$ follows showing Paul's practice for this phrase. I am disinclined to see the variant as an assimilation to this occurrence.

4:11 του $\overline{IY}$: του $\overline{IY}$ $\overline{XY}$ D* F G ; $\overline{XY}$ C; om. 1311. It is interesting to note that D F G here and in the preceding reading show a tendency to favour expanded forms. The omission of IY by 1311 is likely to be a careless error.

4:14sec. $\overline{IY}$: + $\overline{XY}$ 216 242 326 385 440. This too looks like a later expansion. IC *simpliciter* after a preposition may be seen at 2 Cor. 4:11pr.

5:18 (not shown in the apparatus of NA) $\overline{XY}$: $\overline{IY}$ $\overline{XY}$ D[2] K L 049 056 075 0142 0151. 056 0142 seem to be prone to adjusting the *nomina sacra*. $\overline{XC}$ with $\overline{IC}$ follows in the next verse—perhaps that shows Pauline usage but may equally show that the reading here was influenced by or assimilated to that later, fuller title.

C.

We may now be in a position to resolve the variants where the order of 'Jesus' and 'Christ' is disputed:

1 Cor

1:1 $\overline{XY}$ $\overline{IY}$ P[46] B D F G; $\overline{IY}$ $\overline{XY}$ א A L P Ψ

2:2 $\overline{IV}$ $\overline{XV}$: $\overline{XV}$ $\overline{IV}$ F G 2 1827 2143

3:11 I̅C̅ X̅C̅: X̅C̅ I̅C̅ C² D 0150 (and *v.l.* om. I̅C̅ C*)
9:1 I̅V̅ (X̅V̅): X̅V̅ I̅V̅ F G

2 Cor.
1:1 X̅Y̅ I̅Y̅ A D mins; I̅Y̅ X̅Y̅ P⁴⁶ B (and *v.l.* om. both names F).
Thrall, *Commentary* pp. 81f. accepts X̅Y̅ I̅Y̅.
1:19 I̅C̅ X̅C̅: X̅C̅ I̅C̅ ℵ* A C 0223 (and *v.l.* om. X̅C̅ 33). Thrall,
Commentary, ad loc note 219 keeps an open mind on this variant (unlike
her comment on 2 Cor. 4:5pr. see below).
4:5pr. I̅V̅ X̅V̅ K̅V̅ P⁴⁶ ℵ A C etc (= NA²⁷); X̅V̅ I̅V̅ K̅V̅ B H maj
(= NA²⁵). Thrall, *Commentary* note 855, prefers the order I̅V̅ X̅V̅
because that 'conforms to the confessional formula in Phil 2:11 and
Acts 11:17', although fails to point out that *v.ll.* reverse the order at
Phil. 2:11, and that a *v.l.* in A has K̅C̅ precede at Acts 11:17. On
the *v.ll.* omitting K̅Y̅ and I̅Y̅ see above.
4:6 I̅Y̅ X̅Y̅: X̅Y̅ I̅Y̅ D F G 0243 (and *v.l.* om. I̅Y̅ A B). Metzger
and Wikgren in dissenting notes in the *Textual Commentary* prefer the
reading by A B; they draw the comparison with 2 Cor. 2:10 where
the phrase 'the face of Christ' occurs. They claim that the name
'Jesus' was added later either before or after and they ask why an
original 'Jesus' would have been omitted. NA brackets I̅Y̅. Thrall,
Commentary, ad loc note 876 prefers X̅Y̅ arguing that *v.l.* + I̅Y̅ is a
pious expansion. (Cf. 2 Cor. 2:10 above, under B ii.)
13:5 I̅C̅ X̅C̅ B D Ψ maj; X̅C̅ I̅C̅ ℵ A F G P 0150 0243. Thrall,
Commentary, ad loc note 152, prefers I̅C̅ X̅C̅.

Read X̅Y̅ I̅Y̅ at 1 Cor. 1:1; 2:2; 2 Cor. 1:1: K̅Y̅ does not preceed,
thereby unambiguously showing the case, so X̅Y̅ has to take
precedence before I̅Y̅ to show that this is genitive.[9] Read I̅C̅ X̅C̅ at
1 Cor. 3:11; 2 Cor. 1:19pr.; 13:5 because I̅C̅ first shows the case
unambiguously. Likewise read I̅V̅ X̅V̅ at 1 Cor. 9:1; 2 Cor. 4:5pr.
Ev seems to require 'Christ' to precede 'Jesus', a point recognised
by Thrall, *Commentary* pp. 81f. 1 Cor. 1:4 serves as a firm example.
This usage would rule out the *v.l.* εν I̅Y̅ X̅W̅ at 2 Cor. 2:17 by 38.
Obviously an exhaustive survey would ideally look at all comparable examples in the authentic Pauline corpus, but I doubt if such
a further study would overturn the conclusions just reached on the
basis of examples found in only 1 and 2 Corinthians.

---

[9] As proof of this practice note that at 1 Cor. 1:10 instead of του K̅Y̅ ημων
I̅Y̅ X̅Y̅ ms. D reads X̅Y̅ I̅Y̅ του K̅Y̅ ημων

D.
$\overline{XC}$

$\overline{XC}$ alone is found some 30 times in 1 Cor., and *c*.19 times in 2 Cor. excluding the formula εν $\overline{XW}$ already covered above, but there are variants at the following:

1 Cor.

1:6 $\overline{ΘΥ}$ B* F G. This reading is likely to be original given the parallel use of $\overline{ΘΥ}$ after μαρτυριον at 1 Cor. 2:1 (*v.l.* μυστηριον).

2:16 $\overline{KΥ}$ B D* F G due to assimilation to $\overline{KΥ}$ preceding.

9:12 $\overline{KΥ}$ C* acc. Lyon; $\overline{ΘΥ}$ 056 0142. As we have already noted above the two uncials 056 0142 are often indiscriminate in their treatment of the *nomina sacra*. ευαγγελιον is often unqualified but where it is qualified it is followed by $\overline{XY}$ at 1 Cor. 2:12 *v.l.*; 9:13; 10:14 *v.l.*; and see 1 Cor. 9:18 following.

9:18 + του $\overline{XY}$ D² F G K L P Ψ (*pace* NA27) etc. Possibly this reading is the result of assimilation to 1 Cor. 9:21.

9:21 $\overline{ΘW}$ 056 0142. Again, we are disinclined to follow the lead of these two mss. in such variants.

10:9 $\overline{XV}$: P⁴⁶ D F G etc. $\overline{KV}$ ℵ B C P; $\overline{ΘV}$ A; om. 927 1729 1985 2102 2659. The likeliest reading is $\overline{XV}$. It is the more difficult reading because readers found the concept of Christ in the wilderness strange. Origen read $\overline{XV}$ and based Christological arguments on it. Marcion also knew $\overline{XV}$. $\overline{ΘV}$ seems to be a reading that was assimilated to the LXX.[10]

10:16sec. $\overline{KΥ}$ D* F G. $\overline{KC}$ is ambiguous and that may indicate its originality here. αιμα $\overline{XY}$ however occurs at Eph. 2:13; Heb. 9:14; 1 Pet. 1:2, 19. The rare αιμα $\overline{KΥ}$ is not firm at 1 Cor. 11:27.

2 Cor

2:12 $\overline{ΘΥ}$ 33 38 1912 cf. 1 Cor. 9:12; 2 Cor. 9:13; 10:14 for the author's preference for $\overline{XY}$ with ευαγγελιον.

4:4 $\overline{XY}^1$: $\overline{KΥ}$ C; $\overline{ΘΥ}$ 255. Pauline practice is varied: δοξα + $\overline{ΘΥ}$ 2 Cor. 4:6 *v.l.* $\overline{KΥ}$; + $\overline{KΥ}$ 2 Cor. 3:18; 8:19; + $\overline{XY}$ 2 Cor. 8:32 (a different idea).

4:4 $\overline{XY}^2$: $\overline{KΥ}$ C; $\overline{ΘΥ}$ 255. Christ is God's εικων at Col. 1:15-20. $\overline{ΘΥ}$ may have come in accidentally on account of $\overline{ΘΥ}$ following.

---

[10] For a full discussion on this verse see C.D. Osburn, "The Text of 1 Corinthians 10:9" in E.J. Epp and G.D. Fee (eds.), *New Testament Textual Criticism: Its Significance for Exegesis. Essays in Honour of Bruce M. Metzger* (Oxford: Clarendon Press, 1981), 201-21.

5:14 $\overline{\Theta Y}$ C P. αγαπη $\overline{\Theta Y}$ occurs at 2 Cor. 13:13 and indicates our author's usage.

5:15 και[1] + $\overline{XC}$ F G 206 823 *pc.* This looks like an explanatory addition.

10:14 $\overline{XY}$ (after ευαγγελιον): $\overline{\Theta Y}$ Ψ cf. 1 Cor. 9:21 above.

11:2 $\overline{KW}$ 642 1311; $\overline{\Theta W}$ 69. The context needs $\overline{XW}$—see next verses. $\overline{\Theta Y}$ earlier in the sentence may have caused the change.

11:10 om. D*. This may be a sheer error.

E.
$\overline{IC}$

$\overline{IC}$ alone occurs at 1 Cor. 12: 3pr. in a confessional formula. 1947 reads $\overline{IV}$ $\overline{XV}$. At 12:3sec. 606, 1718, 1929, 2523 read $\overline{IV}$ $\overline{XV}$ but neither variant is likely to be original, as it is probable that the formula reads only 'Jesus' alone both times. $\overline{IC}$ is also firm at 2 Cor. 4:11pr. At 2 Cor. 11:4 in the distinctive expression 'another Jesus' the *v.l.* $\overline{XV}$ occurs in FG (these two mss. are not reliable in this regard).

F.
$\overline{\Theta C}$

Although this name occurs frequently there are, surprisingly, a large number of variants:

1 Cor

1:4 om. του $\overline{\Theta Y}$ A* 056 0142 (056 0142, already noted as unreliable witnesses to the original text of the *nomina sacra*, also omit $\overline{IY}$ at 1 Cor. 1:2, and see 2:9; 3:10; 4:15 below); cf. 1:14 om. ℵ* B 424[c]. At 1:14 the noun follows ευχαριστεω as at 1 Cor. 1:4; 14:18 where the noun is firm. At 1 Cor. 1:4 the noun qualifies χαρις (cf. 1 Cor. 3:10 below). The noun could have been omitted accidentally at 1:14 through hom: ευχαρισTWTW$\overline{\Theta W}$. NA inconsistently brackets τω $\overline{\Theta W}$ at 1:14 because of the external witnesses for the omission.

1:29 $\overline{\Theta Y}$: αυτου C* Ψ. $\overline{\Theta C}$ occurs three times in the context and is probably original here too because εξ αυτου following needs its antecedent.

2:9 om. ο $\overline{\Theta C}$ 056 0142. See 1:4 where we indicate our reluctance to follow these particular mss.

2:14 om. του $\overline{\Theta Y}$ 2 216 255 330 440 823 *pc.* (after πνευμα). A careless omission; this noun is commonly—but not invariably—qualified.

3:10 om. του Θ̄Ῡ P⁴⁶ (see 8:3 below) 056 0142 (see 1 Cor. 2:9). Although there are *v.ll.* concerning the noun qualifying χαρις at 1 Cor. 1:4; 3:10, Θ̄Ῡ is firm after χαρις at 1 Cor. 15:10; 2 Cor. 6:1; 9:14.

4:4 + Θ̄C̄ D*. This looks like an addition to explain Κ̄C̄ εστιν.

7:40 Χ̄Ῡ P¹⁵ 33 after πνευμα cf. 1 Cor. 2:14. In the N̄T̄ πνευμα is qualified by ῙῩ, Κ̄Ῡ, Χ̄Ῡ, and Θ̄Ῡ.

8:3 om. P⁴⁶. This ms. omits υπ' αυτου later in this sentence. Both the noun (and the pronoun) are needed in the context. The omissions may be mere carelessness.

8:6 om. Θ̄C̄ ℵ*. An omission through homoioteleuton: ειϹΘϹΟ.

11:3 Χ̄C̄ C (a nonsensical reading here).

12:3 om. Θ̄Ῡ P after πνευμα. This reading could be either a careless omission or an explanatory addition.

12:6 Κ̄C̄ 1738; om. 177 337 618; Χ̄C̄ 1354 1736 1890; Κ̄C̄ και Θ̄C̄ 1943. Θ̄C̄ makes better sense alongside ο ενεργων.

2 Cor.

1:1 om. 489. Cf. 1 Cor. 1:1 where the noun is firm in the same formula.

2:15 om. τω Θ̄W̄ K 0151. Possibly scribes found this concept difficult and therefore dropped the name deliberately.

2:17 Θ̄Ῡ: Χ̄Ῡ Ψ. λογος του Θ̄Ῡ occurs at 1 Cor. 14:36; 2 Cor. 4:2. λογος του Χ̄Ῡ occurs only twice in the NT (in Col. and Heb.). Χ̄C̄ follows and may have influenced the scribe to place it here too.

3:7 θανατου: Θ̄Ῡ ℵ* !

4:4sec Χ̄Ῡ 378. The term εικων του Θ̄Ῡ occurs at Col 1:15 and may indicate it is original here too.

4:6 του Θ̄Ῡ: αυτου P⁴⁶ C* D* F G cf. Eph. 1:12, 14: 3:6. After δοξα (as in next variant): this noun is qualified by Θ̄Ῡ at 1 Cor. 10:31; 11:7. Possibly αυτου is original here and Θ̄Ῡ is a later explanatory change. At 4:15 Κ̄Ῡ is read by 056 0142 (and again we are disinclined to accept their reading as potentially original) .

5:18 om. του Θ̄Ῡ 0243. One would need good arguments before considering accepting the reading of only one ms. in such a variant. Other such variants may be seen at 2 Cor. 6:16 (Κ̄C̄ 69); 10:4 (Χ̄W̄ 0209); 11:2 (om. Θ̄Ῡ 0243).

9:12 $\overline{XW}$ B 181. For the use of $\overline{\Theta W}$ after ευχαριστεω cf. 1 Cor. 1:4 *v.l.*; 1:14 *v.l.*; 14:18.

12:19 $\overline{\Theta Y}$: $\overline{XY}$ 436 642. Possibly $\overline{XY}$ has been accidentally written here because εν $\overline{XW}$ follows.

G.
$\overline{KC}$

$\overline{KC}$ is firm some 79 times in 1 and 2 Cor. In addition to those variants already dealt with (under B i above) there are variants at:
1 Cor.

7:17 $\overline{KC}$....$\overline{\Theta C}$ P⁴⁶ ℵ A B; $\overline{\Theta C}$... $\overline{\Theta C}$ Ψ 629 1881; $\overline{KC}$.... $\overline{KC}$ ο $\overline{\Theta C}$ G; $\overline{\Theta C}$.... $\overline{KC}$ maj.; $\overline{KC}$...$\overline{KC}$ 1319 2004. Fee, *Commentary* says God is the one who assigns in Rom. 12:3; 2 Cor. 10: 13 but that theological subtlety here requires the Lord (= Jesus) to assign and God to call. That subtlety seems to have been lost on scribes.

7:23 $\overline{KW}$: $\overline{\Theta W}$ F G. The context requires $\overline{KC}$ to be repeated, but that is possibly what a scribe thought.

11:23 απο του $\overline{KY}$: παρα $\overline{\Theta Y}$ F G. The variant removes the ambiguity because $\overline{KC}$ following = Jesus.

11:27 $\overline{KY}$²: $\overline{XY}$ A 33 489. The sentence as originally constructed is well-balanced, suggesting $\overline{KY}$ is original.

11:29 σωμα: + του $\overline{KY}$ ℵ² C³ D F G etc; + του $\overline{KY}$ $\overline{XY}$ Ψ. Both variants seem to be explanatory glosses. Fee, *Commentary* thinks that the additions destroy the sense and come from the influence of v.27. There is, as we have noted earlier, no firm occurrence of $\overline{KC}$ $\overline{XC}$ in the Corinthian letters, but see Col. 3:24.

14:37 $\overline{KY}$: $\overline{\Theta Y}$ A 1739ᶜ 1881. εντολη του $\overline{KY}$ occurs at 1 Cor. 7:19 and may indicate this variant is original.

15:47 ανθρωπος²: $\overline{KC}$ 630; + ο $\overline{KC}$ ℵ² A D¹ K L maj. $\overline{KC}$ is an exegetical addition which makes Paul's original soteriological or eschatological statement Christological. The replacement of ανθρωπος² with $\overline{KC}$ loses the balanced structure of the sentence.

2 Cor.

5:6 $\overline{KY}$: $\overline{\Theta Y}$ D* F G . The addition removes the ambiguity as is also the case at 2 Cor.

5:8 $\overline{\Theta V}$ D* (again); 5:11 $\overline{\Theta Y}$ 1611 1867 2005*; 8:21 του $\overline{\Theta Y}$ P⁴⁶; 11:17 [$\overline{\Theta V}$] a f r t; $\overline{KY}$ 326; 12:1 $\overline{XY}$ F G.

6:17 om. λεγει $\overline{KC}$ K 1739 but cf. 6:18 and the phrase is likely to be there twice in these quotations.

8:5 $\overline{\text{KW}}$: $\overline{\Theta \text{W}}$ P[46] 547 a f r. Scribes have probably been influenced by $\overline{\Theta \text{C}}$ following.

The above examination reveals on many occasions the carelessness of scribes concerning the reproduction of the divine names. Some variants, however, are deliberate to provide explanations or to avoid apparent ambiguity. Sometimes an expansion may be due to piety and the influence of liturgical formulae. But in general it is the sheer interchangeabilty and flexibility of these names that is striking, and it seems to have been there from the beginning of the textual transmission.

THE CORINTHIAN CORRESPONDENCE AND THE BIRTH OF PAULINE HERMENEUTICS[1]

Margaret M. Mitchell

I. *Introduction of Thesis*

The epistolary archive preserved in canonical 1 and 2 Corinthians constitutes an inestimably valuable resource for the reconstruction of early Christian missionary tactics and conflicts, the social composition of the Pauline churches, and the development of Paul's theology in the crucible of dispute, debate and distrust which came to characterize his relationship with this key collection of house churches in the Roman province of Achaia. Scholars have drawn upon this raft of source material abundantly in recent research, which in the last decades has focused significant attention on the social history of the early Pauline communities.[2] The data these documents contain, however, do not merely lie on the surface of the text ready to be plucked and statistically applied to demographic or social-historical

---

[1] It is an honor to contribute this essay to celebrate the scholarship of Margaret E. Thrall, whose commentary on 2 Corinthians is a model of patient, painstaking research and clarity of vision in untangling the multiple threads of the puzzles inherent in this letter (*A Critical and Exegetical Commentary on the Second Epistle to the Corinthians* [ICC; 2 vols.; Edinburgh: T. & T. Clark, 1994, 2000]). The argument of the present essay, especially in regard to the literary composition of 2 Corinthians, differs from that of Dr. Thrall, but it stands in the same spirit of ongoing conversation as the remark with which she prefaces her commentary: "What is presented here is one possible reading of 2 Corinthians. There are certainly other plausible interpretations, and other methods of studying the epistle. I offer my own understanding of it simply as a contribution to the continuing debate concerning this highly complex document" (p. xi).

[2] The seminal works were Gerd Theissen, *The Social Setting of Pauline Christianity. Essays on Corinth* (ed. and trans. J.H. Schütz; Philadelphia: Fortress, 1982) and Wayne Meeks, *The First Urban Christians. The Social World of the Apostle Paul* (New Haven: Yale University Press, 1983). Much research has followed, and the discussion continues in vigorous fashion, as evidenced by the recent debate over Justin J. Meggitt's *Paul, Poverty and Survival* (Edinburgh: T. & T. Clark, 1998); see the reviews by Theissen and Dale B. Martin, and Meggitt's reply, in *JSNT* 84 (2001) 51-94. The relevant point for this essay is that the evidence of the Corinthian correspondence continues to dominate the debate, even as its meaning and generalizability are vigorously disputed.

questions. A single exemplar of this fact is the surface-simple but much disputed sentence in 1 Cor 1:26—"not many (of you) are wise according to the flesh, not many powerful, not many of noble birth"— which has led to a range of interpretive options about the social status and economic power of these early urban Christians.[3] What this single case (which can be multiplied exponentially) shows is that historical research cannot proceed without astute and careful literary and rhetorical analysis of the source texts in question. Hence all interpreters, regardless of the major focus of their particular questions, stand before the Pauline letters asking what these words mean.

In this connection I would like to propose another distinction for the Corinthian archive, namely that it also marks, to a large degree, the inauguration of Pauline interpretation itself—both in terms of the meaning of specific utterances and of hermeneutical perspectives on that art itself. It is in 2 Corinthians that we have the first unambiguously attested piece of interpretation of Paul's letters (albeit a not entirely complimentary one) from a reader in the early church (in 10:10). But what is perhaps even more remarkable, 1 Cor 5:9-11; 2 Cor 2:3-9 and 7:8-12 contain Paul's *explicit interpretation of his own letters*. Hence, and this is my thesis, Pauline interpretation begins with Paul himself, in the very act of composing those letters which still continue, at quite some distance, to preoccupy our interpretive energies. Moreover, Paul's self-interpretive work in the Corinthian letters comprises not just the determination of meaning in individual cases (though it does include that), but also very valuable reflections on hermeneutics in general. The following three passages more than adequately illustrate this point:

1. 2 Cor 3:1-3 is a sustained reflection on the nature of "text," reader and author, and the art, function and politics of reading.[4]

---

[3] See, for example, discussion in Dieter Sänger, "Die δυνατοί in 1 Kor 1,26," *ZNW* 76 (1985) 285-91; Andreas Lindemann, *Der Erste Korintherbrief* (HNT 9/I; Tübingen: Mohr/Siebeck, 2000) 49-50.

[4] Richard Hays gives an important discussion of the ways in which the entire chapter of 2 Corinthians 3 is and is not focused on hermeneutics, particularly arguing against the traditional interpretation of the passage as providing a justification for allegorical over literal exegesis, concluding: "2 Cor. 3:12-18, though it does not aim at providing hermeneutical guidelines, certainly is a text laden with hermeneutical implications" (*Echoes of Scripture in the Letters of Paul* [New Haven: Yale University Press, 1989] 146). I agree wholeheartedly, and would add to Hays' subtle interpretation, which emphasizes the passage's reflections upon the nature of textual exegesis in relation to ecclesiology and ethics, that on an even more primary level it concerns the question of what is a text, what is an author, and who are its

2. 2 Cor 10:10-11 explores the central ancient (and modern) epistolary and textual dynamics of παρουσία and ἀπουσία, λόγος and ἔργον, as well as the requirement for an author to have an integrated self, and to be responsible for the effect of his words on others.

3. 2 Cor 2:4-9; 7:8-12 constitutes a Pauline exegesis of both the wording and the textual effects of his earlier letter, focusing on the hermeneutics of temporality (how the meaning of a text shifts in time as its purposes either do or do not come to pass) as well as how authorial intention—both at the time of composition and in later reflection—impacts the meaning of a text.

These few examples stunningly document the fact that the letters now found in 1 and 2 Corinthians are not only documents which *require* hermeneutical attention,[5] but they are themselves sophisticated and spirited reflections on the art,[6] science, work, and difficulty of interpretation—i.e., of comprehensible communication between human persons as mediated, facilitated, and confused by written texts and oral utterances about them.[7] The concurrence of these two hermeneutical preoccupations in this particular correspondence is not accidental, for it is the actual debates over textual meaning which have (not surprisingly) occasioned Paul's more abstract and general hermeneutical expositions which figure so conspicuously in his interactions with this Achaean community.

Proceeding from serious consideration of these facts, the goal of this paper is to demonstrate that the Corinthian letters are themselves a striking illustration of a crucially important fact not always sufficiently recognized in Pauline scholarship: that the meaning of Paul's letters *is not and never was* a fixed and immutable given awaiting discovery, nor was it transparent in the moment of their initial reading, but it was (and is) negotiated in the subsequent history of

---

readers—basic hermeneutical elements which are less developed in Hays' discussion.

[5] It is quite remarkable, for instance, that all the topics in the methodological reflection on "Hermeneutics and 2 Corinthians" in Frances Young and David F. Ford, *Meaning and Truth in 2 Corinthians* (Grand Rapids: Eerdmans, 1988) 139-65 are at stake already *in the letter itself*, between Paul and his earliest readers.

[6] I have argued that Pauline interpretation needs to be taken seriously as an artistic endeavor in *The Heavenly Trumpet: John Chrysostom and the Art of Pauline Interpretation* (*HUTh* 40; Tübingen: Mohr/Siebeck, 2000; Louisville: Westminster/John Knox, 2002).

[7] One simple index of this is that the term ἔγραψα occurs eight times in the Corinthian letters, but only four other times in the Pauline corpus (Rom 15:15; Gal 6:11; Philem 19, 21; cf. προέγραψα in Eph 3:3).; see also n. 54 below.

the relationship between Paul and those he addressed by his letters, who individually and together wrangle with the text and its possibilities of meaning. Meaning emerges through the living and ongoing relationship between epistolary author and readers who together in their subsequent conversations and encounters register, assess and volley different perceptions of the text as they engage in their ongoing relationship. While this process of negotiating meaning must have attended each Pauline letter (think of Galatians, for instance!), it is only in the Corinthian correspondence[8] that we have the astonishing opportunity to watch it unfold before our very eyes, and hence can explore some of the interpretive strategies at play in the process of the development of Pauline hermeneutics at its inception.

II. *The Corinthian Correspondence as an Inner-Interpretive Process*

A. *The Literary Composition of 1 and 2 Corinthians*

The Corinthian archive provides us with the fullest body of evidence in the Pauline corpus of a succession of letters and verbal exchanges back and forth between Paul and his correspondents; this amounts to a history of reception, interpretation and reinterpretation of the letters themselves, which have been the vehicle for a long-distance relationship at risk. However, in order to avail ourselves of this remarkable opportunity to trace not only *Corinthian readings* of Paul's letters, but also *Paul's own* retrospective interpretations of them, one must formulate a literary-critical hypothesis toward a reconstruction of the original documents. In an earlier article I have proposed the following reconstruction of the letter fragments which have been redacted to form canonical 1 and 2 Corinthians:[9]

---

[8] This is true if one holds, as I do, that 2 Thessalonians is a pseudepigraphon, and that 1 Thessalonians and Philippians are single, not composite, letters. Wayne Meeks has also pointed out that Paul "is interpreting himself" in Rom 14:1-15:13, which Meeks convincingly maintains is a revision of 1 Corinthians 8-10 ("The Polyphonic Ethics of the Apostle Paul," *In Search of the Early Christians* [Allen R. Hilton and H. Gregory Snyder, eds.; New Haven: Yale University Press, 2002] 196-209, 204). But because the addressees of the two letters are different, the hermeneutical process of self-interpretation is necessarily not the same as the succession of letters to the Corinthians themselves.

[9] Margaret M. Mitchell, "Korintherbriefe," *Religion in Geschichte und Gegenwart*, 4th ed. (Hans Dieter Betz, et al., eds.; Tübingen: Mohr Siebeck, 1998-) 4.1688-94.

1. *A Previous Letter from Paul to the Corinthians*, not extant (mentioned in 1 Cor 5:9)

2. 1 Corinthians (entire, 1:1-16:24) *A Deliberative Letter Urging Concord*

3. 2 Cor 8:1-24 *Fund-raising Follow-up Letter*

4. 2 Cor 2:14-7:4 (minus 6:14-7:1) *Self-defense of the Maligned Messenger*

5. 2 Cor 10:1-13:10 *The Letter of Tears—Ironic Self-Defense of Apostolic Legitimacy*

6. 2 Cor 1:1-2:13; 7:5-16; 13:11-13 *The Letter toward Reconciliation*

7. 2 Cor 9:1-15 *Final Fund-raising Letter to Achaia*

My partition theory is based upon the foundational research by J.H. Kennedy, Johannes Weiss, Günther Bornkamm and Hans Dieter Betz.[10] What is unique about my proposal (in addition to the characterizing titles, which give some hint of how I regard each letter rhetorically and exegetically) is the placement of 2 Corinthians 8 in the succession of letters. I shall not here repeat the insights of Bornkamm and Betz about the literary and historical disruptions and connections which point to these seven missives as having been originally separate,[11] but shall give a brief summary of the main

---

[10] James Houghton Kennedy, *The Second and Third Epistles of St. Paul to the Corinthians* (London: Methuen, 1900); Johannes Weiss, *Earliest Christianity* (2 vols., trans. F.C. Grant; New York: Harper, 1959 [German original 1917]) 1.344-49; Günther Bornkamm, "Die Vorgeschichte des sogennanten zweiten Korintherbriefes," *Sitzungsberichte der Heidelberger Akademie der Wissenschaften, Philologisch-historische Klasse* (Heidelberg: Winter, 1961) 7-36 (I cite the original pagination; this essay was twice republished: in Bornkamm's *Gesammelte Aufsätze*, vol. 4 [*Geschichte und Glaube* (vol. 2; *Beiträge zur evangelischen Theologie* 53; Munich: Kaiser, 1971) 162-190, with a Nachtrag on pp. 190-94], and in an abbreviated English version published as "The History of the Origin of the So-Called Second Letter to the Corinthians," *NTS* 8 [1962] 258-63); Hans Dieter Betz, *2 Corinthians 8 and 9: A Commentary on Two Administrative Letters of the Apostle Paul* (Hermeneia; Philadelphia: Fortress, 1985). For a comprehensive summary of the evidence and arguments, and of the history of research, which goes back to Johann Salomo Semler in 1776, see Betz, *2 Corinthians 8 and 9*, 3-36; Thrall, *Second Epistle to the Corinthians*, 1.1-77, and Victor Paul Furnish, *II Corinthians* (AB32A; Garden City, NY: Doubleday, 1984) 29-55. On the proposition that 1 Corinthians is a single deliberative letter, not a collection of fragments, see Margaret M. Mitchell, *Paul and the Rhetoric of Reconciliation: An Exegetical Investigation of the Language and Composition of 1 Corinthians* (HUT 28;Tübingen: J.C.B. Mohr Siebeck, 1991; Louisville: Westminster/John Knox, 1993).

[11] The key issues have to do with the independent status of chaps. 10-13, which most critical scholars accept, and, less universally held, the isolation of 2:14-7:4 (leaving aside 6:14-7:1) as a letter separate from chaps. 1-7 (or 1-8 or 1-9). For the arguments, see Weiss, *Earliest Christianity*, 1.344-49 (whose complete partition theory

arguments in support of my novel proposal that 2 Corinthians 8 was the first portion of 2 Corinthians to be sent.[12]

B. *The Place of 2 Corinthians 8 in the Corinthian Correspondence*

The strongest piece of evidence for the historical placement of 2 Corinthians 8 is the exact parallelism in both content and expression between 2 Cor 12:17-18 and 2 Cor 8:6, 18:

12:18: παρεκάλεσα Τίτον	καὶ συναπέστειλα τὸν ἀδελφόν
8:6 παρακαλέσαι ἡμᾶς Τίτον[13]	8:18 συνεπέμψαμεν δὲ μετ' αὐτοῦ τὸν ἀδελφόν

If 2 Cor 12:17-18 is a retrospective reference to Titus' being sent by Paul, along with an unnamed brother, to Corinth on the financial business of the collection, as occurs exactly in 2 Corinthians 8, then that missive must have *preceded* 2 Corinthians 10-13.[14] Since allegations of financial malfeasance appear already in 2 Cor 2:14-7:4, it seems likely that 2 Corinthians 8 came before it. Once placed between 1 Corinthians and 2 Cor 2:14-7:4 on this inference, further strong exegetical connections appear in both directions (back to 1 Corinthians, forward to "The Self-Defense of the Maligned Messenger") which also resolve some significant historical puzzles. 2 Corinthians 8 is a continuation of the same deliberative rhetoric Paul employed in 1 Corinthians,[15] in which he praises the Corinthians for their attainments but pushes them to a next step (see the remarkable parallel and progression in 1 Cor 1:5 and 2 Cor 8:7). Indeed, the

---

of both letters is more complex than the seven letters argued for here), Bornkamm, "Vorgeschichte," 21-23; and Thrall, 1.20-25 (who after weighing the considerations on both sides decides against the separation of 2:14-7:4). The other major consideration is the literary integrity and independence of chapters 8 and 9 (on which see Betz, *2 Corinthians 8 and 9*; Thrall, *Second Epistle to the Corinthians*, 1.36-43).

[12] The full proof for this placement of 2 Corinthians 8 will be found in my forthcoming essay "Paul's Letters to Corinth: The Interpretive Intertwining of Literary and Historical Reconstruction," in the volume, *Urban Religion in Roman Corinth*, edited by Daniel Schowalter and Steven Friesen (which will publish the papers from the conference held at Harvard in January, 2002).

[13] Cf. 8:17: τὴν μὲν παράκλησιν ἐδέξατο.

[14] "The coincidence in wording as well as substance makes it virtually certain that Paul is here looking back ... upon the mission planned in chapter viii" (C.K. Barrett, *The Second Epistle to the Corinthians* [Harpers New Testament Commentaries; San Francisco: Harper & Row, 1973] 325).

[15] See Mitchell, *Paul*, 20-64 on 1 Corinthians, and Betz, *2 Corinthians 8 and 9*, 41-70 on 2 Corinthians 8:1-15 as "the advisory section" (he regards 8:16-23 as "the legal section: commendation and authorization of the envoys").

two letters share, almost word for word, three deliberative appeals
that are found nowhere else in the Corinthian correspondence—or,
for that matter, in the entire Pauline corpus (1 Cor 7:6//2 Cor 8:8;
1 Cor 7:25//2 Cor 8:10; 1 Cor 7:35//2 Cor 8:10). This rhetorical
consistency in employment of deliberative argumentation of persuasion
(toward unity in the first instance, toward contributing to the collection in the second) reflects the same outlook by Paul on the Corinthian
situation, and hence may logically be an indication of temporal
proximity. By marked contrast, the rest of the letters in 2 Corinthians
(except chap. 9) will engage in forensic defense arguments, because
the conditions have devolved into an atmosphere of distrust, accusation and alienation.

My proposed placement of 2 Corinthians 8 can also contribute to
what may be the largest puzzle on the landscape of Corinthian studies:
what accounts for this deterioration in Paul's relationship with the
Corinthians? I propose that the perceived shift in the situation between 1 and 2 Corinthians can in large part be explained by the
effects of 2 Corinthians 8 itself,[16] for Paul changed the original plan
he had set in motion for the proper administration of the collection
in 1 Cor 16:1-4, in particular by usurping the prerogative he had
promised the Corinthians, namely to δοκιμάζειν the envoys to bring
the collection to Jerusalem. In 1 Cor 16:3 Paul promised that those
he would send would be οὓς ἐὰν δοκιμάσητε; in 2 Cor 8:22 συνεπέμ-
ψαμεν δὲ αὐτοῖς τὸν ἀδελφὸν ἡμῶν ὃν ἐδοκιμάσαμεν. This act—of
taking it upon himself to write a letter of recommendation[17] for Titus
and the brothers to carry out Paul's long-distance financial business—
engendered Corinthian enmity against Paul on precisely the matters at issue in the next letter, 2 Cor 2:14-7:4: *letters of recommendation*
and who needs them (2 Cor 3:1-3; cf. 5:12; 6:4); identification of
those who have been legitimately entrusted with a divine διακονία
(2 Cor 3:5-8; 4:1; 6:3-4, etc.; cf. 2 Cor 8:4, 19, 20);[18] and, above all,
financial malfeasance cloaking itself as gospel-proclamation (2:17; 4:1-
5; 6:8-10; 7:2). There are, therefore, many good reasons to think
that 2 Corinthians 8 was the first of the documents in the letter
collection now preserved in 2 Corinthians to have been sent, and
that it played a crucial role in the escalation of the conflict.

---

[16] And 1 Corinthians (see pp. 24 ff. below).

[17] For a formal analysis 2 Corinthians 8, especially 8:16-24, see Betz, *2 Corinthians
8 and 9*, 70-86.

[18] And therefore has the right to make bold requests (with παρρησία [3:12; 7:4]).

C. *The Corinthian Correspondence as a History of Negotiated Epistolary Meaning*

All reconstructions of the literary development of the Corinthian correspondence depend upon the crafting of a plausible historical scenario for the progression of events within which they were situated. My proposal for the succession of letters takes very seriously the role each missive itself played in the ensuing events and seeks to highlight the agency of the letters themselves in the unfolding crises and their (eventual) resolution. We shall see how this assumption allows us to follow the train of events revealed when one reads the letters according to the chronological succession I am proposing, and see how in each letter Paul was responding to a reading or readings of his prior missive.

Sometime in the early 50s Paul founded the Christian cells or house churches in Corinth, where he engaged in a ministry of sufficient duration that his financial support (or refusal of such) became an issue. He reports that his "foundational preaching" was met with belief and acceptance (1 Cor 2:1-5; 3:10f.; 15:11); and the evidence of 1 Cor 1:22-24 suggests that success was among Jews and Gentiles, though 1 Cor 12:2 seems to indicate a preponderance of the latter. After Paul left Corinth he wrote a letter back to the new Christ-believers there which (presumably among other things) told them not to associate with πόρνοι, "the sexually immoral." We cannot know if this letter was a response to an actual instance of immoral conduct known to Paul and the Corinthians, or a proleptic warning stemming from Paul's previous experience enculturating Gentiles into the new moral code of the God of Israel (cf. 1 Thess 4:3: ἀπέχεσθαι ὑμᾶς ἀπὸ τῆς πορνείας).[19] This first letter was either misunderstood, disobeyed, or both, for when Paul next wrote, within a very long and carefully composed letter urging the divided Corinthian house churches to become reunified, he alludes to it (5:9) in the course of his censure of a man "who has his father's wife" (5:1). What role might Paul's previous letter have played in the escalating factionalism at Corinth? Certainly it had a hand in it, for one issue around which the church had become divided by the time Paul wrote 1 Corinthians was πορνεία, which Paul treats at great length in chaps.

---

[19] From this it is clear that Paul associates πορνεία and εἰδωλολατρία with the Gentiles (μὴ ἐν πάθει ἐπιθυμίας καθάπερ καὶ τὰ ἔθνη τὰ μὴ εἰδότα τὸν θεόν [1 Thess 4:5]), a view common in Hellenistic Judaism (as, e.g., in Wisd 14:12: Ἀρχὴ γὰρ πορνείας ἐπίνοια εἰδώλων).

5-7 (and again, by allusion, in connection with the idol meat controversy, in 10:8). This can be seen also in Paul's description of their
response to the notorious act of πορνεία (τοιαύτη πορνεία ἥτις οὐδὲ
ἐν τοῖς ἔθνεσιν, 5:1) as "puffed up" (πεφυσιωμένοι ἐστέ, 5:2) and
"boasting" about it (οὐ καλὸν τὸ καύχημα ὑμῶν, 5:6), both of which
are stock elements of Pauline and general Greco-Roman rhetoric
about contentiousness.[20] Another clue that Paul's earlier letter had
troubled at least some Corinthians is to be found in 7:1—they wrote
him back addressing the precise topic of sexual behavior (περὶ δὲ
ὧν ἐγράψατε), and perhaps, if 7:1b is a quotation, included their
own definition of sexual boundaries that even exceeded Paul's call
to shun πόρνοι—καλὸν ἀνθρώπῳ γυναικὸς μὴ ἅπτεσθαι (7:1). We
do not know to what extent this view is consonant with that expressed
in Paul's earlier letter, but at the least it served to move his earlier
epistolary teaching closer to the middle, by contrast, and invited
further, more conciliatory teaching on marriage and partnership in
his own, now third missive in succession between the epistolary
partners, in 1 Corinthians 7.

Paul wrote 1 Corinthians to urge the house churches, which were
divided on many levels (historically, geographically, ethnically, socio-
economically, ritually, theologically) to become reunified as the single
temple of God or body of Christ. His argument employed a careful
and somewhat conventional strategy of shared praise for spiritual
attainments (1:4-9), then common censure of factionalism in general (1:11-4:21), followed by conciliatory treatments of the key issues causing division, seeking throughout to unite the ἐκκλησία in
the face of the outside world.[21] The consistent rhetorical strategy of
the letter is an appeal to Paul himself as the exemplar of loving,
sacrificial concession for the sake of the greater good—unity and
peace—whom he calls upon *all* Corinthians to emulate (see especially 4:16 and 11:1, but also throughout the letter).[22] The final chapter
of 1 Corinthians shows that, in addition to this appeal in the body
of the letter (repeated as an ἀνακεφαλαίωσις in 16:13-14), Paul is-
sued some concrete commands which would later prove controversial. The first was the elevation of his partisans, Stephanas and his
house, to positions of authority in the ἐκκλησία, and the second was
the inauguration of an administrative plan and structure for the ex-

---

[20] Mitchell, *Paul*, 91-95, 228-230.
[21] Ibid., 184-295.
[22] Ibid., 49-60.

ecution of a fund-raising effort "for the saints" in Jerusalem (16:1-4). The way Paul introduces the topic (περὶ δὲ τῆς λογείας τῆς εἰς τοὺς ἁγίους) shows that this was not the Corinthians' first exposure to the collection,[23] but that Paul was now inaugurating an ongoing plan for deposit and delivery *after* Paul had left Corinth (ἵνα μὴ ὅταν ἔλθω τότε λογεῖαι γίνωνται, 16:2). Both these moves, and perhaps the rhetorical strategy of self-appeal throughout 1 Corinthians, would come back to bite Paul.

We do not know how much time elapsed between the sending of 1 Corinthians and Paul's next letter, 2 Corinthians 8, which is a deliberative letter urging the Corinthians to complete the collection which also formally includes (8:16f.) an introduction and authentication of the envoys Paul has dispatched to convey the funds to Jerusalem. The only clue is 2 Cor 8:10, which says the Corinthians began the work on the collection ἀπὸ πέρυσι, "a year ago." At most, then, the interval was one year, but it may have been less, since 1 Cor 16:1-4 may not signal the very *start* of the collection, but instead a second phase occasioned by Paul's now-absent status, and hence long-distance administration of the fund. Whatever the time gap between Paul's letters to Corinth, it was filled by the Macedonians' tremendously successful monetary efforts, of which Paul here writes to inform the Corinthians (γνωρίζομεν δὲ ὑμῖν, ἀδελφοί), and, by lauding them, to stir them to do likewise (as explicitly stated in 8:8). It is quite possible, even likely, that Paul was personally in Macedonia directing that effort (having travelled there from Ephesus, his locale when writing 1 Corinthians [16:8]), especially if Titus' "beginning" refers to his local efforts in the province of Macedonia, from which Paul now sends him personally to Achaia (8:6, 17). If Paul was in Macedonia as he wrote 2 Corinthians 8, then he has apparently deviated—unaccountably, from the Corinthians' point of view—from the promise to come he made in 1 Cor 16:5-7 ('Ελεύσομαι δὲ πρὸς ὑμᾶς) after "passing through" Macedonia (ὅταν Μακεδονίαν διέλθω· Μακεδονίαν γὰρ διέρχομαι), to stay for a long visit in Corinth (πρὸς ὑμᾶς δὲ τυχὸν παραμενῶ ἢ παραχειμάσω ... οὐ θέλω γὰρ ὑμᾶς ἄρτι ἐν παρόδῳ ἰδεῖν, ἐλπίζω γὰρ χρόνον τινὰ ἐπιμεῖναι πρὸς ὑμᾶς ἐὰν ὁ κύριος ἐπιτρέψῃ). That his absence was justified by the great success

---

[23] περὶ δέ is a conventional formula for introducing a topic readily known to both author and readers (see Margaret M. Mitchell, "Concerning ΠΕΡΙ ΔΕ in 1 Corinthians," *Novum Testamentum* 31[1989] 229-56).

of the collection among Macedonian churches may have been less self-evident to the Corinthians than it seemingly was to Paul (witness the triumphant tone of 2 Cor 8:1-5). Consequently his trumpeting of the Macedonians as the model to emulate may have exacerbated the sense of grievance the Corinthians already had at being less favored by the apostle than their territorial rival. When this offense is joined with the Corinthians' umbrage that Paul took upon himself the very task he had promised would be their prerogative—i.e., of attesting and dispatching envoys for the collection— we can easily see how 2 Corinthians 8 could have contributed mightily to the increasing breakdown of the relationship between apostle and church.

Paul wrote 2 Corinthians 8, as we have noted above, as another deliberative appeal to the Corinthans to add to their prodigious list of spiritual attainments (of πίστις, λόγος, γνῶσις, σπουδή, apostolic ἀγάπη [8:7]) a crowning virtuous act: the generous completion of the collection, which will serve as an outward and definitive proof of *their love* (8:8: τὸ τῆς ὑμετέρας ἀγάπης γνήσιον δοκιμάζων; 8:24: ἔνδειξιν τῆς ἀγάπης ὑμῶν ... ἐνδεικνύμενοι). In these respects his letter resumes the rhetorical strategy of 1 Corinthians,[24] and depends upon its success at instilling that unifying inner-ecclesial love which was its central purpose (as summed up in the final appeal of 1 Cor 16:14: πάντα ὑμῶν ἐν ἀγάπῃ γινέσθω).[25] But here that love is still waiting to be actualized in the collection.[26]

How did the Corinthians react to 2 Corinthians 8? As we have begun to examine above, from the next letter, in 2 Cor 2:14-7:4 (leaving aside the likely interpolation in 6:14-7:1),[27] we can see precisely how the letter of 2 Corinthians 8 occasioned Corinthian anger and suspicion about Paul. First, his appropriating to himself the

---

[24] Though significantly it does not refer to *any* prior missive, perhaps to sidestep the fact that Paul's administrative arrangements have deviated from the plan outlined by him in his previous letter. Instead, Paul retains a focus on the personal: the beginning with Titus (8:6) and with the Corinthians themselves (8:10).

[25] Mitchell, *Paul*, 294.

[26] Note that the love the Corinthians are said to "abound in" is ἡ ἐξ ἡμῖν ἐν ὑμῖν ἀγάπη in 8:7; cf. the anomalous ἡ ἀγάπη μου μετὰ πάντων ὑμῶν ἐν Χριστῷ Ἰησοῦ with which Paul ended 1 Corinthians (16:24).

[27] As is well known, there are many theories about this section, from those who accept its genuineness to those who think it a misplaced Pauline fragment, a non-Pauline interpolation, or even an anti-Pauline intrusion (for the issues and extensive bibliography see Thrall, *Second Epistle to the Corinthians*, 25-36).

authority to test (δοκιμάζειν) and write letters of recommendation for others (Titus, the brothers) has led at least some Corinthians to ask about *his own lack of such letters* (ἢ μὴ χρήζομεν ὥς τινες συστατικῶν ἐπιστολῶν πρὸς ὑμᾶς ἢ ἐξ ὑμῶν; [3:1-2]). The charge was likely fomented further by the fact that Paul had been, especially in 1 Corinthians, holding himself up as an example for imitation,[28] a strategy now recast by (at least some) Corinthian readers as πάλιν ἑαυτοὺς συνιστάνειν (3:1; cf. 5:12; 6:3). The doubts are enflamed also by the perceived inconsistency in Paul's behavior—one he had left on the surface of 1 Corinthians—that while present he refused financial remuneration (1 Corinthians 9), but when absent he wrote arranging for an ambitious monetary collection (16:1-4) and, a year later, its delivery by his own hand-picked strangers to a place very far away from their homeland of Greece (2 Corinthians 8). This discrepancy in behavior led to suspicions that he was behaving ἐν πανουργίᾳ, δολοῦντες τὸν λόγον τοῦ θεοῦ, acting in a "veiled" way (κεκαλυμμένον τὸ εὐαγγέλιον ἡμῶν, in sum: καπηλεύοντες τὸν λόγον τοῦ θεοῦ), acting without εἰλικρινεία, "sincerity" (4:1-3; 2:17). The main topic of this letter, which I term "Self-Defense of the Maligned Messenger," is Paul's *own* διακονία (the term and cognates are found in 3:3, 6, 7, 8, 9; 4:1; 5:18; 6:3, 4).[29] If 2 Corinthians 8 is the immediately prior letter, the referent of that διακονία is more pointed than has been realized—for fully three times in 2 Corinthians 8 the term (or the participial form of the cognate verb) is used to refer to the monetary collection for the saints (8:4: καὶ τὴν κοινωνίαν *τῆς διακονίας* τῆς εἰς τοὺς ἁγίους; 8:19-20: σὺν τῇ χάριτι ταύτῃ *τῇ διακονουμένῃ* ὑφ' ἡμῶν πρὸς τὴν αὐτοῦ τοῦ κυρίου δόξαν καὶ προθυμίαν ἡμῶν ... ἐν τῇ ἁδρότητι ταύτῃ *τῇ διακονουμένῃ* ὑφ' ἡμῶν). This very insistence on his own role as divine emissary entrusted with the collection may have set the Corinthians to wondering by what authority

---

[28] See Mitchell, *Paul,* 49-60.

[29] 3:3: ἐστὲ ἐπιστολὴ Χριστοῦ *διακονηθεῖσα* ὑφ' ἡμῶν; 3:6: ὃς καὶ ἱκάνωσεν ἡμᾶς *διακόνους* καινῆς διαθήκης; 3:7-9: ἡ *διακονία* τοῦ θανάτου ... ἡ *διακονία* τοῦ πνεύματος ... εἰ γὰρ τῇ *διακονίᾳ* τῆς κατακρίσεως δόξα, πολλῷ μᾶλλον περισσεύει ἡ *διακονία* τῆς δικαιοσύνης δόξῃ; 4:1: ἔχοντες *τὴν διακονίαν ταύτην* ...; 5:18: τὰ δὲ πάντα ἐκ τοῦ θεοῦ ... δόντος ἡμῖν *τὴν διακονίαν* τῆς καταλλαγῆς; 6:3-4: Μηδεμίαν ἐν μηδενὶ διδόντες προσκοπήν, ἵνα μὴ μωμηθῇ ἡ *διακονία*, ἀλλ' ἐν παντὶ συνιστάντες ἑαυτοὺς ὡς *θεοῦ διάκονοι.* The ubiquity of the term and its importance for understanding this letter have been demonstrated in the significant works of Dieter Georgi, *The Opponents of Paul in 2 Corinthians* (Philadelphia: Fortress, 1986) 27-32, and especially John N. Collins, *Diakonia: Re-interpreting the Ancient Sources* (New York: Oxford University Press, 1990).

he could claim these divine endowments.[30] One way of phrasing this question apparently was: "from where does his ἱκανότης come?" (2:16; 3:4-6). The connection can be nicely seen in the long list of contrasts beginning in 6:3, between external and internal realities, which echoes precisely the preemptive rhetoric of the prior letter (and shows that it did not quell the disquiet):

6:3-4 Μηδεμίαν ἐν μηδενὶ διδόντες προσκοπήν,
ἵνα μὴ μωμηθῇ ἡ διακονία, ἀλλ᾽ ἐν παντὶ
συνιστάντες ἑαυτοὺς ὡς θεοῦ διάκονοι

8:20 στελλόμενοι τοῦτο, μή τις ἡμᾶς μωμήσηται
ἐν τῇ ἁδρότητι ταύτῃ τῇ διακονουμένῃ ὑφ᾽ ἡμῶν.

The reconstruction I am proposing can largely account for the shift between 1 and 2 Corinthians without having to place the full responsibility for the conflict, as Georgi and others do, on a speculatively reconstructed outside incursion into the Corinthian church.[31] We can see that to a large extent it is quite plausible that Paul's own letters set up failed expectations and engendered doubts about the basis of his authority. But the letter of 2:14-7:4 *is* set within a travel motif, of Paul "being led in triumph" (θριαμβεύειν) by his God as an ambiguous prisoner (2:14) who at the end of the letter calls for his acceptance and welcome upon arrival in Corinth: Τὸ στόμα ἡμῶν ἀνέῳγεν πρὸς ὑμᾶς, Κορίνθιοι, ἡ καρδία ἡμῶν πεπλάτυνται ... πλατύνθητε καὶ ὑμεῖς. Χωρήσατε ἡμᾶς (6:11-13; 7:2). This letter has as its dominant motif the procession, a traveling parade of Christ's

---

[30] The connection between this doubt and Paul's action in writing a letter of recommendation is to be found in the cultural basis of that very practice: delegated authority depends entirely upon that of the person by whom they were sent (see Margaret M. Mitchell, "New Testament Envoys in the Context of Greco-Roman Diplomatic and Epistolary Conventions: The Example of Timothy and Titus," *JBL* 111 [1992] 661-82, esp. 647-51). Paul's acting as sender of Titus and the brothers quite naturally raised the question of by whom *he* was sent.

[31] Georgi postulated the arrival of Hellenistic Jewish-Christian missionaries between 1 Corinthians and the next piece of the correspondence, 2:14-7:4 and 10-13. See, for example, *Opponents of Paul*, 17-18: "During the visits of Timothy and Titus the situation in the Corinthian church seems to have been calm, whereas tensions existed before and after. This break must be placed between the time period described in 1 and 2 Corinthians." But there is actually little evidence of a sudden arrival of "outside opponents" between 2 Corinthians 8 and 2:14-7:4, for all the charges Paul defends himself against in that letter can reasonably have arisen from the Corinthians' own reading of 2 Corinthians 8 and 1 Corinthians. But we should also beware of assuming that non-Pauline missionary "presence" at Corinth must have been a single, datable event (see discussion below, pp. 30-31).

ambassador (5:20) on his way to Corinth.[32] 2 Cor 2:14-7:4 was
probably sent on ahead of Paul as he traveled southwest from
Macedonia to Corinth.

The next piece of the correspondence, 2 Corinthians 10-13, makes
a quick and bitter allusion to a most unpleasant visit (παρὼν τό
δεύτερον) in which Paul was "humbled" (his version) and "found
lacking" (their version), a time marked by "contention, partisan zeal,
wrath, divisiveness, backbiting, whispering, bloated self-importance,
factional disputes" (12:20). Having left Corinth after this "second
visit" (13:2; cf. 12:14), stung by insults, probably at the hand of one
distinct individual,[33] but also from the church in general, by either
active or passive acquiescence to this person's castigations against
the visiting apostle, Paul reentered the fray from a distance in his
chosen (though itself controversial) medium[34]—the letter of 2
Corinthians 10-13. It is here that we see the clearest possible evidence of outsiders influencing the Corinthian conflict, in 11:4, and
perhaps 10:12-18. But it would be a mistake to assume that the
appearance of outside missionaries *in Paul's letter* must correspond to
a single historical event which has just taken place—i.e., these itin-
erant preachers' sudden arrival in Corinth. We know already from
1 Corinthians that other missionaries were going in and out of Corinth
from the earliest period (Apollos, possibly Cephas), and that the
Corinthians had knowledge of "the other apostles" and "the brothers of the Lord" (1 Cor 9:5; cf. 15:5, 7). Although an historically

---

[32] This has been persuasively demonstrated by Paul B. Duff in a series of articles: "The Transformation of the Spectator: Power, Perception, and the Day of
Salvation," *SBLSP* 26 (1987) 233-43; "Metaphor, Motif, and Meaning: The Rhetorical Strategy Behind the Image 'Led in Triumph' in 2 Cor 2:14," *CBQ* 53 (1991)
79-92; "The Language of Processions in 2 Corinthians 4.7-10," *Biblical Theology
Bulletin* 21 (1991) 158-65; "The Mind of the Redactor: 2 Cor 6:14-7:1 in Its Secondary Context," *Novum Testamentum* 35 (1993) 160-80. This is why I think Michel
Quesnell's idea ("Circonstances de composition de la seconde épître aux Corinthiens,"
NTS 43 [1997] 256-67, 264-65), that Paul wrote an advance letter as preparatory
to the "second visit," is correct, except that the letter in question is 2:14-7:4, not
chap. 9, which does not have either a travel motif, an ambassadorial governing
metaphor, or a final call for welcome (cf. 2 Cor 6:11-13; 7:2).

[33] I.e., the subject of φησίν in 10:10, who can be seen, then, as identical to ὁ
ἀδικήσας of 7:12, the man who "has caused the grief" [λελύπηκεν] in 2:5.

[34] I have argued in "New Testament Envoys" against Robert Funk's often-cited
view that personal presence was always Paul's most favored medium ("The Apostolic *Parousia*: Form and Significance," *Christian History and Interpretation: Studies Presented
to John Knox* [ed. W.R. Farmer, C.F.D. Moule, and R.R. Niebuhr; Cambridge:
Cambridge University Press, 1967] 249-69).

datable "arrival" of outside missionaries (particularly some abrupt and serious event that drastically upset the equilibrium of the Corinthian community) remains speculation, what is certain from the evidence of Paul's letter is that other missionaries have "rhetorically arrived," in the sense that they have been invoked by a local Corinthian as the standard for apostolic authority, a comparison that set Paul's position and legitimacy in serious doubt.[35] The debates about who these figures are who "compare themselves with themselves" (10:12), and whether the "super-duper apostles" (οἱ ὑπερλίαν ἀπόστολοι) themselves (or only others who claim their authority) were actually in Corinth are extensive,[36] and they will no doubt continue. What is most significant for the present argument is that in the "Letter of Tears" in 2 Corinthians 10-13 Paul responds not to the threat that outside detractors would turn the Corinthians to new teachings,[37] but instead to *the accusations against himself* occasioned by the "humbling" self-contradictions that were so sharply manifest on the basis of two συγκρίσεις, "comparisons", which his visit brought to sharp public expression: 1) Paul's diminishing status when in direct contrast with the competing missionaries, and 2) Paul the author (of four "weighty" missives to the church) appearing rather differently in the flesh in the city (on his second visit).[38] *His own letters* are now acting

---

[35] It is possible that these are the same persons Paul had in mind already when speaking of τινες in 3:1 who require letters of recommendation, but the rhetorical approach of that letter is pointedly different from what we find in 2 Corinthians; 10-13. In the latter Paul constructs a σύγκρισις between himself and other missionaries, but in the earlier letter a different σύγκρισις: between Paul perceived and Paul actual (as signaled in the opening in 2:14-16, and manifested quite clearly in the blatant contrasts in 6:3f.).

[36] See the classic essay by C.K. Barrett, "Paul's Opponents in 2 Corinthians," *Essays on Paul* (Philadelphia: Westminster, 1982) 60-86, and Furnish, *II Corinthians* 48-54; Thrall, *Second Epistle to the Corinthians*, 2.671-76.

[37] Against the idea that outside missionaries are currently in Corinth, seeking the wholesale defection of the Corinthians to them, stands 2 Cor 12:20-21, where the worst prospect Paul can imagine for the future is more humiliation for himself and further division among the Corinthians. There is no mention here that he is worried about "finding" them going over to "another Jesus" (11:4, whatever that would mean!) when he comes for the third time.

[38] This can be seen from the way in which the argument of the letter 2 Corinthians 10-13 is set up. The thesis to this argument is plainly advanced in 10:7-11, and it focuses on *Paul*, not on outside missionaries. Paul neither confronts the rival missionaries directly, nor does he combat their teaching at all (as commentators have noted), but instead engages in a duel of competing συγκρίσεις with a Corinthian spokesman (10:7, 10) who has incorporated the standard of οἱ ὑπερλίαν ἀπόστολοι in his critique of Paul. It appears that in response to the argument in the previous

as an agent in his condemnation, for they, in juxtaposition with the weak and paltry (perhaps sickly) condition of his body, through their very "weightiness and might" (αἱ ἐπιστολαὶ μέν, φησίν, βαρεῖαι καὶ ἰσχυραί, ἡ δὲ παρουσία τοῦ σώματος ἀσθενὴς καὶ ὁ λόγος ἐξουθενημένος [10:10]) have set to contrastive shame their author's personal appearance. Significantly, this charge of personal inconsistency depends upon a recent visit *after* Paul had been away and writing letters; this is another argument in favor of the placement of the "second visit" subsequent to the letter of 2:14-7:4. After leaving Corinth, probably for Ephesus in Asia Minor, taking the land route through Macedonia (this may be the journey described in Acts 20:3, after a mere three month visit in Corinth),[39] Paul wrote the letter of 2 Corinthians 10-13 to argue that the apparent incongruity of his weak body with his weighty letters is in fact fully consonant with the logic of the gospel (13:3-4; cf. 11:30-12:10), in which what looks to the naked eye like weakness is really a sign of *power*, divine power (see esp. 12:6-10). The framing sections of the letter signal clearly Paul's new intent, as he seeks to accomplish textually what he was so embarrassingly unable to do in person: to bring the Corinthians to repentance of their disloyalty and a return to obedience (see especially the conclusion to the προοίμιον in 10:5-6; cf. the ἐπίλογος in 13:5-10). To do this he must answer their own test (δοκιμή) of his

---

letter (2:14-7:4), in which Paul claimed the divine basis of his status as a διάκονος δικαιοσύνης (see 3:6-9), some at Corinth have brought forward other διάκονοι Χριστοῦ (11:23), setting up a comparison meant to put Paul to shame (Thrall, *Second Epistle to the Corinthians*, 2.697, also noted this logical connection). Paul responds by flipping the rhetorical σύγκρισις on its head. He counters that, by seeking to set up such a comparison with himself, both the Corinthians who do this and the rival missionaries they offer in service of the point demonstrate that it is *they* who are over-reaching, who are seeking—not to hold Paul to *their* standard, but to lay claim to *his* (11:12). These are the ones Paul stigmatizes as τινες τῶν ἑαυτοὺς συνιστανόντων ... αὐτοὶ ἐν ἑαυτοῖς ἑαυτοὺς μετροῦντες καὶ συγκρίνοντες ἑαυτοὺς ἑαυτοῖς. Their role in the situation arises from the fact that a powerful Corinthian spokesman is invoking them as the rhetorical standard of those possessing τὰ σημεῖα τοῦ ἀποστόλου (12:12), a κανών which Paul simultaneously rejects and seeks to demonstrate that he meets.

[39] On this point I agree with Quesnell's reconstruction, for he, too, places the second visit immediately before the letter of 2 Corinthians 10-13 ("Circonstances," 265). Where Quesnell and I part company is in regard to the identification and chronology of 2 Corinthians 10-13; he regards it as emphatically *not* the "Letter of Tears," and as the *last* piece of the Corinthian correspondence. As will be seen below, for various reasons I think 2 Corinthians 10-13 is the "Letter of Tears," which Paul later exegeted in 1:1-2:13; 7:5-16; 13:11-13.

apostolic legitimacy (13:3) with an acerbically sarcastic self-defense which he hopes will lead them to question their own legitimacy to issue such judgments against him (ἑαυτοὺς δοκιμάζετε ... εἰ μήτι ἀδόκιμοι [13:5]). This angry "Letter of Tears" escalates the defense of apostolic weakness and the refutation of the charge of financial malfeasance by a grudging and ironic engagement with an external criterion of apostolic status: the authenticating σημεῖα τοῦ ἀποστόλου (11:12). Still laboring under the accusation that he stands in Corinth as one who only "recommends himself" (10:18: οὐ γὰρ ὁ ἑαυτὸν συνιστάνων, ἐκεῖνός ἐστιν δόκιμος), Paul now counters with the "Fool's Speech," an intricate and inverted proof that he is ὃν ὁ κύριος συνιστάνων—through ἀσθένεια, "weakness," as an apostle's authenticating sign, not marvels and spectacular wonders (11:12, etc.).[40] He insists repeatedly that his past, present and future financial conduct are fully consistent: "I was not, and will not be, a fiduciary burden upon you" (a claim he makes in 11:7-10; 12:13-16). And, furthermore, his discrepancy in allowing such aid from the Macedonians (11:7-9; cf. Phil 1:7; 4:10-20) was not a sign that he favored the Philippians and Thessalonians, but rather an index of prudence (11:12f.) precisely because of his love for the Corinthians, which, Paul avers, can itself be divinely attested (διὰ τί; ὅτι οὐκ ἀγαπῶ ὑμᾶς; ὁ θεὸς οἶδεν). This letter of 2 Corinthians 10-13 was sent with the mutually esteemed envoy Titus, whom Paul recognizes as so trusted by the Corinthians for his prior work among them on the collection[41] that he can, by means of a rhetorical question—μήτι ἐπλεονέκτησεν ὑμᾶς Τίτος;—seek to extend the Corinthians' confidence in Titus' integrity to himself (οὐ τῷ αὐτῷ πνεύματι περιεπατήσαμεν; οὐ τοῖς αὐτοῖς ἴχνεσιν; [12:18]).

The rhetorical stance of 2 Corinthians 10-13 is self-consciously belligerent (overtly signaled in the abrupt and bellicose opening of 2 Cor 10:1-6), a "risk all" bargain aimed at shaming the Corinthians back to allegiance to Paul himself as their true apostle. The alienation that had intensified in an exchange of a least four letters to this point, coupled with one unsavory "Zwischenbesuch," was now

---

[40] The most penetrating analysis of this composition remains that of Hans Dieter Betz, *Der Apostel Paulus und die sokratische Tradition: Eine exegetische Untersuchung zu seiner 'Apologie' 2 Kor 10-13* (BHT 45; Tübingen: Mohr Siebeck, 1972).

[41] In this regard, it is noteworthy that in 2:14-7:4 there appears to be no issue with Titus (or either of the brothers), but just with Paul.

at its height. Paul sent the letter with Titus, and then waited for missive
and missionary to do their reconciliatory work.⁴²

The next letter in the Corinthian archive, the remarkable "Letter
toward Reconciliation"⁴³ in 1:1-2:13; 7:5-16; 13:11-13, because it
mirrors the diplomatic conventions for retrospective reportage on
an envoy's mission, gives us an astonishingly full, even fulsome account of the receipt of 2 Corinthians 10-13 and its bearer in Corinth.
After its author paced and stewed, first en route to Troas, and then
to Macedonia, fitfully awaiting news of its success or failure, Titus
arrived with the happy tidings that the letter had had its desired effect:
μετάνοια (7:9-10), and expressions of fealty to Paul (ὁ ὑμῶν ζῆλος
ὑπὲρ ἐμοῦ), described in such language as ἐπιπόθησις (7:11), φόβος
(7:11, 15), and ἐκδίκησις (7:11). The picture we can reconstruct from
these terms is that some single person, probably the voice behind
φησίν in 10:10 (and τις in 10:7 and τοιοῦτος in 10:11) who had done
Paul an injustice (ὁ ἀδικήσας versus ὁ ἀδικηθείς in 7:12), had been
punished.⁴⁴ This scenario therefore accounts for the perceived problem
for the identification of the "Letter of Tears" with 2 Corinthians 10-
13—that the massive outside incursionists such as the "super-duper
apostles" are missing in the retrospective account—for, as we have
argued, the individual (τις, τοιοῦτος) was the one championing the
rhetorical strategy of σύγκρισις between Paul and the legendary great
apostles (who were not necessarily themselves directly or actively
involved in the conflict). Most significantly, the focus on internal
Corinthian obedience, and not on the actions of the outsiders, is
consistent between the two missives (2 Cor 10:5-6; 2:9; 7:15). Furthermore, the correlation between 2 Corinthians 10-13 and the "Letter
toward Reconciliation" is exact in the later letter, in 2:5f., where τις
has caused some unnamed grievesome injury (λελύπηκεν),⁴⁵ but the

---

⁴² See Mitchell, "New Testament Envoys," 651-62.

⁴³ My title deliberately counters Bornkamm's "Versöhnungsbrief" or "Freuden-
brief" (see "Vorgeschichte," 23, 32; the latter title comes from Walter Schmithals,
Gnosticism in Corinth [trans. John E. Steely; Nashville: Abingdon, 1971] 97) who
regarded it as a letter which Paul wrote to celebrate the complete restoration of
the relationship. As I have argued in "New Testament Envoys," 653-662, this letter
is a requisite piece of the diplomatic process, in which Paul defends himself against
lingering doubts, and meets their offer of reconciliation with his own attestation
of goodwill for them. It seeks to *effect*, not celebrate, full reconciliation between
the estranged parties.

⁴⁴ ἐκδίκησις as the last term in 7:11a heightens its importance, especially since
τὸ πρᾶγμα (7:11b) is described with the cognates ἀδικεῖν, ἀδικεισθῆναι (7:12).

⁴⁵ Paul is quite circumspect about the harm caused to himself, since to admit

majority has laid a punishment (ἐπιτιμία) on τοιοῦτος (2:6 and 7). Paul regards this as the consequence of their obedient reading of his letter (2:3-9; 7:8-12)—an appropriate judicial reprimand which demonstrates the δοκιμή and ὑπακοή which were his very purpose for writing the risky letter (2:9; cf. 10:5-6; 13:5-7). A majority of the Corinthians (οἱ πλείονες) had themselves enacted the ἐκδίκησις that Paul had threatened in his prior letter would be brought against the disobedient when the Corinthians returned to obedience to him (ἐν ἑτοίμῳ ἔχοντες ἐκδικῆσαι πᾶσαν παρακοήν, ὅταν πληρωθῇ ὑμῶν ἡ ὑπακοή [10:6; pronounced as fulfilled in 7:15]).

Yet the letter that achieved the μετάνοια and ὑπακοή Paul sought also raised some problems of its own. Because of its angry, bombastic tone and content, "The Letter of Tears" had generated λύπη among the Corinthians, which endangered their friendship with Paul, for it seemed to contravene the solemn definition of ancient friendship well known to both[46]—unification in the same joys and same sorrows. If Paul could (and did) write a letter that so grieved the Corinthians, even if they agreed on their part that he was an apostle, what did that say about *his* disposition for them? Did he "tar them" with the fault of ὁ τοιοῦτος, and regard them as enemies? Did the severe "Letter of Tears," and the fact that he sent a letter in lieu of a visit (despite his promise 12:14 and 13:1) not prove that he held them in less esteem—once again showing his preference for the Macedonians (cf. his own acknowledgement of their difference in treatment in 11:9)? The burden of the "Letter toward Reconciliation" in 1:1-2:13; 7:5-16; 13:11-13 is for Paul to demonstrate that he has acted sincerely, and not with the "fleshly wisdom" of barbs and taunts, in his dealings with the Corinthians, both by letter and in person (this is signaled clearly in the rhetorical πρόθεσις, or proposition to the argument, in 1:12-14). To do that *he must exegete the letter in question* to show that it was really a friendship letter written out of love, not malice. He must meet their sorrow with a record of his own, and show that in the interval bridged only by letter and envoy, he and the Corinthians were in fact completely unified in the same affliction and grief (as signalled so emphatically in the προοίμιον of 1:3-7), just as they now, exuberantly, share the same joy. This letter is

---

it would be to allow the very vulnerability of which he was accused, so instead he uses elliptical language (see 2 Cor 2:5; 7:12).

[46] The commonplace was invoked in previous correspondence (see 1 Cor 12:26; cf. 2 Cor 7:3).

intended to meet halfway the Corinthians' first step toward reconciliation (the "olive branch" offered through Titus), and is meant to
complete the process of restoration of the relationship.

The last piece of the Corinthian correspondence is 2 Corinthians
9, a separate letter addressed to all the Christ-believers in the province of Achaia, to spur them to the final wrap-up of the collection
effort, and announce Paul's imminent arrival with delegates from
Macedonia (9:4). This final extant letter begins with the same refrain with which Paul had ended the prior missive: his boasting on
their behalf (οἶδα γὰρ τὴν προθυμίαν ὑμῶν ἣν ὑπὲρ ὑμῶν καυχῶμαι
Μακεδόσιν [9:2-3; cf. 7:14]),[47] and it gingerly echoes the now-re-
solved concerns with an assurance that the offering requested is not
to be ἐκ λύπης (9:7). But in 2 Corinthians 9 Paul does not engage
in hermeneutical reflections on his earlier letters and their meanings, for those have, at least for now, been brought to a state of
negotiated equilibrium with the addressees directly involved.[48] With
the doubts about Paul's financial misdealings and illegitimacy at last
behind them, the collection effort, now termed a εὐλογία,[49] continues in earnest, providing the final δοκιμή of the Corinthians' faithfulness and submission (9:13).

III. *The Birth of Pauline Hermeneutics*

Once the sequence of the Pauline letters to the Corinthians has been
established,[50] and the key role played by the letters and their reception in the unfolding of events has been illustrated, we have the
resources to investigate in more detail some of the strategies by which
meaning in the Pauline letters was negotiated. Meaning is negotiated *continually* as an extended process between epistolary partners—

---

[47] A rhetorical commonality between the two letters is that in both cases Paul
plays boasting and shame off one another (compare 7:14 and 9:4), in the prior
letter as a completed action (Paul has not been put to shame) and in the second
as a possible, though unlikely one, since (he strongly insinuates) the Corinthians
are ready with their contribution.

[48] I.e., the Corinthians, as distinct from all Achaeans, who are the recipients
of the letter in 2 Corinthians 9 (with Betz, *2 Corinthians 8 and 9*, 91-97, 139-40).

[49] 2 Cor 9:5-6; compare also Rom 15:29, written just after this, probably from
Corinth, in the act of execution of the plan set in motion in 2 Cor 9:4.

[50] The ensuing analysis depends upon my partition theory, but the procedure,
of tracing successive readings and rereadings, and many of the observations given
here, may I hope be applicable or adaptable to other compositional hypotheses.

but not at random, or without some consistent and deliberate methods. We shall focus here on three key stages of negotiated meaning in any Pauline letter, beginning with the first Pauline interpreter in what has become a long history of exegesis—Paul himself.

A. *Stage One: Paul's Self-Interpreting Moves in the Very Act of Composition*

The interplay between author and readers about what the text they share means does not begin only after the text is written and sent. Paul, like any author (and especially a subtle or sophisticated one) self-consciously wrestles with his hermeneutical control over the possible meanings of his text even as he is writing it. This is a stage in Pauline interpretation that is rarely considered, at least on these terms. One can of course subsume the full panoply of Paul's rhetorical choices under this category, for they are all ways in which Paul attempts to steer his readers to react to his discourse in certain prescribed ways. Here I shall focus within that array upon a few specific hermeneutical strategies by which Paul attempts to locate and prescribe the meaning of his text even as he writes it:

1. *Choosing to write in a fashion that is either clear or opaque for the audience intended.* We know unequivocally from a passage like 2 Cor 10:1 that when he so wishes, Paul can be extremely direct about what it is that he wants to say: Αὐτὸς δὲ ἐγὼ Παῦλος παρακαλῶ ὑμᾶς κ.τ.λ. Naturally the meaning of a statement like this depends upon the wider context, both literary and historical, in which it is located, and upon the words which follow this opening salvo. Such a sentence may intentionally (as it does in the present instance) stand in some relief against the background of more convoluted arguments or expressions which are already a subject of controversy among Paul's readers (as is indicated in 2 Cor 10:10-11). Yet in the "Letter of Tears" Paul begins and ends with such overt statements of literary purpose (see 13:10: Διὰ τοῦτο ταῦτα ἀπὼν γράφω ...), in all likelihood because it was on the grounds of authorial overbearing and cunning that he was under attack.

But Paul does not always present himself as writing in a direct fashion. For example, at 1 Cor 4:6 Paul directly states that he was employing the rhetorical figure of "covert allusion"[51] [μετεσχημάτισα]

---

[51] See Benjamine Fiore, "'Covert Allusion' in 1 Corinthians 1-4," *CBQ* 47 (1985) 85-102.

to deal with the factions in the church, and he offers a most convoluted argument by "the curious indirection of polyphony"[52] in 1 Cor 8-10 on idol meats. Hence the Corinthian correspondence, in which Paul and his Corinthian readers volleyed their different interpretations of his letters, contains a careful and perhaps bewildering mix of plain-speaking, innuendo, and utterances that were to be found capable of a double entendre. One way Paul presents himself as forthright and direct (that is, exemplifying παρρησία)[53] is his frequent use—over eighteen times—of the formula λέγω δὲ τοῦτο, or something synonymous (φήμι, γράφω).[54] Consider, for example, the double explication formula in 1 Cor 15:50-51: Τοῦτο δέ φημι, ἀδελφοί, ὅτι σὰρξ καὶ αἷμα βασιλείαν θεοῦ κληρονομῆσαι οὐ δύναται οὐδὲ ἡ φθορὰ τὴν ἀφθαρσίαν κληρονομεῖ. ἰδοὺ μυστήριον ὑμῖν λέγω· πάντες οὐ κοιμηθησόμεθα, πάντες δὲ ἀλλαγησόμεθα. Even the "mystery" here is declared as being articulated in the simplest (if experience-defying) of terms.[55]

2. *Clarifying unclear or possibly ambiguous points even as they are being made.* Paul can use a formula like λέγω δὲ τοῦτο to provide sharp accent or clarification to an idea he has already been expressing, as in 1 Cor 1:11-12: ἐδηλώθη γάρ μοι περὶ ὑμῶν, ἀδελφοί μου, ὑπὸ τῶν Χλόης ὅτι ἔριδες ἐν ὑμῖν εἰσιν. λέγω δὲ τοῦτο ὅτι ἕκαστος ὑμῶν λέγει· ἐγὼ μέν εἰμι Παύλου κ.τ.λ. In such an instance the phrase could be translated, "what I mean is ...." At other times Paul acts as his own commentator or glossator in clarifying what might be a cryptic referent, such as in 1 Cor 10:28-29: μὴ ἐσθίετε δι᾽ ἐκεῖνον τὸν μηνύσαντα καὶ τὴν συνείδησιν· συνείδησιν δὲ λέγω οὐχὶ τὴν ἑαυτοῦ

---

[52] This marvelous phrase is from Meeks, "Polyphonic Ethics," 203.

[53] Cf. 2 Cor 3:12; 7:4.

[54] This is a notable feature of the Corinthian correspondence, which points to the conspicuous focus upon hermeneutical issues in these letters. See 1 Cor 1:12; 6:5; 7:6, 8, 12, 29, 35; 10:15, 19, 29; 15:50, 51; 2 Cor 8:8; 6:13; 7:3; 11:16, 21a, 21b; 13:2; 9:4; cf. 1 Cor 4:14; 9:15; 2 Cor 13:10; 2:3. Other formulas which have the effect of directness of speech are the common epistolary disclosure formulas, such as γνωρίζω/γνωρίζομεν δὲ ὑμῖν (1 Cor 12:3; 15:1; 2 Cor 8:1) and οὐ θέλω/θέλομεν ὑμᾶς ἀγνοεῖν (1 Cor 10:1; 12:1; 2 Cor 1:8), as well as other statements which attribute already to the reader the information which is to follow (γινώσκετε [2 Cor 8:9] or οἴδατε, often as the verb of a rhetorical question expecting the answer "yes" [1 Cor 3:16; 5:6; 6:2, 3, 9, 15, 16, 19; 9:13, 24; 12:2]). Rhetorical questions (which are ubiquitous in the Corinthian correspondence) are of course an overt strategy for "negotiating meaning" by the author. Space precludes following this inquiry to the next step here: to see if Paul's level of "directness" decreases (or increases) as the correspondence progresses.

[55] See also 1 Cor 7:29: Τοῦτο δέ φημι, ἀδελφοί, ὁ καιρὸς συνεσταλμένος ἐστίν.

ἀλλὰ τὴν τοῦ ἑτέρου. Elsewhere he directs the pertinence of his instructions to segments of his readership, thus clarifying his meaning by overtly limiting the sphere of reference of a given injunction (1 Cor 7:8-12: Λέγω δὲ τοῖς ἀγάμοις καὶ ταῖς χήραις ... Τοῖς δὲ γεγαμηκόσιν παραγγέλλω, οὐκ ἐγὼ ἀλλὰ ὁ κύριος ... Τοῖς δὲ λοιποῖς λέγω ἐγὼ οὐχ ὁ κύριος).[56] Sometimes he "volunteers" the motivation he has in mind while writing, which is another way to circumscribe the sphere of interpretive possibilities that the Corinthians might later impute to the words (for example, contrast 1 Cor 6:5, πρὸς ἐντροπὴν ὑμῖν λέγω[57] and 2 Cor 7:3, πρὸς κατάκρισιν οὐ λέγω (see also 1 Cor 7:35: τοῦτο δὲ πρὸς τὸ ὑμῶν αὐτῶν σύμφορον λέγω). In these cases Paul does not name directly what construal would constitute errant "counter-interpretations" of the words he has just written, but the sure implication of his procedure is to concede the possibility of multiple readings, even as he proactively seeks to disqualify some of them.

3. *Overtly naming and preemptively rejecting a false or misleading (but possible!) interpretation of the words he has just written.* At other times Paul will overtly name the "false" interpretation some might make of his words, and mount a counter-offensive against that interpretive option.[58] A simple example is 1 Cor 1:14-15, where Paul corrects his own inaccurate claim in midstream—twice, in fact—in order to avert a readerly response which he even goes so far as to name, and thereby disqualify: οὐδένα ὑμῶν ἐβάπτισα εἰ μὴ Κρίσπον καὶ Γάϊον, ἵνα μή τις εἴπῃ ὅτι εἰς τὸ ἐμὸν ὄνομα ἐβαπτίσθητε. ἐβάπτισα δὲ καὶ τὸν Στεφανᾶ οἶκον, λοιπὸν οὐκ οἶδα εἴ τινα ἄλλον ἐβάπτισα. Sometimes the wrong effect can be due to tone. For example, after censuring the Corinthians in 1 Cor 3:1-4:13, a passage which cultimates in a stinging paradoxical encomium of the apostles at the expense of the "wise, strong and famous" Corinthians, Paul prophylactically corrects the (hardly far-fetched!) impression these words might give that he is writing with such vehemence for sport or spite: οὐκ ἐντρέπων ὑμᾶς γράφω ταῦτα ἀλλ' ὡς τέκνα μου ἀγαπητὰ νουθετῶν (1 Cor 4:14; cf. 2 Cor 7:3). At other times the interpretive dilemma has to do

---

[56] Paul uses a congruent strategy in propounding his own scriptural interpretations in 1 Cor 9:8-10 and 10:11, wherein he argues that the passage in question was indeed written with "us" in mind.

[57] Cf. 1 Cor 11:17: τοῦτο δὲ παραγγέλλων οὐκ ἐπαινῶ.

[58] That Paul recognizes the possibility of misunderstanding is signaled also by his admonitions against being deceived or deceiving oneself (1 Cor 3:1; 6:9; 15:33).

with the scope and prerogative of a given instruction. For instance, on two different occasions Paul circumscribes the authoritative weight of given statements even as he is making them, by insisting that his advice is not to be taken as absolute command (see, e.g., 1 Cor 7:6 and 2 Cor 8:8: τοῦτο δὲ λέγω κατὰ συγγνώμην οὐ κατ' ἐπιταγήν [Οὐ κατ' ἐπιταγὴν λέγω]). Sometimes the "false interpretation" of a line of argument is countered by an appeal to authorial intention, as in 1 Cor 9:15 (Οὐκ ἔγραψα δὲ ταῦτα, ἵνα οὕτως γένηται ἐν ἐμοί), or a direct defense against a specific, negative assessment of his intention, as in 2 Cor 11:11 (διὰ τί; ὅτι οὐκ ἀγαπῶ ὑμᾶς; ὁ θεὸς οἶδεν).[59] Sometimes, as in 1 Cor 9:15, Paul averts an unfavorable reading of his rhetorical purpose, perhaps due to a reader's anticipated premature judgment on a complicated argument even while in progress (cf. the ironic statement in 2 Cor 11:16 Πάλιν λέγω, μή τίς με δόξῃ ἄφρονα εἶναι).[60] In such cases Paul can even in anticipation acknowledge sticky points of logic in what he has written which may seem to the reader to involve self-contradiction, as in 1 Cor 10:19: Τί οὖν φημι; ὅτι εἰδωλόθυτόν τί ἐστιν ἢ ὅτι εἴδωλόν τί ἐστιν (cf. 1 Cor 8:5-6). This rhetorical question (even without direct attention to the logical or mythological problem at issue) is meant to silence that line of interpretation as categorically wrong. The corrective follows: ἀλλ' [φημι] ὅτι ἃ θύουσιν, δαιμονίοις καὶ οὐ θεῷ θύουσιν (1 Cor 10:20).

A most subtle use of this technique of naming and denying a possible interpretation of his words even in the midst of composition is found in 2 Cor 5:12.[61] Replying to what he knows to be an actual Corinthian reaction to other things he has written (cf. 3:1), Paul explicitly denies that πάλιν ἑαυτοὺς συνιστάνομεν ὑμῖν, "that we are recommending ourselves to you again." Fascinating here is that Paul in fact wishes his missive to have the effect of registered praise, but without the opprobrium of περιαυτολογία, "self-praise"[62] (part of his rhetorical conundrum, given that he must provide his own ἐπιστολαὶ συστατικαί). So he steers the agency of that effect away from his text and onto his *readers*, whom he directs to carry out his

---

[59] The contrastive claims about οἰκοδομή versus καθαίρεσις which frame "The Letter of Tears" in 10:8 and 13:10 should be understood in the same way.

[60] See also 2 Cor 12:19: Πάλαι δοκεῖτε ὅτι ὑμῖν ἀπολογούμεθα (cf. 10:9).

[61] I thank Paul Duff for pointing me to the importance of this passage for my argument.

[62] On some of the dynamics involved in Pauline self-praise and its rhetorical acceptability, see Margaret M. Mitchell, "A Patristic Perspective on Pauline περιαυτολογία," *New Testament Studies* 47 (2001) 354-71.

intent: ἀλλὰ ἀφορμὴν διδόντες ὑμῖν καυχήματος ὑπὲρ ἡμῶν, ἵνα ἔχητε πρὸς τοὺς ἐν προσώπῳ καυχωμένους καὶ μὴ ἐν καρδίᾳ. The text's intention will be carried out, the author hopes, when the readers do the work he insists he is not (actually) doing in the letter, since that would be rhetorically inappropriate. The "null-text" (a paraleiptic strategy if ever there was one!) becomes the full text when appropriated—and deployed—by the readers as instructed by the ("reluctant") author.

4. *Attaching an oath formula to attest to the veracity of the words just written, or about to be written, as a way to urge acceptance of them*, as in 2 Cor 11:31 (ὁ θεὸς καὶ πατὴρ τοῦ κυρίου Ἰησοῦ οἶδεν, ὁ ὢν εὐλογητὸς εἰς τοὺς αἰῶνας, ὅτι οὐ ψεύδομαι), or 2 Cor 1:23 (Ἐγὼ δὲ μάρτυρα τὸν θεὸν ἐπικαλοῦμαι),[63] or insisting upon the ecclesial or divine authority that lies behind and within words that Paul proactively senses may be controversial (e.g., 1 Cor 11:16, Εἰ δέ τις δοκεῖ φιλόνεικος εἶναι, ἡμεῖς τοιαύτην συνήθειαν οὐκ ἔχομεν οὐδὲ αἱ ἐκκλησίαι τοῦ θεοῦ; or 14:37, Εἴ τις δοκεῖ προφήτης εἶναι ἢ πνευματικός, ἐπιγινωσκέτω ἃ γράφω ὑμῖν ὅτι κυρίου ἐστὶν ἐντολή). In the latter two cases the real conditionals demonstrate that Paul thinks he is dealing with a *possible*, though (to him) undesirable, interpretive stance toward his words. Elsewhere Paul will adamantly claim a spiritual authority for what he is writing and they will read (1 Cor 5:3-4: παρὼν δὲ τῷ πνεύματι ... συναχθέντων ὑμῶν καὶ τοῦ ἐμοῦ πνεύματος ...; 7:40: δοκῶ δὲ κἀγὼ πνεῦμα θεοῦ ἔχειν).[64]

5. *Promising proof and arguments beyond the present text which will even further substantiate the point being made.* We see this, for instance, in 1 Cor 4:17f. where a visit from Paul's envoy Timothy is promised which will serve as an extension of the instructions given, and a demonstration that they constitute customary teaching in all the assemblies (καθὼς πανταχοῦ ἐν πάσῃ ἐκκλησίᾳ διδάσκω), and hence are worthy of most serious attention by this particular ἐκκλησία (cf. also 1 Cor 7:17).[65] Paul also promises future counsel in 1 Cor 11:34b, and forthcoming visits in 1 Cor 4:19; 16:5-9; 2 Cor 12:14; 13:1. This

---

[63] See also 2 Cor 8:3 (μαρτυρῶ); cf.1:12 (τὸ μαρτύριον τῆς συνειδήσεως ἡμῶν).

[64] Cf. earlier in the same argument, at 7:25: γνώμην δὲ δίδωμι ὡς ἠλεημένος ὑπὸ κυρίου πιστὸς εἶναι.

[65] This appeal to authorial consistency as a basis for credence will be challenged later in the correspondence (see esp. 2 Cor 10:10-11, and also in regard to Paul's differential treatment of the Macedonians in regard to money [2 Cor 11:7-11]).

strategy deliberately places the words of the text within a wider communicative plan in which (it is implied) *fuller meaning* will eventually be disclosed.

6. *Creating a rhetorical document that either invites or does not invite further conversation about its meaning.* For example, sometimes Paul engages in aporia, pretending that he is unsure about what to say, and inviting his readers in on the compositional choice. But this is a pretense for rhetorical effect, as in 1 Cor 11:22: τί εἴπω ὑμῖν; ἐπαινέσω ὑμᾶς; ἐν τούτῳ οὐκ ἐπαινῶ.[66] However, at other times Paul can either invite or squelch continuing conversation or debate about what he has written, as the following contrast illustrates:

> 1 Cor 10:15 ὡς φρονίμοις λέγω· κρίνατε ὑμεῖς ὅ φημι[67]
> 1 Cor 14:37 ... ἐπιγινωσκέτω ἃ γράφω ὑμῖν ὅτι κυρίου ἐστὶν ἐντολή

One can imagine that this vacillation in hermeneutical invitation—within the same letter—left Paul's readers somewhat unsure of their interpretive freedom in relation to texts written by this author.

B. *Stage Two: Negotiation of Meaning by the Initial Readers*

For their part, Paul's original Corinthian readers also had to make choices in their reactions and responses to the text addressed to them, which are part of the complex of meaning of that text and of the ongoing dialogue within which each subsequent letter is situated.[68] That this is true is shown graphically in the fact that, if someone had not decided to preserve these letters, they would have no contemporary meaning to be disputed! The decisions made by the original readers (who may not, of course, have been responsible for the complete preservation of the archive) include some of the following crucial steps toward developing meaning, which are registered in the correspondence:

---

[66] Cf. 1 Cor 14:26: τί οὖν ἐστιν, ἀδελφοί;

[67] Cf. 11:13 Ἐν ὑμῖν αὐτοῖς κρίνετε.

[68] See Wolfgang Iser, *The Act of Reading: A Theory of Aesthetic Response* (Baltimore: Johns Hopkins University Press, 1978) 107: "Of course, the text is a 'structured prefigurement', but that which is given has to be received, and the *way* in which it is received depends as much on the reader as on the text." Iser's argument, which is based upon the study of novels, has a particularly sharp relevance in epistolary literature, which is an especially lively communicative conversation between active partners.

1. *Deciding to read, and what kinds of readers to be* (attentive, careless, enthusiastic, suspicious, etc.). The Corinthian correspondence is the most famous locus in the Pauline correspondence for recognizably significant shifts in such readerly dispositions as the correspondence proceeds.[69] First, on a mere practical level, potential readers must have some means of finding and reading the text or having it read to them, either individually or collectively, in some context. We do not know the precise situations within which Paul's letters were originally read to their intended addressees. It is possible that envoys did this (in 1 Corinthians, perhaps the co-sender Sosthenes would play this role, or Stephanas and his delegation, or Chloe's people [1 Cor 1:2; 16:15-18; 11:1]). A public, rather than private, reading is consonant with the plural address throughout, and the common designation ἀδελφοί for the readers. The best piece of evidence in that regard is 1 Cor 5:4 which, though not a direct description of Corinthian reading habits, may, in its embedded assumptions by Paul, tells us that he assumes they will read his letter collectively, perhaps in a liturgical setting, or some other corporate context wherein Paul's disciplinary sentence could be pronounced, and an offender cast out. None of the extant forms of Paul's many letters to Corinth contains a command or adjuration to read the letter publicly "to all the brothers and sisters," as does 1 Thess 5:27. Did Paul follow that practice in Corinth, also, such that he as author *mandated* the reception of his text, or were the Corinthians in some sense free to read it or not, depending upon any number of considerations? This must remain an open question, but we may say in general that all readers at some point, whether at the moment of first declamation or of optional rereading, had to determine at least provisionally *whether or not the text with which they were faced was something which deserved their attention*, either by seeking out this text or by choosing to focus on it when pronounced aloud in their presence, or following up by thinking about it afterwards.

2. *Seeking authorial clarification*, in writing (1 Cor 7:1), via envoys or in person (1 Cor 1:11; 16:17; 2 Cor 7:5-16 and 1:15, etc.). The

---

[69] For example, Reimund Bieringer, "Paul's Divine Jealousy: The Apostle and His Communities in Relationship," in idem and Jan Lambrecht, eds., *Studies on 2 Corinthians* (BETL 112; Leuven: Peeters, 1994) 223-53, whose argument for the unity of 2 Corinthians because it pursues throughout the theme of Paul's relationship with the Corinthians, however, is not convincing (for details, see my review in *Theologische Literaturzeitung* 121[1996] 354-56).

Corinthians were not just passive receptors of Paul's words, but there is good evidence that they sought better understanding of these letters through further conversation about the text and the subjects which they engaged. This raises many intriguing and important questions about who within the Corinthian house churches might especially have been involved in these hermeneutical discussions (but they would move us well beyond the scope of this essay, and rather swiftly beyond the extant evidence).

3. *Deciding whether to follow the instructions in the text in some way, or not.* The Corinthian readers' reactions qualify the meaning of Paul's epistolary instructions by demonstrating whether they were reasonable, compelling, attractive or persuasive. 1 Cor 11:2 may be Paul the author's positive registering of their acquiescence to his earlier texts' instructions (Ἐπαινῶ δὲ ὑμᾶς ὅτι πάντα μου μέμνησθε καί, καθὼς παρέδωκα ὑμῖν, τὰς παραδόσεις κατέχετε). The disciplinary act carried out against the offender mentioned in 2 Cor 2:5-11 and 7:12 seems to be another such case. But there are also instances where the Corinthians apparently rejected Paul's advice, arguments or directives, the most obvious being the case of πορνεία in 1 Corinthians 5 which apparently followed a letter by the apostle counseling μὴ συναναμίγνυσθαι πόρνοις (5·9). Naturally, what constitutes a πόρνος is precisely the problem, but it is not unreasonable to imagine that the malefactor knew his interpretation of the matter was different from Paul's, but he "took his father's wife" anyway.

4. *Making evaluative pronouncements to other readers* (and perhaps the author himself, at least by dissemination) about the quality and effect of the writing. Readers can have all kinds of impressions of a text, but keep them to themselves. Yet Paul could not have quoted back the piece of Pauline criticism in 2 Cor 10:10 if it had not somehow reached his ears. In that case Paul had either been confronted by the statement publicly during the disastrous visit (12:21), or some Corinthian travelers had spread the message to Paul that such a thing was being said by τις (surely naming names). The Corinthian readers, or at least a good body of them (cf. οἱ πλείονες in 2:6), also communicated to Paul via Titus their readerly reception of his "Letter of Tears," which led them to λύπη, on the one hand, and ἐπιπόθησις, ὀδυρμός, ζῆλος ὑπὲρ Παύλου (7:7), on the other (cf. the more extended list of effects in 7:11). All these interpretive reactions were somehow shared with others to form enough of a group consensus

that it could be communicated back to the author as having collective weight in the interpretive negotiations.

5. *Engaging in historical contextual interpretation* of the text by contrasting the writing with other things known about the author to see if one interprets the other—or not. This is the method used to such stinging effect by the Pauline critic τις (2 Cor 10:10-11), who highlighted what he saw to be a considerable inconsistency between Paul's personal presence and oratorical effectiveness and the bombastic nature of his textual communications. This hermeneutical move was also essential to the Corinthians' growing distrust of Paul's financial dealings, for his refusal to accept payment while in Corinth (as even invoked by him as an exemplum in 1 Corinthians 9) stood in stark contrast, on the one hand, to his arrangements with the Macedonian churches (2 Cor 11:9), and with his later epistolary appeals to the Corinthians for the collection (1 Cor 16:1-4; 2 Corinthians 8), on the other.[70]

6. *Engaging in literary contextual interpretation* by reading Paul's letters in the light of a wider net of literary texts, including other documents and authors they have read (or heard about). This step lies behind 2 Cor 10:10, for the judgment of τις was based upon some comparative process by which Paul's letters were assessed as βαρεῖαι καὶ ἰσχυραί and his oral rhetorical performance as worthy only of an ἰδιώτης (this involved a double comparison between Paul and other writers and orators, on the one hand, and between the Paul of each medium with himself, on the other). The comparative hermeneutic itself comes up for critique by Paul in 2 Cor 10:12-18, though he is not able to carry off the argument for his own legitimacy without likewise employing the σύγκρισις motif (see especially 11:22f.). And even in his defense against the concerns of the Corinthians that the "Letter of Tears" had caused them λύπη, Paul sets up a comparative construct of another sort of letter (one that he assumes exists) which generates ἡ τοῦ κόσμου λύπη; as compared with this literary standard, Paul's letter, which brought about ἡ κατὰ θεὸν λύπη, stands superior, and therefore exonerated of any blame.

---

[70] Conversely, Paul uses the same strategy himself in defending his vascillating travel plans, where he appeals to other instances of his own λόγος as binding the meaning of these utterances about his itinerary: the mouth which spoke the cosmic divine "yes" of the gospel could hardly have mixed up his "yes" and "no" (i.e., prevaricated) in the case of his intended travel plans (2 Cor 1:17-20).

7. *Disparaging the text by rejecting its author*—his legitimacy, his authority, his character, and/or his authorial skill (2 Cor 13:3; 11:6, etc.), and therefore lowering the currency of esteem of the writing itself. Some of the Corinthian readers came to have a low opinion of Paul in the course of the events and communications we can trace in the Corinthian archive. To some degree it is a "chicken and egg" argument as to whether the letters caused the disparagement of Paul or whether a negative view of the author led to a dismissal of the writings, for surely the two operations were inextricably linked. And Paul's ubiquitous self-reference in the letters themselves, in service of both deliberative[71] and apologetic arguments, placed this hermeneutic always in the immediate forefront of meaning of the texts in the Corinthian archive.

C. *Stage Three: Pauline Retrospective Hermeneutics in Dialogue with His Readers*

The readers' strategies of textual reception, reaction and reportage become part of the record of negotiated meaning of the text. Especially because the Corinthians at key moments registered questions, doubts, worries and objections to Paul's earlier letters (per strategy 4 above), Paul in response engages in a secondary or even tertiary level of self-interpretation as part of the process of communication. In doing so Paul interprets his earlier missive in the light of its reception, and of other hermeneutical assumptions that *he* brings to the process and invokes (sometimes overtly, sometimes by implication) in order to substantiate his own retrospective version of the meaning of his letters. In doing so via an epistolary medium, the new interpretive letters become themselves further stages in the ongoing process of communication.[72] Accordingly both Paul and the Corinthians as textual interpreters shape meaning in two temporal directions: as they cogitate about the meaning of past writings they create the texts that will become the subject of future hermeneutical deliberations. In his own participation in this process Paul employs such steps and strategies as the following:

---

[71] On the centrality of Paul's appeal to his own example in 1 Corinthians and its rhetorical function, see Mitchell, *Paul*, 49-60.

[72] One might bring this notion fruitfully to a discussion of Pauline pseudepigraphy, particularly in relation to 2 Thessalonians (which is apparently the only extant, canonical pseudepigraphon that is overtly cast as a sequel to an existing piece of correspondence).

1. *Quoting back the words of his own earlier text, and clarifying referents that were unclear* (or are no longer desirable in the present?), sometimes with a reason why the earlier statement could not be interpreted in the way taken or possibly taken. The clearest example of this is 1 Cor 5:9-10: Ἔγραψα ὑμῖν ἐν τῇ ἐπιστολῇ μὴ συναναμίγνυσθαι πόρνοις .... From the later vantage point Paul now adds to the citation the phrase οὐ πάντως, together with an interpretive comment based upon the presumption that surely Paul would not have written instructions for them to do something that was logically or practically impossible (οὐ πάντως τοῖς πόρνοις τοῦ κόσμου τούτου ἢ τοῖς πλεονέκταις ... ἐπεὶ ὠφείλετε ἄρα ἐκ τοῦ κόσμου ἐξελθεῖν).

2. *Quoting back the words of the earlier text,*[73] *juxtaposed with a fresh interpretive statement.* Here we are on less sure ground, for Paul does not mark all these with quotation formulas, both because he assumes his readers will recognize phrases that are already part of their shared communication history, and also because he is engaging in new arguments which he seeks elegantly to ground on shared opinions or principles presented as uncontestably true (for which, therefore, extensive defense or documentation would be unsuitable). Despite this qualification, we can identify a likely example of this technique in 1 Cor 6:12 and 10:23, where Paul re-cites his earlier statement, πάντα μοι ἔξεστιν, but adds to it the all-important qualification ἀλλ᾽ οὐ πάντα συμφέρει. Then in both instances Paul formulates a new retelling of the earlier textual citation in parallel fashion in such a way as to move the slogan forward into the present historical and rhetorical context—in the first instance, to introduce the concept of ἐξουσία, which will be so important in the entire subargument (πάντα μοι ἔξεστιν ἀλλ᾽ οὐκ ἐγὼ ἐξουσιασθήσομαι ὑπό τινος), and in the latter to coordinate that language into the syllogistic terminology of "upbuilding" which is so central to his unifying argument throughout 1 Corinthians (πάντα ἔξεστιν ἀλλ᾽ οὐ πάντα οἰκοδομεῖ).[74]

3. *Quoting back the words of a Corinthian critique, either as a rhetorical question or part of a self-defense of that criticism.* The clearest instance of this is 2 Cor 10:10, which is the most direct quotation imaginable of a negative reading of his letters: ὅτι αἱ ἐπιστολαὶ μέν, φησίν, βαρεῖαι

---

[73] Paul also quotes back words of uncertain provenance that may have been oral (or written, but are not found in any existing text), such as in 2 Cor 7:3 (προείρηκα γὰρ ὅτι ἐν ταῖς καρδίαις ἡμῶν ἐστε εἰς τὸ συναποθανεῖν καὶ συζῆν); cf. 13:2, which is clearly oral (προείρηκα καὶ προλέγω, ὡς παρὼν τὸ δεύτερον).

[74] For these exegetical arguments, see Mitchell, *Paul*, 232-58 and 99-111.

καὶ ἰσχυραί, ἡ δὲ παρουσία τοῦ σώματος ἀσθενὴς καὶ ὁ λόγος ἐξουθενημένος.[75] Paul had in this case evidently made the decision that bringing this piece of critical reaction to his letters into the light and re-broadcasting it *himself* would be more effective than letting it linger, unstated but implied, over the reading of his present letter. But elsewhere Paul is less direct, and rather than *quoting* readerly reactions makes allusions to them, unmistakable to the Corinthians no doubt, but less certain for the modern scholar. Yet a quite probable example is to be found in 2 Cor 3:1: Ἀρχόμεθα πάλιν ἑαυτοὺς συνιστάνειν;—a refrain repeated no less than three more times in this letter: that Paul's prior letter(s) involved inappropriate self-recommendation.[76] The tone of incredulousness with which this objection is quoted here by Paul is meant to deflect both the prior criticism and the possibility that Paul will get the same reaction from the new text he is now composing. Here Paul chooses not to go back to 1 Corinthians or 2 Corinthians 8 to give an exegetical defense of how those documents do not entail self-recommendation. Instead he shifts the exegetical conversation away from the earlier disputed missives and onto a new text he now conjures up with his pen: the Corinthians themselves as ἡ ἐπιστολὴ ἡμῶν or ἐπιστολὴ Χριστοῦ. Over *this* text Paul claims absolute hermeneutical control (for the Corinthians are no longer *readers* but *text*, which, ironically, takes away their role as interpreters!), as he is both subject, material (ἐγγεγραμμένη ἐν ταῖς καρδίαις ἡμῶν), publisher (διακονηθεῖσα ὑφ᾽ ἡμῶν), publicist (γινωσκομένη καὶ ἀναγινωσκομένη ὑπὸ πάντων ἀνθρώπων) and, as the larger argument shows, arbiter and facilitator of its interpretation. The proper exegesis of this rival new text (deflecting attention from both the "null texts" of Paul's missing letters of recommendation, and alike the "real text" of 2 Corinthians 8 in which

---

[75] A direct quotation of some Corinthian reactions to Paul's letters likely also lies behind the preceding verse: ἵνα μὴ δόξω ὡς ἂν ἐκφοβεῖν ὑμᾶς διὰ τῶν ἐπιστολῶν.

[76] Cf. 5:12: οὐ πάλιν ἑαυτοὺς συνιστάνομεν ὑμῖν; 4:2: συνιστάνοντες ἑαυτοὺς πρὸς πᾶσαν συνείδησιν ἀνθρώπων; 6:4: ἀλλ᾽ ἐν παντὶ συνιστάντες ἑαυτοὺς ὡς θεοῦ διάκονοι; and 4:5: οὐ ... ἑαυτοὺς κηρύσσομεν (cf. in the next letter, 10:12; 12:11). Paul refers to Corinthian critiques throughout this letter (2:14-7:4), but in most cases we do not have enough evidence to argue for direct quotation (but likely some key phrases, like καπηλεύειν τὸν λόγον τοῦ θεοῦ in 2:17, περιπατοῦντες ἐν πανουργίᾳ and δολοῦντες τὸν λόγον τοῦ θεοῦ in 4:2, are at least partial quotations). I regard the first epithets in each of the contrasting pairs of 2 Cor 6:8-10, as well as the series of denials in 7:2, as reflecting some Corinthians' interpretation of Paul.

he wrote a letter of recommendation for others) by definition, he argues, belongs to the realm of spirit-hermeneutics which he presents himself as having been appointed by the deity to promulgate.[77] The only alternative allowed for, either to what Paul defines as "text" (the Corinthians [3:2 f.], and τὸ εὐαγγέλιον ἡμῶν [4:3=ὁ λόγος τοῦ θεοῦ in 4:2]) or the reading thereof, is the "blinded minds," veiled hermeneutic of Moses (3:12-18; 4:4).

Elsewhere Paul apparently quotes back the words of some Corinthian Pauline interpreters in the ironic allusions of 2 Cor 10:1 (Αὐτὸς δὲ ἐγὼ Παῦλος ... ὃς κατὰ πρόσωπον μὲν ταπεινὸς ἐν ὑμῖν, ἀπὼν δὲ θαρρῶ εἰς ὑμᾶς), and, of course, the charges of 10:2 (... τοὺς λογιζομένους ἡμᾶς ὡς κατὰ σάρκα στρατευόμεθα), 10:8 and many other places in regard to boasting (ἐάν τε γὰρ περισσότερόν τι καυχήσωμαι περὶ τῆς ἐξουσίας ἡμῶν ...),[78] 11:5 and 12:11 on the comparison with the super apostles (λογίζομαι γὰρ μηδὲν ὑστερηκέναι τῶν ὑπερλίαν ἀποστόλων. εἰ δὲ καὶ ἰδιώτης τῷ λόγῳ ... οὐδὲν γὰρ ὑστέρησα τῶν ὑπερλίαν ἀποστόλων), and the serious accusations of financial misconduct occasioned by his epistolary fund-raising as contrasted with his refusal of payment in person, as in 11:8 (ἄλλας ἐκκλησίας ἐσύλησα), 12:14 (οὐ γὰρ ζητῶ τὰ ὑμῶν) and 12:16 (ἀλλὰ ὑπάρχων πανοῦργος δόλῳ ὑμᾶς ἔλαβον). He does the same in the "Letter toward Reconciliation," which likely contains a Corinthian stigmatization of Paul's non-adherence to his written travel plans as τῇ ἐλαφρίᾳ χρῆσθαι and παρ' [αὐτῷ] τὸ ναὶ ναὶ καὶ τὸ οὒ οὒ (2 Cor 1:17). Paul responds first with an outright denial, likely phrased in their own terminology: ὁ λόγος ἡμῶν ὁ πρὸς ὑμᾶς οὐκ ἔστιν ναὶ καὶ οὒ (1:18), and then offers proofs from earlier experience about the truthfulness and divine source of his λόγος, which (he asserts) would make *any* act of prevarication impossible (1:19-22).

4. *Writing a new text which supersedes the old.* While the last example (2 Corinthians 3) shows that Paul can do this in a most imaginative, even fantastic way (turning his readers into the text they wish to read), elsewhere Paul more simply writes a new letter which extends and corrects the prior one. After referring to an earlier letter in 1 Cor

---

[77] ὃς καὶ ἱκάνωσεν ἡμᾶς διακόνους καινῆς διαθήκης, οὐ γράμματος ἀλλὰ πνεύματος (3:6; see the full argument in 3:1-18, and beyond).

[78] This Corinthian reading of Paul's previous letters is alluded to frequently in the "Letter of Tears," in regard to boasting, as in 10:13 (ἡμεῖς δὲ οὐκ εἰς τὰ ἄμετρα καυχησόμεθα); 10:15 (οὐκ εἰς τὰ ἄμετρα καυχώμενοι ἐν ἀλλοτρίοις κόποις); 10:16 (οὐκ ἐν ἀλλοτρίῳ κανόνι εἰς τὰ ἕτοιμα καυχήσασθαι).

5:9 (Ἔγραψα ὑμῖν ἐν τῇ ἐπιστολῇ), in 1 Cor 5:11 Paul sets up the overt contrast: νῦν δὲ ἔγραψα ὑμῖν μὴ συναναμίγνυσθαι ἐάν τις ἀδελφὸς ὀνομαζόμενος ᾖ πόρνος κ.τ.λ.). This is an interpretive strategy that is only available to the author (or to one holding supreme authority above the author)—to severely compromise and limit the influence of the earlier text—but it still depends upon the presumed authority of the sender in *both* the missives mentioned. Notably, Paul preserves the integrity of the first text in his careful emendation in the second round, for he retains the syntax and substance of the first, but supplements that (still authorized) wording with an important addition (ἐάν τις ἀδελφὸς ὀνομαζόμενος ᾖ).

5. *Making a direct appeal to the exact wording of the text in question*, highlighting some words or phrases that the readers may not have emphasized or appreciated in their reading of the text.[79] In 2 Cor 2:4-9 Paul explains in the most painstaking way why he had written what he had written (καὶ ἔγραψα τοῦτο αὐτό ... εἰς τοῦτο γὰρ καὶ ἔγραψα). This passage of Pauline self-exegesis brings into relief three key terms in 2 Corinthians 10-13 which, he argues, were its main purpose: ἀλλὰ τὴν ἀγάπην ἵνα γνῶτε,[80] εἰς τοῦτο γὰρ καὶ ἔγραψα, ἵνα γνῶ τὴν δοκιμὴν ὑμῶν, εἰ εἰς πάντα ὑπήκοοί ἐστε.[81] This form of textual hermeneutics assumes that the words of the text are primary sources to be drawn upon in the arbitration of its meaning. They are the publicly verifiable body of data available to both readers and writer in subsequent discussions and debates about texts' meanings. Here Paul finds enough evidence (culled, it is important to note, largely from

---

[79] This procedure would likely depend upon Paul having kept copies of his letters, which I regard as likely (as does Harry Y. Gamble, *Books and Readers in the Early Church: A History of Early Christian Texts* [New Haven: Yale University Press, 1995] 101: "The tangled correspondence of Paul with the Corinthians, if not typical, certainly indicates that Paul needed to and did keep track of what he had written"). Yet it is also possible that Paul is at times quoting his own letters from memory. That would be an interesting situation, for it would mean that the Corinthians would have possession of the text, and Paul only of his memory of it! Either way, "the text, once placed in the hands of the recipients, was no longer under Paul's control and might be used as the community or its members saw fit" (Gamble, *Books and Readers*, 96).

[80] 2:4; cf. 2 Cor 11:11; 12:15.

[81] 2 Cor 2:9; cf. 2 Cor 13:5-7 on the δοκιμή, especially 13:5: ἑαυτοὺς δοκιμάζετε· ἢ οὐκ ἐπιγινώσκετε ἑαυτοὺς ὅτι Ἰησοῦς Χριστὸς ἐν ὑμῖν; εἰ μήτι ἀδόκιμοί ἐστε; and on the ὑπακοή see 10:5-6: αἰχμαλωτίζοντες πᾶν νόημα εἰς τὴν ὑπακοὴν τοῦ Χριστοῦ, καὶ ἐν ἑτοίμῳ ἔχοντες ἐκδικῆσαι πᾶσαν παρακοήν, ὅταν πληρωθῇ ὑμῶν ἡ ὑπακοή (cf. also the retrospective retelling of their proper receipt of the letter in 7:15: ἀναμιμνησκομένου τὴν πάντων ὑμῶν ὑπακοήν).

the rhetorical proem and peroration of the argument) to set forward an interpretation of the "Letter of Tears" as one predominantly written to show the author's love and provide an opportunity for the readers to demonstrate their "testworthiness" and obedience—both of which goals, Paul claims, were successfully achieved by the missive.

6. *Appealing to authorial intention at the time of composition* to adjudicate between the now-stated purpose of a text and its actual effects on the readers at the time. In the case of the "Letter of Tears," as we have just noted, although Paul is able to generate an exegesis of that text that reads much more positively than the Corinthians' actual experience of it (2:4-9; would ἀγάπη be the strongest impression a reader would take away from 2 Corinthians 10-13?), he still must respond to the grief the text did cause them (which he states was not his purpose [2:4: ἔγραψα ὑμῖν ... οὐχ ἵνα λυπηθῆτε]). The underlying problem here is encapsulated in the cultural commonplace shared by the Corinthians and by Paul, that friends are those who have the same joys and the same griefs (whereas by definition enemies are those who rejoice while you mourn).[82] It is in this context that we must appreciate the retrospective exegesis of chapters 10-13 in 2:1-4 and 7:8-13. Paul's first step is to acknowledge the bitter irony that the letter he had sent to avoid λύπη had in fact *caused* λύπη (ἵνα μὴ ἐλθὼν λύπην σχῶ ἀφ' ὧν ἔδει με χαίρειν [2:3]), even though that was expressly not his intention (ἔγραψα ὑμῖν ... οὐχ ἵνα λυπηθῆτε [2:4]). This would involve an incommensurability among the partners which could only be attributed to hidden enmity on Paul's part, unless, that is, he had in fact been in λύπη just as the Corinthians were. Paul had already prepared for his argument in the repetitive but rhetorically effective epistolary blessing in 1:3-7 which insists resoundingly that Paul and the Corinthians are united in the same griefs and the same promise of comfort (1:7: εἰδότες ὅτι ὡς κοινωνοί ἐστε τῶν παθημάτων, οὕτως καὶ τῆς παρακλήσεως). But what of the past, when there seemed to be disparity in this regard? Initially Paul maintains vigorously that his purpose in writing was not grief, but love (2:4, note how far τὴν ἀγάπην is pulled out of its own clause to emphasize this). This authorial intention is supported by his self-description at the moment of composition as weeping, filled with affliction and distress of the heart (2:4). His self-portrait as the agonizing author is meant to hang ponderously over the text and color

---

[82] For documentation, see Mitchell, *Paul*, 162.

the meaning of it as a missive produced by a man in such a state.[83]
The intent must be the meaning; the authorial emotion at composition, he claims, indelibly imprints the meaning of the text for all
time.

But Paul must still account, by several different arguments, for
the fact that despite his intention the Corinthians *were* greatly sad-
dened by what he wrote. First he emphasizes that he was in turmoil,
not just while writing the painful letter, but even at the very moment that they were reading his letter (this is the purpose of the
"travelogue" of 2:12-13 and 7:5-6—to show that he and the Corinthians were united in grief even at that crucial moment of distance-
mediated communication). Second, he concedes, if only conditionally,
that the Corinthians *may have been grieved* by his letter ("Ὅτι εἰ καὶ
ἐλύπησα ὑμᾶς ἐν τῇ ἐπιστολῇ [2:8]), and then follows up with an
empirical acknowledgement of the fact that they were (βλέπω γὰρ
ὅτι ἡ ἐπιστολὴ ἐκείνη εἰ καὶ πρὸς ὥραν ἐλύπησεν ὑμᾶς [2:8]).[84] Next
Paul engages in a clever argument of definition to demonstrate that
the grief his letter caused was not ἡ τοῦ κόσμου λύπη, but ἡ κατὰ
θεὸν λύπη, and hence not a grief born from his enmity for them,
but of divinely inspired love which has as its goal repentance and,
ultimately, salvation (7:10). So Paul does not regret having written
the "Letter of Tears," because that salvific outcome has been effectively carried out by his letter, and as a result of the full hermeneutical process, Paul claims, they are now united in the same παράκλησις,
"comfort" (7:6-7, 12-13). So even if Paul's original proximate intention—not to cause grief—was in fact not brought about, he is satisfied and vindicated (he asserts) by the fact that his *ultimate intention*—to ensure
the Corinthians' salvation [σωτηρία ἀμεταμέλητος (7:10)]—has been
promoted by this controversial text. In this way Paul seeks decisively
to characterize, not just the meaning of his own composition, but
also its *Wirkungsgeschichte*.

---

[83] In essence, the redactor of the Corinthian correspondence has brought Paul's
wish to perpetual fulfillment. As far as we know, 2 Corinthians 10-13 was never
published disconnected from this authorial self-portrait (in 2:4).

[84] Though he does also slip in mention that the grief was only temporary (εἰ
καὶ πρὸς ὥραν).

IV. *Conclusion*

The preceding overview of reading strategies used by Paul and the
Corinthians in the course of negotiating the meaning of his letters is
not meant to be exhaustive, but to represent some essential ways
the two partners dialogued about the legacy and effects of these texts.
That such strategies were necessary demonstrates that both this author
and his readers realized that hermeneutics is no easy business, and
texts are not translucently clear or unambiguous—but they are nonetheless worth spending time on. That the Corinthian correspondence
was the locus for the birth of Pauline hermeneutics means that it is
also in a very real sense also the birthplace of Pauline misunderstanding. It is in the light of the frustrations of negotiated meaning that
our author, near the end of this whole correspondence course in the
agonies of interpretation, provides an ironic authorial exclamation
of exhaustion at the complexities of the hermeneutical tasks via a
claim that is both naive and emphatically disproved in the texts
themselves: οὐ γὰρ ἄλλα γράφομεν ὑμῖν ἀλλ' ἢ ἃ ἀναγινώσκετε ἢ
καὶ ἐπιγινώσκετε, "for we do not write to you things other than what
you read and recognize" (2 Cor 1:12-14). But of course the birth of
misapprehension is simultaneously the offer of interpretive complexity
and richness,[85] which perhaps does much to account for the fact that
these texts continue to lure interpreters into their whirlwind—readers who stay for more than one conversation in Pauline hermeneutics, because the promise of discerning profound meaning is there
even amidst the more than ample demonstrations of its inherent
elusiveness.[86]

---

[85] Paul's crucial role in the creation of a Christian intellectual culture in this
regard has been astutely appreciated by Averil Cameron: "Paul, who had never
seen Jesus and whose writings are earlier than the first of the Gospels, established
the precedent that Christianity was to be a matter of articulation and interpretation. Its subsequent history was as much about words and their interpretation as
it was about belief and practice" (*Christianity and the Rhetoric of Empire: The Development of Christian Discourse* [Sather Classical Lectures 55; Berkeley: University of
California Press, 1991] 13-14).

[86] I would like to thank Hans Dieter Betz, Scott Bowie, Paul Duff, Hans-Josef
Klauck, Wayne Meeks and Calvin Roetzel for their most perceptive remarks and
valuable critiques of earlier drafts of this essay.

PAUL AND JESUS TRADITION: THE EVIDENCE OF 1 CORINTHIANS 2:9 AND GOSPEL OF THOMAS 17

Christopher Tuckett

The debate about the relationship between "Paul and Jesus" is a perennial and wide-ranging one, with many different issues potentially at stake. One (and only one) aspect of the debate concerns the possible extent to which Paul may have known and used traditions about Jesus in his own letters. The identification of such traditions might give us insight into Paul and his own tradition as well as possibly providing a valuable source for the Jesus tradition itself. For many too, the existence of such traditions is important in establishing how far there is substantive continuity between Paul's teaching and the teaching of Jesus. However, even when parallels between Paul's words and Jesus tradition can be established, one must be wary of deducing too much too quickly. Modern gospel study has long accepted as axiomatic the possibility that some traditions in the gospels were read into the Jesus story and placed on the lips of Jesus secondarily. Thus a parallel between Paul and Jesus tradition might not necessarily show that Paul was dependent on the Jesus tradition and/or the historical Jesus himself. Rather, the line of dependency may go the other way: sayings may have been read into the gospel tradition from the Pauline letters.[1]

In a few instances, Paul himself makes clear that he is quoting, or alluding to, Jesus tradition (cf. 1 Cor 7:10; 9:14; 11:23). In other instances, Paul's language is less clear and it is uncertain whether he is intending to allude to Jesus tradition or not (cf. Rom 14:14; 1 Thess 4:15).[2] Much of the debate then focuses on a number of instances where Paul's words provide a parallel to similar words or ideas in the Jesus tradition, with discussion then on whether Paul

---

[1] Cf. M.D. Goulder, *Midrash and Lection in Matthew* (London: SPCK, 1974) 153-70, on the parallels between Matthew and Paul as perhaps going from Paul to Matthew (though not necessarily directly), rather than vice versa.

[2] Rom 14:14 ("I know and am persuaded in the Lord Jesus ...") and 1 Thess 4:15 ("this we say by a word of the Lord") can both be taken as referring to alleged teaching of Jesus, but need not do so.

might have been aware of the existence of such parallels or not.[3]

In many of the discussions to date,[4] the possibility that Paul might have used Jesus tradition is often discussed in relation to possible parallels between Paul and the synoptic gospels. It has however been a feature of recent studies of the historical Jesus that more openness is now shown to non-canonical sources as possibly providing just as valuable access to the historical Jesus as the canonical gospels in (what later became) the "New Testament".[5] Above all the Gospel of Thomas (GTh) has been seen by many as a source independent of the synoptics and incorporating valuable early tradition. In the light of these new developments in Jesus research, the question of "Paul and Jesus" may take on rather different contours if one takes seriously the possibility that the 'Jesus' side of the balance should not be confined to the canonical texts alone. Thus James Robinson has (in my view rightly) criticised the approach of N. Walter in his discussion of the issue of Paul's possible use of Jesus traditions, where Walter focuses solely on canonical material to identify possible Jesus traditions.[6] Robinson's cited example of one piece of evidence omitted in this way was 1 Cor 2:9, a saying apparently quoted as scrip-

---

[3] The closest parallels are probably Rom 12:14 cf. Matt 5:44 par.; Rom 12:17 cf. Matt 5:39-41 par.; Rom 13:7 cf. Mark 12:13-17 pars.; Rom 13:8-10 cf. Mark 12:28-34 pars.; 1 Cor 13:2 cf. Matt 17:20; 21:21 pars.; 1 Thess 5:2 cf. Matt 24:43 // Luke 12:39.

[4] E.g. most recently, N. Walter, "Paulus und der urchristliche Tradition", *NTS* 31 (1985) 498-522 (ET in A.J.M. Wedderburn [ed.], *Paul and Jesus. Collected Essays* [JSNTSup 37; Sheffield: JSOT, 1989] 57-80); F. Neirynck, "Paul and the Sayings of Jesus", *Evangelica II* (BETL 99; Leuven: Peeters, 1991) 511-68; idem, "The Sayings of Jesus in 1 Corinthians", in R. Bieringer (ed.), *The Corinthian Correspondence* (BETL 125; Leuven: Peeters, 1996) 141-76; M. Thompson, *Clothed with Christ. The Example and Teaching of Jesus in Romans 12.1—15.13* (JSNTSup 59; Sheffield: JSOT, 1991); J.D.G. Dunn, "Jesus Tradition in Paul", in B. Chilton & C.A. Evans (eds.), *Studying the Historical Jesus. Evaluations of the State of Current Research* (Leiden: Brill, ²1998) 155-78; D. Wenham, *Paul. Follower of Jesus or Founder of Christianity* (Grand Rapids: Eerdmans, 1995).

[5] Cf. H. Koester, "Apocryphal and Canonical Gospels", *HTR* 73 (1980) 105-130; idem, *Ancient Christian Gospels* (London: SCM, 1991); J.D. Crossan, *The Historical Jesus. The Life of a Mediterranean Jewish Peasant* (Edinburgh: T. & T. Clark, 1991); and the work of the Jesus Seminar, especially R.W. Funk & R. Hoover (eds.), *The Five Gospels. The Search for the Authentic Words of Jesus* (New York: Polebridge, 1993). See also the collection of essays entitled *The Historical Jesus and the Rejected Gospels* in *Semeia* 44 (1988).

[6] J.M. Robinson, "The Study of the Historical Jesus after Nag Hammadi", *Semeia* 44 (1988) 45-55, esp. p. 47-8. Cf. Walter, "Paulus und der urchristliche Tradition" (n. 4 above).

ture by Paul:[7] "What no eye has seen, nor ear heard, nor the human heart conceived, what God has prepared for those who love him". A very similar saying is ascribed to Jesus in GTh 17: "Jesus said 'I shall give you what no eye has seen and what no ear has heard, and what no hand has touched and what has never occurred to the human mind'".[8] S. Patterson has taken this further and suggested that a number of sayings now found in GTh alone may lie behind Paul's words at various points in his letters.[9]

Methodologically, Robinson and Patterson are quite right to question the restriction to canonical texts in discussing the issue of Paul and Jesus tradition. Nevertheless, while all such parallels should in principle be discussed, it remains to be seen what such parallels might imply. Further, one clearly cannot make a blanket judgement covering every instance. Each case must be considered on its own merits. For this essay I shall confine attention to the parallel noted by Robinson between Paul's words in 1 Cor 2:9 and GTh 17.

Paul's apparent quotation in 1 Cor 2:9 has long been a notorious crux. Paul appears to imply that he is quoting a text from scripture (cf. καθὼς γέγραπται) and yet the words used do not correspond precisely with any known version of a single scriptural text. The closest parallel is often said to be the words from Isa 64:4 (LXX 64:3): "From ages past no one has heard, no ear has perceived, no eye has seen any God beside you, who works for those who wait for him". This contains the reference to no eye seeing and no ear hearing; but it does not contain an equivalent to "what has never occurred to the human mind" (literally "what has not arisen in the heart of man"),[10] and it has a quite different object of what it is that no eye has seen and no ear heard: in Isaiah it is any other God beside

---

[7] It is introduced with καθὼς γέγραπται "as it is written", which is usually taken as a fairly standard indication on Paul's part that he is intending to cite scripture. See below.

[8] ET from B. Layton (ed.), *Nag Hammadi Codex II,2-7 together with XIII,2, Brit. Lib. 4926(1) and P. Oxy. 1, 654, 655* (NHS 20; Leiden: Brill, 1989) 61. The saying is not extant in the Greek fragments and hence only available in Coptic. Any comparison involving the finer detail of the wording is thus impossible.

[9] S.J. Patterson, "Paul and the Jesus Tradition: It is time for another look", *HTR* 84 (1991) 23-41.

[10] There is a similar phrase in Isa 65:17 (LXX 65:16): cf. C.K. Barrett, *The First Epistle to the Corinthians* (London: A. & C. Black, 1971) 73; A.C. Thiselton, *The First Epistle to the Corinthians* (NIGNTC; Carlisle: Paternoster, 2000) 251 and others.

Yahweh himself, in Paul it is the things that God has prepared for
those who love him.[11] The location of the apparent quotation has
been a problem since very earliest times: and as early as Origen the
claim was made that Paul was citing a lost apocryphal work of Elijah
("in secretis Eliae prophetae"),[12] though this has now been shown
to be rather implausible.[13]

The "quotation", together with its parallel in GTh 17 (and possible parallels elsewhere, e.g. in Q 10:23-24 and DialSav 140), has
however been a key element in the theories of H. Koester (and, following him to some extent, S. Patterson). In a number of different
publications over several years, Koester has argued that Paul here
may be using a saying which was known to both himself and the
Corinthians, the latter using it to justify their own theological perspective. In some of his publications, Koester implies quite clearly
that this saying was known to Paul and to the Corinthians as a saying *of Jesus*, stemming from a sayings collection which is more primitive than the canonical gospels and which may underlie the sayings
source Q. Thus in a much quoted section of an early essay, originally published in 1968, Koester states:

> The basis of the *Gospel of Thomas* is a sayings collection which is more
> primitive that the canonical gospels... The relation of this "sayings
> gospel," from which the *Gospel of Thomas* is derived, to the synoptic
> sayings source Q, is an open question...But it must have been a ver-
> sion of Q in which the apocalyptic expectation of the Son of man was
> missing, and in which Jesus' radicalized eschatology of the kingdom
> and his revelation of divine wisdom in his own words were dominant
> motifs. Such a version of Q is, however, not secondary, but very primi-
> tive. At least Paul's debate with his opponents in 1 Corinthians seems
> to suggest that the wisdom theology which Paul attacked relied on this
> understanding of Jesus' message. These opponents propagated a real-
> ized eschatology. They claimed that divine wisdom was revealed through

---

[11] See all the standard studies of Paul's use of the OT: e.g. O. Michel, *Paulus
und seine Bibel* (Gütersloh: Bertelsmann, 1929) 34-6; E.E. Ellis, *Paul's Use of the Old
Testament* (repr. ed. Grand Rapids: Baker, 1981) 34-5; D.-A. Koch, *Die Schrift als
Zeuge des Evangeliums. Untersuchungen zur Verständnis der Schrift bei Paulus* (BHT 69;
Tübingen: Mohr, 1986) 37-8; C.D. Stanley, *Paul and the Language of Scripture*
(SNTSMS 69; Cambridge: CUP, 1992) 188-9.

[12] *Comm.in Matth.* 27,9 (GCS 38, 250).

[13] See the very full and detailed study of J. Verheyden, "Origen on the Origin
of 1 Cor 2,9", in R. Bieringer (ed.), *The Corinthian Correspondence* (BETL 125; Leuven:
Peeters, 1996) 491-511. Verheyden also gives very full details of modern discussions of the origin of Paul's "citation" here.

Jesus. And at least one saying which Paul quotes in the context of his refutation is indeed found in the *Gospel of Thomas* 17 (1 Cor 2:9).[14]

The same theory is propounded in his more recent *Ancient Christian Gospels*[15] where Koester discusses the case of 1 Cor 2:9 under the rubric of "The Collection of the Sayings *of Jesus*. Sayings *of Jesus* in early Christian writings" (my stress). He also claims here that the saying is quoted frequently ("in Gnostic writings") elsewhere (p. 59) and that "it has made its way into the Synoptic Sayings Source in a somewhat altered form in which it appears in Matt 13:16-17/Luke 10:23-24" (ibid.). Koester concludes this section by claiming that "wisdom sayings *of Jesus* must have been the vehicle by which the Corinthians claimed to have received this salvation [= the revelation communicated to them through 'wisdom']... A collection of such sayings must have been known to both Paul and the Corinthians" (p. 60, my stress).

However, in an essay published in 1980, Koester argued rather differently. He again referred to the similarity between 1 Cor 2:9 and Q 10:23-24 (as well as other parallels, e.g. between 1 Cor 2:7 and Matt 13:35), but here he claimed that these might go back to a lost sapiential book that "circulated under the authority *of an Old Testament figure*", and then (only) "at a *subsequent* stage of the development, material from this sapiential book—*once it had been used* by gnosticizing Christians in the time of Paul—was incorporated into the tradition of sayings of Jesus whence it eventually came to Matthew and Luke and to the *Gospel of Thomas*".[16] This suggests a rather different model: Paul and the Corinthians may have used a common saying, but this was known to them not as a saying of Jesus but as a saying attributed to an OT figure; the attribution to the saying to Jesus was then a feature of the later tradition (although this had already happened by the time of Matthew/Luke).

Patterson's model seems to be closer to that of the early and late (rather than the middle) Koester. For Patterson, "Paul quotes a saying

---

[14] H. Koester, "One Jesus and Four Primitive Gospels", *HTR* 61 (1968) 203-247, repr. in J.M. Robinson & H. Koester, *Trajectories through Early Christianity* (Philadelphia: Fortress, 1971) 158-204, quotation here from p. 186.

[15] H. Koester, *Ancient Christian Gospels*, 58-9.

[16] H. Koester, "Gnostic Writings as Witnesses for the Development of the Sayings Tradition", in B. Layton (ed.), *The Rediscovery of Gnosticism. Vol. I. The School of Valentinus* (Leiden: Brill, 1980) 238-261, on p. 249-50. Again my stress.

[i.e. of Jesus?] from the *Gospel of Thomas*",[17] and the omission of the attribution to Jesus is considered to reflect a natural change in the course of oral transmission: "The version of the saying quoted here by Paul is not paralleled word-for-word in Thomas but reflects the sort of differences one would expect to have resulted from oral transmission."[18]

There are here a number of issues which should perhaps be separated logically. First, what is 'the' saying which is under discussion? Second, was the saying quoted in 1 Cor 2:9 known to Paul as a saying *of Jesus*? Third, was the saying known also to the Corinthians? If so, did they know it as a saying of Jesus? Fourth, has Paul modified the quotation in citing it, perhaps adapting it to suit his own argument? What then is the relationship between Paul's version of the saying in 1 Cor 2 and that in GTh 17? Some of these questions may of course be unanswerable. But if so we should perhaps have the courage to say so (or at least admit to the speculative nature of any answers we might give).

1. What is "the" Saying in Question?

It is widely recognised that Paul's saying which he "quotes" is both (a) unusual in relation to previous (scriptural) texts, but also (b) has many parallels in other writings.[19] Its unusual nature has already been noted above: in particular, the extra phrase "what has not arisen in the heart of man" serves to distinguish the saying from any known single OT text. Further, the many parallels noted in other texts are usually identified as such on the basis of the unusual collocation of the references to "eye has not seen/ear has not heard" and "has not

---

[17] "Paul and the Jesus Tradition", 36. Similar in general terms is C.L. Mearns, "Early Eschatological Development in Paul: The Evidence of 1 Corinthians", *JSNT* 22 (1984) 19-35: "...in 1 Cor. 2.9 Paul cites the *Gos. Thom.* 17, showing he could have known this sayings-source as well as Q" (p. 31).

[18] Ibid., 37. Patterson does not specify any further about the changes he has in mind. However, the statement appears to imply that all the major differences are to be explained in this way.

[19] These are most fully set out in M.E. Stone & J. Strugnell, *The Books of Elijah, Parts 1-2* (Missoula: Scholars, 1979) 42-73. Many are also discussed in Verheyden, "Origen". See too W.D. Stroker, *Extra-Canonical Sayings of Jesus* (Atlanta: Scholars, 1989) 184-90; there are also a number of parallels in apocalyptic texts noted by K. Berger, "Zum Diskussion über die Herkunft von 1 Kor ii. 9", *NTS* 24 (1978) 270-83.

arisen in the heart of man" (or some close equivalent). Without such a collocation, it is rather hard to maintain that one still has the "same" saying in view.[20]

In particular, it is hard to justify the claim that a common reference to eyes seeing (or not) and ears hearing (or not) is on its own enough to claim that one is dealing with the same saying. This simple collocation is by no means unique and there are many examples of such a juxtaposition in texts throughout Jewish and Christian scripture.[21] This then makes it rather hard to see any close connection between the saying of 1 Cor 2:9 and the Q saying in Q 10:23-24. Q 10:23 ("Blessed are the eyes which see the things which you see" (Luke) / "Blessed are your eyes because they see, and your ears because they hear" (Matthew)) has a common reference to eyes seeing and ears hearing. However, such a conjunction is scarcely very distinctive,[22] and on its own is barely enough to justify any claim that one has here the same underlying tradition. Further, I argued in an earlier publication that the contents of the two sayings are rather different: 1 Cor 2:9 refers to things which people have not even been able to conceive and which still lie in the future; Q 10:23-24 speaks of things which people did conceive of (especially v. 24[23]) and longed for in the past, and which have now materialised in the present experience of Jesus' disciples.[24] It thus seems unjustified to refer to Q

---

[20] Clearly there are problems in identifying an exact form of a saying which must have changed in the course of oral transmission and/or repetition. (Cf. especially the work of J.D. Crossan, *In Fragments: The Aphorisms of Jesus* [San Francisco: Harper & Row, 1983], and also his *Historical Jesus*.) Nevertheless one does need some common features to justify any claim that one is indeed dealing with different forms of a single identifiable saying, rather than simply separate sayings.

[21] Cf. Ps 115:15; Isa 6:10; 66:8, 19; Jer 4:21; 5:21; 42:14; Lam 1:18; Ezek 1:27f.; 12:2; Matt 11:4 and par.; Mark 4:12 and pars.; 8:18 and pars.; Luke 12:20; Acts 4:20; 1 John 1:1, 13; Rev 9:20; 22:18; see also Berger, "Diskussion", 277.

[22] Cf. D. Wenham, *Paul. Follower of Jesus or Founder of Christianity* (Grand Rapids: Eerdmans, 1995), who is generally very ready to see parallels between Paul and Jesus, and also accepts that the two sayings (Q 10:23f. and 1 Cor 2:9) are "thematically rather similar" (p. 132) concedes that "the overlapping terminology is commonplace—hearing, seeing, eyes" (p. 133).

[23] "Many prophets desired to see the things which you see". Koester in fact argues that this may be a secondary elaboration of the saying, but the first part of the saying (Q 10:23) "parallels 1 Cor 2:9 ... very closely" (*Ancient Christian Gospels*, 59). In fact it is v. 24 which speaks of people *not* seeing or hearing things; v. 23 is worded entirely positively in terms of people ("you") actually seeing (and possibly hearing). Of this there is only a hint in 1 Cor 2:9 (though it is implied more clearly in what follows in 1 Cor 2:10ff.: see below).

[24] See my "1 Corinthians and Q", *JBL* 102 (1983) 607-619, on p. 616. One

10:23-24 as another version of the same saying as 1 Cor 2:9.

So too any alleged parallel in the Nag Hammadi tractate The Dialogue of the Saviour (DialSav) is doubtful. At one point, this (very fragmentary) text reads "The Lord said, [You have] asked me for a word [about that] which eye has not seen, nor have I heard about it, except from you..." (140:1-4). Again we have a joint reference to (not) seeing and hearing but nothing equivalent to the "arising in the heart of man". The content is not dissimilar to that of 1 Cor 2:9 in one way, at least with respect to "eyes seeing" as implying that what is under discussion has not been conceived ("seen") by humans before. Yet the reference to ears/hearing is unusual in that apparently here the speaker (= Jesus) says that he has *not* heard of it, although his disciples have ("except from you")! Given the highly fragmentary nature of the text, and given too the lack of any parallel corresponding to the "arise in the heart of man" phrase, it seems hard to claim with any certainty that DialSav here provides a genuine parallel to the saying in 1 Cor 2:9.

But in any case it is uncertain how much value this would have in the present discussion. I have tried to argue elsewhere that DialSav appears to show a rather developed form of the tradition of sayings of Jesus and to presuppose at least the final redacted forms of the gospels of Matthew and Luke.[25] It may thus be a relatively late witness to any form of the sayings tradition. Any parallel between DialSav and Q 10:23f. may simply be due to the dependence (probably at a number of stages removed) of DialSav on the canonical gospels of Matthew and Luke. DialSav thus does not necessarily provide any independent attestation for the early provenance of the saying.

The same may apply to GTh. It is well known that there is a great debate about the relative age of the gospel and/or of the traditions it preserves.[26] A case can be (and on many occasions has been) made for regarding GTh as a relatively late text, presupposing the redacted

---

might also note that, if one were to look for an OT background which might illuminate Q 10:23-24, it is more likely to be in a text such as Isa 6:9-10 rather than Isa 64:4 (probably the closest OT parallel to 1 Cor 2:9: cf. above): see e.g. D.C. Allison, *The Intertextual Jesus. Scripture in Q* (Harrisburg: Trinity Press International, 2000) 116.

[25] See my *Nag Hammadi and the Gospel Tradition* (Edinburgh: T. & T. Clark, 1986) 128-135.

[26] The two are not of course identical!

forms of the synoptic gospels.[27] But in any case, hopefully enough
has been said to show that the claim of e.g. Patterson, that the saying in GTh is "a saying whose antiquity is assured by its independent multiple attestation in Q (Matt 13:16-17//Luke 10:23-24), 1
Cor 2:9, DialSav 140.1-4, as well as in many other sources of later
date",[28] is at least questionable. It is doubtful whether Q 10:23-24
represents the same saying at all; the same might apply in the case
of DialSav, but in any case the nature of this text may not imply
any independent attestation at all.

The fact that "the" saying is widely attested is unquestionable: there
are many instances (including the distinctive combination of "eyes
[not] seeing + ears [not] hearing" and "not arising in the heart of
man") in a wide range of sources. Most of these are relatively late
and some may well reflect influence from 1 Cor 2:9 (or GTh 17: cf.
below): certainly such influence cannot be excluded very easily given
the relative dates of the sources concerned. This is not to say that
all such parallels are dependent on Paul (or Thomas). At least one
version of the saying is agreed as providing independent attestation,
viz. PsPhilo 26:13.[29] Others too *may* provide independent attestation of the saying, but this is rather less certain.[30] We have then a

---

[27] I myself have argued for this in my "Thomas and the Synoptics", *NovT* 30
(1988) 132-157; also "Das Thomasevangelium und die synoptischen Evangelien",
Berliner Theologische Zeitschrift 12 (1995) 186-200.

[28] *The Gospel of Thomas and Jesus* (Sonoma: Polebridge, 1993) 233.

[29] Cf. Koch, *Schrift*, 37-8; W. Schrage, *Der erste Brief an die Korinther* (EKKNT
7/1; Zürich: Benzinger, 1991) 246; also B.A. Pearson, *The Pneumatikos-Psychikos Terminology in 1 Corinthians* (SBLDS 12; Missoula: Scholars, 1973) 35; M. Philonenko,
"Quod oculus non videt. 1 Cor 2.9", *TZ* 15 (1959) 51-2.

[30] Fee's suggestion (*The First Epistle to the Corinthians* [Grand Rapids: Eerdmans,
1987] 109) that the fact that the saying appears to be reflected in AscIsa 11:34
indicates that Paul cannot have created this de novo is scarcely convincing, given
that this part of AscIsa is almost certainly written under Christian influence: whether
Paul created the saying himself is another issue, but the occurrence of the parallel in AscIsa is probably simply due to dependence on Paul (cf. Verheyden,
"Origen", 510). (In any case the allusion is only present in some versions of the
text [one Latin version and the Slavonic: see M. Knibb, in J.H. Charlesworth,
Old Testament Pseudepigrapha 2 [New York: Doubleday, 1985] 176.)

Others have suggested that e.g. the slightly different forms of the saying apparently reflected in ApostConst 7.32.5 and Clement *Protr.* 10.94.4 may reflect
Paul's possible source here rather than Paul himself (cf. E. Schürer et al, *The History of the Jewish People in the Age of Jesus Christ* Vol. III.2 [rev. ed. Edinburgh: T. &
T. Clark, 1987] 800; Schrage, *Erste Brief*, 246 n. 139 suggests that the Clement
passage and also 2 Clem 11:7 may be independent of 1 Cor 2:9.) The version in
ApostConst 7 has also been suggested as perhaps witnessing to the (probably lost)

form of the saying attested at least in Paul, PsPhilo and in Thomas. But what form was it known as: in particular, was it known as a saying *of Jesus*? Clearly if we allow the possibility that PsPhilo 26:13 provides an independent attestation of the tradition, we cannot say that it was known to the author of PsPhilo as a saying of Jesus! PsPhilo is usually dated far too early to allow such a possibility,[31] and no Christian influence has (as far as I am aware) been detected in the work. Thus PsPhilo indicates that the "saying" was probably known independently of the Christian tradition.[32]

The evidence seems clear that a version of "the" saying (defining the saying as comprising references to eyes seeing, ears hearing and also the reference to "arising in the heart...") did exist. However, apart from PsPhilo, most of the evidence is rather late. Further, there is no evidence that is unambiguously early where the saying is explicitly placed on the lips of Jesus. What then can we say of Paul?

2. *Did Paul Know the Saying as a Saying of Jesus?*

It is very difficult to establish any case that Paul knew the saying as stemming from Jesus. Certainly any suggestion that this is implied by anything Paul says explicitly can surely be dismissed very quickly. As has been pointed out by many commentators and others, the introductory formula used by Paul suggests that he at least thinks that he is (or claims to be) quoting Jewish scripture. There is no other instance in Paul's letters where he implies that any saying of Jesus has scriptural status. We have already noted that Paul does (occasionally) refer to Jesus traditions; but these references are quite different in form from his references to scripture. For Paul, all the ref-

---

ending of the Didache (so A. Garrow, *The Gospel of Matthew's Dependence on the Didache* [Oxford D.Phil. thesis, 2000] 53-9). However, all this is a little speculative and difficult to establish with any certainty. The relative dates of the material make it difficult to exclude the possibility that the parallels are simply due to dependence on the text of 1 Cor itself, with the variations simply arising from inexact 'quotations'.

[31] "A date around the time of Jesus seems most likely", according to D.J. Harrington, in Charlesworth, *OT Pseudepigrapha* 2, 299.

[32] It is though not "quoted" as a specific saying, from scripture or elsewhere, but simply presented as part of the words of God to Kenaz: "And then I will take those and many others better than they are from where eye has not seen nor has ear heard and it has not entered into the heart of man, until the like should some to pass in the world."

erences to Jesus tradition include verbs of speaking (or equivalent) attributed to Jesus.[33] By contrast, references to scripture are generally introduced by a verb implying writing (e.g. γέγραπται). The Jesus tradition for Paul thus recalls things "said" or done by Jesus. It is not yet a written text. It is thus very difficult to see how the evidence of 1 Cor 2:9 itself can be taken as implying that Paul thought that he was reproducing a saying *of Jesus*.

3. Was the Saying Known to the Corinthians? If So, Was it Known as a Saying of Jesus?

Both questions are extremely hard to answer with any degree of certainty. It is widely agreed that at some points in 1 Corinthians, Paul appears to take up words and ideas of the Corinthians he is addressing in order to modify them, at times probably quoting what they have said or claimed (cf. e.g. at 7:1; 8:1, 4). The section in 2:6-16 (within which the saying appears) presents particular difficulties of interpretation. Paul here suddenly seems to go back on what he has said up to this point in the letter in denying the value of any kind of special 'wisdom'. Thus in 2:6 Paul appears to perform a volte-face and claims that there *is* a form of "wisdom" for the "mature". Many have argued that Paul here may be taking up the language and argumentation of the Corinthians, perhaps to invert such arguments later by denying that they have any claim to this special wisdom (cf. 3:1). Further, perhaps Paul himself would claim that, however much he may use the language of the Corinthians in apparently speaking of a higher form of wisdom, at the end of the day the only true wisdom is that of the gospel of Christ crucified. Hence for Paul, the rhetorical question of 2:16 "who has known the mind of the Lord?" is answered positively in relation to *Christ*, who is and remains the crucified one.[34]

---

[33] Cf. 1 Cor 7:10 (implying that Jesus "said"); 9:14 ("commanded"); 11:23 ("said").

[34] See, with varying nuances, the commentaries on 2:6-16, e.g. H. Conzelmann, *1 Corinthians* (Hermeneia; Philadelphia: Fortress, 1975) 57-60; Fee, *First Epistle*, 100; Thiselton, *First Epistle*, 252; also D. Lührmann, *Die Offenbarungsverständnis bei Paulus und in paulinischen Gemeinden* (WMANT 16; Neukirchen-Vluyn: Neukirchener, 1965) 133-40; R.W. Funk, "Word and Word in 1 Cor 2:6-16", *Language, Hermeneutic and Word of God* (New York: Harper & Row, 1966) 275-303; Pearson, *Pneumatikos*, 30-35; J. Murphy O'Connor, *Paul: A Critical Life* (Oxford: Clarendon, 1996) 283 and many others (some listed in Schrage, *Erste Brief*, 241 n. 95; though see Schrage's

In all this, it is indeed possible to see Paul perhaps modifying the Corinthian viewpoint by the end of the section. The fact that Paul may be taking up Corinthian language suggests that it is at least plausible (though one cannot say more!) to think of the saying in 2:9 already being part of the Corinthian armoury.[35] But in what form? Might the Corinthians have thought that this was a saying of Jesus?

There is a strong case to be made for the belief that the use of Jesus tradition was a critical issue at Corinth and that the Corinthians were at times appealing to Jesus tradition to legitimate their views.[36] However, there is nothing in Paul's language, on the surface at least, to suggest that the saying cited in 2:9 was regarded by the Corinthians as a saying of Jesus. As we have seen, Paul himself cites the saying as one from scripture. On the surface, therefore, there is simply no evidence to suggest that the Corinthians believed that this was a saying of Jesus.

Yet the question just considered could be raised in a slightly different form. Could it be that Paul has deliberately changed the form of the quotation as used by the Corinthians in order subtly to subvert their position? Could it be that many, if not all, the differences between 1 Cor 2:9 and the version of the saying in (say) GTh 17 are due to such Pauline modifications?

4. Pauline Modifications? The Relationship of 1 Cor 2:9 to GTh 17

There are three main differences between 1 Cor 2:9 and GTh 17. These are (i) the extra phrase "what no hand has touched" in GTh 17 and missing in 1 Cor 2:9, (ii) the phrase "the things which God has prepared for those who love him" in 1 Cor 2:9 and absent from

---

own comment on the passage as a whole: "eine deutliche Auseinandersetzung wird aber nicht erkennbar" [241]). The unusual nature of Paul's language has led at least one scholar to argue that the whole section is a non-Pauline interpolation: cf. W. Widman, "1 Kor 2.6-16: Ein Einspruch gegen Paulus", *ZNW* 70 (1979) 44-53; for a reply, see J. Murphy O'Connor, "Interpolations in 1 Corinthians", *CBQ* 48 (1986) 81-94, on 81-4.

[35] However, Lührmann, *Offenbarungsverständnis*, 136, claims that it is in vv. 8b and 9 that Paul introduces his own correction to the Corinthian viewpoint.

[36] Cf. J.M. Robinson, *Trajectories*, 40-43; also my "1 Corinthians and Q", 619. One can point to the unusually high number of explicit references to sayings of Jesus by Paul in 1 Corinthians compared with the other letters; also 4:8 and 13:2 may be allusive reflections by Paul of appeals by others to sayings of Jesus.

GTh 17, and (iii) the fact that the saying is ascribed to Jesus in GTh, but not in 1 Cor 2:9. I take the final point first.

4.1 *A Saying of Jesus?*

In general terms it would seem very unlikely that Paul would modify a Jesus tradition in this way. It may also be worth noting that the saying is not always clearly attributed to Jesus in the subsequent tradition. It is true that the Manichean Turfan fragment M 789 has a version of the saying which is very similar to that in GTh 17 ("I will give you what you have not seen with your eyes, nor heard with your ears, nor grasped with your hand"),[37] attributing the saying to Jesus and also having the extra phrase about hands touching/grasping, as well as omitting the final phrase as it appears in 1 Cor 2:9. This does however simply serve to show the link between Manicheans and GTh, a fact which few today would dispute. The close parallel here simply shows the influence of the GTh upon later Manicheans and it can scarcely show anything about an earlier form of the saying.

Elsewhere however it is sometimes less clear whether the saying is attributed to Jesus or not, since the saying (or the activity implied in the last phrase) is attributed to an ambiguous "Lord" who could be God or Jesus.[38] In AcPeter 39 (10), the saying is (probably) regarded as one of Jesus. In many other cases the situation is unclear (cf. 1 Clem 34:8; 2 Clem 14:5) or the context seems to be more theocentric than christocentric (cf. 2 Clem 11:7; AcThomas 36; AscIsa 11:34; ApConst 7.32.5).[39] It certainly seems highly unusual that a saying attributed to Jesus in the earlier tradition should develop secondarily to become one where no reference to Jesus is mentioned and the saying is implicitly predicated of God.[40] Rather, an attribution to Jesus seems more likely to be a feature of the secondary development of the tradition.[41]

---

[37] See E. Hennecke (ed.), *New Testament Apocrypha I* (London: SCM, 1963) 300.

[38] As e.g. in EpTitus (in Hennecke [ed.], *New Testament Apocrypha II* [London: Lutterworth, 1965] 144).

[39] There is thus no clear evidence that by the time of 1 Clement the saying was regarded as a saying of Jesus.

[40] Patterson's implied claim that this is a natural stage in the development of an oral tradition (n. 18 above, if indeed that is what he intends) is undocumented.

[41] Cf. J. Jeremias, *Unknown Sayings of Jesus* (London: SPCK, 1957) 29, in relation to the saying "where I find you, there I will judge you", attributed to Jesus in

Could it be though that it is Paul who has made the change away
from a saying of Jesus, as part of his attempt to undermine the
Corinthian viewpoint?

There is however nothing in the text of 1 Cor 2 to suggest that
Paul is trying to undermine a Corinthian appeal to specifically Jesus
tradition here. Two points may be noted. First, the fact that Paul
introduces the saying with καθὼς γέγραπται would probably en-
hance, but certainly not undermine, the status of the saying. It is
true that elsewhere Paul can at times adopt a position of critical
distance in relation to Jesus tradition,[42] but there is no evidence that
he is doing so here. Indeed the second point to made here is that
Paul here gives no indication at all that he is seeking to undermine
a possible use of the saying to support a Corinthian viewpoint. We
have already seen that, in the passage as a whole (2:6-16), or in relation to the passage placed within its broader context (2:6-16 within
2:1-5 and 3:1-4), there may be some critique by Paul of the
Corinthians. But there is no hint of such a critique in the appeal to
the saying or its immediate context. Indeed, if there is any kind of
modification implied in Paul's flow of argument in going from v. 9
to v. 10, it could be argued that v. 10 might be seen to modify v. 9
in a way that would be even more conducive to the Corinthians'
views by speaking of the revelation which God has given them
through his Spirit.[43] Elsewhere, where Paul cites a quotation of the
Corinthians and critiques it, the critique is clear and (usually) im-

---

Justin *Dial.* 5.47, and widely attested elsewhere but *not* as a saying of Jesus. Cf.
too R. McL. Wilson, *Studies in the Gospel of Thomas* (London: Mowbrays, 1960) 103;
B. Dehandschutter, "L'évangile de Thomas comme collection de paroles de Jésus",
in J. Delobel (ed.), *Logia. Les paroles de Jésus—The Sayings of Jesus* (BETL 59; Leuven:
Peeters, 1982) 507-515, on p. 513.

[42] Cf. 1 Cor 9:14-15: Paul cites a saying of Jesus, claiming that Jesus had "commanded" Christian missionaries to receive payment for their work (v. 14); but then
immediately says that he will ignore this command in his own case.

[43] The precise relationship between vv. 9 and 10 is debatable, partly because
of a textual variant at the start of v. 10: some manuscripts read δέ while others
have γάρ. Hence v. 10 could be seen as perhaps in contrast with v. 9 (if one reads
δέ and takes it in an adversative sense) or as simply clarifying v. 9 (if one reads
γάρ, or indeed if one reads δέ but without a strong adversative sense). For the
latter, see e.g. Lührmann, *Offenbarungsverständnis*, 116; Schrage, *Erste Brief*, 256 (both
reading γάρ). But either way, there is no evidence that what Paul says in v. 10
constitutes any kind of critique by Paul of the Corinthian viewpoint, whether as
expressed in the use of v. 9 or otherwise. Thus Thiselton, *First Epistle*, 252, argues
that Paul's argument is closest to the Corinthian viewpoint in vv. 10, 11 (and hence
any case that Paul might be citing the *Corinthians*' words is strongest at this point
in the section).

mediate: thus in 1 Cor 8:1-2 the Corinthian slogan about "know-ing" is immediately qualified in v. 2 by the counter claim that knowl-edge, which "puffs up", is inferior to love, which "builds up". Of this there is nothing in 1 Cor 2:9 or its immediate context.[44]

This may be supported by the introduction to the quotation in the use of ἀλλά at the start of v. 9. The force of the ἀλλά here has been much debated, though it would seem clear that, in some sense at least, the citation introduced in this way is regarded positively in contrast with some aspect regarded negatively in the immediately preceding context.[45] Frid has argued persuasively that the contrast is with the lack of knowledge (by the "rulers") mentioned in v. 8: thus there is an implied "but *we know*" presupposed in the (some-what elliptical) ἀλλά.[46] But whatever the precise nuance implied, it seems clear that the quotation is being used positively, not negatively, by Paul in his argument at this point.

All this suggests that the quotation as cited by Paul is used thor-oughly positively; further, there is no suggestion that, if it were also being used by the Corinthians, its use is being questioned by Paul. Nor is there the slightest hint that the fact that this is not presented as a saying of Jesus has any significance, positive or negative, at all.

4.2 'What No Hand Has Touched'

As we have seen, GTh 17 contains this phrase, whereas 1 Cor 2:9 does not.

Again a glance at the broader picture may be revealing. The phrase (or an equivalent to it) appears only in the Turfan fragment (apart from GTh). None of the (many) other occurrences of what are nor-mally regarded as examples of 'the' saying contain it.[47]

---

[44] Cf. Schrage's comment on the whole passage, that there is no "deutliche Auseinandersetzung" identifiable here (n. 34 above).

[45] For the ἀλλά as implying a contrast with, rather than support for, what pre-cedes, see Lührmann, *Offenbarungsverständnis*, 116; Schrage, *Erste Brief*, 247, 255-6.

[46] B. Frid, "The Enigmatic ΑΛΛΑ in 1 Corinthians 2.9", *NTS* 31 (1985) 603-11.

[47] I remain unpersuaded by the argument of T. Onuki, "Traditionsgeschichte von Thomasevangelium 17 und ihre christologische Relevanz" in C. Breytenbach & H. Paulsen (eds.), *Anfänge der Christologie* (FS F. Hahn; Göttingen: Vandenhoeck & Ruprecht, 1991) 399-415, arguing that 1 John 1:1 represents an affirmation in positive terms of the saying expressed negatively in GTh 17. See the detailed re-ply by I. Dunderberg, "John and Thomas in Conflict?", in J.D. Turner & A. McGuire (eds.), *the Nag Hammadi Library after Fifty Years. Proceedings of the 1995 So-*

Further, the presence of the extra phrase may imply a rather different meaning for the saying as a whole compared with the version of the saying in 1 Cor 2. In Paul, the stress is on the fact that the things referred to are inconceivable by human beings. The Thomas version suggests rather that what is in mind is essentially nothing to do with this world.[48] As such, this would be all of a piece with the generally negative attitude to the world which pervades much (if not all) of GTh.[49]

If GTh's version were primary and Paul's secondary, one would have to argue that the subsequent tradition (with the exception of the Turfan fragment) has been heavily, if not exclusively, dominated by the Pauline version. On the other hand, the fact that the difference here is thoroughly in line with Thomas's own viewpoint makes it perhaps easier to regard the extra phrase as due to Thomas's own redaction of the saying, bringing it into line with his own theological perspective.

Certainly it is hard to envisage the reverse process and to see the omission of the phrase as being due to Paul's redaction of the saying. In very general terms, one might argue that the GTh version, with its somewhat world-denying stance, might have been congenial to the Corinthians and would correlate with their apparent radical asceticism in relation to marriage as reflected in 1 Cor 7:1. However, it is hard to see any of this behind Paul's citation here. The context in 1 Cor 2 has nothing to do with asceticism at all. It is about the true nature of "wisdom" which evidently for the Corinthians is being located in concerns about thoroughly *this*-worldly status and esteem. Further, even if asceticism were an issue here, it is hard to see that simply deleting the 'hands not touching' phrase would be

---

ciety of Biblical Literature Commemoration (NHMS 44; Leiden: Brill, 1997) 361-80, on 365-70. Any overlap in language is scarcely significant, and in any case 1 John does not have a reference to "arise in the heart". If there is any literary relationship involved, it might be *from* 1 John *to* GTh: GTh's version could simply represent an amalgam of 1 Cor 2:9 and 1 John 1:1. Also any possible "parallel" in the *Muratorian Canon*, lines 29-31, is surely just coincidental (see Dunderberg, ibid., 369). I am grateful to Dr Dunderberg for making his article available to me.

[48] Cf. B. Gärtner, *The Theology of the Gospel of Thomas* (London: Collins, 1961) 147-9; also Dunderberg, "John and Thomas", 366: "This clause adds conveniently to the non-concrete nature of what Jesus promises to give to his followers."

[49] See A. Marjanen, "Is *Thomas* a Gnostic Gospel?", in R. Uro (ed.), *Thomas at the Crossroads* (Edinburgh: T. & T. Clark, 1998) 107-139. Marjanen shows well the pervasive negative attitude to the world in GTh. Whether this is "Gnostic" is partly a matter of semantics and how one defines the term "Gnostic".

regarded as significant. Even without the phrase, the saying is open to the interpretation it seems to have in Thomas. It is thus hard to see that the omission of the phrase on its own would have been read as changing any overall interpretation of the saying very radically.

It is then very doubtful whether the extra phrase in GTh about hands not touching represents an original, or earlier, form of the saying which Paul has abbreviated. There are no clear reasons why Paul should have done so; conversely, it seems entirely plausible to posit Thomas as having added the phrase as it coheres so well with the overall outlook of GTh. Given the very uneven occurrence of the phrase in versions of the saying elsewhere, it seems easiest to assume that the version in GTh is a secondary development of the tradition (with subsequent influence in a limited sphere) and that, in this instance, the version in 1 Cor 2:9 is more original.

4.3 *The Final Clause in 1 Cor 2:9*

Pearson has argued that the final clause in 1 Cor 2:9 ('what God has prepared for those who love him') may be a Pauline addition to the saying, arguing partly on the basis of the absence of the clause from GTh 17.[50] In addition he argues that this addition can be seen as part of Paul's correction of the Corinthian viewpoint by implicitly supplying an "eschatological reservation" to critique the Corinthian claims to possess everything in the present: Paul's extra clause emphasises the *future* possession ("the things that God has *prepared*") of the blessings promised for those who love God.[51]

Once again, such a theory is hard to sustain in precisely this form. Whilst it may be the case that elsewhere in 1 Corinthians Paul is anxious to stress the futurity of aspects of Christian existence, especially resurrection (cf. 1 Cor 15),[52] there is no indication that this is

---

[50] Pearson, *Pneumatikos*, n. 69 on p. 108: "Note also that in *Thomas* 17, the last part of the quotation is missing, another indication that Paul is adding this to a form of the quotation used by his opponents. The use of this quotation in *Thomas* and by Paul's opponents is probably very similar." On p. 35 he also appeals to the redundant ὅσα at the start of the phrase as an indication that the phrase is a secondary addition. For at least the last phrase as a Pauline addition, see too J. Reiling, "Wisdom and the Spirit. An Exegesis of 1 Corinthians 2,6-16", in T. Baarda et al. (eds.), *Text and Testimony* (FS A.F.J. Klijn; Kampen: Kok, 1988) 200-11, on 204-5.

[51] Cf. Pearson, *Pneumatikos*, 35

[52] I am aware that this is disputed. See my "The Corinthians Who Say 'There is No Resurrection of the Dead'", in R. Bieringer (ed.), *The Corinthian Correspon-*

an issue here in 1 Cor 2. In fact all the stress (by Paul!) in this context is on what Christians *have* received. This is clear in v. 10: the
things that God has "prepared" for those who love him *have* been
"revealed" to "us" through the Spirit. As already noted, there is debate about whether v. 10 simply expands v. 9 or contrasts with it
(cf. above). But either way, v. 10 makes it clear that, for Paul, the
"things prepared" referred to in v. 9 are a matter of present reality
and *not* just a matter of future hope. There could be an element of
critique implied by Paul in claiming that these things are revealed
through the Spirit: the Spirit (for Paul at least) is common to *all*
Christians, not just an elite group (cf. 1 Cor 12-14);[53] but the
Corinthians' own behaviour may be disqualifying them already from
being regarded as "spiritual" (cf. 3:1!). Nevertheless, Paul's contrast
here is not between present and future but between (truly) spiritual
and non-spiritual.

There thus seems to be no justification for the theory that Paul
himself adds the final clause to bolster his own critique of the
Corinthians by stressing the future nature of the hope expressed in
v. 9. That there is some critique of the Corinthians in the passage
as a whole seems very likely. But Paul's critique is not apparently
mounted at this point in the argument,[54] nor is it sustained by arguments about the future nature of eschatological hope. The argument then that Paul adds the final clause in v. 9 for reasons such as
those suggested by Pearson seems unsustainable.

To conclude, the saying in 1 Cor 2:9 *may* have been known and used
by the Corinthians. But there is nothing to suggest that it was known
as a saying of Jesus. Equally, there is nothing to suggest that Paul

---

dence (BETL 125; Leuven: Peeters, 1996) 247-75 for a defence of this view.
    [53] Cf. Lührmann, *Offenbarungsverständnis*, 135. On p. 138f., Lührmann also sees
a similar critique of the Corinthians in Paul's phrase "those who love God": since
"loving God" is essentially a gift from God, it is a matter of divine grace, not something which can be claimed by the Corinthian pneumatics as a right. But in that
case one might at least expect a passive verb (e.g. "loved by God")! If there is
really a critique here, it is very veiled.
    [54] Hence I am less persuaded by e.g. Lührmann, *Offenbarungsverständnis*, 134-9,
that Paul is mounting a subtle critique of the Corinthians at almost every point in
this section. E.g. he argues that, in v. 9, Paul is implicitly critiquing the Corinthians
by insisting that any dualism is not a cosmological one separating God and those
with the Spirit from the demons, but rather the radical divide between God and
all human beings (p. 139). This seems unnecessarily complicated and forced. Cf.
too Schrage, *Erste Brief*, 246.

knew the saying in the form of a saying of Jesus. Further, there is no evidence to suggest that Paul has modified the saying in any way as part of his attempt to "correct" and modify the Corinthians' behaviour. The different form of the saying in GTh 17 may well be due to Thomas' own redaction: the addition of the 'hands not touching' clause is in line with the general attitude to the world shown in GTh generally. That the ascription of the saying to Jesus represents a secondary development is also likely (though not provable with any degree of finality); certainly a reverse development seems intrinsically implausible and is not paralleled elsewhere. In sum, it appears that the version of the saying in GTh 17 represents a secondary development of the tradition compared with the version which Paul gives in 1 Cor 2:9. Any line of development between the Pauline epistles and the gospel tradition thus seems to have gone in this case *from* Paul *to* the gospel tradition and not vice versa. In any study of "Paul and Jesus", this particular parallel will probably tell us more about the developing Jesus tradition than it will about Paul.[55]

---

[55] Margaret Thrall has, as far as I am aware, not addressed the broad issues raised in this essay in any of her published work. This small study is however offered here, with thanks for her friendship and personal kindness shown on many occasions, and in deep appreciation for her many contributions to study of Paul and of the New Testament.

OBSERVATIONS ON THE JEWISH BACKGROUND OF 2 CORINTHIANS 3:9, 3:7-8 AND 3:11

Nina L. Collins

As modern commentaries remark, the verses that are listed in the title above are statements *a fortiori*, a category of rhetoric which was common among the Jewish sages of tannaitic and amoraic times.[1] In its simplest form, this consists of two subjects, one of which is considered 'stronger' or 'heavier' in relation to the other, which is 'weaker' or 'lighter'. These subjects are placed in relation to a quality or characteristic which is the same for them both. The latter is introduced by (x) in the discussion below. For example,

> Now if when God is angry [with the righteous] (x) he is full of mercy
> how much more so,
> When He is not angry![2]

The two basic subjects are: (A) God's anger against the righteous (when they do wrong), the 'lighter' subject and (B) God's pleasure with the righteous (when they are righteous), the 'heavier' subject. The quality that they share is the mercy of God, which, for reasons of style, is unexpressed in the second section of the statement. Symbolically therefore this statement may be expressed

> If (A) has X, then [all the more so—*a fortiori*] (B) has X![3]

---

[1] See for example, Margaret E. Thrall, *A Critical and Exegetical Commentary on the Second Epistle to the Corinthians* (2 vols; Edinburgh: T. & T. Clark, 1994) 1.239. There are many discussions of the rabbinic statement *a fortiori*, often called a statement *kal va-chomer*, from the Hebrew phrase often used as a bridge between the two main sections of the statement. For example: M. Mielziner, *Introduction to the Talmud*, 3rd ed.(New York: Bloch,1925) 131-32, para.13; L. Jacobs, "The Aristotelean Syllogism and the Qal Wa Ḥomer" *JJS* 4 (1953) 154-57, *Encyclopaedia Judaica*, Vol 8 (Jerusalem: Keter, 1971) s.v. 'Hermeneutics'; W. Sibley Towner, "Hermeneutical Systems of Hillel and the Tannaim: A Fresh Look", *HUCA* 53 (1982) 101-35; Menachem Elon, *Jewish Law, History, Sources, Principles* (4 vols.; Philadelphia: JPS, 1994) 1.350.

[2] *Siphre* 105. For the Hebrew text see H.S. Horovitz, *Siphre D'Be Rab* (Jerusalem: Wahrmann, 1966) 103, lines 2-3. For other translations, see Paul P. Levertoff, *Midrash Sifre on Numbers* (London: SPCK, 1926) 86; Jacob Neusner, *Siphré to Numbers* (3 vols.; Brown University: BJS, 1986) 2.127.

[3] Based on the symbolic statement of L. Jacobs (see n. 1 above) 155. The

This basic understanding of a statement *a fortiori* leads to some interesting observations on the interrelationship between the three statements of Paul at Cor. 3:9, 7-8, and 11, and the correct text of 2 Cor. 3:9.

Let us begin with 2 Cor. 3:9. This text declares:

εἰ γὰρ τῇ διακονίᾳ τῆς κατακρίσεως δόξα, πολλῷ μᾶλλον περισσεύει ἡ διακονία τῆς δικαιοσύνης δόξῃ.[4]

Translated literally and analytically, this text states:

9a For if for the covenant[5] of condemnation, (x) [there was] splendour,
9b all the more so (*a fortiori*)
   does the covenant of righteousness (x) abound with splendour.

As scholars note, this text remarks that the glory manifested at the Mosaic covenant ('the covenant of condemnation') was also manifest at the Christophany ('the covenant of righteousness').[6] In other words, splendour (δόξα) is the quality which both covenants share, although, as will be noted below, the verb περισσεύω strongly hints that the Christophany is more endowed with this quality than the covenant from Sinai.

Let us now turn to 2 Cor. 3:7-8. This text states:

7. εἰ δὲ ἡ διακονία τοῦ θανάτου ἐν γράμμασιν ἐντετυπωμένη λίθοις ἐγενήθη ἐν δόξῃ,
ὥστε μὴ δύνασθαι ἀτενίσαι τοὺς υἱοὺς Ἰσραὴλ εἰς τὸ πρόσωπον Μωϋσέως διὰ τὴν δόξαν τοῦ προσώπου αὐτοῦ τὴν καταργουμένην,
8. πῶς οὐχὶ μᾶλλον ἡ διακονία τοῦ πνεύματος ἔσται ἐν δόξῃ;

---

symbolic statement of Towner (see n. 1 above) 115 assumes that A and B are linked through law, which is not always the case. Thus: If A, the laws governing which are known to be less rigorous [than B], requires Y, it makes sense that B, the laws governing which are known to be more rigorous [than A], will require Y.

[4] All texts from the *New Testament* in this article are taken from Nestle-Aland, *Novum Testamentum Graece* (Stuttgart: Deutsche Bibelgesellschaft, 1988).

[5] The term διακονία is translated here as 'covenant' (rather than the more common 'ministry'), in accordance with the commentary of Carey C. Newman *Paul's Glory-Christology* (Leiden: E.J. Brill, 1992), 218, 233. Thrall (see n. 1 above) 237 translates 'agency'. Newman also refers to the 'covenant of righteousness' as the 'Christophany'. This terminology will also be used.

[6] See for example: Ralph P. Martin, *2 Corinthians*, WBC 40 (Dallas: Word, 1991) 63; Newman (see n. 5 above) 233: 'The Sinaitic revelation of כבוד to Moses and the Christophanic revelation of δόξα to Paul are ... comparable: in both cases the revelation of Glory serves to legitimize authority'.

An analytical and literal translation follows below:

7. Now if the covenant of death, carved in letters on stone,
(x) took place with [such] splendour that the Israelites could not
look at Moses' face because of its brightness, fading[7] as this was,
all the more so *(a fortiori)*
8. the covenant of the Spirit (x) will be viewed with splendour!

The main contrasting subjects are again: (1) the covenant of death,
that is, the Mosaic covenant and (2) the covenant of the Spirit, that
is, the Christophany. The main characteristic which these subjects
share is again "splendour'. The basic statement as a whole may thus
be expressed:

If the covenant of death (x) had splendour
how much more
the covenant of the Spirit (x) will have splendour!

When the above *basic* statement is compared with 2 Cor. 3:9, it is
clear that apart from one stylistic change and several additions, 2
Cor. 3:7-8 is merely an expansion of 2 Cor. 3:9. Expansions (or,
elaborations) of the components of an argument *a fortiori*, which are
not in themselves necessary for the argument, are obviously an option
for an author, and are typical of rabbinic, *aggadic* statements, that
is, in statements which are not related directly to Jewish law. For
example, the statement of the tanna Rabbi Simeon below notes that
if a man is rewarded because he refrains from the kind of sins that
he would instinctively avoid, then, all the more so, a man should
be rewarded if he refrains from sins which he longs to commit.[8] This
thought could thus be simply expressed:

If a man who refrains from sins he does not want to commit (x) receives reward,
all the more so—*a fortiori*
A man who refrains from sins that he wants to commit (x) should receive
reward.

---

[7] Newman (see n. 5 above) 234, notes that τὸ καταργούμενον refers to 'the
process of eschatological decay'.

[8] Mishnah, m. Makk. 3.15. For English translations see Herbert Danby, *The
Mishnah* (Oxford: Clarendon Press, 1938) 408; Philip Blackman (7 vols.; New York:
Judaica, 1963) 4.328-29. Blackman has a parallel Hebrew text.

This text could be expanded to include an identification of the specific sins in each category, such as the sins of murder, which most people are not tempted to commit, along with other sins, that are hard to resist. We might also learn about types of reward. The author might also describe the attitude of his subject to specific sins, for example, his attitude towards a sin that he hates (and therefore is not likely to commit) could be described as a sin 'which the soul abhors'. Likewise, the attitude of a man towards sins to which he is tempted to commit could be described as 'that for which a man's soul longs after and covets'. It is thus no surprise that the statement of Rabbi Simeon is indeed embroidered in these ways. The main expansions and elaborations are italicised in the translation below:

> If a man keeps himself apart from that which *a man's soul abhors*, [*for example*] *blood* [*=murder*] (x) he receives reward,
> all the more so
> if he keeps himself apart from that which *a man's soul longs after and covets*, [*for example*] *robbery and incest*, (x) shall he gain merit for himself *and his generation and the generations of this generation to the end of all generations*!

Similarly, Paul has expanded and elaborated the (relatively) simple text of 2 Cor. 3:9 to produce the fuller version of 2 Cor. 3:7-8. This occurs mainly in the first section of the statement. Paul tells us here that 'the covenant of death' was carved in letters of stone (it is surely unlikely that this detail was included in the original statement *a fortiori*), and notes that the glory of the Mosaic revelation was so bright that the Israelites could not look at Moses' face, even though the brightness of the glory was fading. This latter addition emphasises the inferior status of the Mosaic revelation in relation to the Christophany. Paul thus reverses his description—instead of the *superiority* of the Christophany to which he refers at 2 Cor. 3:9, he refers here to the *inferiority* of the covenant from Sinai. But this reversal does not effect a change of basic meaning when 2 Cor. 3:7-8 is compared with 2 Cor 3:9, and apart from this one stylistic change, it is clear that Cor. 3:7-8 is an expanded version of the verse which *follows* in Paul's text, namely 2 Cor. 3:9.

We now turn to 2 Cor. 3:11:

> εἰ γὰρ τὸ καταργούμενον διὰ δόξης, πολλῷ μᾶλλον τὸ μένον ἐν δόξῃ.

For if what faded away (x) [was] with splendour
all the more so *(a fortiori)*
what is permanent (x) [is clothed] in splendour.

When this text is compared with 2 Cor. 3:7-8, it is difficult to avoid
the conclusion that 2 Cor. 3:11 is a later version of 2 Cor. 3:7-8.
The reference to the Mosaic revelation that has 'faded' in 2 Cor.
3:7 has become an allusion in 2 Cor. 3:11, which would be difficult
to understand without the earlier verse. Similarly, 'what is permanent' in 2 Cor. 3:11 amplifies Paul's reference to the 'covenant of
the Spirit' in 2 Cor. 3:8. In other words, we need the text of 2 Cor.
3:7-8 to understand *fully* the statement at 2 Cor.3:11—the intervening
text in Paul's letter is too abstract, and not sufficiently explicit to
make this meaning clear. This suggests that the shorter text of 2 Cor.
3:11 is a condensed, later version of the longer 2 Cor. 3:7-8. This
relationship is however obscured by the intervening verses, particularly 2 Cor. 3:9, which is obviously itself closer in thought to the
verse which *precedes*, namely 2 Cor. 3:7-8, than it is to the *subsequent*
statement of 2 Cor. 3:11.

This points to the conclusion that Paul first composed 2 Cor. 3:9,
the simplest of the verses analysed above. Subsequently he composed
2 Cor. 3:7-8, and this verse was the later inspiration for 2 Cor. 3:11.
If this is correct, these statements could not have been composed in
the order that they now appear in Paul's text, which is the order of
composition we would naturally assume. This further suggests Paul's
statements were not composed at the same time as his second letter
to the Corinthian, but were expressed earlier and were then preserved in some way, probably in writing, perhaps in a notebook of
some kind, and later used when Paul wrote the text in which they
now lie. It is also perhaps possible that Paul rearranged segments of
his letter *after* an earlier draft. Whatever the case, although clear
strands of development and unity can be claimed for the overall
pericope of 2 Cor. 3:7-11, which is usually delimited by commentators as a discrete unit in itself,[9] this continuity is no more than the
achievement than can be expected from an intelligent writer who
compiled a continuous text (as far as his readers are concerned) from

---

[9] See for example: Victor Paul Furnish, *II Corinthians: A New Translation with
Introduction and Commentary*, AB 32A (Garden City, New York: Doubleday, 1984),
226, 'These verses [3:7-11] are bound together because they manifest a common
thesis and because the form of argumentation is the same throughout...'; the translation of Martin (see n. 6 above) 57; Thrall (see n. 1 above) 239.

more than one source. A detailed analysis of the statements *a fortiori*
suggests however that this impression of continuity does not conform
to the order in which individual texts were actually composed. These
observations can now be added to those of many others who have
cast doubt on the compositional integrity of 2 Cor. 1-7 as a whole.[10]

Paul and the Rabbinic Rule of Dayyo:

The Variants τῇ διακονίᾳ *and* ἡ διακονία *at 2 Cor 3:9a*

One important detail of a rabbinic statement *a fortiori*, which has not
yet been discussed, relates to the parity that must exist between the
premise and the conclusion of such a statement, that is, the parity
which must exist for the common characteristic or quality which both
topics in the statement must share. For example: If a student with
a second class degree (the 'lighter' or 'weaker' subject) (x) deserves
a prize of £100, then all the more so (*a fortiori*) a student with a first
class degree (the 'stronger' or 'heavier' subject) (x) deserves a prize
of £100. The parity here is the equality of the prize that each student receives. This conclusion may be surprising in view of natural
justice which loudly proclaims that a better student should collect a
better prize. But on the basis of a classic rabbinic statement *a fortiori*, this is not possible, since the conclusion of such a statement is
not permitted to go beyond the terms stated in the premise. Otherwise, there is uncertainty, there being no limit to the amount that
the better student might receive.

This limiting rule in Hebrew is called *dayyo*, literally, 'it is sufficient'. This defining term is taken from the expression דיו לבא מן
הדין להיות כנדון, 'it is sufficient that the result derived from an inference is equivalent to the law from which it is drawn', as expressed
in *Sifre* 106, cited below.[11] The rule is justified by the rabbis from
Num 12:14, which defines the maximum length for the punishment
of Miriam, when she defamed her brother Moses, the leader of the
Israelites, and thus the representative of God, according to rabbinic
thought:

---

[10] For a summary of opinions see Linda L. Belleville, *Reflections of Glory: Paul's
Polemical Use of the Moses-Doxa Tradition in 2 Corinthians 3. 1-18*, JSNTSup 52
(Sheffield: JSOT Press, 1991) 20-23, 85-103.

[11] For more on the rule of *dayyo*, see Mielziner (see n. 1 above) 134-35; Hyam
Maccoby, *The Philosophy of the Talmud* (London: RoutledgeCurzon, 2002) 196, 217-
18.

Num 12:1: And Miriam . . . spoke against (i.e., slandered) Moses
. . .

Num 12:14: And the Lord said unto Moses: If her father had but spit
in her face, should she not have been punished for seven days? Let
her be shut out from the camp for seven days, and after that let her
be received in again.

Since Moses was the representative of God, Miriam's insult to Moses
was considered as slander of God himself. But for how long should
she be punished? The answer can be discovered from Num 12:14
which states that if Miriam had slandered her father, she would have
been punished for seven days. According to a rabbinic argument *a
fortiori* based on this fact, she could not therefore be punished for
this type of crime for longer than seven days, *even though she had committed a more serious offence.* In other words, the conclusion which is
valid for a 'weak' situation (here, slandering a father) must also be
valid for a 'strong' situation (here, as it were, the slandering of God).
This is formally discussed in the tannaitic commentary on Numbers,
Sifre 106:

ר' אתי בר' יאשיה אומר שתי נתיפות נזפה אלו אביה ב״ו נזפה עד שתהא
מוכלמת שבעה או מה אביה ב״ו שבעה מי שאמר והיה העולם ארבעה
עשר דיו לבא מן הדין להיות כנדון   מה אביה ב״ו שבעה אף מי שאמר
והיה העולם שבעה

Rabbi Achay in the name of Rabbi Joshia says: She (=Miriam) [could
have] uttered two [possible] insults. If her human father she had insulted she would have been shamed for seven days. [Thus], if [by
insulting] her human father [she would have been shamed for] seven
days [then we might expect that if she had insulted] the One Who
Created the World [she would have been insulted for] fourteen days.
[But] *it is sufficient* (ויד) for the conclusion [of the argument] to be
[equivalent] to the premise (= the thing being judged). If [by insult-
ing] her human father, she was shamed for seven days, then [by in-
sulting] Him Who Created the World, [she should not also be shamed
for] seven [days]![12]

Does Paul keep to this rule in his statements from Corinthians ex-

---

[12] *Sifre* 106. For the Hebrew text, see Horowitz (see n. 2 above) 105, lines 1-
3. For more traditional English translations, see: Levertoff (see n. 2 above) 88-89;
Neusner (see n. 2 above) 2. 131. The same statement is elaborated at *b. B. Qam.*
25a.

amined above? Or, as this question is usually posed by Christian scholars, does Paul equate the glory of the covenant from Sinai (in the premise of his statements) with the glory of the Christophany (in the conclusion), or does he exalt the glory of the Christophany *over* that of the covenant from Sinai?[13] The answer to this question can be found in the words of his texts, especially in the changes that he makes to his statements, which, almost without exception, focus on this point.

Thus, at 2 Cor. 3:9, probably the earliest of his three statements, Paul uses the verb περισσεύω in relation to the Christophany.[14] However, this is a rather obvious insertion particularly in the absence of a 'balancing' verb in the first part of his statement in relation to the Mosaic revelation (the lack of any verb is discussed further below). In the next of his statements, 2 Cor. 3:7-8, Paul is more subtle. He first changes the name for his two subjects, using terms of much broader appeal—θάνατος 'death' as opposed to πνεῦμα 'spirit', in comparison with the more esoteric 'condemnation' as opposed to 'righteousness' in 2 Cor. 3:9. This surely gives his verse much greater appeal. More significantly, as far as Paul's praise of the Christophany is concerned, instead of the direct, verbal reference to the superiority of the Christophany in 2 Cor. 3:9b, Paul instead uses a midrashic reference to refer to the fading glory of the Mosaic event. This reference is inserted into a descriptive section of the verse, so that it does not affect the main argument *a fortiori*, as can be seen from the *basic* expression of 2 Cor. 3:7-8 above. Paul is thus less open to the charge of the infringement of *dayyo*. The descriptive reference to the diminishing glory of the Mosaic covenant also more subtly alludes to the superior glory of the covenant from Christ. Finally, in 2 Cor. 3:11, Paul finds yet another method of achieving this aim. In this verse, the superiority of the Christophany is established in the very fabric of the statement, by the abstract names that Paul invents for the two covenants, namely τὸ μένον 'the thing that remains' and τὸ καταργούμενον 'the thing that has paled'. The names

---

[13] The argument is summarised by Thrall (see n. 1 above) 239-41.

[14] Originally noted by H. Müller, "Der rabbinische Qal-Wachomer-Schluss in paulinischer Typologie", *ZNW* 58 (1967) 73-92, especially pp. 79-80; see also J.F. Collange, *Enigmes de la Deuxième Épître de Paul aux Corinthiens*, SNTSMS 18 (Cambridge: Cambridge University Press, 1972) 79, and the references of Thrall (see n. 1 above) 240, n. 341.

of the two subjects are thus themselves the bearers of the underlying message of his text. Furthermore, whereas in his earlier statements, Paul limits his references *either* to the superiority of the Christophany *or* to the inferiority of the Mosaic revelation, 2 Cor. 3:11 refers to *both* these ideas. Paul thus finds increasingly sophisticated methods to hint that the revelation of Jesus Christ was superior to the revelation that was given at Sinai, and the successive changes in his statements are almost exclusively devoted to promoting this cause. There is also some indication however, especially at 2 Cor. 3:7a (in which there is an allusion to the superior nature of the Christophany which dos not impinge on the main argument of the statement) that Paul attempts to work within the rule of *dayyo*.

It is possible moreover that this allusion is encouraged by Paul from his knowledge of an accident of translation, by which the Greek phrase which links the two main sections of his arguments— πολλῷ μᾶλλον,[15] or πῶς οὐχὶ μᾶλλον[16]—is the standard translation for the several Hebrew alternatives, קל וחומר or על אחת כמה וכמה or—אינו דין ש, which are used in rabbinic statements *a fortiori* formally to link the two main sections of the text. These Hebrew phrases are almost always translated with an expression that includes a comparative term, for example, 'all the more so', or '*a fortiori*', or, as just noted, the phrases used by Paul, although in keeping with the rabbinic tradition (where there is no intention to compare the two chosen subjects with reference to their stated common quality or characteristic), there is no term of comparison in the Hebrew phrase. Thus, *kal vaḥomer* קל וחומר (the expression often used to name the statement itself) means literally 'light and heavy' or 'light and serious', על אחת כמה וכמה means literally 'on one, how much and how much', and—אינו דין ש means 'can it not be deduced that ..?' It is however obvious that an expression which includes a term of comparison might lead the author or reader to expect a comparison between the two subjects, although no such intention is even hinted by the corresponding terminology in the Hebrew texts. An example of such a tendency can be seen in the comment of one scholar on the meaning of περισσεύω at 2 Cor. 3:9: "*Perisseuo* must mean 'to abound' If the verb were merely to express the compara-

---

[15] 2 Cor.3:9, 11. Also Rom. 5:9,10,15, 17; Phil. 12:2.
[16] 2 Cor. 3:7-8. Paul also uses the phrase πόσῳ μᾶλλον at Rom. 11:12, 24; Phlm. 16.

tive ('be still greater than') it would be redundant with 'mallon'."[17] But the term μᾶλλον, in this context may *not* mean 'more'. If indeed Paul is constructing a classic rabbinic statement *a fortiori*, the phrase that he uses, πολλῷ μᾶλλον, could best be translated along the lines 'is it not logical', rather than by a phrase that includes a comparative term. On the other hand, if Paul hoped or expected that the natural tendency of the reader would lead him to assume the usual understanding of the common term μᾶλλον, this comment, and those of many others, might well be correct.[18] This would also explain the comparatively tentative reference of Paul to the superiority of the Christophany at 2 Cor. 3:8, since he felt that he could rely on the technical terminology of his statement to further the message he intended for his verse.

However, a further method that Paul almost certainly used to promote his belief emerges from a detailed examination of 2 Cor. 3:9. The textual history of this verse includes two much discussed variants—τῇ διακονίᾳ or ἡ διακονία—in the premise of Paul's statement at 2 Cor 3:9a. The reading τῇ διακονίᾳ has support from important Alexandrian and Western witnesses, and is accepted by the editors of the *Greek New Testament*, rather than ἡ διακονία, which occurs in the majority of Byzantine texts.[19] As can be seen from the translations below, both variants are acceptable, as far as sense is concerned.[20] Square brackets surround the terms which are not

---

[17] Jean Héring, *The Second Epistle of Saint Paul to the Corinthians* (London: Epworth, 1967) 24.

[18] Translations of 2 Cor. 3:9, such as those found in the *RSV* may therefore be justified, although they ignore the rule of *dayyo*. Thus: "For if there was splendour in the dispensation of condemnation, the dispensation of righteousness must far exceed it in splendour". Similarly, Furnish (see n. 9 above) 201: "For if there is splendor with the ministry of condemnation, how much more does the ministry of righteousness abound with splendor". The observations here, in which the text of 2 Cor. 3:7 is considered in relation to the rule of *dayyo*, taking account of a convention of translation from Hebrew to Greek, may contribute towards eliminating the distracting possibilities (for example, the Palestinian exegetical tradition regarding the glory that surrounded Moses at the revelation on Sinai) in the discussion summarised by Thrall (see n. 1 above) 1. 239-40, regarding whether Paul intended to emphasise the *greater* glory of the Christophany, or merely to note the *similar* glory of the two revelations from Moses and Jesus Christ.

[19] For details, see Nestle-Aland (see n. 4 above) ad loc. Scholarly opinions are summarised by: Furnish (see n. 9 above) 204, who notes that most translators and commentators prefer the nominative; and by Thrall (see n. 1 above) 248-49, n. 398.

[20] Ralph P. Martin, *2 Corinthians* (Dallas, Texas: Word, 1991) 58; Collange (see n. 14 above) 79, 'le sens reste tout à fait le même'.

represented in Greek but are necessary for a smooth English translation.

> 2 Cor 3:9, reading τῇ διακονίᾳ:
> For if [there is] splendour with the ministry (τῇ διακονίᾳ) of condemnation, how much more so does the ministry (ἡ διακονία) of righteousness abound with splendour![21]

> 2 Cor 3:9, reading ἡ διακονία:
> For if the ministry (ἡ διακονία) of condemnation [was a matter] of glory, much more shall the ministry (ἡ διακονία) of righteousness abound in glory.[22]

The variants can be explained when we take into account Paul's Jewish background, especially his alleged knowledge of Hebrew or Aramaic, which accounts for the several semiticisms noticed in his text.[23] It has even been suggested that Greek may have been the *second* language he spoke.[24] If then Paul was even moderately familiar with Hebrew, the dative noun τῇ διακονίᾳ can be explained as a translation into Greek of the prefixed Hebrew preposition ל, meaning 'to, for, in regard to', thus, *For if in regard to the covenant of condemnation there is glory, all the more so ...* .[25] Or else, the dative case can be

---

[21] Trans. Furnish (see n. 9 above) 201, with p. 204, n. 9. See also Martin (see n. 6 above) 57-58, "If there was glory in the ministry that leads to condemnation ...".

[22] Trans. C.K. Barrett, *A Commentary on the Second Epistle to the Corinthians* (London: Adam & Charles Black, 1973) 109, 116. Similarly, Furnish (see n. 9 above) 201, 'For if there is splendour with the ministry of condemnation ..'; Martin (see n. 6 above) 57: 'For if the ministry that leads to condemnation was glorious ...'.

[23] F. Blass and A. Debrunner, *A Greek Grammar of the New Testament and Other Early Christian Literature* (Chicago: University of Chicago, 1961) s.v. index, 'Semitisms', esp. para. 189, Dative of Possession. According to Acts 22:2-3, 26:5, Paul was a pupil of Gamaliel and spoke 'in the Hebrew language', although Paul himself does not make this claim, stating only that he was 'a Pharisee'.

[24] The suggestion of R. Dean Anderson Jr, *Ancient Rhetorical Theory and Paul* (Kampen, the Netherlands: Kok Pharos, 1996) 250, on the basis of documented Greek solecisms and a 'general lack of literary sophistication', along with a possible foreign accent (Luc. Nav. 2).

[25] Francis Brown, S.R. Driver and Charles A. Briggs, *A Hebrew and English Lexicon of the Old Testament* (Oxford: Clarendon, 1953) 510. This seems also to be the conclusion of commentators working only from Paul's Greek, see for example Newman (See n. 5 above) 322: '[with reference to 2 Cor. 3:7, 9, 11] The series of genitives and datives with the prepositions ἐν should all be construed as means: it was by means of the appearances of God's Glory that the covenant (of Death) was established'.

explained as a dative of possession,[26] a function also served in Hebrew by the prefix לְ.[27]

The impression of a Hebraic background for 2 Cor. 3:9a is further strengthened by the lack of a Greek equivalent for the verb 'to be' in the first section of the statement *a fortiori*, although it is a complete clause in itself, and would normally be present in a sentence in Greek. (The missing verb is supplied in square brackets in the translations above.) The absence of such a verb is however is normal for biblical and mishnaic Hebrew (the latter is the language in which the tannaitic *a fortiori* texts were recorded, and thus the language in which they were probably expressed at the time of Paul) since the Hebrew of these (and later) times does not possess a simple verb which corresponds to the Greek present tense of εἶναι or γίγνεσθαι. An example of a statement *a fortiori* introduced with a term prefixed by לְ, which corresponds with the Greek dative case, and which is also placed at the beginning of the clause in which there is also no term for the verb 'to be', can be seen in the Mishnah at m. Shebi. 7.2.[28] This concerns the rules applicable to the disposal of plants in the seventh year, when no cultivation of crops is allowed. All the more so, claim the sages, profit from the sale of such crops is disallowed:

לְהֶן אֵין בִּיעוּר
קַל וָחוֹמֶר
לִדְמֵיהֶן.

For them [= the plants] the law of removal (בִּיעוּר) [does] not apply.
All the more so
to the money of their sale [the law of removal does not apply]!

It is of course the case that omission of a verb, especially the copula ἐστίν is tolerated in Greek, especially in short, proverb-like sentences, in which category the first section of statement *a fortiori* must surely fall.[29] But the *absence* of a verb in the first section of Paul's text is further emphasised by the *presence* of a verb in the second half of Paul's

---

[26] Thus Thrall (see n. 1 above) 1.248-49, nn. 398, 399, citing Blass and Debrunner (see n. 23 above) para.189.

[27] Brown, Driver and Briggs (see n. 25 above) s.v. לְ, 5.

[28] The text is repeated with a small variant in the Tosefta, t. Shev. 5.4.

[29] For example, 1 Cor. 15:27, Δῆλον ὅτι ...; G; 1 Thes. 5:3, ὅταν λέγωσιν· εἰρήνη καὶ ἀσφάλεια, τότε ...; G; Matt. 10:10, Ἄξιος ὁ ἐργάτης τῆς τροφῆς αὐτοῦ. For many other examples in the NT, see Blass and Debrunner (see n. 23 above), para. 127.

statement, at 2 Cor. 3:9b, περισσεύω, 'to be superior'. This verb of course is optional—if the first part of Paul's statement makes sense without a verb, so also would the second. Moreover the presence of the verb mars the symmetry of the statement, which appears to be the aim of Paul in other statements he makes. The superfluous nature of the verb in the second half of Paul's statement can clearly be seen when Paul's words are arranged analytically, when it is clear that the presence of the verb in the second section of the statement means that the latter is longer than the first, having three main sense units instead of two:

εἰ γὰρ
(1) τῇ διακονίᾳ τῆς κατακρίσεως (2) δόξα,
πολλῷ μᾶλλον
(1) περισσεύει (2) ἡ διακονία τῆς δικαιοσύνης (3) δόξῃ.

This can be compared with 2 Cor. 3.11 which is perfectly constructed as far as the symmetry of units is concerned:

εἰ γὰρ
(1) τὸ καταργούμενον (2) διὰ δόξης,
     πολλῷ μᾶλλον
(1) τὸ μένον (2) ἐν δόξῃ.

Similarly Rom. 5:9, in which the two related topics are νῦν, 'now' (the 'lighter' subject) and ἀπὸ τῆς ὀργῆς, literally, 'from the wrath to come', that is, 'the future' (the 'heavier' topic). The quality with which both these topics are compared is the saving effected by Jesus Christ. This is expressed in the first part of Paul's statement as 'having been justified by his blood' and subsequently, in the second section of Paul's statement, as 'we shall be saved by him'. The words of Paul have been re-arranged below to draw attention to symmetry of the number of units. Since this is the most straightforward order, it is possible that it follows more closely the order in which the statement was first drafted (in thought or in writing) by Paul:

πολλῷ οὖν μᾶλλον
(1) νῦν   (x) (2) δικαιωθέντες (3) ἐν τῷ αἵματι αὐτοῦ
(1) ἀπὸ τῆς ὀργῆς (x) (2) σωθησόμεθα (3) δι' αὐτου

all the more
[If] now (x) having been justified by his blood
from the wrath to come [=in the future] (x) we shall be saved by him!

The balance between the two sections of a statement, combined with
the lack of any representation of the verb 'to be', in which Paul could
have included a verb, such as περισσεύω (had he so wished), is very
clear in his following remarks based on simple analogy. In these
statements, the adjective in the first subject functions also for the
second, although it is unexpressed. This can be compared to the
Hebrew statements cited above, and at the beginning of the article,
which also carry over the sense of the premise, so that the final
conclusion is unexpressed :

> Rom. 11:16a:
>
>   εἰ δὲ ἡ ἀπαρχὴ ἁγία,
>   καὶ τὸ φύραμα·
>
>   If the initial-offering [of the dough] [is] holy,
>   so-also [is] that-which-is-mixed [= the mixture as a whole]
>   [is holy]!

> Rom 11:16b:
>
>   καὶ εἰ ἡ ῥίζα ἁγία,
>   καὶ οἱ κλάδοι.
>
>   If the root is holy,
>   so-also the branches [are holy]!

It seems that Paul aimed whenever possible, and almost always in
short statements, for an elegant parity of units between the two main
sections of his statement. Thus it must be significant that there is
only a *near* parity of the two sections of 2 Cor. 3:9, when parity could
so easily have been achieved by the *absence* of the verb περισσεύει,
since the presence of this verb is not needed to complete the sense
of the clause. The function of this verb—to allude to the superiority of the covenant from Christ—could surely have been achieved
by other means. Why then did Paul write in this particular way?

   With the omission of a verb 'to be', along with Paul's use of a
construction which corresponds with the use of the Hebrew preposition l, the first section of Paul's statement reproduces a Hebrew
clause in Greek, so that a clause with flawed *Greek* is thereby produced. Paul thus alludes idiomatically and grammatically with imperfect Greek to the flawed and inferior quality of the Hebrew
revelation of Moses at Sinai.

A similar example of this technique, whose imperfections can be related to the influence of Hebrew and Jewish thought rather than the wish to prove the superiority of one concept over another, again appears in the same letter of Paul, at 2 Cor. 6:14. As many commentators note, this verse is inspired by the Septuagint's version of Lev. 19:19, which forbids the mating of cattle which 'require a different yoke', the latter qualification stated with the adjective ἑτερόζυγος. This verse is interpreted by anonymous tannaitic rabbis—that is, rabbis who could well have been contemporaries of Paul—as both a prohibition against the mating of different species, and also as a prohibition against yoking different species to the same plough at the same time. The latter is clearly stated in Hebrew, in an unattributed (thus, possibly early, pre-second century) mishnaic text: 'One kind of cattle with another kind of cattle ... it is forbidden to plough ... with them'.[30] At 2 Cor. 6:14, Paul turns this ruling into a metaphor in order to prohibit association between the Christian Corinthians and those whom Paul labels ἄπιστοι:

> Μὴ γίνεσθε ἑτεροζυγοῦντες ἀπίστοις· τίς γὰρ μετοχὴ δικαιοσύνη καὶ ἀνομία ἢ τίς κοινωνία φωτὶ πρὸς σκότος

Literally translated, this text may read:

> Do not be yoked-together with unbelievers. For what [is] participation with-respect-to-righteousness and with-respect-to-lawlessness. Or [what is] fellowship with-respect-to-light with darkness?

This verse can of course be translated into smooth English, for example, 'Do not be incongruously yoked with unbelievers. For what have righteousness and lawlessness in common? Or what fellowship has light with darkness?'[31] Nevertheless, such translations should not obscure those features of Paul's Greek which can be related to the Hebrew language and to Jewish thought. Firstly, there is Paul's periphrastic construction in which γίνεσθε is combined with the present participle ἑτεροζυγοῦντες, which means essentially 'coupling together', a *hapax legomenon* which, as modern scholars note, is related to adjective ἑτερόζυγος in the Septuagint.[32] Paul's construction and terminology corresponds with the similar periphrastic use of the verb הזדווג at m. San. 5.5: היו מזדווגין, 'they went in pairs'.

---

[30] Mishnah, m. Kil. 8.2.
[31] Thrall (see n. 1 above) 1.471.
[32] The periphrasis is noted by Furnish (see n. 9 above) 361, with references.

The simple past tense of this verb (a hypothetical הַזְדְּווּג) does not appear in the tannaitic texts. The verb הִזְדַּוֵּוג means 'to be joined' and can be used for humans or animals.[33] The root of this verb is זוּג, *zug*, which has an obvious acoustic similarity with the stem ζυγ- in Greek. Can it be a coincidence that Paul uses a verb with a simi- lar sound and meaning compared with a term in Greek, in a simi- lar periphrastic construction? A second Hebraic feature in Paul's text is Paul's use of the dative of respect,[34] which (as noted above) is a common function of the Hebrew preposition ל. Thirdly, as is shown by the square brackets round 'is' in the literal translation above, there is a lack of the verb 'to be'. The last two features replicate those in the text of 2 Cor. 3:9a. Finally, it should be noticed that both 2 Cor. 6:14 and 2 Cor. 3:9a are expressed in relation to a concept of Jew- ish origin, which was voiced originally in Hebrew, the former in an allusion to the law of mixed species (to which the whole tractate, *Kilaim*, is devoted in the Mishnah) and the latter in relation to the covenant from Sinai.

Paul further emphasises his Hebraic allusion in 2 Cor. 3:9a by placing this text in parallel with 2 Cor. 3:9b, the latter composed in perfect Greek. Paul thus corrects his imperfections, as far as Greek grammar is concerned, in the second part of his statement *a fortiori* (2 Cor. 3:9b) , using the nominative ἡ διακονία as the simple sub- ject of a clause in Greek, and using a verb which both completes the sense of this clause and provides a meaning which alludes to the superiority of the revelation from Christ. With this perfect Greek grammar and careful choice of words, Paul thus demonstrates by comparison the perfect nature of the revelation from Christ. Work- ing in Greek, Paul thereby exploits the grammar and vocabulary of two languages, Hebrew and Greek, to show the imperfection of the covenant from Sinai, in contrast with the perfection of the covenant from Christ. It is also clear that Paul has used the perfect medium for his purpose, since it is impossible to avoid the fact that the two main sections of a statement *a fortiori* are indissolubly paired, and stand in contrast with each other, even though, according to rab- binic principles, they are not themselves compared.

It is unlikely however that Paul's audience would have appreciated

---

[33] See Marcus Jastrow, *Dictionary of Talmud Babli, Yerushalmi, Midrashic Literature and Targumim* (London: Luzac, 1903; repr. Israel, 1972) 383.

[34] Stanley E. Porter, *Idioms of the Greek New Testament*, 2nd edn. (Sheffield: JSOT, 1994) 98.

the linguistic subtleties of his text. Perhaps for this reason, Paul abandoned such a technique when he later composed 2 Cor. 3:7-8, and subsequently 1 Cor. 3:11.[35] It seems moreover, that as far as his readers were concerned, Paul was correct. At least one Greek scribe who copied Paul's work failed to understand the subtlety of Paul's text and adjusted the dative ἡ διακονία for a smoother, more satisfactory nominative, from the Greek point of view. This was done either to remove the *lectio difficilior*, even though acceptable in Greek, or perhaps to 'correct' the reading, especially in view of the repeated nominative cases for the subjects of the two surrounding statements *a fortiori*, (2 Cor 3:7-8, ἡ διακονία τοῦ θανάτου / ἡ διακονία τοῦ πνεύματος; 2 Cor. 3:11, τὸ καταργούμενον / τὸ μένον), or even perhaps for both reasons combined.[36]

With regard to Paul's statements and the rule of *dayyo*, it is thus clear that the Paul develops his statement in order to proclaim the greater superiority of the covenant from Christ. This is achieved by Paul's management of the Greek language and the changes that he makes to successive statements, which are almost exclusively devoted to this aim. Paul thus announces not only that both covenants had glory—the basic conclusion of his *a fortiori* texts—but that the glory of one was greater than the other. He thereby consistently contravenes the rule of *dayyo*. As far as the logic of Paul's statement is concerned, this weakens his argument as a correct statement *a fortiori*, because his conclusions are foreseen. This is because there would be little point in the premise that *if X, the 'lighter' subject (because it has less or inferior glory), has glory; then, all the more so, it can be concluded that Y, the 'heavier' subject (because it has more or superior glory), has glory*, since,

---

[35] It is however difficult to avoid the observation that Paul was still influenced by Hebrew when he composed 2 Cor. 3:8. Scholars note that 'the ministry of the Spirit' ἡ διακονία τοῦ πνεύματος is contrasted with 'the ministry of Death' ἡ διακονία τοῦ θανάτου, thus for example, Furnish (see n. 9 above 204). But translations and commentaries do not make this contrast clear, especially when πνεῦμα is translated 'Spirit', in accordance with the understanding of Pauline thought, for example, see Thrall (see n. 1 above) 237, 244 with n. 370. But if πνεῦμα is a translation from Hebrew נפש, the contrast with 'the ministry of Death' can be made, since one of the meanings of נפש is 'life', see Brown, Driver and Briggs (see n. 25 above) s.v. נפש, 3c.

[36] It is possible that the nominative ἡ διακονία results from a comparatively simple scribal assimilation to the preceding and following nominatives, see B.M. Metzger, *A Textual Commentary on the Greek New Testament* (London and New York: United Bible Societies 1971) 578. See the references in Thrall (see n. 1 above) 249, n 398 for authorities who propose a scribal alteration from *lectio difficilior*.

if something with less glory is set aside something with more glory, they both clearly have glory, which is the conclusion of Paul. Fore-knowledge of the existence of the quality of glory in both his subjects thus means that Paul's conclusion can be anticipated, is superfluous, and does not teach. It seems however that although in at least one instance (2 Cor. 3:7) Paul tried to accommodate the rabbinic rule, he in general ignored this lapse of logic, in order to promote his principle aim—the proclamation of the superiority of the covenant from Christ. As one scholar notes: 'Paul's primary intent ... is not to interpret a biblical text, but rather to use text, tradition, and haggada (and perhaps whatever else was at hand) to interpret his own current situation'.[37] The deliberate misuse of a rabbinic statement *a fortiori* from which to promote his own intense belief is surely a part of 'whatever else was at hand'.

---

[37] Belleville (see n. 10 above) 298.

PART TWO

CULTURE, CONFLICT AND THE RHETORIC OF PAUL

PAUL'S ROLE AS 'FATHER' TO HIS CORINTHIAN 'CHILDREN' IN SOCIO-HISTORICAL CONTEXT (1 CORINTHIANS 4:14-21)*

Trevor J. Burke

Commentators have often drawn attention to the sudden change in Paul's tone in 1 Cor. 4:14-21, but few, if any, have remarked on the frequency of familial expressions. Of special note is Paul's relationship to the Corinthians as that of a 'father' (γεννάω 4:16) to his 'children' (τέκνα, 4:14), an affinity he contrasts with other familial roles such as 'guardians' (παιδαγωγούς, 4:15) and other so-called 'fathers' (πατέρας, 4:15) of his day. As the Corinthians' *pater*, Paul in his absence dispatches Timothy, his associate and beloved 'child' (τέκνον, 4:17), as a reminder of his ways.[1] Why does Paul use these family terms at the conclusion of the first major section of the letter (1:10-4:21) where divisive issues predominate? More important, from where do these expressions originate and how would they have been *heard* and understood by his Corinthian readers? It is sometimes argued that Paul's use of family terminology reflects a re-socialisation of conversion where the ἐκκλησία, the 'new "family of God"',[2] functions as a replacement for the natural family ties severed by conversion. Rarely, however, have scholars sought to make a con-

---

* This essay is written in honour of Dr Margaret Thrall's scholarly contribution to New Testament Studies and with whom I have had the privilege of researching. While I was teaching in S. Wales, Dr Thrall supervised my MPhil thesis entitled, "Adoptive Sonship (HUIOTHESIA) in the Pauline Corpus" (University College of North Wales, Bangor, 1994). This interest in Paul's family metaphors led to doctoral research on other fictive kinship terms in the corpus Paulinum (see n 5) which Prof. John M.G. Barclay (University of Glasgow) supervised. I am especially grateful to Prof. Barclay for reading and commenting on the present essay.

[1] Paul makes reference to father-child relations in many of his letters (e.g. 1 Thess. 2:11-12; Phil. 2:22) but does so more frequently in his troubled correspondence with the Corinthians (cf. 2 Cor. 6:11-13; 12:14-15). In 1 Corinthians, Paul also uses maternal imagery (1 Cor. 3:1-3a) and refers to siblings (i.e. ἀδελφός/ἀδελφή on 40 occasions.

[2] E.g., W.A. Meeks, *The Moral World of the First Christians* (London: SPCK, 1986) 129.

nection between the social institution of the family in the ancient world and the notion of early Christian communities as 'families' or fictive kinship groups.[3] In this essay I propose that Paul's use of the father-child metaphor derives its meaning from the socio-historical context of his day. More specifically, when the apostle employs these terms he is drawing on the *common assumptions* or *normal social expectations* of household members in the ancient world.[4] That is to say, there were in Paul's day conventional attitudes or presuppositions regarding how fathers, children (and brothers) *ought* to conduct themselves towards one another.

In the first part of this paper, a cognitive approach to metaphor is pursued where Christian relations as a family are understood in terms of biological family relations in antiquity. In the second part of the paper, a broad range of ancient sources are sampled in order to identify a number of stock meanings or associations of the parent-child relationship. In the third part it is argued that Paul uses these common assumptions in regulating and controlling relations between himself and the Corinthian Christians.[5]

In order to lay some groundwork for the topic in hand, it is necessary to engage first in a brief discussion of metaphor theory.

---

[3] See J.H. Neyrey, "Loss of Wealth, Loss of Family and Loss of Honor: The Cultural Context of the Original Makarisms in Q," in P.F. Esler (ed.), *Modelling Early Christianity: Social-Scientific Studies of the New Testament in its Context* (London: Routledge, 1995) 139-58 (156-7).

[4] H. Moxnes ("What is Family?: Problems in Constructing Early Christian Families" in H. Moxnes (ed.), *Constructing Early Christian Families: Family as Social Reality and Metaphor* (London: Routledge, 1997) 13-41 [18]) states: 'What are the sources for studies in the context of early Christianity? The major sources are texts, Christian as well as Jewish, Greek and Roman authors. *It is common among all these sources* that they offer statements of ...*norms*, not just data on people's actual behaviour...The emphasis is upon these *shared presuppositions...regarding families'* (emphasis added); see also S.J.D. Cohen (ed.), "Introduction," in *The Jewish Family in Antiquity* (BJS 289; Atlanta: Scholars Press, 1993) 1-5 (3); H. von Lips, *Glaube—Gemeinde—Amt: Zum Verständnis der Ordination in den Pastoralbriefen* (Göttingen: Vandenhoeck & Ruprecht, 1979) 126.

[5] For a fuller defense of this methodology see Trevor J. Burke, "Family Matters: An Exegetical and Socio-Historical Analysis of Familial Metaphors in 1 Thessalonians", unpub. Ph.D. diss. University of Glasgow, 2000 36-41 (forthcoming as part of the JSNT Sup Series).

I. *Metaphor and Meaning*

I do not intend here to review the vast body of theoretical literature on metaphor, but will confine myself to some of the main points
relevant to our inquiry. Aristotle's classic definition of metaphor is
a useful starting point—he characterises metaphor as 'the application of an alien name by transfer' (*Poet.* 21.7). Alternatively, metaphor can be defined in terms of its cognitive content[6] and, according
to one recent definition advanced by Lakoff and Johnson, metaphor
is defined as 'understanding and experiencing one kind of thing in
terms of another kind of experience'. On the basis of this definition,
we could say Paul is using metaphor, since he takes familial expressions from one sphere, that of the ancient social world, and applies
them in another (quite different) sphere—the sphere of Christian
relationships, by the use of analogy. In this case, the family in antiquity is the 'donor' field and the relationship between Paul (as
'father') and the Corinthians (as his 'children') is the 'recipient' field.
All this assumes that the correspondence between the two is sufficiently strong and meaningful to be an adequate basis for a metaphor (I shall return to this below).

Metaphor comprises two parts: the first is the imprecise element
which is to be explained, and the second is the alien, or unexpected
element which is used to supply the explanation. In accordance with
Lakoff and Johnson's earlier definition of metaphor (an understand-
ing/experience taken from one sphere and transferred to another),
different terms are employed to describe the realm from which a
metaphor is taken e.g. the 'source domain', 'vehicle', or 'donor field'.
Likewise, different terms are used to describe the realm or 'thing'
to which the metaphor is then applied e.g., the 'target domain',
'tenor' or 'recipient field'.

As stated above, when Paul uses familial metaphors the assumption is that a sufficiently strong correspondence exists between 'the
one kind of thing' and 'another' to serve as a basis for a metaphor.
When Paul (or anyone) explicitly refers to himself as a 'father' (ὡς,

---

[6] G. Lakoff and M. Johnson, *Metaphors We Live By* (Chicago: Chicago University Press, 1980) 5. Contemporary metaphor theory continues to be debated, especially the issue of the cognitive content of metaphor. For arguments for and
against see E.F. Kittay, *Metaphor: Its Cognitive Force and Linguistic Structure* (Oxford:
Clarendon Press, 1987) and D. Davidson "What Metaphor Means," in S. Sacks
(ed.), *On Metaphor* (Chicago: University of Chicago, 1978) 29-46.

1 Cor. 4:14; cf. 1 Thess. 2:11) a set of common notions or associations are triggered in our twenty-first century minds but what is
required is for us to grasp the first century meaning and the stereotypical attitudes of such a term. If metaphors are to be a useful means
of communication 'the *person using the figure* and the *person...hearing
the words* [must] give the words the same content'.[7] Thus, if Paul's
usage of familial nomenclature is far removed from what was commonly associated with family members in antiquity, the correlation
would be weak and the impact lessened and our findings rendered
less useful. As I shall argue, Paul's use of family metaphors in general and the father-child metaphor in particular are replete with
meaning and stem from the family in the ancient world. To test this
hypothesis and to enable us to grasp the sense of these metaphors
we need to look beyond Paul (see part 2 of this essay) to check
whether his Jewish assumptions re family are likely to be consistent
with those of his non-Jewish hearers.

Linguists also grade metaphors according to their 'quality' and in
doing so make a distinction between 'live' and 'dead' metaphors. In
this respect, Peter Macky points out that the phrase 'run for election' was once a novel and thus a living metaphor: it was understood only by reference to the more common sense of the word 'run'
(as in 'running a race'). However, the expression 'run for election'
has become so commonplace that 'users of English apply the verb
without having to think about physical running first'.[8] Hence, we
may describe 'run' as in 'run for election' as a dead metaphor. So,
is it the case that when Paul uses images such as 'father' or 'child'
they were so traditional as to convey little or no meaning? I think
not. We know that at the beginning of the Christian era family
metaphors, certainly as far as ancient Roman society was concerned,
permeated the religious, social and political spheres.[9] This is especially so because Roman life and society was often perceived as a
society of fathers and sons[10] where 'the metaphor father held a

---

[7] F. Lyall, *Slaves, Citizens and Sons: Legal Metaphors in the Epistles* (Grand Rapids:
Zondervan, 1984) 20 (emphasis added).

[8] P.W. Macky, *The Centrality of Metaphors to Biblical Thought: A Method for Interpreting the Bible.* Studies in the Bible and Early Christianity 19 (Lewiston, NY: Edwin
Mellen, 1990) 53.

[9] E.M. Lassen, "The Roman Family: Ideal and Metaphor," in Moxnes (ed.),
Early Christian Families, 103-120 (110).

[10] Y. Thomas, 'Vitae necisque potestas' in Y. Thomas (ed.), *Du Châtiment dans
la Cité. Supplices Corporels et Peine de Mort dans la Monde Antique* (Rome: École Française
de Rome, 1984) 195-230.

particularly important position among family metaphors in the...
Republic and later on in imperial Rome'.[11] So, family metaphors
were a very useful vehicle for the communication of the Christian
faith in the ancient world.

In the final analysis, in order to determine whether a metaphor
is 'live' or not we need to understand the context (or cotext as it is
called) and how metaphor is being used 'by this particular author
on this particular occasion'.[12] Only on two occasions in 1 Corinthians
does Paul refer to real fathers (5:1) and children (7:14) and from the
context of 1 Cor. 4:14-21 it is obvious Paul is not the biological father
of the Corinthians; moreover the way he uses these terms here and
elsewhere in his correspondence with the Corinthians (cf. 2 Cor. 6:13;
12:14-15) suggests in the metaphorical sense they are still very much
alive.[13] Indeed, there is an intensive use of the metaphor in 4:14-
21, it is utilised in unusual ways (not set formulae), and the final
reference to 'rod' (v. 21) makes good sense only if the Corinthians
have heard the resonances of the metaphor of father-children in the
previous verses. In my view there is good reason to believe that by
using familial metaphors Paul is working with what *he* considers to
be a familiar source-field and that there is a shared world of meaning about families from which he is drawing.

I will now illuminate a number of aspects of the parent-child
relationship from a broad selection of ancient texts. This will not
only situate Paul in his rightful socio-historical milieu but will also
provide a comparative context against which to understand his
paternal role. It should also enable us to determine how he may have
used such aspirations for clarifying his own relationship with his
converts. I will restrict my discussion of the primary evidence (Jewish and non-Jewish)[14] to aspects which impinge directly upon 1 Cor.
4:14-21.

---

[11] Lassen, "The Roman Family," 114.

[12] G.W. Dawes, *The Body in Question: Metaphor and Meaning in the Interpretation of Ephesians 5:21-33* (Leiden: Brill, 1998), 77.

[13] See O.L. Yarbrough, "Parents and Children in the Letters of Paul," in L. Michael White and O.L. Yarbrough (eds.), *The Social World of the First Christians: Essays in Honor of W.A. Meeks* (Philadelphia: Fortress Press, 1995) 126-41 (131-38).

[14] I shall combine my presentation of the primary evidence since there is general agreement among scholars that, as far as the *norms* or *presuppositions* of parent-child relations in antiquity are concerned, there is not much difference between Jewish and non-Jewish families. Cohen ("Introduction," 3) comments: 'The Jewish val-ues and expectations governing parent-child relationships were entirely consonant

II. *The Normal Social Expectations of Father-Child Relations in Antiquity*

(a) *Hierarchy*

Undergirding every discussion of family[15] life in antiquity is the common assumption that parent-child relations were hierarchical in nature. For example, Aristotle maintains that all households are hierarchically structured and comprise three relationships: father-child, master-slave, and husband-wife (*Pol.* 1.3.2). In order for the *oikos* to function well proper account must be taken of this hierarchy since some are better fitted to rule (e.g., fathers) while others (e.g., children) are to serve (*Pol.* 1.1.2). A father governs his children in a hierarchical relationship, but nonetheless one between free people (*Nich. Eth.* 8.11.2).

Aristotle's assumptions are echoed by Philo whose theoretical framework was basically hierarchical. The parent-child relationship is one expression of this order evident in Philo's remarks on the fifth commandment where parents are described as 'rulers' and 'seniors' and children as 'juniors' and 'learners' (*Spec. Leg.* 2.226). Elsewhere Philo states that 'parents belong to the superior class…while children occupy the lower position [as]…subjects' (*Dec.* 165-66). Other near contemporaries of Paul, Josephus and the first century Jewish poet Pseudo-Phocylides, also view parent-child relations as hierarchical. Josephus' references to family relationships illustrates the chain of hierarchy where obedience is required of the various members: God is over humankind and elders, while fathers and rulers are over children, subjects and wives (*Ap.* 2. 201).[16] Pseudo-Phocylides regards the honour due to one's parents as ranking second only to the honour due to God (*Sent.* 8).

---

with, and almost indistinguishable from, that of Greco-Roman society'; see also A. Reinhartz, "Parents and Children: A Philonic Perspective" in Cohen, *The Jewish Family*, 61-88 (87).

[15] In any study of the ancient family we are faced with the difficulty of which nomenclature to employ. Part of the problem is that no Greek, Latin or Hebrew words directly translate the English term and meaning of 'family' or 'house'; see C. Osiek and D.L. Balch, *Families in the New Testament World: Households and House Churches* (Louisville/Kentucky: Westminster John Knox Press, 1997) 6.

[16] C.B. Kittredge (*Community and Authority: The Rhetoric of Obedience in the Pauline Tradition* (Pennsylvania: Trinity Press International, 1998, 37-51) has recently shown how the semantic range of obedience language (i.e. ὑπακούειν and ὑποτάσσεσθαι) in ancient Jewish and non-Jewish writers serves the purpose of upholding the hierarchical structure of the family.

The above Jewish presuppositions are widely shared by Graeco-Roman authors of the period. Only a few pertinent examples need be cited. Plutarch the first century Greek-born rhetorician states that it is natural for children to be subordinate to their parents since 'Nature, and the Law which upholds Nature, have assigned to parents after Gods, first and greatest honour'(*Frat. Amor.* 4/479F). Cicero and the Stoic writer Hierocles concur but they differ from the above writers in that the honour due to parents ranks *third* after the honour due to the gods and one's country (*De Off.* 1.160; Hierocles, 3.39.34). Indeed, Hierocles even goes as far as to suggest that not only are parents 'most like the gods' but are 'far superior' because 'their nearness to us [means] we honour them more highly than the gods'(4.25.53).[17]

(b) *Authority*

Closely associated with the notion of hierarchy is that of authority. According to Aristotle, authority and subordination are essential and it is the male who is considered the most rational, the woman less rational, and the child immature (*Pol.* 1.13.6-7). In his *Nichomachean Ethics* Aristotle compares the authority exercised in the state with the authority administered in the household where he reasons it is natural for a father to exercise authority. However, there are right and wrong ways to do this—it is wrong for a father to exercise tyrannical authority, but hierarchical authority is right and just in and of itself (*Nich. Eth.* 8.11.6). In Aristotle's opinion, throughout life a child is regarded as never being separated from the father and is always dependent upon him (*Nich. Eth.* 5.6.8). Philo is in general agreement with these aspirations and recognises that both parents have authority over their offspring (*Spec. Leg.* 2.231) even though he concludes 'the father [is] the head of the house' (*Mut. Nom.* 217).

Pseudo-Phocylides' recommendations on the rearing of children, however, are strikingly milder. The poet warns parents not to be severe with their offspring: 'parents are not to be harsh with their children but gentle (ἤπιοι, *Sent.* 207).[18] Cicero even likens himself to a mild father (*De domo*, 94). Plutarch's views on authority are also

---

[17] References to Hierocles are taken from A.J. Malherbe, *Moral Exhortation: A Graeco-Roman Sourcebook* (LEC, 4; Philadelphia: Westminster Press, 1986).

[18] There is an interesting linguistic parallel here with Paul, if one accepts the variant reading, ἤπιοι 'gentle' (1 Thess. 2:7).

lenient, evident in the way he directs his remarks towards the male parent: 'fathers...should not be harsh and utterly austere' towards their offspring (*De Lib.* 13/E).[19]

As noted above, the parent-child relationship in antiquity was one of unequal power and authority. Basic to this relationship was the powerful principle of reciprocity where children were expected to render obedience to their parents. A string of Jewish and non-Jewish authors could be cited. For example, Philo insists that children should be 'willing to hearken to their [parents'] commands and to obey them in everything' (*Spec. Leg.* 2.236; cf. Josephus, *Ant.* 1.222). Likewise Seneca the Roman Stoic tells children of the need to 'obey...parents...[and] give way to their authority...whether it was unjust or harsh' (*De Ben.* 3.37:1-3; cf. Epictetus, *Diss.* 2.10.7).[20]

(c) *Imitation*

Imitating some kind of moral exemplar (e.g. teachers-pupils) was another stereotypical attitude in ancient society. Fathers in particular expected to model appropriate behaviour for their children, especially sons, to imitate. Isocrates exhorts Demonicus to follow the example of his father Hipponicus: 'I have produced a sample of the nature of Hipponicus after whom you should pattern your life as after an ensample, regarding his conduct as your law, and striving to imitate and emulate your father's virtue' (Isocrates, *Dem.* 4.11). Plutarch stresses that 'fathers above all' should not misbehave in front of their offspring but should instead 'make themselves a manifest example to their children, so that the latter, by looking at their fathers' lives as at a mirror, may be deterred from disgraceful deeds and words' (*De Lib.* 20/14B). In Jewish literature of the period, imitation of the father extended to imitation of their fore-fathers i.e. the fathers of the people of the nation. Josephus writes in relation to the Law that 'children shall be taught to read, and shall learn both the

---

[19] The comments by these authors are indicative of this time when 'paternal severity and filial duty gave way to mutual affection and devotion in the late republic or early empire'; see, for example, R.P. Saller, *Patriarchy, Property and Death in the Roman Family* (Cambridge: Cambridge University Press, 1994), 104.

[20] I am aware that in the case of Stoic writers the higher call to the philosophical life did not always sit easily alongside the need for marriage/parenthood. However, in the case of Seneca and Epictetus this tension is not irreconcilable (cf. Seneca, *Ep.* 9.17-19; Epictetus, *Diss.* 2.23.37-38).

laws and deeds of their fore-fathers in order that they may imitate the latter' (*Ap.* 1.204; cf. Philo, *Sacr. Abel* 68; 1 Macc. 2.51).

(d) *Affection*

The theme of the naturalness of parental love is commonly found in ancient literature, often explicitly in Graeco-Roman writers. Aristotle notes that the love between a parent and their offspring was a mutual but nonetheless hierarchical emotion. Parental love for children 'exceeds that of the child in duration' because they 'love their children as part of themselves' (*Nich. Eth.* 8.12.2). 'Parents love their child as soon as it is born', whereas children love their parents 'only when time has elapsed and they have acquired understanding' (*Nich. Eth.* 8.12.2).

Philo uses very emotive language to describe the relationship between parents and their offspring:

> parents cherish their children with extreme tenderness because they are fast bound by the magnet forces of affection (*Spec. Leg.* 2.240).

Elsewhere Philo, in his *Exposition of the Law*, views parents and their offspring as 'inseparable parts' because they are bound 'by the love ties…of affection which unites them' (*Spec. Leg.* 1.137). Plutarch not only considers parental love as present from inception—('accompan[ies] their first beginnings,' *De Amor.* 3/495C)—but also as the goal of the relationship: 'the end aim of bearing and rearing a child is not utility, but affection' (*De Amor.* 3/496C). Plutarch even goes so far as to suggest that a father places affection for his children above personal honour and achievement: 'No father is fond of oratory or of honour or of riches as he is of his children' (*Frat. Amor.* 5/480C). According to Seneca, affection is the most important tie between parents and their progeny: 'No affection binds us more than the love of children' (*De Clem.* 1.14.2). The same author also states that both parents love their children but makes a distinction between how a father and a mother show affection towards their offspring. A father's love for his children is stricter, but it is no less real for all that: 'Do you not see how fathers show their love in one way and mothers in another? The father orders his children to be aroused from sleep in order that they may start early upon their pursuits, even on holidays he does not permit then to be idle, and then he draws from them sweat and sometimes tears. [On the other hand], 'the mother fondles them in her lap, wishes them out of the sun, wishes them never to be unhappy, never to cry, never to toil' (*De Prov.* 2.5).[21]

(e) *Education*

Parents in antiquity, particularly fathers, were also expected to educate their offspring. Aristotle, whilst recognising the part which the state plays in the education of children also maintains that parents have a didactic role. 'Parents', he writes, 'have bestowed on them [their children] the greatest benefits in being the cause of their existence and rearing, and later of their education' (*Eth. Nich.* 8.12.5). But although it may be the responsibility of all 'parents to train their sons', Aristotle particularly emphasises the importance for children to attend to 'paternal exhortations' (οἱ πατρικοὶ λόγοι, *Eth. Nich.* 10.9.15).

   Both Philo and Josephus enthuse about the early religious teaching of Jewish sons and refer to the laws as having been 'engraved' on the souls of all young Jews (*Leg.* 210; *Ap.* 2.178). In keeping with Jewish custom, the family was the locus for the socialisation and instruction of offspring. Philo states that children are taught by their parents 'from their swaddling-clothes' (*Leg.* 115) and should 'impress upon their young minds...the most essential questions of what to choose to avoid...to choose virtues and vices and the activities to which they lead' (*Spec. Leg.* 2. 228). Josephus shows a particular pride in his Jewish tradition, declaring that it is remarkable because of the place it gives to the 'instruction of children' (παιδοτροφία *Ap.* 1.60). Josephus also revels in the special emphasis placed on teaching within the context of the home (*Ap.* 2.173-74; cf. *Ant.* 8.12).

   Education is a subject which the first century philosopher Musonius Rufus addresses at some length. The instruction of one's children

---

[21] Classical scholars are currently of the view that father-son relations in the ancient world were not devoid of affection. E.M. Lassen ("Fathers and Sons," in B. Rawson (ed.), *Marriage, Divorce and Children in Ancient Rome* [Oxford: Clarendon Press, 1991, 114-43 [119]) writes: 'Paternal love...was a reality in Antiquity'. Also, R.P. Saller ("Corporal Punishment, Authority and Obedience in the Roman Household," in *Marriage, Divorce, and Children in Ancient Rome* [Oxford: Clarendon Press, 1991] 144-65 [165]) rightly makes the point that 'if the father had been the severe and repressive figure in Roman culture...it would have been odd that emperors were so concerned to present themselves as *pater* in contrast to *dominus*...The rationale for this image was surely precisely the fact that *fathers exercised a benign authority*' (emphasis added).

should in Musonius Rufus' opinion begin at the earliest possible moment: 'straight from infancy they ought to be taught that this [virtue] is right and that is wrong…that this is helpful, that is harmful, that one must do this, one must not do that' (*frag.* 4.46.35f.).[22] A similar point is made by Plutarch who states: 'for just as it was necessary, immediately after birth, to begin to mould the limbs of the children's bodies in order that these may grow straight and without deformity, so, in the same fashion, it is fitting from the beginning to regulate the characters of children' (*De Lib.* 5/3E). What is striking about all these views on the education of children is the fact that although Jewish and non-Jewish authors differed as regards the *content* of instruction, the responsibility for fathers to teach their offspring was a commonly held one in the ancient world.

In summary: our brief survey of the conventional attitudes of ancient writers re father-child relations reveals considerable agreement between Jewish and non-Jewish writers. The evidence for the most part shows that as far as the typical expectations of father-child relations are concerned, Jewish families were little different to their non-Jewish counterparts at the turn of the eras.

Having isolated a number of stock meanings of the father-child relationship we now turn to consider the passage. It is my view that Paul uses an array of cultural assumptions of the father-child relationship in regard to how he and the Corinthians ought to conduct themselves towards one another.

III. *Paul's Dysfunctional Family in Corinth*

1 Cor.4:14-21 concludes the first major unit of the body of the letter (chps. 1-4) where Paul has been primarily addressing the issue of divisions in the church at Corinth. In 1:10f. Paul explicitly refers to a number of factions, factions which centred around the Corinthians' appeals to different authority figures (e.g., "I belong to Apollos" 1:12).[23] To be sure, there were other authority figures in

---

[22] Meeks (*Moral World*, 61) writes: 'Education began of course within the family. Even though schools had become common by imperial times, the *father* remained primarily responsible…for educating his dependants' (emphasis added).

[23] M.M. Mitchell (*Paul and the Rhetoric of Reconciliation: An Exegetical Investigation of the Language and Composition of 1 Corinthians* [Louisville/Kentucky: Westminster/ John Knox Press, 1991] 85-86) has shown that these formulaic appeals are commonly used to describe relations between a *parent* and a *child*, the force of which

the Corinthian community, evident by the way the church met in the house of Stephanas (τὴν οἰκίαν Στεφανᾶ, 16:15). Paul also mentions Crispus and Gaius (1:14) in whose households church groups would probably have met. This points up the fact that the early churches in general and the Corinthian community in particular (cf. καὶ οἶκον αὐτῶν ἐκκλησίᾳ 16:19) was socially and structurally organised as different household units.[24] Moreover, the fact that Paul refers to 'the *whole* church' (ἡ ἐκκλησία ὅλη, 14:23), which only occasionally came together (11:18), suggests there were a number of separate house churches. Not only did each of these appeal to different authority figures but the rivalry and divisions which existed in the community were primarily between the household heads who hosted churches in their houses.[25] It is highly probable that these house churches were operating independently of each other, a practice which would have contributed to the disunity in the community.[26] Thus, it is ironic that whereas the Corinthians' relationships with outsiders were healthy, their relationships with one another were in disarray.[27] Irony also pervades the verses immediately preceding 4:14-21 where Paul contrasts the elevated position of the Corinthians with his own debased rank: they are 'kings', 'rich', 'wise', 'strong' and 'in honour' (4:10) whereas he is 'scum', 'a fool', 'weak', and 'in dishonour' (4:12). In 4:14-21 Paul applies this to the moment in hand and in his absence takes the necessary action to curb the household divisions by having already sent Timothy to further his interests (4:17).

1 Cor. 4:14-21 therefore marks a crucial turning-point in the letter

---

is to suggest there are those within the Corinthian church who are acting childishly (3:1-3a). This being so, these appeals stand in stark contrast to Paul's call in 4:14-21 for the Corinthians to become *child-like* in their conduct and relationship to him.

[24] L.M. White, *Building God's House in the Roman World: Architectural Adaptation among Pagans, Jews and Christians*, (Valley Forge, PA: Trinity Press International 1990, 105) posits as many as six or more house churches in Corinth in Paul's time.

[25] S.C. Barton, "Paul's Sense of Place: An Anthropological Approach to Community Formation in Corinth," *NTS* 32 (1986) 225-46 (238).

[26] E.g., E. Dassmann, "Hausgemeinde und Bischofsamt," *JAC* 11 (1984) 82-97 (88). Historically, there may never have been an actual unity in the church at Corinth but as Mitchell (*Paul*, 1 n 1) rightly points out: 'Paul's rhetorical stance throughout 1 Cor is to argue that Christian unity is the...*sociological expectation* from which the Corinthians have fallen' (emphasis added).

[27] J.M.G. Barclay, "Thessalonica and Corinth: Social Contrasts in Pauline Christianity," *JSNT* 49 (1992) 49-72, has shown how two churches founded in close succession to one another can develop differently in terms of their relationships *to each other* and *to outsiders*.

where Paul lays claim to a self-description superior to those just mentioned by the introduction of his paternal metaphor. Against the prevailing background of household dissension and rivalry, Paul uses paternal imagery to call for unity between the different 'household factions by representing the church to itself as *one household* with Paul himself as its father'.[28] To achieve this goal, Paul assumes a role similar to that of a *paterfamilias* in the ancient world who was responsible for exercising authority as well as maintaining order, peace and concord within his own family.[29] In brief, Paul here is about the business of household management.

At the outset Paul states that his aim is not to shame the Corinthians—they are his 'beloved children' (v. 14)—but to 'admonish' (νουθετέω, v. 14) them—a verb he uses elsewhere (cf. 1 Thess. 5:12) and one which frequently describes a *father's* admonishment of his *offspring* (e.g. Wisd. 11:10; Pss. Sol. 13:19; Josephus, *Bell. Jud.* 1.481). Mention of the Corinthians as his 'beloved children' paves the way for Paul to explicitly introduce his 'father' metaphor by declaring that he had 'given birth' (ἐγέννησα, v. 15; cf. Phlm.10) to the Corinthians through the gospel. The notion of (spiritual) 'begetting' stresses the fact that Paul had been with the Corinthians from the very beginning in that he was the *first* to proclaim the gospel to them and establish the community (cf. 2 Cor.10:4, RSV), a note he had struck earlier in 3:6a ("I planted"). However, even though this act of fathering had taken place at a specific moment in time[30] Paul, in keeping with the common attitudes of fathers in antiquity, viewed his paternal role as a continuous and on-going concern (e.g. instruction, imitation, etc.).

The term 'father' highlights the superordinate position between Paul and his spiritual offspring and as we observed earlier accords with the normal social expectations of leading household members in relation to their dependants. Paul's hierarchical stance is accentuated, in the first instance, by the way in which he contrasts his paternal role with other inferior familial roles such as παιδαγωγοί, "guardians", whose obligations were short-lived and whose author-

---

[28] Barton, "Paul's Sense of Place," 239 (author's own emphasis).
[29] S.J. Joubert, "Managing the Household: Paul as paterfamilias of the Corinthian Household", in P.F. Esler (ed.), *Modelling Early Christianity: Social-Scientific of the New Testament in its Context* (London: Routledge, 1995) 213-23.
[30] B.R. Gaventa, "Our Mother St. Paul: Toward the Recovery of a Neglected Theme," *Princeton Seminary Bulletin* 17 (1996) 29-4 (34f.).

ity was strictly limited.[31] The juxtaposition of these two metaphors
emphasises Paul's attachment to the Corinthians as 'their progenitor into the gospel' and not as some 'post-natal appointee'.[32] This
contrasting imagery underscores Paul's 'greatly superior claim... [as]
... father of the family'.[33] By describing himself thus Paul relativizes
the position of all others (i.e. Apollos, Cephas) and asserts his own
vital role.

'Father' is Paul's preferred self-designation and by referring to himself in this way he situates himself above his converts.[34] It is instructive to note that when Paul describes *himself* by way of familial terms
in his letters he never uses the sibling metaphor. It is instructive because Paul does not primarily see his relationship to the Corinthians—or any of the churches which he had founded—as a brother
but as a πατήρ.[35] Although the Corinthians had a myriad (μυρίους,
lit. ten thousand) of other so-called 'fathers' or teachers, Paul occupies the unique position of having exclusive claim over his converts
because he is their principal father in the gospel.[36] To be sure, Paul
is not denigrating Apollos (or any others) with whom he had successfully coaboured among the Corinthians (cf. 3:6; cf. 4:6); rather,
he is stating a plain fact—children can have only *one* real father and
Paul was it.

Paul's senior relationship to the Corinthians, one of the earliest
Christian communities, is one piece of evidence that his churches
did not start out as egalitarian in nature only to 'degenerate' into
patriarchal structures with the passing of time, such as we find in

---

[31] See, for example, Xen. *Lac.* 3.1.

[32] N.H. Young, "Παιδαγωγός: The Social Setting of a Pauline Metaphor," *NovT*
29 (1987) 150-76 (170).

[33] M.E. Thrall, *The First and Second Letters of Paul to the Corinthians* (Cambridge:
Cambridge University Press, 1965) 37.

[34] E.g., D.B. Martin, *Slavery as Salvation: The Metaphor of Slavery in Pauline Christianity* (New Haven: Yale University Press, 1990) 122; Joubert, "Managing the
Household," 216.

[35] R. Aasgaard "My Beloved Brothers and Sisters!: A Study of the Meaning
and Function of Christian Siblingship in Paul, in its Graeco-Roman and Jewish
Context," DTh diss. University of Oslo, 1998, 327. The Corinthians are Paul's
brothers and by implication Paul is their brother but nowhere does Paul actually
say the latter. The only New Testament reference we have of this is in 2 Pet. 3:15
where the author *refers to Paul* as '*our dear brother*'.

[36] E.g., C.K. Barrett, *The First Epistle to the Corinthians* (HNTC; New York: Harper
& Row, 1968) 115; G.D. Fee, *The First Epistle to the Corinthians* (NICNT; Grand
Rapids: Eerdmans, 1987) 185.

the Pastoral epistles.[37] Rather, some form of hierarchy was there from the inception of these communities and this is also seen in the varying functions of leading members in the church (cf. 1 Cor. 12:28). Moreover, the number of leading household members who embraced the gospel in Corinth (e.g., Stephanas) coupled with Paul's predilection for household terms to describe these communities show that the household was not merely a model but that the structure of the 'household imposed its own quiet hierarchy on the proceedings'.[38]

The expression 'father' also implies Paul's authority over the church, an authority that was being undermined by some (τινες 4:18b) from within and which Paul needed to re-establish (cf. 4:3-5).[39] Paul's authority is made clear in a number of ways: first, it is generally evident in this pericope by the deliberate shift from the first and second person plurals in 4:9-13 to the repeated use of the first person singular: '*I* am not writing this to shame you' (4:14); '*I* gave birth to you' (4:15); '*I* exhort you' (4:16); '*I* sent Timothy' (4:17); '*I* teach' (4:17b); '*I* come to you' (4:18); 'Shall *I* come to you with a rod?'(4:21). Clearly Paul will not tolerate or entertain any rivals. In actual fact, if Paul is mirroring the stereotypical attitudes of fathers who exercised total control over their offspring he may have viewed the Corinthian church as in some sense 'belonging'[40] to him (cf. Aristotle, *Nich. Eth.* 8.12.2; Hierocles, 4.25.53).

Secondly, his authority is apparent in the manner in which he expects his convert-children to obey him through imitation.[41] The logic of the connecting particle οὖν (v. 16) should not be over-looked and points up the fact that whilst sons in twenty-first century western

---

[37] See Burke, "Family Matters," 172-174, 204, 294-299, 330; B. Witherington, *Conflict and Community: A Socio-Rhetorical Commentary on 1 and 2 Corinthians* (Eerdmans/ Paternoster: Grand Rapids/Carlisle, 1995) 35, 453; *contra*, Elizabeth Schüssler Fiorenza, *In Memory of Her: A Feminist Reconstruction of Christian Origins* 2nd ed. (London: SCM, 1994), p. 279

[38] R.A. Campbell, *The Elders: Seniority Within Earliest Christianity* (SNTW; Edinburgh: T. & T. Clark, 1994) 119.

[39] N.A. Dahl, "Paul and the Church at Corinth according to 1 Corinthians 1:10-4:21," in (eds.), W.R. Farmer, C.F.D. Moule and R. Niebuhr, *Christian History and Interpretation: Studies Presented to John Knox* (Cambridge: Cambridge University Press, 1967) 313-35; Yarbrough, "Parents and Children," 131-132.

[40] S.H. Polaski, *Paul and the Discourse of Power* (Gender, Culture, Theory, 8; Sheffield: JSOT Press, 1999) 31-32.

[41] B. Holmberg, *Paul and Power: The Structure of Authority in the Primitive Church as Reflected in the Pauline Epistles* (ConB; New Testament Series, 11; Lund: CWK Gleerup, 1978) 78.

society are not expected to imitate their fathers, they were not exempt from doing so in the ancient world. It is with this '*cultural expectation* controlling his analogy'[42] that Paul urges his spiritual offspring to follow his example. However, even though the apostle expected his Corinthian progeny to conform to his pattern, this ought not to be construed as a strategy of coercion[43] or manipulation[44] or authoritarianism on Paul's part. On the contrary, whenever Paul has occasion to use his authority amongst the churches which he founded he never stresses his apostolic status or credentials but prefers instead a softer approach of exercising paternal authority.[45] Moreover, Paul later sounds an important Christocentric note to inform his readers that to imitate him is merely to imitate Christ (11:1) whom he serves.

But to what does Paul refer when he calls upon the Corinthians to imitate him? Evidently the Corinthians were aware of what Paul has in view since he had sent Timothy to *remind* them of his manner of life and teaching. Nevertheless, the plural expression τὰς ὁδούς, μου ("my way*s*") would seem to indicate that there are general moral categories of Paul's life which are worthy of imitation and that these stood in contrast to the ways of the Corinthians.[46] More particularly, if 4:14-21 concludes the first part of the epistle, and in light of the existing household factions in the church, Paul may (in part) be

---

[42] D.A. Carson, *The Cross and Christian Ministry: An Exposition of Passages of Corinthians* (Grand Rapids: Baker, 1993) 110 (emphasis added).

[43] E.A. Castelli (*Imitating Paul: A Discourse of Power* [LCBI; Louisville: Westminster/ John Knox Press, 1991] 101) is right when she states that the 'image of father must be read in cultural context, that is, in relationship to the paternal role in Graeco-Roman society'. But she is mistaken when she concludes in relation to 1 Corinthians: 'The paternal metaphor does not necessarily evoke a sense of kindness or love' (*Imitating Paul*, 109); see T.J. Burke, "Pauline Paternity in 1 Thessalonians," *TynB* 51.1 (2000) 59-80. Moreover, Paul's paternal role *vis-à-vis* his spiritual offspring is highly complex and variegated and should not be reduced to a *single* expression of his hierarchical stance channeled through his call to imitate him. Castelli's emphasis upon 'sameness' is also problematic and if followed to its logical conclusion leaves us with Pauline churches lacking in initiative and so uniform they can only be described as clone-communities. Paul is more concerned with *unity* than uniformity in the churches he had established; see A.C. Thiselton, *The First Epistle to the Corinthians* (Grand Rapids/Carlisle: Eerdmans/Paternoster, 2000) 372.

[44] G. Shaw, *The Cost of Authority: Manipulation and Freedom in the New Testament* (London: SCM, 1983) 35.

[45] E. Best, "Paul's Apostolic Authority?," *JSNT* 27 (1986) 3-25 (16 & 18).

[46] A.D. Clarke, "'Be Imitators of Me': Paul's Model of Leadership," *TynB* 49.2 (1998) 329-60 (345).

alluding to the agricultural metaphors (planting, watering) used earlier to underscore the harmonious manner in which he and Apollos had co-laboured (3:6). The unanimity which characterised Paul's own working relations with Apollos should also distinguish relations between the different household churches in Corinth. When we consider the premium placed upon family concord and harmony in the ancient world we have some appreciation of Paul's concern for unity among his spiritual offspring (e.g. Plutarch, *Frat. Amor.* 2/479A).

To facilitate the Corinthians in this matter of mimesis, Paul has sent Timothy his 'faithful and beloved child in the Lord' (v. 17a). Paul's depiction of Timothy also as his 'child' again underscores his authority and as we noted in part II carries the (fatherly) assumption that the latter will submit to his request. Timothy's role is strategic in that he is not only dispatched as Paul's emissary but also as the embodiment of his ways. Given that Paul is no longer physically present with the Corinthians Timothy is Paul's conduit and didactic tool, representing the apostle's power and authority to the Corinthians. Certainly Timothy was well placed to be Paul's ambassador since he had been with him (Acts 18:5) during the apostle's lengthy 18 month stay of 'instruction' (Acts 18:11) in Corinth. Thus, the apostle's confidence in him is not misplaced since Paul knows that Timothy's manner and conduct accords with what he had 'taught in all the churches' (ἐν πάσῃ ἐκκλησίᾳ διδάσκω, v. 17b). This latter phrase probably refers to a common core of Pauline instruction (cf. 7:17; 11:16; 14:33) which Paul passed on to all his nascent congregations. But given that Paul is the *paterfamilias* of the whole Corinthian community his teaching responsibilities are wide-ranging and tailored specifically to the needs of these convert-children. This included instructing them on a raft of moral issues (e.g. sexual immorality, 1 Cor. 5:1-5; civil litigation, 1 Cor.6:1-11) as well as answering the many questions upon which they were divided (e.g. marriage, 1 Cor. 7; idol meat consumption, 1 Cor 8, church meals, 1 Cor. 11, worship, 1 Cor.12 etc.), an approach consonant with our ancient sources adduced earlier and crucial if the Corinthians are to grow and mature in the Christian faith (cf. 1 Cor.3:1-3a).

In vv.18-21 Paul's tone appears to harden as he contrasts the 'power' (δύναμιν, v. 18) of the kingdom of God with the mere 'talk' of certain 'arrogant people' whom he wishes to discipline—by so doing, Paul implicitly asserts his paternal power (v. 19f.). The arro-

gant whom Paul has in mind may be some of the leaders[47] of the
various house-churches who by their conduct were instrumental in
causing the rivalry and divisions. However, Paul's words not only
address the house-church leaders but also the entire community,[48]
evident by the way in which he re-introduces the father-child relationship (v. 21) which effectively ties vv. 14-17 to vv. 18-21. As we
have seen, Paul's paternal strategy is to employ different methods
to get his point across to his converts (e.g. irony) and it is only as a
last resort that he threatens to use the vast power at his disposal.
Clearly Paul believes he has the ability to influence and effect change
in the community and his language strikes a chord with his contemporary Philo who states: 'parents must have power over their children to...tend them carefully' (*Hyp.* 7.3). Paul's power however is
not manifested in a dictatorial or authoritarian manner[49] and in any
case we should not assume an (over-simplistic) one-to-one correspondence between the social reality of a father in antiquity and Paul's
metaphorical use of this term. In the case of the former a father's
power could (in theory) be demonstrated in the exposure of unwanted
children; Paul as *pater* to the Corinthians cares too much to throw
them on the slag heap.

    The above warning is coupled with the explicit threat to use the
'rod' (ῥάβδος, v. 21) and conveys something of Paul's authority as
well as the disciplinary measures he is prepared to take to check the
household divisions and unite his Corinthian children under his
common paternity. Paul's language is severe and his fatherly role
appears stricter than that found in 1 Thess. 2:10-12 or 2 Cor. 8-9
(although cf. 1 Cor. 16:1-4). But the apparent contrast between his
coming 'in love' and in a 'gentle spirit' ought not to be over-played
since what is in view here is not the motive but the *manner*[50] of Paul's
coming. Crucially, it is as their father that Paul now promises to come
to the Corinthians and whatever action he has to take will demonstrate his paternal affection for them. Although Paul as a loving parent
presents his converts with a choice as to whether or not he should
come with a rod (v. 21a) *he* as their father will decide on the necessary action he should take when he arrives. By referring to his coming

[47] Witherington, *Conflict and Community*, 147.
[48] Fee (*Corinthians*, 190) suggests that the *whole community* was at fault because
it had either 'tolerated' or 'adopted' the behavioural patterns of the arrogant.
[49] Holmberg, *Paul and Power*, 79.
[50] Fee, *Corinthians*, 193.

'in love' (ἐν ἀγάπῃ, v. 21b) Paul brings his argument full circle ('be-loved children,' τέκνα μου ἀγαπητὰ, v.14) and reflects the fact that whilst his position as 'father' was a hierarchical one, there is a dia-lectic between this and the undoubted affection he also felt for his spiritual offspring.[51]

In conclusion, the Corinthian church comprised a number of household churches each operating independently of the others. In an effort to prevent further divisions Paul at a strategic point in the letter (chpts. 1-4) employs the father-child metaphor in order to unite the Corinthians under himself as their common *pater*. As the found-ing-father of the community Paul expects his children to heed his position, submit to his authority, follow his example, obey his in-structions and be aware of his love for them. These household di-visions were compounded by the fact that others followed Paul (e.g., Apollos) and although he pays tribute to their work and stresses their co-operation together, his role is preeminent to all others. In his absence Paul has sent Timothy, another of his children but also his associate to not only remind the Corinthians of his ways and teach-ings but to also represent his power and authority to them. Paul's hope is that the Corinthians will amend their ways so that he can avoid using the rod which he as a loving parent has every right to exercise.

---

[51] Dale B. Martin (*The Corinthian Body* [New Haven: Yale University Press, 1995], 85) aptly sums up Paul's relationship with the Corinthians as 'a loving father, kind but superior'.

A RHETORIC OF POWER: IDEOLOGY AND 1 CORINTHIANS 1-4

Charles A. Wanamaker

1. *Introduction*

In her seminal study of the theme of imitation in Paul, Elizabeth Castelli explores the way in which Paul employs this theme in 1 Cor. 4:16.[1] In doing so she places 4:16 within its rhetorical context of 1 Cor. 1:10-4:21 where Paul addresses the problem of factionalism within the community. She argues that between calling for unity in 1 Cor. 1:10-18 and calling for imitation of himself in 4:14-21 Paul introduces a discourse of dualistically determined mimetic examples. The overall thrust of the section pushes for the unity of the community, and this plays a key role in re-inscribing Paul's authority over the community as its leader. Thus 1 Cor. 1:10-4:21, like other mimetic discourses in Paul's writings, "uses rhetoric to rationalize and shore up" Paul's position of power over the community by making it seem completely 'natural.'[2]

Although Castelli is aware that this is an ideological move and that ideological moves are the most powerful available to Paul for establishing and for that matter sustaining his relationships of power with the Corinthian Christians,[3] she has not developed this point with any depth because she has not clearly defined what she means by ideology nor has she explored in any detail the relation between power, domination, and ideology. This may reflect the fact that Michel Foucault, upon whom she draws for her analysis, was not really interested in the question of ideology.[4] Whatever the reason,

---

[1] Elizabeth A. Castelli, *Imitating Paul: A Discourse of Power*, Literary Currents in Biblical Interpretation (Louisville, KY: Westminster/John Knox Press, 1991).

[2] Castelli, *Imitating Paul*, 116.

[3] Castelli, *Imitating Paul*, 123.

[4] Pieter van Veuren, "Review Article: Ideology and Modern Culture," *South African Journal of Philosophy* 12 (1993): 12, argues that two tendencies exist in postmodernist thought on ideology. One tendency is to render ideology otiose by claiming that all discourses are ideological in nature since they mediate "the play of power and specific interests." The other is to define ideology as a system of

however, in this paper I hope to move Castelli's work forward by looking at the ways in which Paul's rhetoric in 1 Cor. 1:10-4:21 functions ideologically to reassert his power in the Corinthian Christian community. In order to do this I will first clarify the understanding of ideology which I will use in this paper before turning to 1 Corinthians 1-4 to demonstrate that the power of Paul's rhetoric resides strongly in its ideological nature, or what Vernon Robbins calls its ideological texture.[5]

2. Ideology and Meaning

The concept of ideology has a long and varied history. Not surprisingly, perhaps, the concept has come to have a variety of meanings depending upon who is using it and for what purpose. John B. Thompson has usefully suggested that the academic study of ideology has two different and competing streams of analysis and interpretation. He refers to these as neutral conceptions and critical conceptions.[6] Neutral conceptions of ideology, which Thompson believes have come to dominate most contemporary discussions of ideology,[7] "characterize phenomena as ideology or ideological without implying that these phenomena are necessarily misleading, illusory or aligned with the interests of any particular group."[8] Effectively ideology has come to be used as a "purely descriptive term" when it is employed in a neutral sense,[9] and often means little more than someone or some group's system of ideas and beliefs or their worldview.

---

ideas which functions as "social cement," but to then argue that in postmodern societies ideologies no longer operate since postmodernity "is characterized by irreducible 'diversity', 'plurality' and 'difference.'"

[5] Vernon K. Robbins, *The Tapestry of Early Christian Discourse: Rhetoric, Society and Ideology* (London: Routledge, 1996), 36-40, 192-236.

[6] John B. Thompson, *Ideology and Modern Culture* (Cambridge: Polity Press, 1990), 52-55. On neutral and critical conceptions in ideological analysis see also Michèle Barrett, *The Politics of Truth: From Marx to Foucault* (Cambridge: Polity Press, 1991), 18-24. T. Eagleton, *Ideology: An Introduction* (London: Verso, 1991), 15, maintains that the term ideology can have a pejorative sense, a positive sense, or a neutral one. Unfortunately he does not develop clear criteria for analyzing these distinctions.

[7] Thompson, *Ideology and Culture*, 55.

[8] Thompson, *Ideology and Culture*, 53.

[9] John B. Thompson, "Communication and Power: A Response to Some Criticisms," *South African Journal of Philosophy* 13 (1994): 134.

Critical conceptions, on the other hand, according to Thompson, "imply that the phenomena characterized as ideology or ideological are misleading, illusory or one-sided,"[10] that is, they are characterized by one or more elements of "negativity."[11] Thompson positions himself in the tradition of critical conceptions of ideology going back to Napoleon Bonaparte and Karl Marx, but he argues that the concept of ideology should be linked to only one criterion of negativity: ideology and ideological phenomena involve symbolic meanings and forms which serve *"to establish and sustain relations of domination."*[12] By limiting the negativity to this it allows him to overcome the epistemological burden that ideological phenomena must of necessity be erroneous, illusory, or in some other respect flawed before they can be ideological, and it allows him to focus on the ways in which symbolic forms serve in certain circumstances "to establish and sustain relations of domination."[13] Thus Thompson conceptualizes ideology as

> the ways in which the meaning mobilized by symbolic forms serves *to establish and sustain* relations of domination: to establish, in the sense that meaning may actively create and institute relations of domination; to sustain in the sense that meaning may serve to maintain and reproduce relations of domination through the ongoing process of producing and receiving symbolic forms.[14]

In this essay I will employ Thompson's understanding of ideology because I believe that his critical conception of ideology offers a valuable tool for the analysis of the ways in which Paul's rhetoric functions to reestablish and maintain his relationship of authority and domination over his converts in Corinth as seen in 1 Corinthians 1-4, and elsewhere for that matter, without suggesting that Paul intentionally sought to deceive the Corinthians while attempting to sustain his power to shape the community as its founder. Before turning to 1 Corinthians 1-4, however, several other aspects of Thompson's work need to be noted, as they are important for my analysis.

In his earlier work on the theory of ideology Thompson identi-

---

[10] Thompson, *Ideology and Culture*, 54.
[11] Thompson, *Ideology and Culture*, 54.
[12] Thompson, *Ideology and Culture*, 56 (emphasis his). He claims that this conception is latent in Marx's understanding of ideology.
[13] Thompson, *Ideology and Culture*, 56-57.
[14] Thompson, *Ideology and Culture*, 58 (emphasis his).

fied language as the "principal medium of the meaning (significa-
tion) which serves to sustain relations of domination."[15] By broadening his understanding of the "medium of meaning" to symbolic
forms Thompson is able to offer the possibility of analyzing the ideological significance of a far wider range of meanings including "*meaningful actions, objects and expressions of various kinds.*"[16] According to
Thompson symbolic forms derive their meaning from "socially structured contexts and processes,"[17] and therefore, their analysis requires
the analysis of the actual social-historical context and processes in
which they occur and are embedded if we are to determine whether the symbolic forms have ideological significance and what that
significance is for creating and sustaining relations of domination.[18]
In the case of Paul, for example, when he identifies himself as the
Corinthian Christians' father in Christ (1 Cor. 4:14-15) the meaning of this symbolic representation of his relationship with his converts must be understood against the cultural conception of what a
father was in both Jewish and Greco-Roman culture of that time.
In the process of this analysis it becomes clear that Paul's application of the father-children metaphor in his relation with the Corinthians has ideological significance in terms of his claim to the right
to exercise power over them and to challenge the claims of com-
petitors to power.[19]

Since Thompson's conceptualization of ideology is closely related
to his understanding of power and domination, it is important to
understand what he means by these terms. Power, according to
Thompson, refers to "a capacity which *enables* or *empowers* some individuals to make decisions, pursue ends or realize interests."[20] Such
power is normally derived from the position which an individual or
group occupies in some or other social sphere or social institution,

---

[15] John B. Thompson, *Studies in the Theory of Ideology* (Cambridge: Polity Press,
1984), 131.
[16] Thompson, *Ideology and Culture*, 136.
[17] Thompson, *Ideology and Culture*, 136.
[18] Thompson, *Ideology and Culture*, 122-62. Within the confines of this paper it
is impossible to do justice to the richness of Thompson's thought regarding symbolic forms, their social-historical contextualization, and the social-historical processes from which they receive their meaning and significance. Suffice it to say
that many of the issues which he raises are not foreign to those working in Biblical studies, particularly those whose work is informed by the socio-rhetorical approach which Vernon Robbins (see, e.g., *Tapestry*) and others have developed.
[19] See below for a full discussion of 1 Cor. 4:14-21.
[20] Thompson, *Ideology and Culture*, 151 (emphasis his).

and often this power stands in socially determined relations to the power of others. When the relations of "power are *systematically asymmetrical*, then the situation may be described as one of *domination*" because some individual or group is endowed with power "which excludes, and to some significant degree remains inaccessible to, other individuals or groups of individuals, irrespective of the basis upon which such exclusion is carried out."[21] Once again an example from Paul may prove helpful. Paul, by virtue of his acknowledged status and position as an apostle of Christ, stood in a position of dominance over the churches which he established because his status as an apostle, on the one hand, was not accessible to ordinary converts (1 Cor. 15:8-11), and on the other, gave him the right to make decisions effecting the church communities which he established.[22]

Another aspect of Thompson's work is of particular relevance for the analysis of ideology from a critical perspective. Thompson identifies five general modes in which ideology operates: 1) legitimation, 2) dissimulation, 3) unification, 4) fragmentation, and 5) reification.[23] But he is quite explicit that these are not the only possible modes in which ideologies operates nor that these modes operate in isolation from one another.[24] Each mode can be associated with a number of "strategies of symbolic construction." For example, legitimation, one of the most widely recognized modes by which ideology functions, may work through rationalization as a set of interconnected reasons are developed to justify or defend social institutions or social relations, or it may work through universalization in which features of institutions which serve some people's interests are portrayed as serving everyone's interests. For reasons of space I am unable to discuss in detail the modes by which ideology operates or all of the possible strategies suggested by Thompson at this point, but I will make use of several of the general modes by which ideology oper-

---

[21] Thompson, *Ideology and Culture*, 151 (emphasis his).

[22] E.g., in 1 Cor. 5:1-5 Paul instructs the community to expel a member whose action Paul deems to be morally outrageous.

[23] Thompson, *Ideology and Culture*, 60. For his discussion of these five modes and their typical strategies see 60-67. Compare Eagleton, *Ideology: An Introduction*, 51-60, who suggests a somewhat similar list of mechanisms by which ideology functions. His list includes rationalization, legitimation, universalization, naturalization, and reification. He seems, however, to confuse modes in which ideology functions with some of the strategies for symbolic construction, to use Thompson's distinction.

[24] Thompson, *Ideology and Culture*, 60.

ates in the analysis of 1 Corinthians 1-4 which follows and show how
several of the strategies discussed by Thompson are embedded in
Paul's discourse.

One final point regarding Thompson's approach requires mentioning. Thompson develops a methodological approach for the
analysis of symbolic forms and ideological phenomena, particularly
those of modern mass media, which he calls "depth hermeneutics."[25]
He draws on the work of a variety of people for this, but Paul Ricoeur
is particularly important since the very name for his approach is
derived from him. I do not have time to discuss Thompson's analytical methodology in this paper, suffice it to say that what he attempts to do closely parallels the methodological approach developed
by Vernon Robbins and others under the name socio-rhetorical criticism. Robbins' approach, which is really something like a methodological toolbox, includes a range of resources that can be applied
to symbolic forms, particularly complex textual forms, for their analysis.[26] In what follows I work from a socio-rhetorical approach paying particular attention to Paul's rhetorical construction in 1 Cor.
1:10-4:21 since rhetoric was the only real cultural means available
to Paul for convincing his readers to accept his authority.[27] To para-
phrase Thompson, Paul's rhetoric was employed in the service of
power in the sense that his power was institutionally understood as
his authority to require obedience from the members of the
Corinthian community which he had established. Thus, the ideological analysis of Paul's text requires rhetorical analysis since it is
through his rhetoric that Paul projects his authority,[28] and therefore his power to the Corinthian community, as he seeks to reestablish his own dominance over the community.[29]

---

[25] Thompson, *Ideology and Culture*, 272-327.

[26] See Robbins, *Tapestry* and Vernon K. Robbins, *Exploring the Texture of Texts:
A Guide to Socio-Rhetorical Interpretation* (Valley Forge, PA: Trinity Press International,
1996) for detailed expositions of socio-rhetorical analysis.

[27] John Howard Schütz, *Paul and the Anatomy of Apostolic Authority*, Society for
New Testament Studies: Monograph Series (26) (Cambridge: Cambridge University
Press, 1975), 9-15, has a very helpful discussion of the relationship between authority and power. He argues that authority is the interpretation of power in a
social group and is characterized by such things as "legitimacy, mandate, and
office."

[28] See Castelli, *Imitating Paul*, 123, for the connection between rhetoric, apostolic authority and ideology in Paul.

[29] Ben Witherington III, *Conflict and Community in Corinth: A Socio-Rhetorical Commentary on 1 and 2 Corinthians* (Grand Rapids, MI: Eerdmans, 1995), 145, rejects

3. *"Meaning in the Service of Power": Rhetoric and Ideology in 1 Corinthians 1-4*

The close link between Paul's rhetoric and his attempt to reestablish his own dominance over the community necessitates us first looking at his rhetorical construction in 1 Corinthians 1-4. Once this has been done, we will then look at the strongly ideological character of Paul's rhetoric in these chapters.

1 Corinthians is a complex rhetorical composition with multiple rhetorical units. Hester identifies four argumentative units: 1:11-6:11; 6:12-11:1; 11:2-14:40; and 15:1-58; as well as an introductory section, 1:1-10; and a concluding section, 16:1-24.[30] Mitchell sees the letter as a single deliberative argument by which Paul seeks to maintain unity in the Corinthian church.[31] According to her, 1 Cor. 1:10 provides the thesis statement for the argument with 1:11-17 serving as a statement of the facts of the case. The argument, according to Mitchell, contains four distinct sections of proof: 1:18-4:21; 5:1-11:1; 11:2-14:40; and 15:1-57. While she does not discuss the overall rhetorical structure of the letter, Castelli argues that 1:10-4:21 is a single unit which builds to a rhetorical crescendo in 4:14-21.[32] Between a call for unity in 1:10-17 and a call for imitation in 4:14-21, Castelli maintains that 1:18 to 2:5, 2:6 to 3:5, and 3:6 to 4:5 "function as mimetic examples."[33] What these three rhetorical approaches show is the considerable diversity of opinion regarding the rhetorical structure of 1 Corinthians and more especially of the opening unit of the argument of 1 Corinthians.

Several factors point to the fact that 1:10-4:21 is a single rhetorical unit. First, in 1:10 Paul begins with an appeal to his readers (παρακαλῶ δὲ ὑμᾶς) which is then repeated with specific reference to imitation of himself in 4:16. These two appeals to the readers seem

---

the view that Paul is seeking to reestablish his authority in 1 Corinthians 1-4, but see Mark D. Given, *Paul's True Rhetoric: Ambiguity, Cunning, and Deception in Greece and Rome*, Emory Studies in Early Christianity (Harrisburg, PA: Trinity Press International, 2001), 94-95, who offers a telling critique of Witherington.

[30] James Hester, "Re-Discovering and Re-Inventing Rhetoric," *Scriptura* 50 (1994): 9.

[31] Margaret M. Mitchell, *Paul and the Rhetoric of Reconciliation: An Exegetical Investigation of the Language and Composition of 1 Corinthians* (Louisville, KY: Westminster/John Knox, J.C.B. Mohr, 1992), 184-85.

[32] Castelli, *Imitating Paul*, 98-111.

[33] Castelli, *Imitating Paul*, 99.

to form an *inclusio* around Paul's discussion of the factionalism within the church at Corinth.[34] Second, as Wire points out, in 1:10 Paul begins with an appeal to return to the unity which he had taught them whereas in 4:21 he threatens to come with the disciplining rod of a parent if they do not return to the ways which they had been taught by himself and Timothy.[35] Thus 4:21 seems to round out the argument which began with an appeal but threatens serious intervention if the appeal is not heeded. Third, 5:1 seems to introduce a new stage in the argument. In 1:11 Paul begins his discussion on factionalism by acknowledging that he is taking up this issue because of the report of Chloe's people. In 5:1 Paul mentions another issue that has been reported to him in the community which he then seeks to address. But this time there is a direct instruction about what needs to be done. This gives the distinct impression that Paul has begun a new line of argument as he addresses a practical problem within the church, but his instructions to the community in 5:1-5 is dependent upon the results of the first argument in which Paul seeks to reestablish his authority among the Corinthians.

Even a cursory analysis of the rhetorical construction of 1 Cor. 1:10-4:21 shows that the rhetorical stasis, or point of the argument, in 1 Corinthians 1-4, if not the whole letter, is to be found in 1:10 where Paul appeals for his readers to overcome their factionalism by being united to one another with a common way of thinking and a common purpose. From a rhetorical perspective this constitutes a *topos* of concord (περὶ ὁμόνοιας) which was a well-known *topos* among both ancient politicians and rhetoricians as Welborn has shown.[36]

Hester, following Wuellner,[37] maintains that the first argument (in his view 1:10-6:11) "serves to *censure* and to *educate*, to re-align loyalty to a gospel received and believed by the Corinthians."[38] He goes on to say that Paul is "indicating that he feels a need to reestablish his ethos with this group, to combat understandings of the

[34] J. Ross Wagner, "'Not Beyond the Things Which Are Written': A Call to Boast Only in the Lord (1 Cor 4.6)," *New Testament Studies* 44 (1998): 281.

[35] Antoinette Clark Wire, *The Corinthian Women Prophets: A Reconstruction of Paul's Rhetoric* (Minneapolis: Fortress Press, 1990), 40, 45-46.

[36] L.L. Welborn, "On the Discord in Corinth: 1 Corinthians 1-4 and Ancient Politics," *Journal of Biblical Literature* 106 (1987): 89-90.

[37] Wilhelm Wuellner, "Greek Rhetoric and Pauline Argumentation," in *Early Christian Literature and the Classical Intellectual Tradition*, eds. W.R Schoedel and R.L. Wilken (Paris: Beauchesne, 1979), 177-88.

[38] Hester, "Re-Discovering," 16.

gospel which are undermining adherence to it, but not necessarily because he has opponents, or because his apostolic status was under question." Hester concludes that Paul's primary rhetorical strategies are epideictic in this section. But as Schüssler Fiorenza observes with respect to Wuellner,[39] Hester in defining 1 Cor. 1:10-6:11 as a work of epideictic rhetoric is drawing heavily upon the views of Perelman,[40] who sought to redefine epideictic rhetoric as having an essentially educational function. This analysis does not seem to take adequate account of the argument in 1 Cor. 1:10-4:21, in particular. In 1:10 Paul appeals to the Corinthians to be united by having a common mind and a shared purpose. This request is reinforced by 4:16 where Paul appeals to his readers to imitate him and by 4:21 where Paul calls on his readers to take a decision about their behavior when he says: "What do you wish? Am I to come to you with a rod or with love in a spirit of gentleness?" These questions call for the Corinthians to make a decision about their future behavior with regard to establishing unity and imitating Paul, and therefore, they clearly indicate that in the first argumentative unit of the letter, Paul's overall argument is closely aligned with deliberative rhetoric. This interpretation is supported by the work of Welborn who has shown clear links between the language used in this section and the language of secular politics.[41] Deliberative rhetoric was especially appropriate in such contexts when a civic body was being confronted with a political decision. Paul confronts the Corinthian Christian community with just such a political decision over their factionalism, and thus Welborn himself designates 1 Corinthians 1-4 as "deliberative in character."[42]

Paul's deliberative argument in 1 Cor. 1:10-4:21 consists of several sub-arguments. In 1:11-17 Paul begins with a shaming narrative, the first of several such shamings in 1 Corinthians,[43] in which he sets forth the rhetorical situation or exigency from his perspec-

---

[39] Elizabeth Schüssler Fiorenza, "Rhetorical Situation and the Historical Reconstruction in 1 Corinthians," *New Testament Studies* 33 (1987): 391.

[40] Ch. Perelman and L. Olbrechts-Tyteca, *The New Rhetoric: A Treatise on Argumentation*, translated by John Wilkinson and Purcell Weaver (Notre Dame: University of Notre Dame Press, 1969).

[41] Welborn, "Discord in Corinth," 85-111.

[42] Welborn, "Discord in Corinth," 89.

[43] David A. deSilva, "'Let the One Who Claims Honor Establish That Claim in the Lord': Honor Discourse in the Corinthian Correspondence," *Biblical Theological Bulletin* 28 (1998): 72. See, e.g., 1 Cor. 3:1-5; 4:8-13.

tive.[44] The exigency is that Paul had learned of the emergence of what he considers to be factions within the church, and he claims these factions were proving highly contentious (ἔριδες) (1:11) to the extent that the body of Christ was being divided (1:13). The "I belong to" (NRSV) slogans in 1:12 suggest that Paul understood the problem to be related to the formation of factions around important external leaders of the early Church.[45] In 1:17 Paul summarizes his own role in the founding of the church in terms of a dissociative move as he claims that he proclaimed the gospel without the use of "σοφία λόγου," that is, without the use of sophisticated rhetorical skill that might have actually rendered void the content of his message regarding the cross of Christ.[46] Castelli observes that 1:17 already places Paul in a privileged position of authority in relation to the gospel since he claims a primary role in mediating the message of Christ crucified to the Corinthians, thereby removing himself from the competition for factional loyalty.[47] This privileged position plays a crucial role throughout 1 Cor. 1:10-4:21 since Paul's claim to unique authority with the implicit right to exercise power is based on his role as the divinely appointed founder of the community. Thus in ideological terms Paul begins at the outset to legitimate his own position of authority through a strategy of narrativizing his unique role as the "creator" of the community, a

---

[44] Hester, "Re-Discovering," 12.

[45] Welborn, "Discord in Corinth," 90-93, convincingly argues that 1 Cor. 1:12 should be understood in terms of the way in which political parties in antiquity formed around individuals. This position seems to be accepted by Raymond F. Collins, *First Corinthians*, Sacra Pagina Series (Collegeville, MN: Liturgical Press, 1999), 79-81, but Anthony Thiselton, *The First Epistle to the Corinthians: A Commentary on the Greek Text*, New International Greek Testament Commentary (Grand Rapids, MI: Eerdmans, 2000), 121-22, following Mitchell, *Paul and Rhetoric*, 84-85, maintains that the Greek construction "ἐγὼ μέν εἰμι Παύλου, ἐγὼ δὲ Ἀπολλῶ, κτλ." does not have political overtones and should be understood as a genitive of relationship. Although it seems unlikely that any of the figures named—Paul, Apollos, Peter, or for that matter, Christ—intended for factions to form around them, it does seem likely that some Corinthian Christians, very probably including some socially prominent members of the community, strongly identified with various of these figures and that that identification from Paul's perspective endangered his own position of authority within the community.

[46] Bruce W. Winter, *Philo and Paul Among the Sophists: Alexandrian and Corinthian Responses to a Julio-Claudian Movement* (Grand Rapids, MI: Eerdmans, 2002, 2nd edition), 187-88. See also L.L. Welborn, "A Conciliatory Principle in 1 Cor. 4:6," *Novum Testamentum* 29 (1987): 339.

[47] Castelli, *Imitating Paul*, 98-99.

position of importance which no one else can claim.[48]

Wuellner has argued that the whole of 1:19-3:21 is a rhetorical digression which functions to "highlight how 'faithful God is' (1:9) to those who wait for the revealing of our Lord Jesus Christ and as such keep or hold themselves 'to the end guiltless in the (last) day' (1:7-8)."[49] This analysis of the point of 1:19-3:20 seems highly problematic since it ignores the fundamental exigence, the factionalism which Paul perceives in the community (1:10-12; 3:3b-4). But as Lampe has observed, the immediate connection of 1:18-2:16 to the problem of factionalism is not obvious.[50] Knowledge of the modes in which ideology functions can help at this point. In 1:18-2:5 Paul presents a series of three interrelated arguments (1:18-25; 1:26-31; 2:1-5) that subtly critique the human valuing system employed by the Corinthian Christians under the banner of wisdom (1:20-25) and then in 2:6-16 Paul presents the divine alternative, true wisdom, which the Corinthians at that stage were not mature enough to receive (3:1-4).[51] 1 Cor. 1:18-2:16 takes on an ideological character since Paul feels compelled to defend his message of the cross and his manner of presentation against the human valuing system of at least some of the Corinthians, a valuing which implicitly called in question his own authority and was responsible for the emergence of factionalism.

Paul puts the proclamation of Christ crucified at the center of his argument in 1:18-25 because the cross is the power of God for salvation. But he also puts himself at the center of the argument because, as he points out, it was his proclamation of Christ crucified that God decided to use for the saving of those who believed in Corinth. From an ideological perspective these are both crucial points. In a situation of partisanship, one of the functions of ideology is to provide unifying symbols. This is precisely what Paul has done in 1:18-25. That which unifies the Corinthians, or at least should be the basis of their unity is the saving power of the crucified Christ. To outsiders this message is both a scandal and foolish-

---

[48] According to Thompson, *Ideology and Culture*, 61-62 narrativization embeds claims to legitimacy in stories about the past. These stories "serve to justify the exercise of power by those who possess it" while reconciling those who do not have power to the fact that they do not possess it.

[49] Wuellner, "Greek Rhetoric and Pauline Argumentation," 185-86.

[50] Peter Lampe, "Theological Wisdom and the 'Word About the Cross': The Rhetorical Scheme of I Corinthians 1-4," *Interpretation* 44 (1990): 119.

[51] Cf. Thiselton, *1 Corinthians*, 224-25.

ness, and therefore it functions, from Paul's perspective, as an identity marker to distinguish the Corinthian Christians from the outside world with its alternative system of values. But how, it may be asked, is this important theological insight ideological? The answer is that it was not simply any version of Christ crucified that was the basis of salvation for the Corinthians, but it was the one proclaimed by Paul (1:21, 23). As Thompson explains, "In practice the symbolization of unity may be interwoven with the process of narrativization, as symbols of unity may be an integral part of a narrative of origins which recounts a shared history and projects a collective fate."[52] 1 Cor. 1:18-25 implies a narrative of origin, the origin of the Corinthians' faith through the preaching of the cross of Christ by Paul. The apostle elaborates the narrative of origin in 2:1-5 when he speaks of the mode of his coming to the Corinthians, and he later narrativizes the origins of the community through the planter and master builder metaphors of chapter 3. Each time his own role in the founding of the community is given prominence as the initiator.

In 1:26-31 Paul offers a second argument. He introduces the argument with what Hester refers to as the Corinthians "call status."[53] In 1:26 Paul reminds his readers that the majority of them were of low social status.[54] This was not an accident. God chose the powerless members of the community, the weak and the lowly, to shame the wise and the strong in order to eliminate any possibility of boast-

---

[52] Thompson, *Ideology and Culture*, 64.

[53] Hester, "Re-Discovering," 9.

[54] Gerd Theissen, "Sociale Schichtung in der Korinthischen Gemeinde: Ein Beitrag zur Soziologie des hellenistischen Urchristentums," *Zeitschrift für die neutestamentliche Wissenschaft und die Kunde der älteren Kirche* 65 (1974): 232-72 (now in English in Gerd Theissen, *The Social Setting of Pauline Christianity: Essays on Corinth*, edited and translated by John H. Schütz [Philadelphia: Fortress Press, 1982], 69-119) argued that the Christian community in Corinth was socially stratified between a group of high social status and a majority of people who were of low social status. This view is now widely held. See, e.g., Andrew D. Clarke, *Secular and Christian Leadership in Corinth: A Socio-Historical and Exegetical Study of 1 Corinthians 1-6*, Arbeiten zur Geschichte des Antiken Judentums und des Urchristentums (Leiden: E.J. Brill, 1993), 41-57, and David G. Horrell, *The Social Ethos of the Corinthian Correspondence: Interests and Ideology from 1 Corinthians to 1 Clement* (Edinburgh: T. & T. Clark, 1996), 91-101. Justin J. Meggitt, *Paul, Poverty and Survival*, Studies of the New Testament and Its World (Edinburgh: T. & T. Clark, 1998), 101-53, critiques what he calls the "New Consensus," but in my view he fails to overturn the consensus because he ignores the cumulative weight of the evidence as well as the social situation of the community implied in the Corinthian correspondence which presupposes significant social stratification of the Christian community.

ing, to eliminate any possibility that the socially strong members of the community might think that their social superiority was the basis of their election to salvation in Christ. Carter suggests that through this argument "Paul thus allies himself directly with the socially disadvantaged in Corinth in an attempt to win their loyalty."[55] This is probably so, but more needs to be said. In 1:26-31 Paul creates a rationalization that serves to legitimate the importance of the socially insignificant members of the community in God's redemptive plan. Their very social status is part of God's plan to eliminate the social status of socially superior members being carried over into the community of faith. Thus "[t]he church is the reverse-image of the dominant cultural value-system."[56] This rationalization has the potential to function in the ideological mode of fragmentation since Paul implies a key differentiation within the community between the socially superior and the socially inferior members of the community, with the latter being God's chosen ones for shaming the socially powerful.[57] By this differentiation, Paul seeks to align the majority in the community with himself as the messenger of God's wisdom against those who are socially prominent and precipitated the factionalism that so concerned Paul.

I have already noted that 2:1-5 can be analyzed as reflecting the narrativization of the origins of the community as Paul sets out the manner of his initial preaching at Corinth. In the narrativization Paul maintains that he made a conscious decision to avoid rhetorical sophistry and instead to preach the unification symbol of Christ crucified.[58] The goal of this, as Paul made clear in 1:18-25, and now in 2:5, was to ensure that the readers' faith would rest on the power

---

[55] Timothy L. Carter, "'Big Men' in Corinth," *Journal for the Study of the New Testament* 66 (1997): 61.

[56] Edward Adams, *Constructing the World: A Study in Paul's Cosmological Language* (Edinburgh: T. & T. Clark, 2000), 116.

[57] Thompson, *Ideology and Culture*, 65, describes the ideological mode of fragmentation as being used to prevent individuals or a group from effectively challenging the dominant group. "Differentiation," is one strategy and emphasizes the differences, the distinctions and divisions between groups and individuals to prevent them from uniting in effective opposition to the existing relations of power or those who exercise it. A second strategy is the "expurgation of the other." This strategy involves the creation of an internal or external foe which a group is called upon to either reject or to resist. Often calls for the "expurgation of the other" take place in the context of strategies for the unification of a group.

[58] For a careful analysis of the anti-sophistic position taken by Paul in 1 Cor. 2:1-5 see Winter, *Philo and Paul*, 143-64.

of God instead of human wisdom, as embodied in rhetorical sophistication. Thus Paul once again connects the central symbol of his
message, the crucified Christ, with himself as the founder-messen-
ger of God. The importance of this for the unity of the community
will become clear later since a key issue for establishing concord in
the community, from Paul's perspective, was the acceptance of his
own authority.

At the same time it needs to be noted that 1 Cor. 2:1-5 is a subtle
attack on the value system of the socially superior members of the
community who almost certainly would have identified with and even
approved of rhetorical sophistication since they appear to have
brought in rhetorically trained teachers who attacked Paul for his
lack of rhetorical sophistication according to 2 Corinthians 10-13.[59]
Paul's implicit critique of the socially elevated members of the community, whose superior education was a hallmark of their position,[60]
are directly challenged in 1 Cor. 3:18-20 to set aside their social
claims to status based on their educational sophistication. As we will
see, this had clear implications for Paul's own claims to authority in
the community.

Although the interpretation of 1 Cor. 2:6-16 has proved problematic for many scholars,[61] a careful reading against the context in
which it occurs allows for reasonable clarity about the overall intention of the section and its possible ideological function. In 2:6-9
Paul claims that he, and others,[62] speak a divine wisdom to mature

---

[59] See Winter, *Philo and Paul*, 203-31 who holds a similar view of 2 Corinthians
10-13 with supporting evidence.

[60] Andrew D. Clarke, *Serve the Community of the Church: Christians as Leaders and
Ministers, First-Century Christians in the Graeco-Roman World* (Grand Rapids, MI:
Eerdmans, 2000), 175, 179-80.

[61] Welborn, "Discord in Corinth," 104, and Thiselton, *1 Corinthians*, 224.
Thiselton thinks that the unusual vocabulary of the 2:6-16, terms like τελείοι,
μυστήριον, πνευματικός and ψυχικός, were catchwords of the Corinthians which
Paul sought to reclaim for the gospel by reinterpreting them in terms of the nature of God and of the gospel.

[62] Both Collins, *First Corinthians*, 122, and Thiselton, *1 Corinthians*, 229, relate
the shift from the first person singular verbs and pronouns in 2:1-5 to the first
person plural verbs and pronouns in 2:6-16 to Paul's inclusion of the community
in those who speak divine wisdom. This needs some refinement. In 3:1-4 Paul argues
that the Corinthian Christians were so spiritually immature and bound to their
human ways of thinking that he could not impart to them the deeper spiritual
things so how could they possibly be equals with Paul in discussions about the
wisdom of God as Collins and Thiselton seem to imply? Thus the "we" in 2:6-8
probably includes Paul, Apollos, and other missionaries, but not the Corinthians

Christians which is fundamentally different from the human wisdom of the current age and the current world rulers who were responsible for the crucifixion of the Lord Jesus. In this Paul is simply picking up a major theme of 1:18-2:5. The second part of 2:6-16 introduces the theme of the Spirit and the gifts of the Spirit (2:10-12), but ends by distinguishing between the response of those who are still determined by their human nature (2:14) and those who are determined by the Spirit of God (2:15). When 2:6-16 is read against the context provided by 3:1-4 it becomes clear that Paul has created a legitimating rationalization to explain his own position of dominance over the Corinthians, as well as that of Apollos and his fellow missionary workers apparently. He has received the gift of God's wisdom through revelation (2:10) which he imparts to the mature (2:6) but which as a gift of the Spirit is not comprehendible to those still living according to their human nature (2:14) any more than it was comprehendible to the worldly political rulers who were responsible for the death of the Lord Jesus (2:6, 8). Moreover, a person like Paul who has the gift of the Spirit (2:12) and is therefore determined by the Spirit is capable of judging or examining everything, but cannot himself be examined because he is determined by the mind of Christ (2:15-16).[63] What follows in 3:1-4, as we shall see shortly, makes it clear that from Paul's perspective the Corinthians are nowhere near being his spiritual equals and hence the yawning gap between his spiritual status and theirs, even if he does not meet their human expectations regarding status.

In 3:1-4 Paul asserts that the Corinthians are too immature to receive the gifts of the Spirit, and he cites as proof for this their factiousness (3:3-4). In making his point he uses a metaphor that portrays the Corinthians as infants who are not old enough to cope with solid food. There can be no doubt that this serves the ideological func-

---

themselves who were spiritually immature according to Paul. While conceptually it is possible to conceive that the first person plural verbs and pronouns in 2:10-12 include the Corinthians, 2:13 clearly seems to refer to Paul's own role in providing spiritual teaching, something which the Corinthians were unable to receive.

[63] Thiselton, *1 Corinthians*, 271-274, claims that Paul is using a theological catchphrase from the Corinthians themselves in 2:15. There is no direct evidence to support this, and in any case it is an unnecessary assumption since as Gordon D. Fee, *The First Epistle to the Corinthians*, The New International Commentary on the New Testament (Grand Rapids, MI: William B. Eerdmans Publishing Company, 1987), 117-19, recognizes, 2:15-16 prepares for 3:1-4 where Paul makes a negative judgment about the spiritual condition of the Corinthians. Thus, Paul is principally talking about himself in 2:15-16.

tion of openly establishing Paul's position of dominance over the community since he is the parent who knows what is best for the Corinthians and reflects the common ideological strategy of dissimulating social relations through metaphors which endow people with characteristics which they do not really possess.[64] In this instance Paul uses the negative characterization of the Corinthians as infants in Christ (3:1), who have remained in an infantile state that keeps them from a more mature faith, in order to underscore his own dominance and control of the relation with his readers.[65] Carter also suggests that Paul may have hoped to encourage the non-elite in the community to dissociate from leaders who engaged in factionalism.[66] If this is correct it would constitute a differentiation strategy such as we saw in 1:26-31 and would imply that unity can only be achieved on Paul's terms.

Having re-introduced the idea of factionalism that almost certainly reflected an Apollos/Paul split in the community (3:4),[67] Paul attempts to provide an ideological basis for re-unification within the community in 3:5-9. He first underscores his own and Apollos' role or function as servants of the Lord (3:5).[68] He does this in an attempt to discourage the factionalism emerging around their supposed leadership.[69] Second, he introduces an agricultural metaphor in which both he as the planter and Apollos as the one who watered share a common purpose in the plan of God, the one who gives the

---

[64] Thompson, *Ideology and Culture*, 63.

[65] Beverly Roberts Gaventa, "Mother's Milk and Ministry in 1 Corinthians 3," in *Theology and Ethics in Paul and His Interpreters: Essays in Honor of Victor Paul Furnish*, eds. Eugene H. Lovering and Jerry L. Sumney (Nashville, TN: Abingdon Press, 1996), 101-13, reads too much into Paul's metaphorical statement that he had given the Corinthians milk to drink when she claims that Paul is actually foregrounding himself as nursing mother or wetnurse to the Corinthians and that this might have called in question his masculinity. She misses the point that Paul's claim, even as nursing mother or wetnurse, is that he took responsibility for deciding when the Corinthians were mature enough for the deeper elements of the wisdom of God and that in his judgment they were not ready for such things as long as they were factious and propagating factionalism in the community.

[66] Carter, "'Big Men'," 60.

[67] Winter, *Philo and Paul*, 172-77, makes a very plausible case that the origins of the factionalism (3:4) and the strife and jealousy (3:3) between supporters of Paul and Apollos was a reflection of the rivalries which emerged in the "secular" sphere around individual sophists and their partisans.

[68] Clarke, *Christian Leadership*, 119 argues that the emphasis in 3:5 is not on who Paul and Apollos are but on what role they play as Christian leaders. Thus, he contends, Paul's leadership model is task-orientated.

[69] Horrell, *Social Ethos*, 135.

growth (3:6-9). From Paul's perspective the symbolic unification of his and Apollos' ministry ("the one planting and the one watering are united," 3:8a) is an attempt to remove one of the possible bases of division within the community since the common purpose and cooperative work of Paul and Apollos should preclude the possibility of factions existing in their names.[70] But in doing this it also allows him to reassert his own authority over people who may have been rejecting it in favor of attaching themselves to Apollos. Subtly, however, Paul does allow for differentiation between himself and Apollos when it comes to the rewards that they will receive from God. The narrativization implied in the planter metaphor once again emphasizes Paul's unique role in the origins of the community. By being the planter Paul inevitably takes priority over Apollos as becomes clear in 3:10-15 and again in 4:14-16.

Having described the Corinthians as a building belonging to God in 3:9, Paul extends the architectural metaphor in 3:10-15, comparing himself to a wise master builder, who had laid the foundations of the community in Corinth. In 3:16 the building is identified as the temple of God. Welborn has observed, "The architectural metaphor lent itself readily to the attempt to promote concord" in the community, not least because it was used in political discourse of the period to stress the fact that the wise politician like the wise master builder needed to chose subordinates who would work cooperatively to perfect his work.[71] Although 3:10-15 to some extent reiterates the point of 3:6-9, Paul goes beyond those verses by developing the theme of judgment found in 3:8. Hollander, focusing on the judgment theme of 3:10-15, has observed that this unit forms an important part of Paul's argument against factionalism in the church since it underscores the fact that "all builders, [that is] all authorities in the Christian community, are servants of God, whose works cannot be approved or disapproved by the members of the church."[72] Faction-

---

[70] Richard A. Horsley, "Rhetoric and Empire—and 1 Corinthians," in *Paul and Politics: Ekklesia, Israel, Imperium, Interpretation. Essays in Honor of Krister Stendahl,* ed. Richard A. Horsley (Harrisburg, PA: Trinity Press International, 2000), 88, implies that Apollos was responsible in someway for the problems which emerged in Corinth, but Paul never says this. In fact 1 Cor. 16:12 suggests that Paul did not view Apollos as a threat nor did he hold him responsible for what had happened at Corinth.

[71] Welborn, "Conciliatory Principle," 337.

[72] Harm W. Hollander, "The Testing by Fire of the Builders' Works: 1 Corinthians 3.10-15," *New Testament Studies* 40 (1994) 89-104. The quotation is from page 96.

alism has its roots in people trying to make just such decisions by virtue of whom they choose to identify with as their leaders, but Paul insists that God alone will judge the quality of the work of the leaders who are building on the foundation laid by him.

The metaphor in 3:10-15 has another significance. By describing himself as the master builder who laid the foundation of community/building Paul highlights his role in establishing the church community at Corinth. At the same time the master builder metaphor underscores his role as the one taking responsibility for supervising the coordination and the overall progress of the project with respect to the other builders.[73] By adding that he took this role "according to the grace of God given to me" (3:10) he offers a divine warrant for his dominant role in the Corinthian community. Thus as the one who marked out and laid the foundation, which he identifies as Jesus Christ, and by implication in the context, Christ crucified, everyone else who exercises leadership in the community must build on the foundation which he laid. There is no other foundation according to Paul; there is no chance for anyone to supercede or replace his work. Ideologically the metaphor dissimulates his relation to the church and to the leaders of the community by subordinating both to him. The judgment theme of 3:12-15 simply heightens the subordination of "community builders" or local leadership, since their work will be tested by God, and they will be rewarded according to how they have built on Paul's foundation, but Paul gives no indication that his own work as "wise master builder" will be subject to similar testing. The logical conclusion that church leaders are intended to draw is that they must work under Paul's supervision to avoid suffering loss for the work which they do.[74]

The building metaphor and the judgment theme of 3:10-15 are carried forward in 3:16-17 in ways which show a strong ideological imprint. The building of which Paul has laid the foundations is identified as nothing less than the temple of God, and he identifies the Christian community in Corinth as that temple. He further adds that as the temple of God the divine Spirit dwells in them, not as indi-

---

[73] Jay Y. Shanor, "Paul as Master Builder: Construction Terms in 1 Corinthians," *New Testament Studies* 34 (1988) 465-66.

[74] In terms of secular leadership Paul's choice of metaphors in 3:5-15 is important. They imply that he and Apollos as well as other church leaders are of low social status since they are compared to manual workers in both the agricultural and the builder metaphors, according to Clarke, *Christian Leadership*, 119-21.

viduals but as the community.[75] This is a powerful symbol of unification because it identifies the church community as the holy dwelling
place of God's Spirit in Corinth, while 1 Cor. 3:17 proceeds to pro-
nounce a dire warning of divine destruction on anyone responsible
for the destruction of the temple-community. In the context of 1 Cor.
1:10 to 3:15 the destroyers of the temple-community are almost
certainly those guilty of fostering factionalism whom Paul refers to
as arrogant people in 4:18. The strong condemnation of 3:17 implicitly invites the community to expurgate or reject any individual
guilty of divisiveness in order to protect the holy temple of God. Since
Paul is the founder-parent (2:1-5; 4:14-15) of the community, 3:17
can only serve to strengthen his position by identifying those who
oppose him as destroyers of the temple of God.

1 Cor. 3:18-23 is sometimes said to summarize the whole line of
argument in 1:18 to 3:17.[76] In particular, 3:18-21a recapitulates the
basic thrust of 1:18-2:16 by calling for an inversion of the dominant
social logic outside the church where human wisdom equates with
social status and influence. Such logic for the Christian is self-deception which must be avoided, according to Paul, and must be
rejected in favor of the wisdom of God (3:18) since the wisdom of
God manifests itself in the seeming foolishness of the cross of Christ
(1:21-25). The imperatives ἐξαπατάτω and γενέσθω in 3:18 and
καυχάσθω in 3:21a clearly indicate that this is a direct instruction
from Paul to each individual member of the community, and by
including the scriptural warrants found in 3:19-20 he significantly
strengthens the force of his instruction.[77] From an ideological perspective 3:18-21a reflects a kind of self-expurgation by demanding
that people change their attitudes and practices in terms of the principal source of division within the community, the elevation of leaders, who manifest human wisdom with its correlatives of social status
and power, to positions of prestige and dominance in the community. To accept Paul's instruction in 3:18-21a is to accept Paul's

---

[75] On the rich imagery of the local church as the temple of God see Fee, *First
Corinthians*, 146-47.

[76] See Hans Dieter Betz, "The Problem of Rhetoric and Theology according
to the Apostle Paul," in *L'Apôtre Paul: Personnalité, style et conception du ministère*, ed.
A. Vanhoye, Bibliotheca Ephemeridum Theologicarum Lovaniensium 73 (Leuven:
Leuven University Press, 1986), 39, and Winter, *Philo and Paul*, 195-96.

[77] Collins, *First Corinthians*, 165, sees 3:19-20 as recalling the apocalyptic paradox of the scriptural quotation in 1:19 and suggests that it forms an *inclusio* with
it.

authoritative status and his legitimation of an inverted system of valuation, what he refers to as the wisdom of God, through his rationalization of it in 1:18-2:16.[78]

In 1 Cor. 3:21b-23 Paul redirects his readers to a theme of unification. This shift is marked in the Greek text by the change from the third person singular verbs of 3:18-21a, which focus attention on individuals who wrongly value human wisdom, to the second person plural pronouns in 3:21b-23 which are intended to include all the readers as a group. The litany of the things that belong to the community as a whole, including Paul, Apollos, and Cephas, creates a sense of common ownership by the community of the very individuals around whom the factionalism of the community has emerged (1:12). But the community itself shares in a powerful common identity by virtue of belonging to Christ who in turn belongs to God (3:23). Thus Paul provides a powerful symbolization of unity in 3:22-23 which has a clear ideological significance of collecting the community together under the banner of Christ, and ultimately of God, in an effort to overcome the divisiveness of the factionalism within the community. Needless to say, by accepting this unity, the community effectively subscribes to Paul's authoritative position as the architect of the community's unity, and therefore, the re-unification of the community re-inscribes Paul's own position of dominance within it.

Paul picks up the theme of unity again in 1 Cor. 4:6-7. Verse 6 in particular has proved a *crux interpretum*.[79] Two aspects of the verse have received considerable attention. First, the meaning of the verb μετεσχημάτισα has been discussed frequently,[80] and second the meaning of the phrase "not beyond what is written." has also received careful examination.[81] However these two interpretative problems are understood, the first two clauses of the verse serve to provide

---

[78] 1 Corinthians 3:21a seems to pick up the theme of 3:1-17 where Paul deals specifically with the problem of leadership and points forward to 3:21b-23 where Paul downplays the importance of leaders, as we shall see.

[79] Wagner, "Not Beyond," 279.

[80] See, e.g., Benjamin Fiore, "'Covert Allusion' in 1 Corinthians 1-4," *Catholic Biblical Quarterly* 47 (1985): 85-102 and David R. Hall, "A Disguise for the Wise: ΜΕΤΑΣΧΗΜΑΤΙΣΜΟΣ in 1 Corinthians 4.6," *New Testament Studies* 40 (1994) 143-49.

[81] See, e.g., Welborn, "Conciliatory Principle," 320-46; Wagner, "Not Beyond," 279-87; and Ronald L. Tyler, "First Corinthians 4:6 and Hellenistic Pedagogy," *Catholic Biblical Quarterly* 60 (1998) 97-103.

reasons for the final clause of 4:6: "so that no one of you be puffed up for the sake of one against another." Clearly this is a call for unity in the practices of the community. It is then carried over into 4:7 with its rhetorical questions that suggest that people should not boast about the gifts which they have received and in fact which they have been using to make distinctions among the members of the community.

Although Paul seems to place himself and Apollos on a similar level through describing himself and Apollos as servants (3:5), fellow workers of God (3:9), and servants and stewards of Christ (4:1-2), in 1 Cor. 4:14-21 Paul reveals a different understanding of himself which sets him off from Apollos and any other leaders in the community, an understanding that is ideologically pregnant. This section, as was shown earlier, concludes the first rhetorical unit of the letter, laying the basis for Paul's authoritarian instruction in 1 Cor. 5:1-5 where he commands the community to expel a member whose behavior is morally outrageous. In 4:14-16 Paul implies a narrative of origin in which he is the "begetter" of the community through the gospel (4:15), and therefore the Corinthian Christians are his beloved offspring (4:14),[82] who should imitate their father (4:16). This claim is of course metaphorical and in ideological terms dissimulates Paul's actual relationship with the community because it has the clear significance of giving him a unique position of unrivalled authority within the community in relation to other leaders whom he describes as mere παιδαγωγοί.[83] A παιδαγωγός was a guardian and disciplinarian for a child, not a teacher, who worked at the behest of the father of the child and whose own position and authority was derived from the father of the child. Thus by virtue of the triad of interconnected metaphors which present Paul as father, other leaders, including Apollos, as guardians and disciplinarians, and the Corin-

---

[82] On the irony of Paul's situation as the low status and abused father of a community (4:9-15) that thinks itself to be of high status (4:8) see Eva Maria Lassen, "The Use of the Father Image in Imperial Propaganda and 1 Corinthians 4:14-21," *Tyndale Bulletin* 42 (1991) 135-36.

[83] Fee, *First Corinthians*, 185, maintains that the description of other leaders as παιδαγογοί was "not intended to be a putdown" of the other "teachers" of the Corinthians. Rather, it was intended to distinguish Paul's relation with the Corinthians from the relation of all the other leaders of the church. While Fee recognizes that Paul is "reasserting his authority and appealing to their loyalty," he is guilty of downplaying the clear implication of the relationships implied by Paul's metaphorical self-designation as the "begetting father" of the community and the subordinate role of other leaders as παιδαγογοί.

thians themselves as children, Paul reasserts his unique authority over
the community in preparation for authoritatively addressing a range
of divisive behavior beginning with the man living in an incestuous
relationship in 5:1-5.[84]

While this authority is benign, even benevolent, in 4:14-15 as Paul
maintains that he is writing to the Corinthians as "beloved children"
in order to admonish them not to shame them (4:14),[85] in 4:18-20
his tone becomes menacing towards any in the community who dare
to challenge him and his parental-like authority.[86] The threat is directed towards those who pride themselves in their rhetorical sophistication and its concomitant social status and power (4:19),[87] and in
turn have apparently demeaned Paul for his lack of eloquence and
social status (2:1-5). Paul invokes a powerful symbol, namely, the
kingdom of God, to suggest that his δύναμις has an altogether different basis from those who equate eloquence in speaking with power.
In doing so, Paul legitimates and intensifies his own authority by
subtly suggesting that his power is derived from the divine sphere,
not the human sphere, unlike those whom he threatens.

4. Conclusion

Confronted by a situation in which he perceived that some members of the church in Corinth were engaged in factious behavior that
threatened the very essence of the gospel which he had preached to
them and at the same time undermined both the unity of the community and his own authority in the community, Paul was forced
into a response. Without any means of physical coercion he engaged
in the one strategy available to him for reclaiming the church from

---

[84] Given, *True Rhetoric*, 93-94.

[85] The ironical tone of 1 Cor. 4:8-13 was almost certainly intended to shame
the Corinthians, but in 4:14-16 Paul softens his tone before becoming more forceful
again in 4:17-21 according to Richard A. Horsley, *1 Corinthians*, Abingdon New
Testament Commentaries (Nashville, TN: Abingdon Press, 1998), 72-73.

[86] The metaphorical use of the image of the father as benevolent and as authoritarian was simply two sides of the same coin in Roman Corinth as Lassen,
"Father Image," 127-36, has shown.

[87] Winter, *Philo and Paul*, 200-01, has developed a case for understanding the
juxtaposition of the key rhetorical terms, λόγος and δύναμις, in 4:19 and Paul's
challenge regarding them as part of his critique of sophists and their disciples.
Winter finds a parallel in Philo's charge that the rhetorical skills of sophists were
not matched by their power in living.

the grips of factionalism, the construction of a rhetoric of persuasion that could reestablish and sustain his authority while re-unifying the community. It is this which gives 1 Cor. 1:10-4:21 its strongly ideological character as Paul uses meaning encoded in language and rhetoric in order to achieve his goals.

Having shown the fruitfulness of examining 1 Cor. 1:10-4:21 from an ideological perspective informed by the work of John Thompson, there is still much more work to be done on the remainder of 1 Corinthians in order to determine the extent to which other parts of the letter serve Paul's goals of community unification and the legitimation and maintenance of his own authority. But in the meantime, I hope that what I have accomplished in this essay may serve as a small tribute to Dr. Thrall who has done so much over her academic career to illuminate Paul and his correspondence with the church at Corinth.

THE 'UNDERLAYS' OF CONFLICT AND COMPROMISE IN 1 CORINTHIANS

Bruce W. Winter

Margaret Thrall has made a major contribution to Corinthian studies, not least in her magisterial commentary on 2 Corinthians. Her early work, *Greek Particles in the New Testament*, included texts relating to 1 Corinthians. Like her learning, that book of one hundred and seven pages published in 1962 was deceptively modest.[1] It reflected her encyclopaedic knowledge of ancient sources from which she draws on apposite examples long before the whole of the Greek corpus was available on a CD Rom. She understood distinctive aspects of Koine Greek grammar and, in particular, the role of particles, well before the study of rhetorical arguments became fashionable for New Testament scholars. Her understanding of the critical role that these particles played in linking the flow of the argument enabled her to resolve exegetical impasses in the New Testament and included 1 Corinthians. Before I had the privilege of meeting her during her sabbatical leave at Tyndale House, Cambridge, I had already benefited enormously from what I still regard as the most seminal contribution to the study of Koine Greek of the New Testament in the past half-century.

It seemed appropriate in this long overdue Festschrift to explore an issue prior to any examination of the pastoral resolutions Paul provides in 1 Corinthians in which particles would play such a critical role in his argumentation. It is proposed to search the letter for the fundamental underlying causes of the various problems of Corinthian Christians. By examining the amount of space Paul devoted to each issue we may see whether the origins of the underlying problems in 1 Corinthians are revealed.

---

[1] E.J. Brill. This published dissertation was undertaken at Cambridge University as one of the first doctoral students of C.F.D. Moule.

I. *Discrete Issues in 1 Corinthians*

The following analysis of the number of lines in a manuscript indicates the length of Paul's discussion of various issues. For this purpose P 46 was chosen.

Number of Lines of Greek Text Devoted to Discrete Issues

Issues	Lines	Percentage
*gifts (12-14)	246	19.26
leadership (1:10-4:21)	237	18.56
*idols temple (8-11:1)	237	18.56
resurrection (15)	148	11.59
*marriage, etc. (7:1-24)	70	5.48
*betrothal (7:25-40)	56	4.38
Lord's supper (11:17-34)	56	4.38
veiling (11:2-16)	43	3.36
incest (5)	43	3.36
litigation (6:1-11)	32	2.5
fornication (6:12-20)	25	1.95
thanksgiving (1:4-9)	14	1.09
*collection (16:1-4)	13	1.
Stephanas, etc 16:15-18	13	1.
travel plans (16:5-9)	12	.9
opening salutation (1:1-3)	10	.93
greetings (16:19-24)	10	.93
Timothy (16:10-11)	7	.54
*Apollos (16:12-14)	5	.39

*Signifies issues on which the Corinthian church wrote to Paul.

The drawback with these figures based on the number of lines in P[46] is that the abbreviations of *Nomina Sacra* mean the percentages are not quite accurate. A word count provides a helpful comparison.

Both approaches yield basically the same results and therefore give a broad indication of the amount of space Paul devoted to arguments in which he sought to resolve the problems in 1 Corinthians. In the above table the descending order of the percentage of space given over to Corinthian issues suggests that spiritual gifts, loyalty to former leaders in the church, food offered to idols and questions surrounding the resurrection of the body are the problems to which Paul devoted most space. Marriage, separation, and singleness occupy significantly less attention, followed by the issue of betrothal, the Lord's supper, and the veiling of men and women.

Surprisingly incest, litigation and fornication occupy the least space,

Number of Greek Words Devoted to Discrete Issues

Issues	Words	Percentage
leadership (1:10-4:21)	1349	19.59
* gifts (12-14)	1276	18.53
* idol temple (8-11:1)	1164	16.90
resurrection (15)	851	12.37
* marriage, etc. (7:1-24)	383	5.56
* betrothal (7:25-40)	307	4.46
Lord's supper (11:17-34)	298	4.33
veiling (11:2-16)	227	3.30
incest (5)	219	3.18
litigation (6:1-11)	173	2.5
fornication (6:12-20)	172	2.5
thanksgiving (1:4-9)	90	1.30
collection (16:1-4)	64	.93
greetings (16:19-24)	62	.90
travel plans(16:5-9)	61	.88
Stephanas, etc. (16:15-18)	60	.87
opening salutation (1:1-3)	55	.79
* Apollos (16:12-14)	39	.56
Timothy (16:10-11)	37	.54

yet in any analysis these are most serious issues for they are sins against the person's own body (6:18). The litigation to which Paul referred resulted in defrauding other Christians whom he declares are brothers. To engage in litigation against an actual family member would have created a legal precedent in the Roman period.[2] Sexual issues were indeed serious; adultery, incest and fornication were acts that would exclude unrepentant Christians who committed them from any inheritance in the kingdom of God (6:9-10).

The conclusions from the above analysis seem to negate the thesis that the amount of space devoted to an issue was an indicator of its importance. How is the methodology flawed? Studies in 1 Corinthians have largely proceeded on the *a priori* assumption that each of the issues addressed forms a discrete unit. It assumes that there is no underlying problem or problems that surface in different situations, no overlap between one issue and another, no cumulative argumentation proceeding in the letter and that Paul never defers the resolution of an issue until later in the letter. Are these assumptions justified on the basis of the text? In the next section another

---

[2] D.F. Epstein, *Personal Enmity in Roman Politics 218-43BC* (London: Routledge, 1989) pp. 27-8 on the family as a sanctuary from civil litigation.

approach will be explored which shows that the discrete issues analysis is not an appropriate one.

II. *Cluster Issues in 1 Corinthians*

There are common problems or clusters of issues in which the same symptoms manifest themselves in different situations in 1 Corinthians. It will be argued in the remainder of this chapter that these relate to two underlying cultural issues in the first century, namely that of conflict and compromise.

a. *Conflicts*

Divisiveness or conflict in the congregation over loyalty to Paul, Apollos and Peter appears as the first issue (1:11-12). It resurfaces in 3:3-6 and is repeated in 4:6 where the Corinthians played Paul off against Apollos and *vice versa*. Given the content and clear flow of the argument based on the particles Paul uses in the whole of 1 Corinthians 1:10-4:21, this section should be seen to be dealing with the problem of strife and jealousy over former teachers.[3]

Paul also hears about divisions in the community at the Lord's Supper and proceeds to condemn the church strongly because of the indefensible selfishness and drunkenness of some (11:18-22). In fact, he argues, they have already experienced divine judgement because of their mistreatment of the 'have-nots' which arose from their divisions.

Divisiveness among members again surfaces in the call to unity in the church—'that there be no division in the body' (12:25), and they are encouraged to adopt the more excellent way, the priority of genuine love (12:31-13:13). It is only in the concluding part of the letter that Paul succinctly raises the matter of the request for the return of a former teacher over whom there had been conflict and substantial discussion—'Now, concerning Apollos...' (16:12)—having examined the outworking of conflict in 1:10-4:21.

The issue of civil litigation in which a Christian took another Christian to court over the smallest matter as the end result of unresolved

---

[3] See "Paul and the Sophistic Conventions" and "Paul's Critique of the Corinthian Sophistic Tradition" in my *Philo and Paul among the Sophists: Alexandrian and Corinthian Responses to a Julio-Claudian Movement* (Grand Rapids, Eerdmans, 2002 2nd ed.), chs. 8 and 9.

conflicts was typical of Roman Corinth.[4] The fact that litigation was over trivial causes indicates that this was a matter of vexatious litigation (6:2). Private quarrels became public ones and civil action was used as an occasion to win finally in a Roman court. The defeated adversary incurred a financial penalty and a loss of face among friends and foes.[5] Plutarch observed:

> disorder in a State is not always kindled by contentions about public matters, but frequently differences arising from private affairs and offences pass thence into public life and…private troubles become the causes of public ones and small troubles of great ones.[6]

This was true not only in the realm of *politeia* but also in the Christian community in Corinth.

Conflict Situations in 1 Corinthians

	Lines	Percentage	Words	Percentage
leadership (1:10-4)	237	18.5	1349	19.59
litigation (6:1-11)	32	2.5	173	2.5
Lord's supper (11:17-34)	56	4.38	298	4.33
*gifts (12-14)	246	19.2	1276	18.53
Apollos/Stephanas (16:12-18)	18	1.39	99	1.43
Total		44.83		46.38

By proceeding on a cluster method rather than one of discrete issues, it emerges from the above analysis that a major portion of the letter is taken up with issues of conflict which seriously threaten to create great havoc in the life of the Christian community.

b. *Compromises*

Was there another underlying problem around which other issues in 1 Corinthians cluster? Sexual conduct, or rather misconduct, appears in a number of situations in 1 Corinthians. Incest and the

---

[4] Dio Chrysostom, *Or.* 8.9 relates the presence of innumerable lawyers touting for business at the Isthmian Games for the purpose of vexatious litigation cases.

[5] On the blackening of an opponent's character (*imfamandam*) see Epstein, *Personal Enmity in Roman Politics*, pp. 102-3 and my discussion on enmity and vexatious litigation in Roman society "Civil Law and Christian Litigiousness" *After Paul left Corinth: the Influence of Secular Ethics and Social Change* (Grand Rapids: Eerdmans, 2001), ch. 4.

[6] *Moralia* 825A.

unwillingness of the congregation to deal with the offender come to
Paul's notice only by way of a report and not a request (5:1). It was
treated as a serious issue in society and was, in fact, a criminal offence under Roman law.[7] In Corinth's criminal court conviction
would have resulted in exile for both parties on separate islands and
loss of citizenship and property had they been exposed to criminal
action.[8] How could the church not have dealt with this matter in
the Christian community? As it was not possible to prosecute a person
of superior rank under Roman law,[9] it has been argued that the
church is boasting not in the man's sin but in his social status which
made him virtually a legal untouchable.[10]

Fornication was seen as a given by young, unmarried men after
they assumed the *toga virilis* which was the Roman rite of passage to
manhood.[11] Paul did not accuse them of adultery, for he argued that
they had formed a one-flesh relationship by engaging in sexual relationships with prostitutes (6:16). Had the offenders already established a one-flesh relationship in marriage, the charge would have
been adultery, and not fornication. They defended their conduct on
the grounds of the secular catch-cry 'all things were permitted for
me'.[12] Furthermore, the reference to food being for the belly and
the belly for food indicates a context, not of a brothel but of a typical dinner given for young men, during which the unholy trinity of
eating, drinking and fornicating occurred (6:13).[13] Cicero poured
scorn on any call to sexual abstinence.

[7] O.F. Robinson, *Criminal Law of Ancient Rome* (London: Duckworth, 1995), 61-
2.
[8] *The Digest*, 48.40.2.
[9] P. Garnsey, *Social Status and Legal Privilege in the Roman Empire*. (Oxford:
Clarendon Press, 1970), p. 182.
[10] A.D. Clarke, "Secular Practices of Christian Leadership, II; Beyond Re-
proach", *Secular and Christian Leadership: A Socio-Historical and Exegetical Study of 1
Corinthians 1-6* (Leiden: E.J. Brill, 1993), ch. 6 and my "Criminal Law and Christian Partiality", *After Paul left Corinth*, ch. 3.
[11] See Plutarch, *Moralia* 37C-D.
[12] For evidence of the catch cry see my *After Paul left Corinth*, pp. 89-90.
[13] Plutarch, *Moralia* 705C "those whose shortcomings are in eating and drinking and sexual indulgence". On the description of this unholy trinity see A. Booth,
"The Age for Reclining and its Attendant Perils" in W.J. Slater, ed., *Dining in a
Classical Context* (Ann Arbor: University of Michigan Press, 1991), p. 105, and
generally on the promiscuous behaviour of young men see e.g. E. Eyben, *Restless
Youth in Ancient Rome* (E.T. London: Routledge, 1993), pp. 231-33.

> If there is anyone who thinks that youth should be forbidden af-
> fairs even with courtesans, he is doubtless eminently austere, but
> that view is contrary not only to the licence of this age, but also to
> the custom and concessions of our ancestors.[14]

After the lengthy opening discussion in 1 Corinthians 15:1-28 the
first injunction 'eat and drink' if death is the end, follows with a
citation from Menander's *Thais*, 'Bad company corrupts good mor-
als' which referred to a prostitute providing sexual favours.[15] The
command that follows was 'to wake out of drunkenness and sin no
more' (15:33-4). This was preceded by Paul's revelation that in
Ephesus he metaphorically 'fought the beasts'—in his day this apho-
rism was a standard analogy to struggling with sexual passions
(15:32).[16] Paul also discloses that he 'dies every day' to them (15:31).
The ethical injunctions (15:32-4) occur immediately before he proceeds with an extended answer to the major objection concerning
the nature of the resurrection body—'but someone will say…' (ἀλλὰ
ἐρεῖ τις), 15:35—in 15:35-57. They are an apposite conclusion to
the opening discussion on the certainty of the resurrection of the
body.

The command (15:33-4) would also have applied to the behaviour
of married men. Some, we learnt earlier, had sat down as a matter
of a 'right' (ἐξουσία) to eat and drink in the idol temple and risen
up to play; the evil they were warned against in the context of idolatry
was immorality (8:9, 10:7-8). It was a civic right of Roman citizens
in Corinth to attend the banquets given by the President of the
imperial games in the court of Poseidon's temple at the Isthmian
games complex.[17] Such great dinners also provided the services of
prostitutes who were part of the travelling brothels that accompanied such important festivals. The catch-cry of those determined to
exercise 'this right' (ἐξουσία) of theirs had been 'everything is al-

---

[14] Cicero, *Pro Caelio* 20.48.

[15] A. Körte and A. Thierfelder, *Menandri quae supersunt* (2nd ed. Leipzig: Teubner,
1964), p. 80 and T.B.L. Webster, *An Introduction to Menander* (Manchester: Manchester
University Press, 1974), pp. 14, 185 for discussion of the setting of prostitution.

[16] A.J. Malherbe, "The Beasts at Ephesus", *JBL* 87 (1968), pp. 71-80.

[17] See the inscription for Lucius Castricus Regulus who first presided over the
Isthmian games when they were moved back to Isthmia after two hundreds absence from the site and "gave a banquet for all the colonists [Roman citizens]",
Kent, *Corinth* VIII.3, no. 153. Plutarch, *Moralia* 723A records that the President
of the Games "several times entertained all the citizens".

lowed' (πάντα ἔξεστιν), (8:9, 10:23).[18] Their conduct was the same
as that of young men at the private dinners where typically, along
with an excess of food and drink, high-class prostitutes were provided as the 'after dinner' entertainment (6:12).[19] The unholy trinity of eating, drinking and the effects of sex with a prostitute occurs
in 15:32-34, just as it does in 6:13-15 and 10:7-8.

The justification for sexual promiscuity was defended philosophically on the basis of a first-century Platonism in which the body
was not the prison house but the soul's house surrounded by the
senses. Nature meant these senses to be enjoyed and this included
sexual indulgence. It was argued that such pursuits could only be
indulged in when one was alive and therefore should be unre-
strained.[20]

Of the issues raised by the Corinthians Paul dealt first with
marriage, stressing the temptation to immorality. It was because of
this that each man was to 'have' his own wife and she her husband,
(7:3).[21] The society's expectation was that married men would in-
dulge in extramarital sex either with their slaves, high-class prostitutes or affairs but would preserve the certainty of the family line
through his wife by her faithfulness in her conceiving only his children.[22] The Corinthians were suggesting the possibility of sexual
abstinence which Paul ruled was only to be exercised for prayer, by
mutual consent and only for a limited period, lest they be tempted
by Satan through lack of sexual control, (7:1-5).

The second issue raised was about marrying or not marrying one's
betrothed at this present time. The problem was inappropriate conduct between a young man and his future wife. As a result the fiancé

---

[18] The noun of the verb, ἔξεστιν is εξουσια. Liddell & Scott.

[19] Tacitus, *Agr.* 21 "The elegant banquet...along with the use of the *toga*...are
enticements of Romanization, to vice and servitude."

[20] For a discussion of this verbatim account of their argument see Philo, *Det.*,
33-4 and my *Philo and Paul among the Sophists*, pp. 202-5, and D.T. Runia, *Philo and
the Timaeus of Plato* (Leiden: E.J. Brill, 1986), pp. 306-8 on this canon of interpretation of the senses as guardians and courtiers of the soul.

[21] ἔχειν τινά = "have intercourse with someone", J.N. Adams, *The Latin Sexual
Vocabulary* (London: Duckworth, 1982), p. 187.

[22] Plutarch, "Advice to the Bride and Groom", 140B on that expectation in a
speech delivered at the marriage bed of two young friends about to consummate
their relationship. See L. Goessler, "Advice to the Bride and Groom", in ed. S.B.
Pomeroy, *Plutarch's "Advice to the Bride and Groom" and "A Consolation to his Wife"*:
English Translations, Commentary, Interpretative Essays (Oxford: Oxford University Press,
1999), pp. 111-20.

was full of sexual passion, and Paul comments, 'thus it is bound to occur' (οὕτως φείλει γίνεσθαι). The following verse contrasts and commends the conduct of the young man because he has fixed in his heart to behave appropriately towards his fiancée and therefore was under no necessity, having his sexual desires under control (7:36-7).[23]

It is suggested that the remaining issue falling under the heading of compromise was that of the veiling of men with the *toga* in Christian worship. This was a pagan custom and well illustrated by the statue types of Augustus. There is a surviving example in Corinth which portrays the emperor with his *toga* pulled over the top of his head offering up a sacrifice as a priest. This office was normally undertaken by the élite in society and was being replicated in the church by Christian men praying and prophesying. They were thereby dishonouring their head, Christ, by drawing attention to their social status (11:3-4).[24] Women, who had been convicted of adultery (which was a criminal offence under Roman law) and those who were prostitutes, did not wear the marriage veil.[25] Paul argues that they should also have their hair cropped if they wish to appear as convicted adulteresses, for the cropping of hair was also part of the punishment (11:6).[26] Here is an example of wives following the convention of those whom some ancient historians have designated the 'new' Roman wife whose economic, social or sexual liberation could result in adultery.[27] The men and women who spoke to God in prayer and spoke to the congregation on God's behalf were copying the Roman male and female customs; they are rebuked in this

---

[23] See my "Puberty or passion? The meaning of ὑπέρακμος in 1 Corinthians 7:36", *Tyn.B.* 49.1 (May, 1998) 71-89 and summary in "The Present Crisis and the Consummation of Marriage", *After Paul left Corinth*, pp. 246-9

[24] The view that covering one's head to pray and prophesy finds its origins in a Jewish custom is rejected on the grounds that not only does Paul not recognise the practice and nor do any of the churches of God—a reference that includes Jewish as well as Gentile congregations.

[25] For a discussion of this little known provision in Roman Law see T.A.J. McGinn, *Prostitution, Sexuality, and the Law in Ancient Rome*, (Oxford: Oxford University Press, 1998), p. 162.

[26] D.W.J. Gill, "The Importance of Roman Portraiture for Head-coverings", *Tyndale Bulletin* 41.2 (1990), pp. 245-60 on the copying of this Roman custom.

[27] For a discussion of this, see my "New Roman Wives and New Rules" and "Contentious Christian Wives", *The Appearance of New Roman Women and the Pauline Communities: the Impact of New Rules and New Roles* (forthcoming, Grand Rapids: Eerdmans, 2003) chs. 1 and 7.

passage for being contentious (11:16). Their behaviour represented a further compromise with the spirit of the age in Corinth.

Here, then, is another cluster of ethical issues that reflect the pressure to compromise with the Roman culture of Corinth. On the basis of this analysis the major portion of the letter is taken up with issues of sexual and other ethical compromises which seriously endangered the future of some Christians and that of their community. Those who were unrepentant about having committed incest, fornication and adultery were threatened with exclusion from the community and from the Kingdom itself (6:9).

Compromise situations in 1 Corinthians

	Lines	Percentage	Words	Percentage
incest (5)	43	3.36	219	3.38
fornication (6:12-20)	25	1.95	172	2.5
*marriage, etc. (7:1-24)	70	5.48	383	5.56
*betrothal (7:25-40)	56	4.38	307	4.46
*idol temple (8:1-11:1)	237	18.56	1164	16.90
veiling (11:2-16)	43	3.36	237	3.3
resurrection (15)	148	11.58	851	12.37
Total		48.67		48.47

This analysis indicates that 18% of the letter is devoted to compromise over idol meat and 12% to the issue of the resurrection of the body and the deeds done in the body, 10% to marriage/betrothal issues, while incest covers 3.5% and fornication 2.3%. Compromises that were over veiling involve 3.5%.

From the statistical data it emerges that conflict issues comprise 44.83% of the lines or 46.38% of the words written in 1 Corinthians with a combined average of 45.60%. Compromise issues occupy 48.67% of the lines or 48.47% of the words with an average of 48.57%. In round figures 45% of the discussion is occupied with matters relating to conflict and its effects in interactions between Christians in the life of the community. 48% of the letter is taken up with matters relating to compromise, primarily in the realm of sexuality.[28] It is concluded that using a model of cluster issues rather

---

[28] The remainder of the issues in 1 Corinthians are taken up with *varia*. The thanksgiving (1:4-9) 14 *ll*. 1.09%, 90 words 1.3%; the collection (16:1-4) 13 *ll*. 1%; 64 words .93%; travel plans (16:5-9) 12 *ll*. .9%, 61 words .88%; opening salutations (1:1-3) 10 *ll*. .93%; 61 words .88%; greetings (16:19-24) 10 *ll*. .93%; 62 words .9%; and Timothy (16:10-11) 7 *ll*. .54%; 37 words .54%. These items total 6.29% of the lines and 5.43% of the words.

than discrete issues is the more appropriate approach because the underlying problems of conflict and compromise surfaced in various areas of the community and the personal lives of Christians.

III. *Implications*

'Underlays' in 1 Corinthians

a. *Conflict*

The cluster approach is appropriate because Paul does not always deal fully with one issue and then proceed to another, never to return to that problem. This is clear from the beginning of the letter with the opening issue (1:10-4:21). As the discussion unfolds the Corinthian's boasting is about Paul and Apollos at the expense of the other (4:6), and has resulted in strife and jealousy (3:3-4). What comes as a surprise is that the Christians, or at least the influential ones, in the church have written asking for the return of Apollos. However, this fact does not emerge until the concluding section of the letter in which Paul deals with their request for his return—'now concerning' Apollos (Περὶ δὲ Ἀπολλῶ), (16:12).

However, the discussion of conflict does not end with chapter 4. The enmity of the parties manifested itself in vexatious litigation, played out in civil actions with the judge and jury awarding damages (6:1-8). The decision handed down would indicate who was judged to be the most powerful of the parties. Even in insignificant matters a just ruling was unlikely.[29] That decision created a new set of enmity relationships between the defeated and the members of the jury who voted against him. The interpersonal conflict could be unending and those connected with the respective parties would inevitably be required to take sides.[30]

The conflict over teachers and between fellow Christians naturally spilt over into the worshipping life of the church. At the Lord's supper (11:17-34) Paul reported, 'I hear there are divisions in your midst' (11:18). In the exercising of spiritual gifts (chs. 12-14), worship had also been affected by divisiveness where some were discriminating in the care they bestowed on their own group to the exclusion of others (12:25).

---

[29] Garnsey, *Social Status and Legal Privilege in the Roman Empire*. p. 187.
[30] Epstein, *Personal Enmity in Roman Politics*, p. 90.

Is the final solution to the conflict issues in 1:10-21, 6:1-8, 11:17-34 to be found in aspects of the teaching about how members of the Christian community are to relate to one another in terms of ministry? The new concept of themselves analogous to different functions of a human body operating in a beneficial way for each other seems to suggest this will resolve conflict and secure its antonym 'unity' (12:12-27). If so, chapters 12-14 may not be simply about the importance of spiritual gifts but how the body of Christ is meant to function harmoniously and to the benefit of all its members in a way that it has not done so to that point.

b. *Compromise*

In the case of sexual compromise, issues such as fornication by young men who had received the *toga virilis*, and those attending the banquets at the Games appear to be separate units. However, the catch-cry of young men was on the lips of all the men involved in the latter event. The discrete approach can overlook the fact that the term 'right' (ἐξουσια) 8:9, 9:4, 5, 6, 12, 15, 18, is the noun for the verb 'it is permitted' (ἐξεστιν), 6:12, 10:23. The issue was, in effect, the same and both defended what they did by sheltering under the same aphoristic saying that Paul repeats in both verses.

Given what is known about the first-century discussion of the relationship between the senses and the soul and the derivative ethical arguments from a Platonic/Epicurean anthropology (see p. 146), it comes as no surprise that Paul has to deal with the sexual misdeeds done in the body. Roman society regarded these as a matter of complete indifference because of its philosophical defence of hedonistic behaviour. It is for this reason that there are two sets of ethical injunctions in 1 Corinthians 15. The first, the response to 'the eating and drinking for tomorrow we die' thesis with the command to 'wake up out of drunkenness and stop sinning', is connected to a lack of control of appetites for food and sexual intercourse (15:32-4). The other, preceded by a long argument on the nature of the resurrection body, is found in the final summing up with the positive call to be 'steadfast, immovable, always abounding in the work of the Lord, knowing that your labour in the Lord is not an empty thing'. The implication is that if they continued to be unstable and open to current sexual mores with the present self-indulgent lifestyle (15:58).[31]

---

[31] Paul uses ὥστε to summarise ethical requirements at the end of the Lord's

Paul had already indicated how assiduously he worked to bring the gospel to them (15:10). By contrast he draws attention to their self-indulgence in order to shame them, because their lifestyle of drunkenness and sexual misbehaviour had deprived others of the knowledge of the truth (15:34). For the Corinthians it was actually a case of the insurrection of their bodies against the Lord's purposes for them as members of the Kingdom and as heralds of the gospel for others. They had been reminded that they were no longer their own and they must glorify God in their bodies (6:20).[32] It is suggested that the extended discussion of the resurrection of the body was meant to remove the 'underlay' that had provided the basis for the sexual compromises of youth and older men which had been discussed earlier in 5:1-5, 6:1-11, 7:36 and 10:8.

'Underlays' in Roman Corinth

Do these findings confirm features of first-century Roman society? There were enormous pressures in society to conform to the cultural norms of one's class. The constitutions of Roman colonies were drawn up by the Senate and reflected the imperial city's ordering of society based on Roman law.[33] Senators wore broad purple stripes, equestrians, plebes, and freedmen were likewise distinguishable, and gold rings were worn by men in the first two classes.[34] After a period of bonded service in Roman households, even manumitted slaves were granted freedmen status along with Roman citizenship, but could acquire the privileged status of priests of the imperial cult of Augustus with a religious connection with the emperor.[35] From the time of Augustus the class system was even more clearly defined and

---

Supper, spiritual gifts and the resurrection of the body, 11:33-4, 14:39, 15:58.

[32] Paul was to subsequently write to the Corinthians (2 Cor. 5:10), "For we must all appear before the judgement seat of Christ, so that each one may receive good or evil, according to what he has done in the body."

[33] J.A. Crook, *Roman Life and Law, 90 B.C.–A.D. 212* (New York: Cornell University Press, 1967), pp. 7-8. For a treatment of this unique aspect of Roman society see my "Roman Law and Society in Romans 12-15", in P. Oakes ed., *Rome in the Bible and the Early Church* (Carlisle and Grand Rapids: Paternoster and Baker, 2002), ch. 3.

[34] For a helpful summary see M. Goodman, "The City of Rome: Social Organization", *The Roman World 44 BC-AD 180* (London: Routledge, 1997), ch. 17.

[35] On the priests of Augustus see D. Fishwick, *The Imperial Cult in the Latin West: Studies in the Ruler Cult of the Western Provinces of the Roman Empire* (Leiden: E.J. Brill, 1987-1993) vol. II.I., pp. 609-16.

one's legal *persona* (πρόσωπον) determined one's place and privileges in society.

There were two significant areas of social life in which rank and status in Rome were clearly seen. The first was in the theatre where seating was assigned according to social status, so that all were well aware of their place in society.[36] As theatre-going was extremely popular with all classes in Roman society, this only heightened class-consciousness in public contexts. The other domain was at public banquets where the person of highest rank took his portion of food first, the remainder taking theirs in descending order. The same applied at private dinners where eating arrangements also draw attention to social status.[37]

It was at private and public dinners that there was the pressure to conform to lax sexual norms. It was presupposed that young men would not be virgins on marriage although it was essential that their new bride should be, and husbands would be sexually unfaithful to their wives who themselves were not to be adulteresses. Social status also meant that those who were guilty of criminal offences could not be persecuted except by equals or superiors.

Under such strong hierarchical and social pressures it is easy to understand how Christians capitulated to culturally acceptable norms and embraced their rights. So strong was the counter-cultural character of much early Christian teaching on relationships that a hiatus developed among Corinthian Christians. Social conformity and the pressure to justify compromise was a trap in which some were ensnared whether at a personal, communal or societal level.

It is also well documented that first-century society was one in which conflict situations were endemic in social relationships whether in the city's 'council and assembly' (βουλὴ καὶ ἐκκλησία), voluntary associations or social relationships generally.[38] The causes of con-

[36] E. Rawson, "*Discrimina ordinum*: the *lex Julia theatricalis*", *PBSR* (1987) pp. 83-114.

[37] J.H. D'Arms, *Commerce and Social Standing in Ancient Rome* (Cambridge, Mass.: Harvard University Press, 1984). On the highly structured dinners, S. Ruden, "Roman Dinner Parties", *Petronius, Satyricon: Translated, with Notes and Topical Commentary* (Indianopolis: Hackett, 2000), ch. 6. On equal and unequal private dinners in relation to the Lord's Supper see my "'Private' Dinners and Christian Divisiveness (1 Corinthians 11:17-34)" in *After Paul left Corinth*, ch. 7.

[38] See generally O.M. Van Nijf, *The Civic World of Professional Associations in the Roman East* (Amsterdam, Gieben, 1997) and on strife T. Seland, "Philo and the Associations of Alexandria" in ed. J.S. Kloppenborg and S.G. Wilson, *Voluntary Associations in the Graeco-Roman World* (London: Routledge, 1996), pp. 117-9

flict could be personal grievances, exclusive loyalty to patrons or the political élite, ambition, violations of trust and obligations, envy towards new people joining a group, and the power and influence of others in it. Conflict was promoted through relatives, friends and clients and was acceptable in society.

> The Roman politician was confronted with potential *inimicitiae* [enmity] in every aspect of his political career, often extending into areas of life we consider strictly personal. Roman society was unusual in allowing *inimicitiae* to compete along with other more conventional values such as patriotism and humanity in guiding a public figure's conduct. A reputation for successfully pursuing *inimicitiae* [in court or the civic council or assembly] was a vital asset to a Roman politician seeking to establish and maintain an influential voice.

Epstein goes on to note that Roman society was never very successful at defining the limits of acceptable behaviour or regulating conduct.[39] Voluntary associations tended to replicate structures and relationships of the civic institutions and it has been argued that Jewish communities also did this.[40] It comes as no surprise that this socially acceptable ethical *modus operandi* should also emerge in the Corinthian church.

IV. *Conclusions*

This exploratory use of a statistical data approach to 1 Corinthians shows that alone it leads to misleading conclusions. However, that data used along an examination of the common problems presenting themselves in different issues in the text of 1 Corinthians helped alert us to two important 'underlays' reflecting the dysfunctional nature of Corinthian society that were the root causes of the present problems in this nascent Christian community.[41]

---

[39] Epstein, "The Causes of Inimicitiae", *Personal Enmity in Roman Politics*, ch. 3. Cit. pp. 62-3.

[40] On associations see n. 38. On synagogues see T. Rajak and D. Noy, "Archisynagogos: Office, Social Status in the Graeco-Roman World", *JRS* 83 (1993), pp. 75-93, T. Rajak, "The Synagogue within the Graeco-Roman city" in S. Fine ed., *Jews, Christians and Polytheists in the Ancient Synagogue: Cultural Interaction in the Graeco-Roman Period* (London: Routledge, 1999), ch. 9. T. Rajak, "The Jewish Community and its Boundaries", in J. Lieu, J. North and T. Rajak, eds. *The Jews among the Pagans and Christians in the Roman Empire* (London: Routledge, 1992), pp. 9-28.

[41] For a full discussion of the influence of the secular ethics on the issues in 1 Cor. see "The Influence of Secular Ethics" in my *After Paul left Corinth*, Part I.

The above investigation demonstrates that the discrete unit approach with a sequential reading of 1 Corinthians does not allow us to see the spread of the two underlying issues. As a consequence it also cautions us against an approach that would seek to divide the letter into an *exordium, narratio, probationes* and the *peroratio* and then conclude that the full extent of Paul's arguments can be explained in each discrete unit, using deliberative or others forms of rhetorical classification.[42] That form-critical straight jacket simply cannot account for the intensity and flow of the different arguments, or indeed the overall ethos of 1 Corinthians. The letter is a highly personal one when compared with those that were 'masterpieces of rhetorical display, paeans to classicism'.[43] What is striking is that Paul makes his appeals on numerous occasions to the Christian community in familial terms addressing the recipients as brothers and sisters. His frequent use of this term reflects his view of Christians as the family of God who were in a primarily spiritual 'sibling' relationship with himself.[44] There are no precedents in rhetorical handbooks for such a letter addressed to this particular *Sitz im Leben*.

This present investigation is but the prolegomenon to exploring how Paul resolved the critical issues of conflict and compromise. It is not within the purview of this essay to determine how he would proceed to pull down every argument and philosophically or culturally entrenched position that determined the social mores of Corinth and which were contrary to the knowledge of God (2 Cor. 10:5).

The next step in determining how Paul sought to resolve the influence of these two 'underlays' is to pay close attention to the

---

[42] E.g. B. Witherington III, *Conflict and Community in Corinth: A Socio-Rhetorical Commentary on 1 and 2 Corinthians* (Grand Rapids and Carlisle: Eerdmans and Paternoster, 1995) See also e.g. M. Bünker, *Briefformular und rhetorische Disposition im 1. Korintherbrief* (GTA 28; Göttingen: Vandenhoeck & Ruprecht, 1983), Margaret Mitchell, *Paul and the Rhetoric of Reconciliation: An Exegetical Investigation of the Language and Composition of 1 Corinthians* (Tübingen: J.C.B. Mohr [Paul Siebeck]/Louisville: Westminster/John Knox, 1991) and A. Eriksson, *Traditions as Rhetorical Proof: Pauline Argumentation in 1 Corinthians* (ConBNT 29; Stockholm: Almqvist & Wiksell, 1998).

[43] P.A. Rosenmeyer, *Ancient Epistolary Fictions: The Letter in Greek Literature* (Cambridge: Cambridge University Press, 2001), section IV, cit. on p. 343.

[44] Paul addressed them on 20 occasions as "brothers" and "sisters" in 1 Cor. and uses the term in another 17 instances as he appeals to them in their relationship with each other, himself and others. It appears to be part of his argument in seeking to resolve the pastoral issues. He uses it more in 1 Cor. than in any other of his letters.

nature of his argumentation and strategies in dealing with their pastoral problems. It is suggested that this requires a re-reading of the earlier sections in the light of what might be called 'final' solutions to conflict and compromise in chapters 12-14 in the case of the former and chapter 15 in the case of the latter. The overall task will involve a careful analysis of sentence structures and the all-important word order for emphasis in Koine Greek if we are to understand something of the intensity and flow of the arguments and their cumulative effect on cluster issues. Of course, in any such investigation the critical role that connectives play in Paul's argumentative style must be included. Margaret Thrall's scholarly, seminal work in this area remains both a paradigm of solid scholarship and an essential tool in this important endeavour of seeking to understand how the two major 'underlays' of conflict and compromise were to be resolved.

"WHO ARE YOU FOR?" 1 CORINTHIANS 1:10-17 AS CHRISTIAN SCRIPTURE IN THE CONTEXT OF DIVERSE METHODS OF READING

Clive Marsh

The Corinthian Factions: A New Look at an Old Problem

1 Cor. 1:10-17 offers itself as an ideal text for considering the value of a reader-response approach to the New Testament.[1] Whoever is reading, a contemporary experience of division in a human community is usually readily available and will be drawn upon by a reader. Whoever is reading the text in a Christian setting will have a contemporary experience of Christian division ready to hand. Go into any church and ask about 'factions' and you are likely to find some. Whatever else they may be held to be, churches are, after all, human organisations. Thinking only of the British scene in recent years, it is easy to list many types of factions which occur regularly in the lives of local churches. To name but a few:
- those who welcome critical thinking in Christian faith and those who would prefer it not to be used
- those who advocate 'free worship' as opposed to highly-structured forms
- those who put social and political action at the top of the Christian's agenda, versus those who mainly want to pray or worship in gathered congregations, or who primarily want to study
- those who accept gay and lesbian relationships as equal to heterosexual relationships and those who don't
- those who favour more recent music over classical hymnody
- those who welcome contact and dialogue with those of other religious traditions, and those who favour distance or detachment.

---

[1] A point readily picked up by commentators keen to look at the question of contemporary relevance and/or writing in a commentary series which looks for 'points for preachers', see e.g. Richard B. Hays *First Corinthians* (Louisville: John Knox Press, 1997), 25-6.

Whether consciously articulated or not, such polarities and factions as these create the contexts out of which, and thus the groups of Christian readers within which, such texts as 1 Cor 1:10-17 are actually read in churches today. Before anyone has asked a historical question about Apollos, Peter or Paul, a contemporary Christian group of any kind knows what it means to be divided. The reception, then, of such a text as 1 Cor 1:10-17 (esp. v.12) sharpens the question of how reader, text, historical context (past and present) and the history of tradition interweave in the act of interpretation. The moment a hearer or reader of the text recognises that what the text is 'about' is division—or at least potential factionalism—within a Christian community, then the *de facto* existence of known contemporary factions is unavoidable as a factor in reading.

The analytical challenge, however, begins precisely here. What is to be done next? One could go in a number of different directions. One could seek to use this experiential starting-point as a means of accessing the author's intention. On this view, the contemporary experience will ultimately be left behind, in the service of clarifying the original meaning: the nature of the division in Corinth. Alternatively, one could be more positive about the contemporary access-point—this present church division really does matter—even whilst maintaining a controlling, normative function for the original meaning. The point here would be to see how the best available historical reading of Paul's sense in 1 Cor 1:10-17 is to be made use of in clarifying and even resolving the contemporary situation. But the priority remains with the original meaning. If there is no real 'fit' between Paul's meaning and the contemporary situation, then Paul's words at this point simply do not help. To try and pretend that the meaning of a biblical passage could be 'applied' to a current dilemma might, in other words, be a misuse of the text. To suggest that Paul could be held to be talking here about those who think differently about forms of worship *may* be permissible. (It would not be wholly unreasonable to suppose that Pauline, Petrine and Apollonian factions favoured different forms of worship, whatever their main emphases may have been.) But we are not likely to be able to prove it. So on this understanding, the contemporary situation may only really be addressed if there is an evident connection between past and present contexts.

There is, however, a third alternative. This alternative prioritises a reader or reading community over any sense of an original meaning of the text, or over any claim that we have grasped the author's intention *in relation to a particular text*, but it is one which nevertheless respects an author's evident *interest* in more general terms. The reading I shall offer of this passage of Paul by no means disregards Paul's apparent intention both in this passage and in the letter as a whole. Furthermore, it refuses to imply that hearers/readers can make of the passage what they want, even though the hearer's/reader's interests are paramount. But I propose that the experiential starting-point of *de facto* division amongst Christians be seen as decisive for the interpretation of this passage, and ultimately as more important than whatever historical conclusions that may be able to be drawn about Peter's, Apollos', Paul's or Christ's party. For only on this basis can the christological unity which Paul appears to want to emphasize be appreciated in real, concrete terms. If, in other words, the christological unity of the Church is perceived only in ideal terms, or only in the context of a discussion about past (first-century) divisions, then the theological import of this passage from Paul's letter is nullified. To *prioritise* the context of contemporary Christian division in the fact of interpretation becomes, somewhat ironically, the means by which Paul's theological emphasis is to be respected and repeated. To express the matter differently: the only meaning worthy of Paul's intention is a theological meaning, and the best way of getting at that meaning, is by beginning from the contemporary experience of Christian division, regardless of whether such division correlates easily with historical knowledge of the specific, Corinthian division to which Paul refers. The theological challenge is then to determine what sense can be made of Paul's call for attention to christological unity when Christian disunity is so evident, in the present as well as in the past.

Being 'true to Paul': The Acknowledgement of Division

The next stage of this exploration must be, then, to proceed from whatever form of Christian disunity offers an experiential starting-point for the reader and to read it in the light of the call for attention to christological unity. What can it possibly mean to be reminded via rhetorical questions (1 Cor 1:13) that Christ has not been 'apportioned out', that Paul was not 'crucified for you' and that no one was 'baptized in the name of Paul'? A concrete example is necessary.

A contemporary Christian community (church) has become divided over a seemingly trivial issue. The community is deciding whether to make a substantial purchase of a data-projector for projecting text and DVD material. The need to make a decision has opened up some deep divisions, which can easily be seen to relate to different emphases within Christian faith and practice, and to divergent resulting priorities. One group (let's call them, for sake of argument, an 'Apollos group') thinks that the purchase is clearly the right move to make. They use three main arguments: if the Church is to make its message relevant to contemporary culture, then it must do so in a contemporary form; as a local church, there have been many major discussions going on as to how better to equip the church to be serving the wider community, and possession of such equipment would not only be for the church's benefit; third, and most importantly, the church has money available for such purchases and should be using some of it.

A second group—shall we say the 'party of Peter'?—also wants the equipment to be bought. Their reasons are not, however, presented as coolly and rationally as the first party. They think the purchase is necessary because there's a Peter who's very good with modern technology, but cannot afford to extend his current range of computer hardware. But there are those in the church who see that here is someone with a particular background and skill which they think the church should help develop.

A third group, however, is very aware of a broader context in which the question of the use of finance should be raised. Very conscious of the current financial squeeze on the whole denominational structure in which this particular church sits, this group wants loyalty to the denomination as a whole to take priority over local needs or desires. They are, in other words, more conscious of the network of churches of which they are a part and want to respect the work being done by those who work across the many different communities. Perhaps it may be right to make such a purchase. But it would be wise, first, to check out whether such a purchase should be made by or for a *group* of churches, if it should even be made at all. Perhaps we might label this group a 'Paul party'.

The fourth group appeals to a broad context too. Unlike 'the Paul party', however, this group thinks that all three other groups have got their priorities very skewed indeed. There is a real danger, in their eyes, that this particular church has lost its way. It is no long-

er focussed on Christ. How can it be when it is considering spending so much money on equipment it does not really need? (It can,
after all, loan most kinds of equipment from a local community group
whenever it needs to.) For this group, prioritizing the teaching of
Jesus within an awareness of God's preferential option for the poor
answers in an instant the question of whether such an expensive
purchase should be made.

This case study could, of course, be worked through in a similar
way in relation to any one of many similar current issues. It does,
however, remind us of how such divisions actually come about, or
at least how they surface. These divisions, which may in fact be
theological at root, rarely surface in explicit forms or in terms of
seemingly abstract theology. And yet what Paul appears to be concerned with when he speaks to the Corinthians relates directly to
what is being talked about here, even if not in any simple 'applied'
sense, or even via any mere merging of two horizons. Authorial
intention clearly did not have the purchase of computer hardware
in view. But authorial intention remains relevant, even if in a different way from what may be expected. *'Being true to Paul', then, may
entail less trying to tease out who the parties 'really were' in the Corinthian church,
and more a matter of being concerned, from a basis of contemporary Christian
disagreement, with what Paul appears to do with such disagreements when they
appear.* And at such a point a strange alliance between a reader-
response approach to the text (with what divisions in mind are readers
actually reading?) and the concerns of the historical critic (but what
did Paul have in mind here?) can be perceived. But first we must
do some more digging in relation to the contemporary situation.

The four groups, or 'parties', which have formed around this tricky
decision about the data-projector may, of course, have formed for
a variety of reasons: age, personality type, gender, degree of involvement at the core of church life. Theological differences may emerge
and be able to be highlighted; but there may not be an explicit
theological reason why a group formed.[2] The Apollos people may have

---

[2] It is interesting to note how commentators differ as to whether the Corinthian
parties should be seen as theological/ideological in focus, or whether their existence is much less programmatic. See e.g. Hays ('The divisions at Corinth should
not necessarily be understood to be clearly organized parties...it is not possible to
assign a distinct ideological program to each of these factions' p.22) as opposed to
Nigel Watson *The First Epistle to the Corinthians* (London: Epworth Press, 1992): 'Parties
have formed around the names of various evangelists, thus reproducing within the
church the rivalries that existed between different philosophical schools' (p.6).

formed around a treasurer: one in possession of the facts about church
finances. Or this may be a young, professional group wanting to move
the church on in its use of modern technology, and clear about the
processes of how you argue your case in relation to given budgets.
Or it may be a group who simply know how committees work, see
this as a useful project, and have gained support because they are
known to be successful in the kinds of things that they do.

The second group might have formed itself around a charismatic, pushy, or plainly gifted individual (who might equally, of course,
be a combination of all three). Less concerned about the structural
or financial aspects of how the church runs, this group will have seen
a need and the pragmatic usefulness of identifying a person's gifts.
The church's resources would be devoted to a highly practical cause,
and the church and its mission thereby be better served locally.

The third group could be a bunch of denominational tradition-
alists who are especially loyal to the many churches of their confes-
sion. But this need not be blind loyalty. There may be some very
good reasons for it. They are concerned, for example, by the tendency amongst congregations—especially newer ones—to be rather self-preoccupied. They see these tendencies emerging in their own
congregation. They notice that it has been happening for some years
in their fund-raising and gift-giving habits. As a church, they now
give a lower percentage of their annual budget to other bodies (char-
ities, world relief agencies and the like). Not only that, questions have
been raised by some other members of their congregation as to
whether they should pay their full quota to the central church administration. To think of spending such a large amount of money
on equipment just for their own use, when such other tendencies
are being displayed too, is thus rather worrying for them.

The fourth group are the activists, but also the purists. They
contain the newest members of the church, including those new to
Christianity *per se*. They can see through the potential factionalism
of the other groups more clearly than any, for they burn with a
passionate loyalty to their saviour, and are much fresher in the way
that they ask again and again how their actions relate to Christ. They
are the ones who nag people with the question 'What would Jesus
do?' They cause others discomfort, but are less able to see that they
themselves are a group in their own right.

The groups' differences could be characterized further, in explicitly theological terms. There are obviously major differences in ec-

clesiology between the groups. The first two are more congregational in focus. The third looks more to a networked (or national or global) church as the primary corporate unit through which God speaks. The fourth group may deem that they are permitting Christology (or perhaps eschatology, via an emphasis on the Kingdom of God) to have priority over ecclesiology. 'Church concerns' are being put in their appropriate place through attention to Christ.

Different understandings of the human being may be implicit in differences between the first and second groups. The first may prize rationality, and consider that the powers of argument entrusted by God to human beings should be used to the full as local churches work out how resources are to be allocated. By contrast, the second may be seeking to identify creative individuals. It may be through such creative individuals, indeed, that God especially 'speaks' today. Those entrusted with ministerial roles should perhaps even arise from amongst such creative people.

The third group may, by contrast, be emphasizing the bonding role of the Holy Spirit which enables Christians to rise above their immediate social location, noting a connectedness with others potentially quite different from them. The fourth group, too, would look for a unity. This would, however, be a unity 'in Christ' by which would be meant a unity of purpose and action, borne out in unified, liberating conduct which demonstrated a clear commitment to the poor.

It is highly unlikely that such theological differences would be articulated in such explicit terms. This would not, of course, mean that they were not present. Nor does it imply that still further theological differences might not also be present. It is important simply to note that differences within Christian communities, however seemingly trivial, will almost always be related to theological divergences.[3] People do not disagree for nothing. Even if psychological, sociological, economic or local historical factors may also come into play when Christians disagree, theologies play their part too. Theology is neither detached from such factors, nor reducible to them. It could not be otherwise in Corinth. It cannot be otherwise now.

---

[3] This will be true, furthermore, without it necessarily being possible to determine whether theology precedes opinion or action.

Being 'true to Paul': Respecting a Past Historical Context

I must, though, account for why I gave the four groups in the case study the same labels as the four 'parties' in Corinth. What am I suggesting by this? It could be held that the four Corinthian parties should be regarded as 'types'[4]: the kinds of groups which are likely to exist in any Christian community. This is scarcely likely to have been Paul's intention in any direct sense. After all, Paul is dealing with detail which has been passed on 'by Chloe's people' (1 Cor 1:11). But this may be how the resulting text is best received. I am, however, not trying to suggest any direct equation between the characteristics of the four groups I sketched and the four groups in Corinth. Is not, then, the use of the four labels little short of misleading? Not quite; though no direct equation can be claimed between a summary of any contemporary situation and the circumstances in Corinth, value can nevertheless be gained from the historical exploration of what those Corinthian groups may have emphasized. But it is important to recognize the *limitations* of the historical enquiry, and therefore the *direction* of the resulting juxtaposition. As Fee notes: 'the exact nature of this quarrelling and how it took shape in the community are matters on which far more certainty is expressed in the literature than is actually warranted by what is explicit in the text'.[5] In other words, despite the many pages devoted to the topic in commentaries and monographs, we cannot really be sure who constituted these groups, or what their particular hobbyhorses were.[6]

The informed guesses do, however, prove fruitful *for the present*. It is not difficult to move from scrutiny of any kind of Christian division in the contemporary Church to the kinds of educated hunch usually offered by scholars about the Corinthian groups. Apollos' party may have had something to with reason, or the employment of wisdom or rhetoric. Peter's/Cephas' party may have been a Jewish/Jewish-Christian group, thus possibly focussing specifically on a

---

[4] The 'types' argument goes back at least to F.C. Baur, who argued for two main 'parties' at work in Corinth, representing the fault-lines of early Christianity (a Pauline and a Petrine type). But even if there is some generalization here, it is unlikely that the parties in Corinth were anything but very concrete groupings.

[5] Gordon D. Fee *The First Epistle to the Corinthians* (Grand Rapids: Eerdmans, 1987), 55-6.

[6] For an extensive recent survey see Anthony C. Thiselton *The First Epistle to the Corinthians* (Grand Rapids: Eerdmans/Carlisle: The Paternoster Press, 2000) 120-133, esp. 123-133.

characteristic, gift or element in the background of an individual or particular individuals. Paul's party may have been one which looked to the 'founder figure' and was thus more conscious than others of a particular tradition or set of practices which people deemed should be standardized across the emergent Christian world. Christ's party could well have been the first-century Jesus-people, the enthusiasts appealing to a minimalism which cuts through all the hassles of structurally-minded Christianity. These are all highly speculative constructions, but they are possible.

Even so, the juxtaposition remains provocative, so long as we recognize which way we then move with it. These are *possible* versions of the historical groupings, and no more than that. They attain a profound plausibility from the perspective of a real, contemporary case study which brings them to life. When expounded around the decision about whether a data-projector should be bought, we see their plausibility all the more clearly.

The point of offering the juxtaposition is to show how historical enquiry at the very least embroiders and embellishes the contemporary situation and not the other way round.[7] The historical possibilities do prove instructive. There are, however, constraints at both ends. Though beginning with a contemporary experience of division enables a connection to happen between readers/hearers and the text, it could, of course, be argued that this would only ever work adequately with particular types of division. Either the divisions must be within an identifiable Christian group, or they must be within a group sufficiently concrete to be able to relate to aspects of the division which seem pressing in the Corinthian context. In other words, not any division will do. The point should also be made that use of the Corinthian correspondence is only likely to work in the context of a group or groups who think the letters of Paul might have something to offer them (be they Christian or not). You don't read things, or listen to things, unless you think they'll do something to or for you (whether this be entertainment, stimulation, education or whatever).

From the opposite end—that of the context in Corinth—our sheer lack of knowledge is the most major constraint. Though historians of early Christianity and biblical scholars are scarcely likely to ad-

---

[7] It needs to be taken as read that present contexts inform and embellish the task of history writing, otherwise history would not be possible.

mit the fact (for it would put them out of business), there remains
the incipient danger that despite the evident reality of (social? economic? theological?) division in the Christian community in Corinth,
overconfidence about what can be known can lead to too much
'reading-in' and thus inappropriate controlling of later interpretations.[8] Being 'true to Paul', then, may potentially happen best, when
creative, playful—though not unruly, unchecked—speculation happens with respect to both interpretative horizons, within a wider
framework of meaning.

Being 'true to Paul': Reading Corinthians as Christian Scripture

I have, though, been implying thus far that the 'wider framework
of meaning' must inevitably be the Christian church. An experiential starting-point of social division will undoubtedly work best, as a
means of access to a possible reading of Paul's text, if the division
is seen to occur within an identifiable Christian community 'then'
and 'now'. Perhaps this whole approach only works when a community reading the work as authoritative text (e.g. as 'scripture')
brings its concerns to it. This may well be true. For who, in any case,
would otherwise be reading the letter these days?[9]

   Even accepting the text as 'scripture', though, does not indicate
in precise terms how, and with what level of authority, the text is
being and should be read in any particular Christian community.
Christians differ as to what 'reading the Bible as scripture' amounts
to, even if almost all accept that this is what is happening, and should
happen.[10] One aspect of the current 'Bible as scripture' discussion

---

[8] There can, however, be little doubt how fruitfully historical speculation can
inform contemporary experience-related, theological readings of the text. To cite
an example: John K. Chow's *Patronage and Power: A Study of Social Networks in Corinth*
(Sheffield: Sheffield Academic Press, 1992) not only supplies useful socio-historical insight as to the possible background to the Corinthian divisions. It invites
contemporary reflection on the many ways that divisive patronage and its current
equivalents operate in different ways in many cultures. In the context of the case-
study I am using, those with local benefactors inside or outside the community of
faith might offer to pay for the data-projector, with all the attendant complica-
tions such patronage might cause.

[9] Though for an example of a contemporary reading of the Corinthian correspondence from within 'the literary community', see e.g. the introduction to *the
epistles of paul the apostle to the corinthians* (Edinburgh: Canongate, 1998), by the novelist
Fay Weldon.

[10] To cite a simple, contemporary example from my own tradition (British

is, though, surely of crucial importance. That is the recognition that for texts to function authoritatively, note needs to be taken of the community or communities which regard and use them as authoritative. The Bible does not function as authoritative merely 'as text' and in relation solely to individuals. It functions authoritatively as a received text amongst a body of people (whether gathered or dispersed) who attach weight to its contents and consider the task of interpreting it a necessary part of their life.

Expressed in this way, the authoritative function of the Bible naturally appears most prominently in religious communities (the Hebrew Bible for Jewish communities, the two-Testament version for Christian communities). It should not, however, be assumed that the Bible has no authority elsewhere. In literary and artistic circles, in political settings, and in the academy, for example, for those that use them Bibles function authoritatively too. The only issue is what *kind* of authority is functioning. Artists who paint biblical themes and stories give the text some claim on their work. Politicians may be couching their references to Bibles within broader ideological concerns (but, then, who doesn't?), but still attach some weight to the text, be that moral or rhetorical, in using it. Academics—whether they are looking at the richness and significance of King James English, or the possible historical value of biblical texts—don't simply start from the assumption that Bibles have nothing to offer them in their work.

At issue, though, as post-liberalism in theology and literary theory

---

Methodism): as one of the ways out of a tense and still unresolved discussion about human sexuality (with particular relation to homosexuality), the annual Conference of the Methodist Church in Great Britain saw the need to work on the question of how the Bible was being understood and used in such discussions. The result was a study document *A Lamp to My Feet and a Light to My Path* (Peterborough: Methodist Publishing House, 1998). It considered the use of the Bible, and framed its discussion material within a consideration of the place and function of authority within the Church. Part of the study document was a presentation of seven different 'models of authority' according to which the Bible was being used. The follow-up report of 2001 drew upon responses received. It found the Church unable to rule out any of the models as possible ways of reading the Bible, even whilst acknowledging that some of the models could be held to stand in tension with the Methodist Church's own doctrinal standards. The only position which could be excluded was any which deemed that the Bible had no place at all in the Christian task of formulating a contemporary understanding of faith. Acknowledgement that the Bible functions 'as scripture', and even that as scripture it functions in some sense authoritatively, may not, then, actually tell us very much. It may simply remind us that the Bible cannot be ignored by Christians.

in biblical and literary study have demonstrated so forcefully, is consciousness of the communities one belongs to as one reads a Bible. Reading the Bible 'as scripture' means at the very least that a reader is consciously reading a biblical text from within a religious community. It should not, however, be assumed that such a reading context excludes attention to the impact of all other reading communities. From this perspective, a contemporary reading of I Corinthians 1:10-17 will not be able to exclude consciousness of many aspects of social, ethical, economic or political division—depending upon the social location of the reader—even whilst the starting-point or focal-point of an act of reading may lie elsewhere.

To put the point differently: starting to read the first chapter of I Corinthians (and especially as Christian scripture) from the perspective of local church discussions about whether or not to buy a data-projector may seem disrespectful, or plainly trivial. But this is an example of a real issue of division. And whether or not the division can be held to relate in any identifiable sense to possible aspects of the historical circumstances in Corinth, this contemporary reading context can be interpreted in the light of the many different reading communities out of which contemporary participants approach the text.[11] Christians disagreeing about the purchase of a data-projector not only read the Corinthian correspondence as Christians reading scripture. They remain voters (which in a British context means for the Labour, Liberal Democrat, Conservative, Green or some other party). Their ethical stances are informed by many different life-experiences and choices. Their jobs—or lack of them—produce different levels of disposable income. Multiple communi-

---

[11] In other words, whether or not the economic aspects of the dispute about the purchase of a data-projector are initially made explicit, they cannot but feature somewhere in the discussion. At this point the social, economic and political 'communities' out of which the Christian readers (here, disputants) receive and read the text of I Corinthians become significant, even whilst the text is read 'as scripture'. Again, the historical work undertaken in relation to the Christian community in Corinth can be informative for the contemporary reading task, without necessarily proving determinative. Theissen's identification of the social stratification of the Corinthian community can, in short, prove useful with respect to contemporary readings whether or not it is in all respects demonstrably 'historically true'; see Gerd Theissen "Social Stratification in the Corinthian Community: A Contribution to the Sociology of Early Hellenistic Christianity" in *The Social Setting of Pauline Christianity* (Edinburgh: T. & T. Clark/Minneapolis: Fortress Press, 1982), 69-119, esp. 94-99 and 106-110.

ties to which a scripture-reader belongs, in short, make claims when the act of reading takes place.[12]

Being 'true to Paul': Reading Corinthians in a Broader Pauline Framework

I am, then, in this chapter prioritizing the reading of the (Christian) Bible as scripture, without wanting to see that task as in any way simplified by the recognition that the text functions 'as scripture'. Nor do I want to pretend that reading the text as scripture, and thus reading it in relation to a religious community, excludes the fact that readers read a text simultaneously out of the context of other (non-religious) communities. In any single act of reading, communities of reading may collide.[13] I have, however, carried forward in this chapter the insight that '..."being true to Paul"...may entail less trying to tease out who the parties 'really were' in the Corinthian church, and more a matter of being concerned, from a basis of contemporary Christian disagreement, with what Paul appears to do with such disagreements when they appear.' It is now time to address this point.

The insight contains two aspects, a historical and a contemporary theological aspect. Perhaps surprisingly, given the tenor of this chapter, the interest in 'what Paul meant' remains a leading concern. This constitutes the historical aspect of the insight brought forward. The contemporary theological aspect ultimately overrides it, but only in the sense that the point of becoming clear about what Paul may have been trying to say is to inform and shape contemporary thinking, believing and acting.[14] The theological question linking past and present, however, is undoubtedly what one is supposed to do when

---

[12] I have been greatly helped here by the work of Etienne Wenger *Communities in Practice: Learning, Meaning, and Identity* (Cambridge: Cambridge University Press, 1998), who notes that 'we belong to several communities of practice at any given time' (6) and 'can participate in multiple communities of practice at once' (105).

[13] Though they may also agree! It is inaccurate to assume that simply because different communities read the same text their readings will automatically be radically different. Different *Christian* communities clearly disagree sometimes in their understanding of biblical passages. Different communities (Christian and not) will sometimes (often?) agree in their reading of texts, biblical and not.

[14] 'The point' from the perspective of reading this text theologically, as Christian scripture. Other reading communities would, of course, have other 'points' in reading.

faced with such division. What, in such a setting, might being 'in
Christ' mean? What should such Christian unity amount to? How
much division can, or should, Christians put up with? How do
Christology and ecclesiology relate? Does, or should, one control the
other and if so, which? Attention to Paul's 'basic line' here, if it can
even be identified, may not, of course, solve the contemporary dilemma. But, as with the historical circumstances of the division in
Corinth, it may prove useful. So what does Paul actually do with
these disagreements?

Given the apparent Christocentrism of Paul's theology as a whole,
it is not difficult to conclude that he undermines these disagreements
christologically. The mocking rhetoric of 1 Cor 1:13 is both possible and powerful because of the emphasis upon Christian unity in
Christ to be found throughout Paul's letters. Difficult though it may
prove to tease out in detail the nature of Paul's corporate Christology,[15] there can be little doubt that disagreements which end up in
division amongst Christians are to be seen as countered and crushed
by the conviction of Christ's capacity to unite. Paul does not say
'whatever happens: do not divide', though the thought may well have
entered his head. The issue of actual, physical division is simply
anathema. Christians are not to do that kind of thing.[16]

At this point, we could push the contemporary case study a stage
further. A disagreement over whether or not to purchase a data-
projector is not an issue to fall out over. This is even something that
all parties may be able to acknowledge. But what of the deeper social,
economic, political or theological reasons for the disagreements? Are
they to be overcome 'in Christ'? Perhaps the case study is merely
one of many which highlight the kinds of disagreements which are
regularly likely to arise. Such a scenario could certainly be borne
out in the life-experience of most local churches.

A Contemporary Christian Reader's Challenge to Paul

Reading Paul this side of the early development of Christianity, the
Great Schism, the Reformation, the Counter-Reformation, the Thirty

---

[15] See e.g. John Ziesler *Pauline Christianity* (rev. edn.; Oxford and New York:
Oxford University Press, 1990), ch.4. esp. 63-5, for one summary amongst many.

[16] Commentators seem to be in general agreement that, even despite 1 Cor
11:18-19, the Corinthian community has not split, but may potentially do so.

Years' War, the Enlightenment, the rise of modernism, missionary
endeavours, colonial expansion, two World Wars and the emergence
of late/post-modernism, it is difficult not to be left wondering whether
Paul's advice to the Corinthians quite works today. There really are
quite a lot of Christians around, and many of them are very different from each other. We can perhaps receive Paul's words more easily
in relation to a particular Christian congregation—linking context
to context in the most obvious way, for Paul was after all speaking
to a defined, local Christian group—but the challenge remains to
see whether and how his christological trump-card can still be played.
Does Christ really still unite? If so, how does this work?

At root, such questions take us well beyond the confines of this
chapter. They invite us to reflect on what kind of Christology will
be viable today. We shall need to reflect who the 'we' are who
articulate it. More accurately, it will need to be recognized that we
shall only be able to speak of Christolog*ies*. A contemporary Christian reader's challenge to Paul, then, must consist in a questioning
of the ease to which an appeal to Christology enables Christians to
handle not just diversity, but also disagreement and division.

The challenge would press Paul for ultimately seeming to play
down the concreteness of the living conditions in Corinth and the
harsh realities of inequality even between Christians. He seems to
commend instead a spiritualized Christology within which ideas and
beliefs are in total harmony (1:10), and which runs counter to his
undoubted emphasis on embodied existence both now and in the
future resurrection (15:35-41).[17] If not a modern 'idealist', then has
not Paul nevertheless so prioritized unity of thought and belief that
he overlooks not only what the Corinthians will have to wrestle with
concretely, but also what other Christians in congregations he is
supporting (and then many other Christians down the centuries) will
have to face? It is, in short, surely harder to maintain a unity 'in
Christ' than Paul implies here. Which 'real world' does Paul think
he is living in?

---

[17] Paul is, in other words, more socially and politically conservative than his
theology suggests he should be. Such a charge is, of course, an old one, and examples are ready to hand: e.g. he did not oppose slavery, but merely assumed that
Christians had to live within it as an accepted socio-economic practice; despite his
recognition that male and female are one in Christ (Gal 3:28), he can scarcely be
regarded as an early champion of women's rights.

Paul Answers Back: A Response from Paul the Unsystematic Systematician

Guessing what Paul might say in response to a contemporary reader's challenge is an exercise in historical imagination. Christology
would always surely be central for him. But it is quite clear that not
any Christology will do. Being 'in Christ' means knowing oneself to
be part of a body of believers to whom one is committed and with
and amongst whom one works out one's salvation in 'fear and trem-
bling' (Phil 2:12). Such participation will be entered into through
baptism (1 Cor 12:13), and kept ritually alive through appropriate,
regular involvement in a shared, symbolic meal (1 Cor 11:23-6).
There is a concreteness here which cannot be denied no matter how
strong the reference to 'Christ as Spirit' in Paul's theology.

Perhaps, though, Paul's Christocentrism gives way too easily to
ecclesiocentrism at this point. In order to be concrete in his Christology, he must point to bodies of believers where Christ is present
('...you are the body of Christ...' 1 Cor 12:27). Christ now *is* the
Church. For this very reason, the division of the Church, and of local
churches, tortures the body of Christ himself. The case is compelling, but is still not the last word. For despite the concreteness and
particularity of the presence of Christ in the Church, the gospel which
it is Paul's task to preach is more important, it seems, even than
baptism (1 Cor 1:17).[18]

Paul's Christology is unfolded, of course, in a distinctly soteriological direction. It is to do with 'the cross of Christ' which usurps
the power claimed by 'eloquent wisdom' (1 Cor 1:17). The 'message about the cross' is the power of God 'to us who are being saved'
(1:18). Is Paul's Christology, then, crucicentric?; not quite. If it would
be futile to argue for a simple balance between crucifixion and resurrection in Paul's understanding of Christ, the importance of addressing both dimensions needs to be stressed nevertheless.

Paul's response to the reader's challenge, then, amounts to this:
– in handling Christian disagreement, even division, Christ sum-
   mons us nevertheless to unity;
– such unity overrides our divisions;

---

[18] Paul may, of course, simply mean that, evangelism is more important in his
own ministry. In addition, it can be argued that evangelism and the fostering of
baptisms changed in their relationship as Christianity expanded. Paul's view here
is thus limited to the earliest phase of Christianity.

- such unity has to be 'lived', at the very least in ritual enactment;
- 'church' is constituted by such enactment;
- despite the evident significance of 'church', church is transcended by 'gospel'.

Admittedly, if we can say that 'gospel' transcends 'church' for Paul, then we are faced again with the prospect of a wholly spiritualized Christology: the folly of the cross does not simply create churches, it cuts through and beyond them in the light of an apparently deeper wisdom.

The Question whether 'being true to Paul' Matters

Why, though, should it matter whether or not contemporary readers are 'true to Paul' when reading his letters? In one sense, of course, it doesn't matter. Or, more accurately, what 'being true to Paul' means will differ in accordance with the interests of readers. A historian's desire to be 'true to Paul' will issue in the attempt not simply to clarify as far as possible 'what Paul meant' but also what the circumstances were in which and for whom he wrote. A Christian believer or Christian theologian's aspiration to be 'true to Paul' may include a historical interest. But it will go beyond this—within a working construal of the use of the Bible as scripture—to include a judgment as to how normative Paul's theology can and should be for contemporary Christianity.

The point of this chapter has been to explore the insight that 'being true to Paul' in relation to 1 Cor 1:10-17 cannot, though, be best achieved via mere historical criticism. The historian's interest may be satisfied by such an approach, but Paul and his text ask for more to be done with it than the historian requires. The text itself requires a theological reading, and invites the theological engagement of the reader/hearer. Paul himself demands that his words be read theologically. Theological interest is, in other words, not only created by the fact of reading the text in a church as scripture, even if an ecclesial context for reading frames the theological act of reading in a particular way i.e. by suggesting that a text be read within a distinct theological tradition. This chapter illustrates, then, the now widely-recognized insight that neither authorial intention nor text, neither past nor present context in itself supplies an answer to the question 'what does the text mean?'

We can, in fact, go further. The christological unity which Paul asserts in response to the emerging factionalism in Corinth needs to be grasped in some way in the present. But what does it actually amount to? Here, the tension which is apparent in Paul's own thinking becomes creative. The concreteness of the division in Corinth and any present Christian context stands in tension with the asserted unity in Christ. Christ is even caught up in the factionalism ('I belong to Christ'). Paul's appeal to unity in Christ will of necessity be repeated by any later Christian group. And it will be Christ, rather than Christology, who will be held in such contexts to unite. But Christians have to live with diverse christologies (and ecclesiologies, and pneumatologies, and more), even if their diversity will not, cannot, be limitless. How, then, does Christ unite? How, then, do Paul's words carry meaning and power?

They do so, I suggest, precisely because of the tension evident in Paul's own thought and practice between the concreteness of the division and the assertion of unity in Christ. God, it may be concluded, may not need division in order to be God, but God may well need difference. The contemporary case-study was used as more than a 'way in' to 1 Cor 1:10-17, for, in truth, it is the decision about the data-projector which has to be made, and the divisive undercurrent which is prominent so often in the life of the local church. But it highlighted the fact that no one group was wholly right, and no one group was wholly wrong. In such a context, Paul's christological undermining of Christian division makes a telling point. But it fails to help the groups in the present reach their decision, or deal with their differences. Concreteness has lost out. Perhaps Paul's insight has to be received differently from the way he intended. Christ is central: yes. Christ unites: yes. But Christ can only be known in the thick of tough, seemingly trivial, discussions about data-projectors. Christ can only be known in relation to decisions about how church communities are to be structured, to views about how 'church' relates to 'world', or to whether the poor matter in society. Paul knows all of this—hence his concern for very concrete issues in the Corinthian community. But he has perhaps left his assertion of unity in Christ, announced in the opening formalities of his letter, more abstract than is helpful.

'Being true to Paul', then, ultimately means respecting the fact that God is the God of the 'in-between': between people, between factions, between author, text, past context, present context and reader. Christ is not divided (1 Cor 1:13). But Christ is always being divided (1 Cor 1:12). And it will presumably always be thus. It is, however, not merely human fallenness which brings this about. Diversity is the consequence of the self-expenditure of God: God has ('foolishly', we might say in the spirit of 1 Cor 1:18) so immersed Godself in the created order, that God chooses only to be known through the fragile, rich mix which is creation. Division is not the same as diversity. Paul is perhaps prone to play down the latter (1 Cor 1:10) because of understandable fear of the former.

1 Cor 1:10-17 in the Real World

1 Cor 1:10-17 is read and studied as Christian scripture around the world in many settings: around kitchen-tables, in church meeting-rooms, in open fields, under the shade of trees. The case study I have used to examine the reception of the text comes from the context of the wealthy North West of the world. It is a limited example. But it has served a useful purpose. In considering the interplay between a historical-critical approach and the *de facto* reception of the text by Christian readers, a number of things have become clear.

First, we are reminded that in both past and present Christian division runs deep, whilst often seeming trivial. In relation to Paul's own context, we simply have no hard evidence for the precise cause and nature of the factions in Corinth. Contemporary reception of the text teaches us that factions emerge over issues which may only be small, and create problems which are easily solved. Equally, small issues may disclose major theological clefts within a community. Theological conviction is clearly entangled with the most mundane of matters.[19]

Second, a conversation with Paul suggests that the Apostle may well be too prone to play down the inevitable concreteness of the divisions that take shape. His theological viz. christological drivenness does lead him to rush to assert the nature and significance of christological unity rather swiftly.

Third, Christian readers belong to multiple communities. If Christian readers may not be uniform, even whilst forming some kind of community, they are also not isolated, however much Christians are

---

[19] But, significantly, theology need not be held to be reducible to sociological factors.

also prone at times to ghettoize themselves in their Christianity. It is precisely the social aspect of reading, from the perspective of belonging to multiple communities and as an expression of the social dimension of what it means to be human, which sharpens the tension which the reading of this text in the context of a real Christian community exposes.

What, then, in conclusion does this text do to and for you if you read it as Christian scripture, in the company of others?

Participants who are willing to bring their experience with them and actually put it to use in the reading of such a text will gain much. Their experience cannot wholly control either the text or any community's use of it. But nor can any community's use (even the community of historians or biblical scholars) inevitably shape the use people make of their life-experience. Reading 1 Cor 1:10-17 could, of course, be used to justify all manner of divisions ('we're only like the Christians in Corinth' '1 Cor 12 is something to be aimed for; it's not the way the world is'). It must also nag Christians to critique their divisions. At its best, though, it seems to me, an historically-informed, experientially-led communal reading of 1 Cor 1:10-17 as Christian scripture invites Bible readers to press on to a more viable sense of what being 'in Christ' means than many of the senses often offered in Christian contexts. In the space between evident division and claimed christological unity, and in the knowledge that every reader of the Corinthian correspondence stands in multiple communities, is the invitation to consider what 'living in Christ' amounts to. It is a social, socio-psychological, ethical and political, as well as religious or theological, challenge to determine what is meant. Such a challenge becomes a good indicator of what Bible-reading, at its best, can achieve.

BOOLEAN LOGIC IN THE CORINTHIAN CORRESPONDENCE

Julie Renshaw

There are three basic conditions in Boolean Logic, namely: AND, OR, NOT (inversion).[1]

1) AND.　　This is a condition whereby two or more events have to be correct for the truth to be known. The logic symbol for this is:

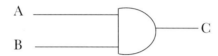

Both conditions A *and* B have to be true, for C to be true.

An example of where Paul uses this kind of argument is in Rom 1:2-4. Paul argues that Jesus is the means of salvation, by being human in the line of David *AND* through the power of the Holy Spirit he was also the Son of God. Both these things are true at the same time, so comparing this with the function of an AND gate: If Jesus was human alone, he would not have had the power of God to effect the Resurrection. If Jesus was God alone, he could not (on a human level) bear the sins of humankind as a means of atonement. Jesus had to be fully human AND the Son of God at the same time for this righteous act of salvation to occur.

2) OR.　　This condition is true when one OR another event is correct.

　　a)　An *inclusive OR* condition can have one event *OR* another

---

[1] R.J. Simpson & T.J. Terrell, *Introduction to 6800/6802 Microprocessor Systems*. (Sevenoaks: Butterworth, 1982), 16-17. D.C. Green, *Electronics, TEC Level II*. (London: Pitman Education Limited, 1982), 118.

event true individually or at the same time. The logic symbol for an inclusive OR condition is:

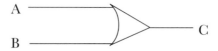

Either A or B or A and B together must be good for C to be true.

Paul uses an argument like this in 1 Corinthians 12. Here Paul describes the various kinds of spiritual gifts which are assigned to Christian believers. God bestows all believers with the Holy Spirit during their conversion and initiation into the Christian faith, and spiritual gifts are a part of this process. Some believers may prophesy or heal or speak in tongues, but each has the same spirit. Some Christians may even have more than one gift at the same time but all spiritual gifts are part of the Christian experience. So the OR function is demonstrated here when one believer has one gift OR another, AND possibly more than one, but the Holy Spirit remains constant. Therefore there is an inclusivity in this condition, which is lacking in the exclusive OR gate considered next.

b)   In an *exclusive OR* gate it is one or another event, but not both at the same time, for the condition to be effective. The logic symbol for an exclusive OR gate is:

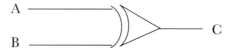

A or B must be true for C to be good, but not both A and B at the same time.

Paul uses a similar argument whilst defending his position as a Christian believer to the Corinthians (2 Cor 11:16-33). Paul is accused of being insane (v. 23) but he points out that he has suffered a great deal during his missionary journeys and all for the sake of preaching the gospel of Jesus Christ. Paul lists a number of occasions where he has been near to death, been imprisoned, whipped, stoned and shipwrecked, amongst many other hardships and misfortunes. Now from a logical point of view, either Paul *is* mad *OR* he genuinely believes in his cause so much that he will endure absolutely anything to put his message across. The conclusion in this case is that Paul is one of the most diligent and hard working of all the apostles in preaching his faith but he is not mad. Yet the point is still being made that he is either insane, *or* so motivated by his love for the Lord Jesus that he is prepared to risk his life to preach about him, but not both those things at the same time! Madness and faith appear to be mutually exclusive.

3) NOT.   This condition gives the exact opposite or inverse of what one might expect in a given situation. The logic symbol for an inverter (NOT gate) is:

B is always the exact opposite of A.

The events surrounding the conversion of Paul create a 'NOT' situation. Paul was previously known as Saul of Tarsus who, as a Jew, persecuted the Christians of the early church (Acts 7:54-59). Then came Saul's miraculous conversion (Acts 9:1-19a), after which he began preaching the Christian faith (Acts 9:19b,20).

   This complete change around in Saul's life, from persecuting Christians to preaching their faith, must have been quite astonishing for onlookers and understandably perplexing for those who witnessed it (Acts 9:21,22). In fact it would have been the opposite behaviour to what they were expecting and thus have created a situation representing the NOT condition.

Logic in the Pauline Epistles

It is appropriate now to consider how logic is specifically used within the Pauline Epistles. Examples of the three main conditions of Boolean Logic, namely AND, OR, NOT, will be considered separately.

1) AND Condition

a) *Christ as Mediator (1 Cor 1:30)*

Paul in 1 Cor 1:17-31 has been contrasting human wisdom with divine wisdom. Christian believers, according to Paul, have the benefit of Christ mediating between themselves and God:

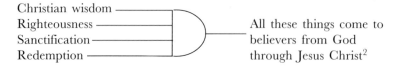

Christian wisdom
Righteousness
Sanctification
Redemption

All these things come to believers from God through Jesus Christ[2]

b) *God's Mystery (1 Cor 2:10)*

The mysteries of God are:

Unseen
Unheard
Unthought

The Spirit reveals the truths about God[3]

c) *Paul's Success as a Missionary, Proves his Apostleship (1 Cor 9:1ff.)*

An example of Paul's use of diatribe as a rhetorical device can be found in 1 Cor 9:1ff., and may be represented by an AND gate which combines a series of rhetorical questions:

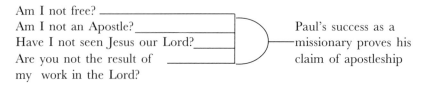

Am I not free?
Am I not an Apostle?
Have I not seen Jesus our Lord?
Are you not the result of
my work in the Lord?

Paul's success as a missionary proves his claim of apostleship

Here Paul is giving the Corinthians evidence of his apostleship, that is a commission from the risen Jesus and his manifest success as an evangelist.[4]

---

[2] C.K. Barrett, *A Commentary on the First Epistle to the Corinthians.* (London: A. & C. Black, 1968), 59-60.
[3] Ibid., 74.

d) *Resurrection (1 Cor 15:20)*

The AND condition is where two or more conditions work together to give a result. For example, it follows that if Christ has been raised from the dead, then his believers are also raised (1 Cor 15:20). So resurrection is not just for Jesus, but for believing Christians also.

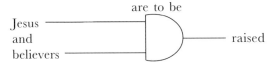

Logic is an important element within Paul's rhetoric and it is obviously one of the stylistic devices which Paul employs to persuade his audience. In 1 Cor 15:1-58, for example, the power and logic of Paul's argument would have been enhanced by the fact that his hearers were used to the Graeco - Roman rhetoric of their culture.[5] Boolean is a form of conditional logic, because all of its outcomes are dependent upon certain initial conditions being satisfied to reach a conclusion.

e) *Forgiveness of Sinners (2 Cor 2:6-11)*

If a member of the church sins and repents then the members are exhorted to forgive and comfort him so that he may not be overwhelmed by grief and remorse. Paul mentions that to be unforgiving may result in "Satan taking advantage" and claiming Christian believers for his own.[6]

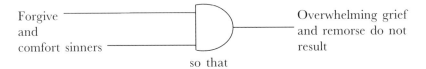

---

[4] Ibid., 200 ff. See also G. D. Fee, *The First Epistle to the Corinthians.* (Grand Rapids. Eerdmans, 1987), 392f.

[5] J.L. Bailey, & L.D.V. Broek, *Literary Forms in the New Testament.* (London: SPCK, 1992), 36. Paul's logic in 1 Cor 15:12-34 is also dealt with in G. Fee., *The First Letter to the Corinthians*, 737-8.

[6] C.K. Barrett, *A Commentary on the Second Epistle to the Corinthians.* (London: A. & C. Black, 1973), 91ff.

f) *Light to the World (2 Cor 4:6)*

Paul sees his ministry as the means of bringing light to the world. The light which illuminates the world in a spiritual sense is knowledge. The knowledge of the glory of God includes his saving acts as well as his majesty, and this can be seen in the person (or face) of Christ. As the image of God, Christ is the location where God himself, the invisible, can be known.[7]

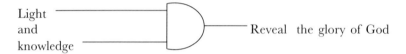

Light
and   Reveal the glory of God
knowledge

g) *Paul's Life as an Apostle (2 Cor 11:16-33).*[8]

Paul considered that it was by the grace of God that he was able to serve God so effectively. 2 Cor 11:16 - 33 gives a picture of Paul's life and how he understood his apostolic vocation in terms of pioneer missionary work.[9] Paul has:

Worked harder
Been imprisoned frequently
Been flogged severely   Paul's apostolic
Been exposed to death   mission continued
Been beaten with rods 3X   despite all these
Been stoned   threats to his life
Been shipwrecked 3X

There were many dangers that Paul encountered on his Christian missionary journeys such as:

---

[7] Ibid., 135.

[8] cf. Gal 1:15,16,17.

Paul did not mix with other men   Therefore his revelation came from
AND   God. (With the consequence that
He did not consult with the   he could preach to the Gentiles).
other apostles in Jerusalem.

[9] There are similarities in this passage with Cynic-Stoic diatribe, cf. C.K. Barrett, *A Commentary on the Second Epistle to the Corinthians*, 295ff.

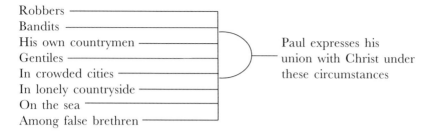

Robbers
Bandits
His own countrymen
Gentiles
In crowded cities
In lonely countryside
On the sea
Among false brethren
— Paul expresses his
union with Christ under
these circumstances

Paul has endured all these things so that the Gospel of Jesus Christ could be preached.

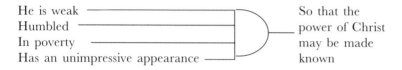

He is weak
Humbled
In poverty
Has an unimpressive appearance
— So that the
power of Christ
may be made
known

h) *Eschatology (1 Thess 1:10)*[10]

The Thessalonians had a real expectation of the imminent Parousia and expected the return of Jesus in their lifetime. The behaviour of some of the Thessalonians was less than honourable from a Christian point of view. So Paul later in the epistle encourages them to see that at the Coming of Jesus, his people would be expected to be blameless, holy (3:15; 5:23), sober, and filled with faith, love and hope (5:8f.). Waiting for the Parousia meant that Christians should seek to manifest these qualities, although their attainment of them might also be attributed to the power of God working in their lives. Therefore the Coming of Jesus was an incentive for moral behaviour, not inaction and laziness.

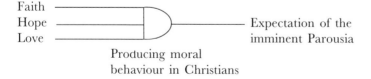

Faith
Hope
Love
— Expectation of the
imminent Parousia

Producing moral
behaviour in Christians

---

[10] I.H. Marshall, *1 and 2 Thessalonians.* (Grand Rapids: Eerdmans, 1983), 58.

i) *The Armour of Christ (1 Thess 5:8)*

Paul likens Christian behaviour to soldiers in that they need the
appropriate Spiritual armour for the battle in which they are engaged, namely the battle with evil. Vigilance concerning the Parousia
is not dissimilar to a soldier on guard—duty. So Christians ought
to put on the armour of Christ:-

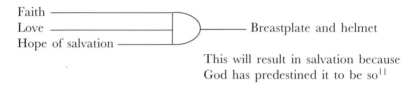

Faith
Love ———————————— Breastplate and helmet
Hope of salvation

This will result in salvation because
God has predestined it to be so[11]

Other Pauline examples of the AND condition such as Gal 4:21-
31; 5:1-12 can be found in Appendix 1.

2) *OR Condition*

This is the condition where one or another of opposing extremes is
true. For example, you either believe in Jesus *or* not; you have faith
in God *or* not; the Holy Spirit is working in your life *or* not. These
examples are exclusive OR conditions because both cannot be true
at the same time. The inclusive OR condition allows for situations
where two or more conditions can be true at the same time, but also
true individually, that is one *or* the other.

Inclusive OR Conditions.

Church Discipline (1 Cor 5:6-13).
In the Corinthian church there appears to be a problem with discipline amongst the members, especially with regard to sexual immorality. Paul compares this situation with the analogy of bread. A
small quantity of yeast is sufficient to impregnate a whole lump of
dough and one corrupt member is sufficient to corrupt the whole
church. The church should therefore exercise discipline in order to
maintain its purity. In other words the Corinthians should avoid
contact with those who have called themselves Christians but whose
behaviour suggests otherwise.[12] For example:

---

[11] I.H. Marshall, *1 and 2 Thessalonians.* (Grand Rapids: Eerdmans, 1983),138-9.
[12] C.K. Barrett, *A Commentary on the First Epistle to the Corinthians*, 127-131.

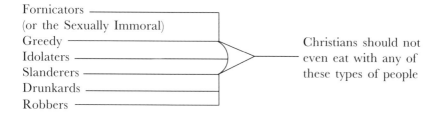

Fornicators
(or the Sexually Immoral)
Greedy
Idolaters
Slanderers   Christians should not
Drunkards   even eat with any of
Robbers   these types of people

Other examples of the inclusive OR condition can be seen in Galatians 2:9[13] and also in Rom 6:1-23; Col 3:18 - 4:1.

Exclusive OR Conditions

A Christian's Response to God is Exclusive (2 Cor 6:14-7:4).
Paul encourages the Corinthians to consider their holiness of life in the fear of God. Paul urges them not to be yoked with unbelievers, and then makes a series of exclusive statements. It follows that if a person is in one state, then he or she cannot be in the other; the conditions are mutually opposite and exclusive to one another.[14]

Free association outside the church is permitted because God judges those outside the Christian community. Conversely, strict discipline within the church is necessary to show to the world a distinctive Christian character. G. Fee, *The First Epistle to the Corinthians*, 194-228.

[13] *Paul's Christian Mission (Gal 2:9).*
Paul's mission to convert people to the Christian faith is an inclusive OR situation. It does not matter if Jewish converts have already been circumcised, nor does it matter if the Gentiles have not been circumcised. Their faith is equally acceptable to God. *Both* groups individually *or* collectively at the same time can have access to God's salvation. (H.D. Betz, *Galatians*, 100).

    Mission to the Jews
    (presupposing circumcision)
                                             Are equally valid
    Mission to the Gentiles   conditions before God
    (presupposing uncircumcision)

[14] C.K. Barrett, *A Commentary on the Second Epistle to the Corinthians*, 192f.

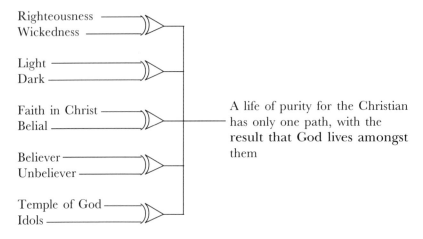

Obviously the opposite or negative states of being have nothing in common with Christians. Paul urges purity of life for Christians because the presence of God requires this as a necessity of self-edification.[15]

Also see Galatians 2:5 for another example of an exclusive OR condition in use by Paul.[16]

3) NOT Condition

In the 1950's Ernst Käsemann wrote an article[17] in which he defined the structure and function of the two-part form found in the New Testament, for example 1 Cor 3:7 "If anyone destroys God's

---

[15] Ibid, 200.

[16] In the Galatian Church there were a number of opponents to Paul's "law-free" gospel. These "false brothers" denied that the Gentile Christians were saved solely by God's grace. Paul's response was that salvation through Christ was not achieved by submission to the "circumcision/law gospel" of the Jewish Christian faction centred in Jerusalem, but by God's grace alone. (H.D. Betz, *Galatians*, 90-6.) Obviously these opposing views are mutually exclusive. Either salvation is by God's grace alone *or* has other prerequisites such as circumcision.

Gospel of circumcision ⎯⎯⎯⎯⎯⟩⟩⎯⎯ Which is true to the Christian
Gospel of uncircumcision ⎯⎯⎯⟩⟩⎯ Gospel?

The Jerusalem Council had to decide the issue of whether circumcision was a necessary part of salvation or not. Both options could not be true together and at the same time. Either a gentile *is* circumcised as a prerequisite condition of his faith *or* he is not to be circumcised as it is not necessary. A person can not be in both states at the same time; it is a mutually exclusive situation.

[17] E. Käsemann, *New Testament Questions of Today*. (London: SCM, 1969), 66.

temple, God will destroy that person." Käsemann proposed that these pronouncements had well-defined features, that is, a conditional logic that reflects an understanding of retributive justice.

Despite criticism of Käsemann's observation (for example, Aune defines this as a two-part statement dealing with men's activity and God's response)[18] Kasemann's definition is useful in identifying types of conditional logic in Pauline literature.

a) *Gospel as Foolishness or Salvation (1 Cor 1:18,19)*

The Gospel is foolishness to those on the way to destruction 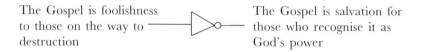 The Gospel is salvation for those who recognise it as God's power

From a sensible point of view it is absurd to find the truth about God in the crucifixion. Wisdom might suggest otherwise. 1 Cor 1:19, turns reason on its head: "I will destroy the wisdom of the wise, the intelligence of the intelligent I will frustrate." Fee argues that this point is crucial to the whole letter. Human dependence on wisdom and devices has ended. The Gospel stands in divine antithesis to such things.[19]

Human wisdom and intelligence 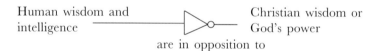 Christian wisdom or God's power
are in opposition to

b) *Contrast of Natural Man with Spiritual Man (1 Cor 2:14)*

In this verse Paul contrasts natural man with spiritual man. Natural man has not received the spirit of God and therefore cannot comprehend spiritual truths. Spiritual man has received the spirit of God, which is the spirit of Christ crucified.

---

[18] D. Aune in J.L. Bailey, & L.D.V. Broek, *Literary Forms in the New Testament.* (London: SPCK, 1992), 58.

[19] G.D. Fee, *The First Epistle to the Corinthian,* 66-9.

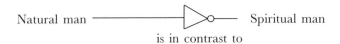

Natural man ————————————▷∘—— Spiritual man

is in contrast to

c) *The New and the Old Covenant (2 Cor 3:3-14)*

The Corinthians were ministers of the new covenant converted by
the Spirit of the living God. The old covenant was represented by
the Law and written on tablets of stone. But the Gospel which stands
over and against the Law is written in men's hearts through the
Spirit.[20]

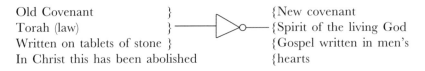

Old Covenant	}		{New covenant
Torah (law)	} ————▷∘———		{Spirit of the living God
Written on tablets of stone	}		{Gospel written in men's
In Christ this has been abolished			{hearts

d) *The Work of Satan (2 Cor 11:13-15)*

Paul's response to the false apostles in Corinth was to point out that
their deception and disguise were the work of Satan. Paul may also
have been thinking about the deception of Eve, where Satan was
disguised as an angel of light. Paul regarded the opposition of his
work to be of Satanic origin, in direct opposition to God.[21]

Work of Satan ————————————▷∘—————— God's work

in direct opposition to

The existence of Satan opposing God's work is also an issue in 1
Thessalonians 2:18;3:5. It was common New Testament teaching that
leading a Christian life would inevitably involve suffering and per-
secution (cf. Matt 5:11f.; Acts 9:16; 1Cor 4:12; 2 Cor 4:9). This
situation is the opposite of what one might expect. Being a Christian does not guarantee an easy passage to eternal life. Quite the
opposite. Paul's theology expresses the view that Satan will frustrate
the plans of those aspiring to lead a Christian life.

---

[20] C.K. Barrett, *A Commentary on the Second Epistle to the Corinthians*, 108-9.
    See also J.D.G. Dunn, *The Theology of Paul the Apostle.* (Edinburgh: T. & T.
Clark, 1998), 147-148.
    [21] C.K. Barrett, *A Commentary on the Second Epistle to the Corinthians*, 286.

e) *Paul's weakness/Power of Christ (2 Cor 12:10)*

Paul contrasts weakness by human standards with the inner strength he gains from the power of Christ which rests within him. So when Paul is persecuted and is in anguish and distress, he endures his sufferings on behalf of Christ because the power of Christ gives him inner strength.[22]

Weakness by human   Strength in the power of
standards   Christ

f) *Diatribe*

Graeco—Roman diatribe was used orally in public preaching by Cynic and Stoic philosophers, but also appeared in written form in the New Testament letters (for example Rom 1-11; 1 Cor 15:29-41). The dialogical style of diatribe makes frequent use of imaginary opponents, hypothetical objections and false conclusions. The questions and objections of the imaginary opponent are answered with a response of censure and persuasion. The diatribe style is a teaching style that he used in dealing with issues relating to the churches he wrote to and preached to. This style appears especially in Romans and occasionally in 1 Corinthians and Galatians and is also in James.[23] This drawing to a false conclusion can easily be reflected by the Boolean logic condition 'NOT', where the opposite of what you would expect is true. For example Romans 3:3-4 asks the question "What if some did not have faith? Will their lack of faith nullify God's faithfulness? Not at all!"

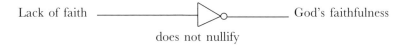

Lack of faith   God's faithfulness

does not nullify

Further examples of the NOT Condition may be found in Rom 5:12-21; 8:1-17; Gal 1:1; 1:6-10; 1:23;6:14; 1 Thess 3:8.

---

[22] Ibid, 317.
[23] D.E. Aune, *The New Testament in its Literarary Environment*. (Cambridge: James Clarke, 1988), 200-201.

Conclusion

As we can see from the examples laid out in this study, it does seem possible to make connections between Boolean Logic and the Pauline theological arguments found in his epistles. Consideration here has concentrated on the Corinthian Epistles but many particular examples can also be found in the other Pauline letters. Undoubtedly Paul was influenced by his Jewish Pharisaical upbringing in a Hellenistic environment. This not only meant that Paul was extremely familiar with the Jewish Scriptures, which he used and freely quoted in his writings and preaching, but he also used argumentation, logic and rhetoric equally well. These skills which are to be found in the culture of the Graeco–Roman world in which he belonged were deployed by Paul in order to convert his listeners to Christianity and to strengthen their faith. Given that the Cross was such an unlikely means of salvation, Paul probably needed all the powers of persuasion available.

APPENDIX 1

FURTHER EXAMPLES OF THE AND CONDITION

a) *Unity (Rom 15:1-6)*

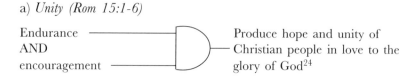

Endurance
AND
encouragement

Produce hope and unity of Christian people in love to the glory of God[24]

b) *Allegorical Interpretation of Scripture (and Typology) Gal 4:21-31*

An example of Paul's use of an allegorical interpretation of Scripture (and typology) can be found in Galatians 4:21-31. The Gentile Christians are the offspring of Abraham's free-born first wife Sarah, rather than the slave wife Hager.[25] Stylistically Paul uses this passage like a Hellenistic diatribe where one part of the letter is assumed to be a dialogue with another, in order to get a point across to Paul's audience.[26]

---

[24] C.K. Barrett, *The Epistle to the Romans.* (London: A. & C. Black, 1991), 247-8.

[25] H.D. Betz, *Galatians.* (Philadelphia: Fortress Press, 1979), 238.

[26] Ibid., 241. Paul contrasts the epochs of before and after Christ here, with

Summary of associations with Hagar are:

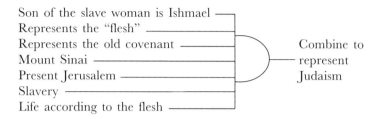

Son of the slave woman is Ishmael
Represents the "flesh"
Represents the old covenant   Combine to
Mount Sinai   represent
Present Jerusalem   Judaism
Slavery
Life according to the flesh

In contrast, the associations with Sarah are:

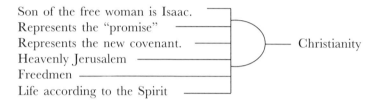

Son of the free woman is Isaac.
Represents the "promise"
Represents the new covenant.   Christianity
Heavenly Jerusalem
Freedmen
Life according to the Spirit

c) *The Jewish Torah (Gal 5:1-12)*

Galatians 5:1-12 has a series of ethical exhortations which warn against the acceptance of the Jewish Torah. Man's freedom was lost when Adam transgressed and sin was introduced into the world. Since Adam, humankind has been living in a state of imprisonment through the power of sin, that is, in a state of deprivation of freedom. Paul describes the human situation outside what Christ did for us as one of slavery by the evil elements dominating the world. The freedom granted to Christians based on God's redemption in Christ is an experience enabled by the gift of the Spirit.[27]

Promise and Law representing the two covenants. J.D.G. Dunn, *The Theology of Paul the Apostle*, 146.

[27] H.D. Betz, *Galatians*, 253-6.

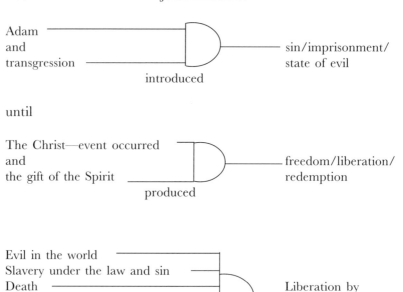

until

Christians participate in Christ's redemptive act of liberation:-

d) *Christian Life (1 Thess 1:3)*

The outward and visible signs that someone has been converted are work, labour and steadfastness. These are the three basic characteristics of Christian life inspired by the spiritual reality of a conversion.[28]

---

[28] I.H. Marshall, *1 and 2 Thessalonians*, 50ff.

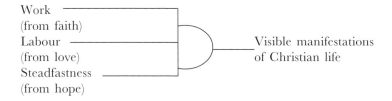

e) *Encouragement (1 Thess 5:12 - 24)*

1Thessalonians ends with general encouragements from Paul to the Thessalonians about life within the church.[29]

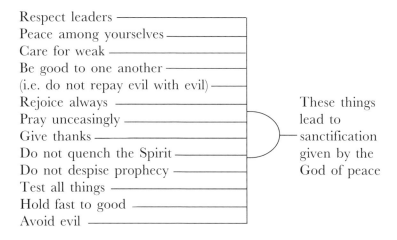

---

[29] I.H. Marshall, *1 and 2 Thessalonians*, 1154ff. See also J.D.G. Dunn, *The Theology of Paul the Apostle*, 585.

PART THREE

THEOLOGY IN THE LETTERS

1 CORINTHIANS 7:1-7 REVISITED

Gordon D. Fee

When the New International Version first appeared in 1978 I was stunned to find that in 1 Corinthians 7:1 the translators had glossed the euphemism "not to touch a woman" as "It is good for a man not to marry." When this was singled out by one reviewer[1] as a good change from the traditional, more literal rendering, I wrote to the committee urging that they change the NIV to something that more closely resembled the consistent meaning of this idiom in Greek antiquity: "not to have sexual relations with a woman." When the committee responded negatively, despite the data, I chose to go public and point out how singular without lexical support this translation was.[2] This was followed up by a full rehearsal of the data and the place of this verse in its context in my commentary in the *New International Commentary on the New Testament*.[3]

With the appearance of many new or updated English translations[4] and of several new commentaries[5] in the last decade of the

---

[1] L. Ryken, *Christianity Today* 23 (October 20, 1978), 16-17 [76-77].

[2] "1 Corinthians 7:1 in the *NIV*," *JETS* 23 (1980), 307-14; reprinted in G.D. Fee, *To What End Exegesis?* (Grand Rapids, Mich.: Eerdmans, 2000), 88-98. It should be pointed out that this rendering had appeared earlier in such translations as the *Twentieth Century* (1898), *Weymouth* (1903), *Goodspeed* (1923), *Williams* (1937), *Amplified* (1958), *Living Bible* (1962), *TEV* (1966). It should also be noted that in the 1984 edition of the NIV, the translation "not to have sexual relations with a woman" appeared in a footnote. This translation now appears in the text of the TNIV (2002) without a note.

[3] *The First Epistle to the Corinthians* (Grand Rapids, Mich.: Eerdmans, 1987), 271-286. Since this commentary was based on the *NIV*, I sought for and received permission to make some changes to the *NIV* in the actual lemmata of the commentary. Thus the passage was altered to "It is good for a man not to *have relations with a woman*," a change that now appears in the *TNIV*, but with the addition of "sexual" before "relations," and thus a total removal of the euphemism.

[4] See e.g., *REB* ("to have intercourse with a woman"); *The NET Bible* ("to touch a woman sexually"), *TNIV*, *ESV* ("to have sexual relations with a woman"); *The Message* ("Is it a good thing to have sexual relations?"); curiously the NRSV chose to stay with the Greek idiom.

[5] E.g., G.F. Snyder, *First Corinthians: A Faith Community Commentary* (Macon, GA: Mercer University Press, 1992); C. Blomberg, *The NIV Application Commentary: 1 Corinthians* (Grand Rapids: Zondervan, 1994); W. Schrage, *Der erste Brief an die Korinther* (EKKNT 2; Neukirchen-Vluyn: Neukirchener Verlag, 1995); B. Witherington, *Conflict*

previous century, it seemed as if the meaning of the Greek idiom
had finally won the day. It was therefore a matter of moderate
surprise a few years back to read C.C. Caragounis's contribution to
The Corinthian Correspondence,[6] where he has taken some exception to
this apparent ground swell and has offered a vigorous defense of the
more traditional position, but with some new twists regarding the
meaning of πορνεία in verse 2 and συγγνώμη in verse 6.[7] Since I
am equally as anxious about a new "consensus"[8] as I am about earlier
ones, I am glad for the opportunity to take a Berean stance toward
this matter ("to see whether these things are so") and to offer this
reevaluation of the data in honor of Margaret Thrall, one of the keen
interpreters of the Corinthian correspondence in our day.

I

Perhaps the best way to get at the issues is to walk through the structure of the paragraph (7:1-7), indicating how the argument works,
and thus also pointing out the areas of agreement and disagreement.

Verse 1 is the presenting statement, which in some way is related
to what the Corinthians have written: καλὸν ἀνθρώπῳ γυναικὸς μὴ
ἅπτεσθαι ("It is good for a man not to touch a woman"). This statement is then immediately qualified in verse 2 (by an adversative δέ),
with the contrasting statement: "However, . . . let each [man/hus-
band] have (ἐχέτω) his own wife and let each [woman/wife] have
her own husband." The reason for this qualifier comes at the be-

---

and Community in Corinth: A Socio-Rhetorical Commentary on 1 and 2 Corinthians (Grand
Rapids: Eerdmans, 1995); R.B. Hays, *First Corinthians* (Interpretation; Louisville,
KY: John Knox, 1997); R.H. Horsley, *1 Corinthians* (AbingdonNTCommentaries;
Nashville: Abingdon, 1998); R.F. Collins, *First Corinthians* (SP; Collegeville, MN:
Liturgical Press, 1999); M.L. Soards, *1 Corinthians* (NIBC; Peabody, Mass.: Hen-
drickson, 1999); A.C. Thiselton, *The First Epistle to the Corinthians* (NIGTC; Grand
Rapids: Eerdmans, 2000).

[6] This is the collection of papers read at the Leuven Conference by this title
held in 1994, edited by R. Bieringer (BEThL; Leuven: Leuven University Press,
1996); Caragounis's paper, "'Fornication' and 'Concession'? Interpreting 1 Cor
7,1-7," appears on pp. 543-59; hereinafter cited in the notes as "C."

[7] Although it must be pointed out that C.'s view is anything but "traditional"
on several other matters, as will be pointed out below.

[8] Cf. Thiselton, *First Epistle*, 498 ("an increasing consensus"); see notes 79 and
80 for a list of those who have espoused this view. This excellent commentary is
notable for the author's thorough interaction with the secondary literature on almost
all issues—much more than I intend to do here, because my focus is so singular.

ginning: διὰ τὰς πορνείας ("because of the sexual immoralities"). This qualifier is then followed up with two sentences that are intended (note the asyndeton) to elaborate on verse 2: that each husband should "pay" what he "owes" his wife, as should the wife to her husband (v. 3); and that the wife does not have "mastery/power of control" (ἐξουσιάζει) over her own body but her husband does, and likewise the husband lacks "mastery" with regard to his body, but rather his wife has it (v. 4).

Next (v. 5a) comes a prohibition with regard to (apparently) all that was said in verses 2-4, namely that in the matter of sexual relations they are not to "defraud/deprive" (μὴ ἀποστερεῖτε) one another. This in turn is followed by a concession (v. 5b) unless perhaps, on mutual agreement, they abstain for a set time; but they should then come back together again lest Satan tempt them because of lack of self-control.

This is followed (v. 6) by τοῦτο δὲ λέγω κατὰ συγγνώμην οὐ κατ' ἐπιταγήν ("now/but I say this as permission/concession, not as command"), with a final reflection (v. 7) on the concession (and probably the whole paragraph) that he could wish all men/people (ἀνθρώπους) were "as I myself also am," which in turn is followed by yet another concession to reality: "Each person has their own gift: one of one kind, another[9] of a different kind."

At issue between the "traditional" view and the present "consensus" view are four basic matters regarding some of these parts:
1. Whose point of view is expressed in verse 1b, Paul's or (some) Corinthians'? All other matters under discussion stem in some way from this one.
2. The meaning of the opening prepositional phrase in verse 2: διὰ τὰς πορνείας
3. The meaning and force of the verb ἐχέτω, which appears twice in verse 2.
4. What is the συγγνώμην ("concession/permission") in verse 6?

On these matters the "traditional" view has it:
1. The point of view is Paul's, and he is "conceding" marriage in verse 2.

---

[9] On the probability that this refers to the differing χαρίσματα, not persons, see Fee, p. 272 n. 22.

2. The reason for concession to marriage is διὰ τὰς πορνείας, which is usually interpreted as a generalized plural, referring to the alleged[10] enormity of the problem in Corinth.
3. The combination τὴν ἑαυτοῦ γυναῖκα ἐχέτω is understood to mean "take a wife" = "get married so as to have his own wife."
4. There is no unanimity in the traditional view regarding the "concession." Usually it is taken to refer to verse 2, sometimes to verses 3-4, and less often to verse 5.

Caragounis brings his own twist to the traditional view:
1. He contends for the tradition, suggesting that "to touch a woman" is a metonymy for marriage; he also offers a considerable argument against the possibility that Paul is quoting the Corinthian letter.
2. Recognizing the difficulty with the traditional view of the prepositional phrase, he argues that it is a metonymy for "lustful thoughts."
3. He argues for the traditional view of the meaning of ἐχέτω.
4. Basically he rejects altogether the meaning of "concession" for συγγνώμη, arguing instead for either "pardon" = "pardon me for intruding into your private life like this" or for "I am saying this with your permission."

It should be noted that Caragounis begins his paper with an energetic denunciation of *both* interpretations as being driven "by the assumption that the Corinthian Christians were uniquely lascivious and that this characteristic is present in Paul's mind as he pens ch. 7" (p. 544). Since he includes me in his denunciation, a few words are in order about this matter at the outset.

Although Caragounis has quite misread me on this matter (n. 10), that is not my concern here, which rather is twofold. First, in contending against this traditional view, he downplays the issue of sexual immorality in this church altogether; indeed, although not condon-

---

[10] In an unfortunate misquoting of my commentary, C. (p. 545 n 6) asserts that "Fee . . . in spite of his caution that 'This aspect of Corinthian life, however, has tended to be overplayed by most NT scholars' (p. 2), still goes on to speak of 'the prevalence of sexual immorality in Corinth . . . the enormity of this evil in Corinth' (p. 277)." But in both of these instances I was representing not my own view, but the traditional view. The full quote in the first instance, for example, reads: "Traditionally it [v. 2] has been held to be a condescension to marriage because of the prevalence of sexual immorality in Corinth." I thought my point would be clear, so here I hope to clarify by the addition of the word "alleged."

ing their sins, he asserts on this matter, "the Corinthian Christians would seem to have been very ordinary Christians, of the sort that have populated Christian Churches throughout the centuries" (p. 544). But to get there he must (a) temper the issue in chapter 5 ("a unique instance for this church") and (b) surprisingly, ignore the issue in 6:12-20 altogether.

At the same time, second, he alleges that all former interpreters, by focusing on Corinth's alleged propensity for sexual immorality, have thus come to this passage "with . . . a pre-understanding . . . which is prejudicial to the Corinthians, and thus a hindrance to a correct understanding" (p. 545). Furthermore, such interpreters are also at fault for interpreting chapter 7 in light of chapters 5 and 6, since beginning with 7:1 Paul is now done with those matters (p. 545). But Caragounis's own deliberate softening of this dimension of a clear "problem" in this church seems just as prejudicial. No one can claim a lack of "pre-understanding" when coming to this text; but the way forward from an extreme position is not to assume another extreme. Caragounis's deliberate toning down of sexual misconduct in this church is to deny the vigorous rhetoric with which Paul takes on Corinthian misconduct in both 5:1-13 and 6:12-20. The life of the church is at stake on these matters, even if they are not the by-product of the well-known "gross immorality" of the earlier Greek city.[11] Roman Corinth, after all, was one of the wealthiest cities in the empire, and one of the busiest "port" cities on the Mediterranean.[12] This combination makes sexual immorality—from a Jewish or Christian point of view, of course—much more accessible,[13] including a generous amount of prostitution, than one would find, for example, in a "backwater" city like Philippi. The importance of this matter will emerge when we reconsider the meaning of verse 2 below.

---

[11] That is, as pointed out in my commentary (pp. 2-3) this common assessment was based mostly on data from the Greek city, which was destroyed by the Romans in 146 B.C.E.; the city to which Paul came ca. 50 C.E. and to which he wrote this letter was founded by Julius Caesar as a Roman colony in 44 B.C.E..

[12] Not because it was an actual port city itself, but because as Strabo remarked (*Geog.* 8.6.23), it held the "keys" to so much commerce: all overland commerce north and south, and, through its eastern and western ports (Lechaion and Cenchrae), much shipping commerce east and west.

[13] So also with Thessalonica further north; sexual immorality is the first behavioral issue taken up in 1 Thessalonians (4:1-8).

II

In embracing the traditional view of verse 1, Caragounis makes two points. First, he contends vigorously against the view that "it is good[14] for a man not to touch a woman" is anything other than Paul's own view; second, he suggests that the phrase γυναικὸς μὴ ἅπτεσθαι is best understood as a metonymy "to signify marriage" (p. 547).

1. I register a degree of confusion regarding the first point. All of Caragounis's energy has gone into one issue: whether the *grammar* of verse 1 can support the option that Paul is actually quoting their letter verbatim. It seems clear that he also believes that if this grammatical point can be proven beyond doubt, he has thereby also rung the death knell to the present "consensus" view, especially as that is represented in my commentary.[15]

But in making this point, Caragounis seems clearly to overstate the case. He has rightly called attention to the grammar that seems to be stretched just a bit if Paul is intending to cite in either a modern or ancient sense. That is, the passage has no "marks" that indicate actual quotation.[16] But at issue in calling this a "quote" from their letter is *not* whether Paul is actually "citing" them verse and line; rather at issue is whether the *content* of this clause represents Paul's own position or that of the Corinthians.

What Caragounis seems to argue is a threefold chain that goes: (a) there is no grammatical justification that Paul is citing the Corinthian letter; (b) thus "the clause constitutes Paul's own *wording*" (italics mine); (c) therefore this is Paul's perspective, not theirs. But this "logic" is suspect, since items (b) and (c) do not necessarily "follow"—and especially so since Caragounis earlier allows that "it is quite probable . . . that in their letter the Corinthians had given expression . . . to some such idea as we find expressed in vs. 1b" (pp. 545-46). At issue, finally, is not whether this is an actual quote

---

[14] He also argues (p. 546), correctly I think but not "beyond possible doubt," that καλόν in this kind of gnomic sentence should be understood to mean "better." On this cf. G.F. Snyder, "The *Tobspruch* in the New Testament," *NTS* 2 (1976), 117-20.

[15] Some caution is needed here, since one is not always sure about some of C.'s expressions, which may be due in part to an issue of second language English; but it is obviously a crucial matter for him, since he picks it up again in an additional note (p. 559) and presses for it even more strongly.

[16] In comparison with 8:1 and 4, e.g., where the combination οἴδαμεν ὅτι . . . ὅτι seems to justify quotation marks as such.

from their letter, but whether it ultimately reflects his or their sentiment (or perhaps both?). But more needs to be said about the "grammar."

Caragounis's case is predicated on all of verse 1 being a single sentence, all in Paul's wording, and therefore reflecting Paul's own perspective. This is based primarily on the lack of any verbal signal that he might be quoting them. But what Caragounis fails to show is how one can make good sense of the sentence from this perspective. What kind of syntactical relationships are involved in a sentence that reads: περὶ δὲ ὧν ἐγράψατε, καλὸν ἀνθρώπῳ γυναικὸς μὴ ἅπτεσθαι? For if one were to *diagram* this sentence grammatically, where would the opening prepositional phrase be positioned (as a modifier) in relation to the main clause (καλόν κτλ.)? The point, of course, is that the sentence *qua* sentence could be diagrammed all right (the preposition would modify the suppressed "is"), but in fact such a sentence makes no sense at all. Thus, to argue from *grammar* on this issue appears to be a dead end, since the sentence as its stands is a *non sequitur*.

In this regard a more careful look at all six occurrences[17] of this formula (7:1, 25; 8:1; 12:1; 16:1, 12) in 1 Corinthians reveals some interesting data. First, in the next five instances the object of the opening preposition has specific content ("the virgins," "food sacrificed to idols," etc.). Second, in three instances the beginning phrase modifies a first person singular verb (7:25: 12:1; 16:12); and in one instance a second person plural (16:1). In 8:1, and its resumption in 8:4, it modifies a first person plural verb; but in this case it is οἴδαμεν ὅτι, where almost everyone is agreed that Paul is indeed citing from their letter.[18] Thus its first occurrence in 7:1 differs from the others in two significant ways: (a) the object of the preposition is not case specific; rather it begins the series by referring to their letter; (b) it is followed by a nominal sentence that has all the appearance of a maxim of some sort. So the grammatical issue is ultimately a red herring. At issue is whether the maxim is Paul's own, which he will then qualify, or theirs, which he will in effect reject altogether in terms of where some of them want to go with it—and this can only be decided, it would seem to me, in conjunction with a careful look at the qualifying sentence in verse 2.

---

[17] Seven, if one were to include the repeated, slightly altered, formula in 8:4.
[18] See the discussion in this regard in Thiselton, *First Epistle*, 498-99.

204 GORDON D. FEE

2. On the second matter,[19] the idiom ἄπτεσθαι γυναικός, Caragounis agrees that it is a euphemism (p. 546); his point of contention is my claim that "the expression always 'without ambiguity . . . refers to having sexual intercourse'" (p. 547). I can be faulted for saying "without ambiguity"; if a text can be taken another way, then of course there is a degree of ambiguity. But Caragounis goes further. In a brief look at three of the eight texts, he concludes that the phrase "is not a set expression for having sexual intercourse, as Fee seems to suppose" (p. 547 n. 15). His reason for this, however, does not seem to be lexical; rather he makes these demurrals because he wants to take the phrase as a metonymy for marriage—a view that presents its own set of problems. The best way to engage this conversation is to list again—and comment on—each of the texts (in roughly chronological order):

1. Plato *Leges* 8.840a: "During all the period of his training (as the story goes) he never touched a woman (γυναικὸς ἥψατο), nor yet a boy." (LCL 11.162-63)

> [This first known appearance of the phrase is an obvious euphemism for sexual relations.]

2. Aristotle *Politica* 7.14.12: "As to intercourse with another woman or man, in general it must be dishonourable (μὴ κάλον) to be known as ἁπτόμενον ("touching" = "participating in sexual relations) in it as long as one is a husband.

> [Granted that the corresponding genitive does not occur, but this use of the verb is clear.]

3. Gen 20:6 LXX (of Abimelech with Sarah): "That is why I did not let you touch her (ἄπτασθαι αὐτῆς).

> [The context indicates that we dealing with sexual relations, as Josephus (#7 below) makes clear by his paraphrase.]

---

[19] There is actually a third as well; but it seems to be something of an irrelevancy. C. argues (p. 547) that had this been a Corinthian slogan that Paul is citing, and had it to do with abstention from sexual relations within *marriage*, then they would have used the specifying ἀνήρ ("husband") rather than the generic ἀνθρώπῳ ("man"). But this seems to miss the point being made by the "emerging consensus," that some Corinthians (esp. women) were arguing precisely from the general (a broader theological perspective, that abstention is always to be considered a better option than engaging in sexual relations) to the particular.

4. Ruth 2:9 LXX: "I have told the men not to touch you" (ἅπτεσθαί σου).

[In the original paper I appended this to the former one with a "cf.". This is the first one Caragounis objects to, asserting, "Ruth 2,9 has nothing to do with sex; the term refers to molestation (cf. vv. 15-16)." This is the one passage which could indeed be ambiguous, which is why I appended it rather than listing it separately. But despite verses 15-16, it seems altogether possible that the language here could just as easily be intended as instruction not to try to have sex with her.]

5. Prov 6:29 LXX: "So is he who sleeps with another man's wife; no one who touches her (ὁ ἁπτόμενος αὐτῆς) will go unpunished." [If the phrase was ambiguous in the Ruth text, the parallelism of this passage makes it certain that it stands in for "have sexual relations."]

6. Plutarch *Alex. M.* 21.7-9: "But Alexander . . . neither laid hands upon these women, nor did he know any other before marriage, except Barsine. This woman . . . was taken prisoner at Damascus. And since she had a Greek education, . . . Alexander determined . . . to attach himself to a woman (ἅπτασθαι γυναικός) of such high birth and beauty." (LCL 7.284-85)

[Here Caragounis argues that this one "is a little problematic, inasmuch as Alexander did eventually marry Barsine." But how is that an objection, one wonders? The context is full of euphemisms for sexual relations ("lay hands on," "know," "touch a woman"), and the euphemistic English translation gets at what Alexander has chosen to do *before* marriage; can one seriously doubt that Plutarch intended this to be taken sexually?]

7. Josephus *Ant.* 1.163 (referring to Gen 20:6): "The King of the Egyptians . . . was fired with a desire to see her and on the point of laying hands on her (ἅψασθαι τῆς Σάρρας). But God thwarted his criminal passion." (LCL 4.8-81).

[Caragounis strangely objects that this "is merely a reference to Gen 20,6, having no corroborative value of its own." It would seem that quite the opposite is true: that the very explicit paraphrasing of the passage so as to include Abimelech's passion for Sarah makes it abundantly clear what the idiom means!]

8. Marcus Aurelius Ant. 1.17.6: "That I did not touch Benedicta or Theodotus (μήτε Βενεδίκτης ἅπτασθαι μήτε Θεοδότου), but that even

afterwards, when I did give way to amatory passions, I was cured of them." (LCL, pp. 22-23)

[Again, as in most of these cases, this is an unambiguous reference to sexual relations, in this case with men.]

Thus we may conclude that this idiom, occurring as it does over a span of at least seven centuries and in many parts of the empire, is a common euphemism for sexual relations.

At the same time, I stand by my earlier assertion, despite Caragounis's objection, that "it cannot be extended or watered down to mean 'It is good for a man not to marry'."[20] Moreover, there is especially good reason to reject the phrase as a metonymy for marriage. For the phrase in all of the known passages is a *euphemism*, pure and simple, and in some cases it sits alongside other such euphemisms that people of many cultures have coined for "sexual intercourse." At issue, then, in terms of human discourse, is why an author would choose to use a *euphemism* for sexual relations as a *metonymy* for marriage, when that could only lead to misunderstanding. How could the Corinthians possibly know that this is what he intended? And such a usage is even more problematic if the "metonymy" is alleged to come from Paul and not the Corinthians, since in this very chapter Paul uses verbs for "marrying" several times without the need to use a euphemism as a metonymy.[21]

But the issue still remains, whose point of view is being expressed here? To answer that we need to proceed to the two issues presented to us in verse 2.

III

All interpreters of 1 Corinthians 7:1-7 must wrestle with the meaning of the prepositional phrase (διὰ δὲ τῆς πορνείας) which stands at the head of Paul's immediate qualification of the maxim in verse 1. By all counts, including Caragounis's (in a very moderate way),

---

[20] Fee, *First Corinthians*, 275, cited by C. on p. 547.

[21] Thus C.'s own conclusion seems highly problematic at several points: "Since vs. 1b. can *under no circumstances be regarded as a quotation in its present context*—the construction would then constitute an *unprecedented barbarism*—one has no longer any grounds for denying the metonymical use of ἅπεσθαι γυναικός to signify marriage. Indeed, this is *the most natural and satisfactory meaning* of the statement" (p. 547) [emphases mine, pointing out the more problematic dimensions of this conclusion].

this stands at the head of sentence as the reason for whatever it is Paul is urging, by way of contrast, in the rest of the sentence. But what does it mean?

The word itself, of course, ordinarily means what all English translations take it to mean—some form of "unlawful sexual intercourse" (BDAG)—and thus it is seen as the reason why Paul qualifies the maxim in verse 1a.[22] The point of contention between the "traditional" and "consensus" views is over whether this plural with its attendant article—which seems plainly to mean something like "because of the cases of sexual immorality"—can ever be stretched to mean something more generic, such as the abundance of sexual immorality in the surrounding culture.[23] This latter view seems to stand behind the KJV's "to avoid fornication" or the NIV's "since there is so much immorality" (cf. REB's "in the face of so much immorality"[24]).

With a circuitous series of objections to both of these views, Caragounis argues for yet another metonymy—that the phrase stands in for "the *sexual urge*, or the *desire for sex*" (p. 551; italics his). The singular support for this option is found in a passage in Tobit 8:7, where before consummating his marriage with Sarah, Tobias has her join him in a prayer which includes the affirmation, "I am now taking this kinswoman of mine, not because of lust (διά πορνείαν), but with sincerity" (NRSV). But here it is not a metonymy, but an extended meaning of the word; that is, the relationship they are about to enter into is not based on what causes others to commit fornica-

---

[22] Even C. admits to "the seeming reasonableness of this position" (p. 549); but from his perspective "certain details have been overlooked" that create "insuperable" problems.

[23] Perhaps one should use more caution here, since this more generic understanding of the plural is supported by Danker in the new BDAG ("the pl. points to the various factors that may bring about sexual immorality"), which he bases on P.J. Tomson, *Paul and the Jewish Law: Halakha in the Letters of the Apostle to the Gentiles* (Minneapolis: Fortress Press, 1990), 106. But this seems to be an unfortunate reference, since Tomson merely glosses the phrase "in view of the dangers of unchastity," without discussion or supporting evidence; cf. the *ESV*'s "but because of the temptation to sexual immorality"! If the word were singular, this would almost certainly be the universal understanding of the phrase; but how does one justify such a translation of this plural?

[24] Thiselton (*First Epistle*, 501) cites this with qualified approval; this must be a matter of how one hears what is being said. I would consider both the NIV and REB to be saying the same thing, and to be suggesting not actual instances of sexual immorality, as the phrase seems clearly to imply, but the more general problem facing the Corinthian church.

tion (thus "lust"), but on a sincere following of God's own command
(v. 7, based on Gen 2:18). What makes Caragounis's view seem
untenable is his assertion following the quote from Tobit: "Tobias'
use of διὰ πορνείαν (singular and [anarthrous) is *to all intents and
purposes an identical construction* with the one under consideration"
(p. 551; italics mine). And so by fiat one removes the obstacles of
the article and the plural!

But that will scarcely do, nor will it do to dismiss the content of
6:12-20 so easily as Caragounis does (p. 549). For in the immediately preceding sentences[25] Paul explicitly refers to a man as "joining himself to a prostitute, so as to become one body with her"
(6:15-16); and it is hard to believe that in an oral culture they would
not have heard the pickup from πόρνης (6:15), πόρνῃ (v. 16), and
τὴν πορνείαν/ὁ πορνεύων (v. 18) to the διὰ τὰς πορνείας of this sentence. But besides objecting to reading the text this way, Caragounis
sees two matters stand in the way of our understanding the present
phrase as in any way related to 6:12-20.

First, if this phrase were to refer to actual (or at least implied) cases
of sexual immorality on the part of a married man, then "the causal
element would have been μοιχείας ('adulteries'), not πορνείας ('for-
nications')" (p. 549). But this is simply to assume more precision to
πορνεία than the evidence allows. There is no question that μοιχεία
always and only refers to actual adultery. But in fact, in the Greek
Bible adultery is also understood as an expression of πορνεία, when
sexual sin is more broadly conceived (see Sir 23:23; Matt 5:32), or,
as in 6:12-20, when the πορνεία takes the specific form of consort-
ing with a πόρνη—whether this was done by an unmarried *or* married man.

Second, Caragounis urges that other views present "an insuperable problem" that "no commentator has ever touched upon" (p.
549, and n. 21): since Paul urges, on the basis of this prepositional
phrase, that *both* partners in a marriage should fulfill their marital
obligations to one another (vv. 3-4), this should mean, under the view
espoused by the "new consensus," that the Christian women of
Corinth also "either were wont to or were in danger of going to the

---

[25] It would be of some interest to know how people read and understood texts
that lacked our markers, not only for major divisions, but also for paragraphs,
sentences, and words. It is certainly arguable that Paul for the very reason that
they might be heard together in such a reading has juxtaposed these two items.

prostitutes" as well (p. 549), a view that he sees as "clearly absurd."

But this seems to be an altogether unnecessary assumption. Under no view of the presenting issue from Corinth[26] is there reason to think that the "cases of sexual immorality" involve the women. In the "traditional view," the women are the beneficiaries of Paul's admonition (they get to be married, which at the same time will hopefully stave off the men's going to the prostitutes); In the "emerging consensus," they are themselves the cause of the problem (by denying sexual relations to their husbands, the latter satisfy their sexual needs elsewhere). This option seems so clear to proponents on both sides that it is no wonder that "no commentator has ever touched upon this problem."

So we may assume that either of the positions Caragounis stands over against can make a reasonable case for their reading of these first two issues, although in either case one will still argue for a given position as having the better of it in terms of the "why" questions. But these two views part company altogether on the rest of verse 2; and here Caragounis rejoins the tradition.

IV

The third major issue in interpreting this passage is the meaning of ἐχέτω and the force (and reason for) the emphatic ἑαυτοῦ/τὸν ἴδιον. The bone of contention is whether or not a verb which very often refers to people as "being married," is also used to mean "get married." Here in particular Caragounis has raised strong objection to my contention that there is no known evidence to support the latter sense. By contrast he asserts that the verb "can certainly be used of 'marrying a wife' as well as 'having a wife', i.e., of being married or living in the state of marriage" (pp. 547-48). Here again it is a matter of exegeting the available evidence.

On this matter Caragounis limits himself to the biblical evidence only. But his argument seems to be flawed considerably. He begins by pointing out that the LXX translators twice render the Hebrew שׁגל with a form of ἔχω, where it is a euphemism for "rape" (Deut 28:30; Isa 13:16), and admits that this evidence is irrelevant to the

---

[26] That is, either getting married to avoid cases of sexual immorality (the "tradition") or cases of sexual immorality because of the denial of sexual relations on the part of some women.

present context. He then turns to the translation of נָשָׂא in 2 Chronicles 11:21, where the LXX translator rendered it with the imperfect εἶχεν. But then he argues what appears to be an irrelevancy, namely that the *Hebrew* word ordinarily means "to take wife," so here the Greek should also be understood to mean, "[Rehoboam] took [i.e., got married to] eighteen wives and sixty concubines." But in this case, the LXX translator was simply doing what an English translation like the NIV has done: turned the Hebrew into a Greek equivalent for the fact that Rehoboam simply "had" all these wives and concubines, in the same way that one would speak of his "having so many treasures in his palace." Thus the NIV (rightly) has it: "In all he *had* eighteen wives and sixty concubines," a sentence that follows the comment that the daughter of Absalom was his favorite. So this hardly counts as an instance of using ἔχω with γυνή to mean "get married." And the same is true of all the other examples brought forward (Ezra 9:12, 17, 18; Isa 54:1; Tob 3:8); in each case the verb is used to refer to someone who is, or has been, married, not to someone heretofore unmarried who is going to "take a wife." Moreover, in the case of Isaiah 54:1, which Paul cites in Galatians 4:27, the emphasis lies specifically on the present state of being married, not on having gotten married.

Perhaps the most problematic of all is the analysis of the LXX of Exodus 2:1. Here the LXX translator has literally rendered the verb לָקַח as ὃς ἔλαβεν (ἐκ τῶν θυγατέρων Λευι) but then adds καὶ ἔσχεν αὐτήν. This is interpreted as the translator supplying the verb phrase καὶ ἔσχεν αὐτήν instead of the more common "as a wife," and thus he intends us to read, "Who took from the daughters of Levi and married her." If this is the case, then it stands alone in the Greek Bible with this meaning. But it seems far more likely that in this instance the translator did not supply the ordinary "as a wife" because the prepositional phrase makes it unnecessary, and that the additional phrase is not a form of "take a wife," but means "and had her [as a wife]." And thus it serves as the lead in to verse 2: "And he had her [as a wife] and she became pregnant and gave birth to a son." Thus it is not a lone exception to the rule (so that in any case Homer nods), but in fact is being used in a very ordinary way.[27]

---

[27] On this usage see further BDAG, 2a and 2b, where it is assumed under the heading "to stand in close relation to someone," and includes the several NT examples where it means to "be married."

Thus my point remains. When Paul, or other Biblical writers, talk about someone who is *already married* they often use a form of ἔχω, which means either to be in a married state, as elsewhere in 1 Corinthians 7 (vv.12-13, 29; cf. Gal 4:27; John 4:17-18), or to be engaged in ongoing sexual relations with one's spouse or partner (1 Cor 5:1). When they wish to speak about "getting married," they use either the verb itself (1 Cor 7:28, 33) or the idiom similar to ours in English, "to take a wife" (Mark 12:19-21 and //'s; cf. the *v. l.* in 1 Cor 7:28 as a substitute for γαμήσης). There is simply no compelling reason to think that the language here has anything other than its normal usage: "let each man continue in relations with his own wife and each wife continue in relations with her own husband."[28]

Finally, it is right at this point that the emerging consensus has so much to commend it over the traditional view. The problem with the latter—and Caragounis has hardly overcome this—is threefold: (a) It has to fly full in the face of the ordinary meanings of the words and phrases because of a prior commitment to an understanding of what the whole chapter is about. (b) It can make almost no sense as to *why* Paul continues on in verses 3 and 4 to elaborate verse 2, especially with the emphasis on mutuality. Here also is where Caragounis's misguided objection to the appearance of both husband and wife in verse 2 comes in. The reason for Paul's concern that each "owes" the other his/her due most likely is that the men are going to the prostitutes precisely because the women are rejecting the marriage bed at home. (c) The traditional view can make almost no sense at all of verse 5; indeed it stands as something of embarrassment to the tradition. For if verse 1b were Paul's own position on marriage, one could make some sense of the "temporary abstinence from sex." But why, under any circumstances, would he begin that allowance with the strong prohibition, "do not defraud one another on this matter"?

Thus verses 2-5 continue to be the Achilles' heel for the traditional view.

---

[28] That this verb means "take a wife" becomes especially problematic for the second half of the clause. The idiom "to take a wife" occurs with some regularity in both Hebrew and Greek; but I am aware of no instance where a "woman takes a husband." The woman appears as the subject of the verb γαμέω (e.g., 1 Cor 7:28, 34), but not of the idiom to "take a husband" (note that this textual variation occurs only with the man in v. 28).

V

The final point of interpretation of this passage that needs some discussion is the meaning and role of verse 6 in the whole argument. Here is the other "Achilles' heel" for the traditional view, namely both the "what" and the "why" of Paul's saying, τοῦτο δὲ λέγω κατὰ συγγνώμην οὐ κατ' ἐπιταγήν. The "what" has to do with the meaning of συγγνώμην; the "why" has to do with *what* is being qualified in what has preceded. None of the views offered has anything to commend it: if it refers to verse 2 only, then what does one do especially with the clear "concession" in the latter part of verse 5?; it is hard to find reasons for limiting it to verses 3 and 4;[29] and to make it refer to all of verse 5 makes little sense, because this verse begins with a clear "command." So in the end, the single clear concession—in verse 5b (εἰ μήτι ἄν = "except perhaps" as NRSV, TNIV)—also happens to be what immediately precedes the τοῦτο of verse 6. So why would one look elsewhere?

But Caragounis does look elsewhere; but now the issue is not with the "new consensus," but with his own new twist on the traditional view, in which he has downplayed the whole passage as not speaking to a real issue in the church in Corinth. He begins by pointing out (correctly) that whatever κατὰ συγγνώμην means, it must stand over against the following οὐ κατ' ἐπιταγήν, which in light of verse 25 must bear the sense of a binding regulation. Since in his view nothing that has preceded could conceivably take the form of an ἐπιταγή, he feels compelled to look elsewhere for the meaning of συγγνώμη. So by means of a careful analysis of the word, he decides on what had come to be a common meaning, namely to seek "pardon" from someone. What Paul is doing, he argues, is asking their pardon for speaking so plainly into a somewhat delicate, personal matter (that people should get married and have regular sexual relations). Thus Caragounis opts for either "Pardon me for intruding; [that is], I just wanted to help. I have only given you advice, not a command," or "But I am saying this with your permission, not as a command!" (p. 558). And with either of these, he can then make it refer to all of verses 1-5.

But it is hard to imagine that the Corinthians could have been able to extrapolate all of this out of a mere κατὰ συγγνώμην, espe-

---

[29] A point also made by Caragounis, p. 555.

cially since the two κατά phrases must be read together as qualifiers of λέγω, and therefore must move from Paul's direction toward them, not ask them to pardon or be indulgent toward him.

On the other hand, one can make perfectly good sense of this sentence if something close to the "new consensus" is what is going on. In this view Paul has first of all insisted, over against the stance of some, that wives and husbands continue in a fully conjugal marriage, both as "obligation" to the other and as an expression of submitting "mastery" over one's own body to the other. Indeed, he insists (v. 5a), they must not deprive/defraud (perhaps "stop defrauding"[30]) one another; but then he softens the impact by (barely) allowing a concession to their perspective—but only briefly, by agreement, and for the purpose of prayer!

Verse 6 then carries a whiff of slight irony. In conceding this much to them, Paul is not going to allow someone to turn his "concession" into a "command." So he concludes by pointing out precisely what he himself has done. Thus he is not seeking their pardon, but offering them a sop—allowing their point of view only as a very circumscribed concession.

Finally, therefore, when all factors are considered, Caragounis's objections to the "emerging consensus" are simply not substantive enough to cause a change of mind on the significant issues in this passage. While one can appreciate his considerable contribution to our overall understanding of συγγνώμη, the application of his findings to our passage appears less than satisfactory. Indeed, I would argue that the "emerging consensus" has become so because it does justice to all the details and in the end seems to make the most sense of all the data.

---

[30] C. takes some exception to my suggesting that here is a case were the present aspect could well carry this sense (p. 553), but my point was not "the present vis-à-vis the aorist," but simply that the present tense could carry this sense. It could, of course, well carry the sense of promoting a lifetime principle; this is a matter of interpretation, not of using verb aspect to make a point. Cf. now Thiselton, *First Epistle*, 507. My main point still remains, that this is a very strong verb for simply denying sexual relations to one's partner; cf. 6:8, where it clearly means "to defraud/cheat" another.

ΚΕΦΑΛΗ AND THE THORNY ISSUE OF HEAD COVERING IN 1 CORINTHIANS 11:2-16

Linda L. Belleville

While a fair amount of effort has been spent on determining the sense of κεφαλὴ δὲ γυναικὸς ὁ ἀνήρ (1 Cor 11:3) and διὰ τοῦτο ὀφείλει ἡ γυνὴ ἐξουσίαν ἔχειν ἐπὶ τῆς κεφαλῆς διὰ τοὺς ἀγγέλους (1 Cor 11:10), far too little attention has been given to how these two clauses fit into the broader context and argument of 1 Corinthians 11:2-16. This is because Paul's overriding concern quite often has been reduced to that of flaunting social conventions thought to be unrecoverable due to ignorance of local Greco-Roman customs.[1] Yet, current socio-historical data indicate that a breach of social etiquette is not really the core issue. Paul's line of argument suggests instead that the concern is theological and that gender based forms of worship are what is in question. If this is so, then it is actually δόξα, and not κεφαλή, that provides the key to understanding Paul's train of thought.

The exegetical issues in 1 Corinthians 11:2-16 are many. Nonetheless, the clear features of the passage are not to be overlooked. Paul's matter-of-fact mention of the prophetic and intercessory activity of women and men at Corinth points to mutual gender roles: πᾶς ἀνὴρ προσευχόμενος ἢ προφητεύων . . . πᾶσα δὲ γυνὴ προσευχομένη ἢ προφητεύουσα (1 Cor. 11:4-5). This accords with Greco-Roman religious practice. Intercession and prophecy were primary activities of cult priests and priestesses. Prayers and invocation were daily rituals. Prophecy, though common, was more localized. Two of the most prestigious cult sites were the oracular shrine at Delphi

---

[1] See, for example, R. Williams, who talks of Corinthian worship leaders being perceived by outsiders and unbelievers as shameless women ("Lifting the Veil: A Social-Science Interpretation of 1 Corinthians 11:2-16," *Consensus* 23 [1997] 53-60); Richard Hays, who evokes "social deacorum" and "a particular cultural code" to explain Paul's teaching in this pericope (*First Corinthians* [Louisville, Kentucky: John Knox Press, 1997] pp. 188-189), and Gail Paterson Corrington, who speaks of subversion of the social order ("The 'Headless Woman': Paul and the Language of the Body in 1 Cor 11:2-16," *Perspectives in Religious Studies* 18 [1991] 224.

and the Olympia Dodona.[2] More, women are affirmed by Paul as equal to the task as liturgical leaders: ἐπαινῶ δὲ ὑμᾶς ὅτι πάντα μου μέμνησθε . . . καθὼς παρέδωκα ὑμῖν, τὰς παραδόσεις κατέχετε; 1 Cor 11:2). This too corresponds with Greco-Roman practice. For example, during the time of Paul's correspondence with the Corinthian church, Iuliane served as high priestess of the imperial cult in Magnesia (*I.Magn.* 158) and Menodora as priestess of Sillyon (*IGR* III, 800-902).[3] There is also every evidence that men and women served as liturgical co-ministers. Although women tended to officiate the cults of female deities and men the cults of male deities, by the second century B.C. there was a growing number of priests and priestesses who served side-by-side. This was especially the case for imported cults such as Isis.[4]

The language throughout 1 Corinthians 11:3-16 evidences gender parity and mutuality.[5] Both male and female bear the image of God—the former explicitly, the latter implicitly: Ἀνὴρ μὲν γὰρ . . . εἰκὼν καὶ δόξα θεοῦ ὑπάρχων· ἡ γυνὴ δὲ δόξα ἀνδρός ἐστιν (v. 7).[6]

---

[2] Priests and priestesses generally served a particular sanctuary with a complex of buildings. They were responsible for its maintenance, its rituals and ceremonies, and the protection of its treasures and gifts. Liturgical functions of officially recognized priests and priestesses included ritual sacrifice, pronouncing the prayer or invocation, and presiding at the festivals of the deity. Prophecy was obtained from oracular shrines such as Apollo's at Delphi and the Olympia Dodona. See Ross Kraemer, *Her Share of the Blessings* (Oxford: Oxford University Press, 1992) and *The Oxford History of the Classical World*, edited by J. Boardman, J. Griffin, O. Murray (Oxford: Oxford University Press, 1986) 266-267.

[3] Inscriptions dating from the first century to the mid-third century place a female high priestess in Ephesus, Cyzicus, Thyatira, Aphrodisias, Magnesia and elsewhere. See R.A. Kearsley, "Asiarchs, Archiereis, and the Archiereiai of Asia," *Greek, Roman and Byzantine Studies* 27 (1986) 183-192.

[4] The Egyptian goddess, Isis, is credited with putting women on the same plain as men: "I invoke thee, who . . . didst make the power of women equal to that of men; . . ." (*P. Oxy.* 1380 c. A.D. 100). Six of twenty-six cultic inscriptions name women as priests of the highest rank. See S.K. Heyob, *The Cult of Isis Among Women in the Greco-Roman World.* (Leiden: Brill, 1973) 81-86.

[5] This is over against those who claim that a patriarchal viewpoint is undeniable. See, for example, J.B. Hurley, "Did Paul Require Veils or the Silence of Women? A Consideration of 1 Cor. 11:2-16 and 1 Cor. 14:33b-36," *WTJ* 35 (1973) 190-220; Bruce Waltke, "1 Corinthians 11:2-16: An Interpretation," *BibSac* 135 (1978) 46-57; John P. Meier, "On the Veiling of Hermeneutics (1 Cor 11:2-26)," *CBQ* 40 (1978) 217-219 and, more recently, Hays, *1 Corinthians*, 184.

[6] Morna Hooker is surely correct in saying that Paul makes no explicit mention of woman in the image of God not because it is unacceptable to him but because it is irrelevant to his purpose ("Authority on Her Head: An Examination

Both were created to be dependent on one another: πλὴν οὔτε γυνὴ χωρὶς ἀνδρὸς οὔτε ἀνὴρ χωρὶς γυναικὸς ἐν κυρίῳ (v. 11). Both historically find their origin in each other. The first woman's physical origin is by virtue of creation ἐξ ἀνδρός (vv. 8, 12), while all men subsequently come διὰ τῆς γυναικός· (v. 12). And both men and women are called on to behave responsibly: Ἀνὴρ μὲν οὐκ ὀφείλει κατακαλύπτεσθαι τὴν κεφαλὴν . . . δε . . . διὰ τοῦτο ὀφείλει ἡ γυνὴ ἐξουσίαν ἔχειν ἐπὶ τῆς κεφαλῆς (vv. 7-10). The language of obligation assumes that women and men could and would do so.

Part of the obligation was that women in liturgical roles wear a head covering (and men forgo one). Whether this head covering was hair or clothing is much debated. Some think that the issue is one of hairstyle. The Corinthian men were letting their hair grow long, while the women were cutting theirs into boyishly short, unruly locks.[7] Or the men were aping the upswept feminine fashion and the women were loosing their plaited buns or braids and letting their hair hang down.[8] However, neither of these fits first century Roman styles and customs. The plaited bun was actually a later hairstyle, and the male youth hairdo was more restrained.[9] Also, long and short hair in public were perfectly acceptable under certain circumstances for both men and women.[10]

---

of 1 Cor. XI.10," *NTS* 10 [1963] 411). The creation of both male and female in God's image is a familiar part of the Synoptic tradition (Mark 10:6; Matt 19:4).

[7] See, for example, Raymond Collins, *First Corinthians* (Sacra Pagina Series 7; Collegeville, Minnesota: The Liturgical Press, 1999) p. 407; W.J. Martin, "1 Corinthians 11:2-26: An Interpretation," in *Apostolic History and the Gospel: Biblical and Historical Essays Presented to F.F. Bruce on his 60th Birthday*, ed. W.W. Gasque and R.P. Martin (Grand Rapids, Michigan: Eerdmans, 1970) 231-41; M. Gielen, "Beten und Prophezeien mit unverhülltem Kopf? Die Kontroverse zwischen Paulus und der korinthischen Gemeinde um die Wahrung der Geschlechtsrollensymbolik in 1 Kor 11,2-16," *ZNW* 90 (1999) 220-249.

[8] See for example, Richard and Catherine Kroeger, "An Inquiry into the Evidence of Maenadism in the Corinthians Congregation," *SBL Seminar Papers* 1978, 2.331-36; Elisabeth Schüssler Fiorenza, *In Memory of Her: A Feminist Theological Reconstruction of Christian Origins* (New York: Crossroad, 1984) 227; F.F. Bruce, *I & II Corinthians* (Grand Rapids, Michigan: Eerdmans, 1971) 105; Gordon Fee, *The First Epistle to the Corinthians* (Grand Rapids, Michigan: Eerdmans, 1987) 496-97, Hays, *First Corinthians* 185-86; Hurley, "Did Paul Require Veils," pp. 197-200; Jerome Murphy-O'Connor, "Sex and Logic in 1 Corinthians 11:2-16," *Catholic Biblical Quarterly* 42 (1980) 488-489; Corrington, "The 'Headless Woman'," 223-231.

[9] See Cynthia Thompson, "Hairstyles, Head-coverings and St. Paul: Portraits from Roman Corinth," *Biblical Archeologist* 51 (1988) 109-110.

[10] For example, Roman men grieved by covering their heads while women

The trend setters at this time were the emperors and their wives.[11] First century portraiture shows that fashionable hairstyles for women involved either twisting the hair into a roll at the top of the head and then looping it to form a raised, lopped ridge or parting it in the middle and winding it into a knot at the back of the head while framing the face with soft waves; the hair on the crown of the head was typically set off by a filet tied at the center-back of the head.[12] Men had short locks combed forward to frame the forehead.[13] The face was typically clean shaven.[14] Youths had slightly curved locks combed forward to frame the forehead.[15] A headband was commonly worn to keep the hair in place.[16]

---

let their hair down without any covering. Greek men grieved by letting their hair grow long, while women cut theirs short. See Plutarch, *Quaest.Rom.* 267A-B. In fact, Plutarch and Paul employ the same Greek infinitive, τὸ κείρεσθαι. (Ibid., 267B; 1 Cor 11:6) Also, Dio Chrysostom notes that farmers, most barbarians, sophists, and devotees of deities such as Zeus and Apollo wore their hair long (*The Thirty-fifth Discourse* 11-12). Long hair became more the style in the A.D. second century. See, for example, the A.D. 150-160 sculpture of a youthful male with locks of long hair extending from the bottom of a close-fitting Attic helmet, over the neck, and around the brow. Vierneisel-Schlörb 1979, 178-87, no. 16, figs. 80-84; Munich, Glyptothek 212. http://www.perseus.tufts.edu/

[11] The general public aped the hairstyles of the emperor and empress. See, *Ibid.*, 99-115; compare David Gill, "The Importance of Roman Portraiture for Head-Coverings in 1 Corinthians 11:2-16," *Tyndale Bulletin* 41 (1990) 252.

[12] See, for example, the Humphry Ward Head, Paris, Musée du Louvre , Louvre Ma 3106, Marianne Hamiaux, *Les sculptures grecques. I. Des origines à la fin du IVe siècle avant J.-C.* (Paris: Musée du Louvre. Département des antiquités grecques, étrusques et romaines, 1992) and Olympia West Pediment, Fig. B (Old Woman; late addition) Olympia, Archaeological Museum, ca. 100 B.C.—ca. A.D. 100. Upper class women had the leisure to have their hair done in ever more elaborate versions of these two styles. http://www.perseus.tufts.edu/

[13] See the Della Valle-Medici relief (Claudian era) in *The Cambridge Ancient History*, edited by S.A. Cook, F.E. Adcock, M.P. Charlesworth, vol. of plates IV (Cambridge: Cambridge University Press, 1934*)* and Ibid. p. 102.

[14] Hairstyles changed with a change of emperor in subsequent centuries. So it is important not to go beyond the apostolic period. Emperor Hadrian, for instance, grew a beard to conceal facial scars. He also wore a bow and tied ribbons that dangled down the back of the neck (A.D. 117-138). See John Matthews, "Roman Life and Society," in *The Oxford History of the Classical World*, edited by J. Boardman, J. Griffin, O. Murray (Oxford: Oxford University Press, 1986) 744-45. Emperor Augustus, on the other hand, "never neglected the razor" (*semper usus est;* Pliny, *Nat.Hist.* 7.59.211)

[15] See, for example, the A.D. 90 head of Ares Ludovisi, Munich, Glyptothek 272. Vierneisel-Schlörb, *Klassische Skulpturen des 5. und 4. Jahrh. v. Chr.* Vol. 2 of Glyptothek München. Katalog der Skulpturen (Munich: Beck, 1979, 424-29, no. 38, figs. 206-209. http://www.perseus.tufts.edu/

[16] See, for instance, the 1st century A.D. head of a Volubilis youth, Munich

The stigma of loose hair in public has been exaggerated. There were occasions, such as weddings, funerals, and religious rites, when it was perfectly acceptable for women to wear their hair down in public.[17] In particular, the commonly cited connection between loose hair and prostitution or the worship practices of cults such as Dionysius, Cybele and Isis has been overstated. The excavation of the Villa of the Mysteries outside Pompeii uncovered Dionysiac rites, where the majority of women are portrayed with their hair tied up.[18] Also, women devotees of Isis near Corinth are described as having their hair "anointed and wrapped in a transparent covering" (*illae limpido tegmine crines madidos obvolutae*; Lucius Apuleius, *Metamorphosis* 11.10).

A commonly overlooked difficulty with hair as a covering is that Paul takes issue with worship leaders, not all congregants. And there is simply no cultural parallel in antiquity for requiring long hair on a priestess, liturgist or other cult leader. It is also a misconception that women covered hair and head in public. Public statuary of women in Corinth and elsewhere are typically shown bare headed. This indicates that the lack of a head covering was socially acceptable in Paul's day.[19] Further, there is the question of language. If a covering of long, human hair were in view, Paul surely would have used the standard Greek term κομᾶ, rather than the oblique κατὰ κεφαλῆς ἔχων.[20] More, hair as a covering does not fit Paul's flow of argument. 1 Corinthians 11:6 demands something else: εἰ δὲ αἰσχρὸν γυναικὶ τὸ κείρασθαι ἢ ξυρᾶσθαι, κατακαλυπτέσθω assumes clothing distinct from long, cutable tresses (v. 6). "A woman ought to have ἐξουσία ἐπὶ τῆς κεφαλῆς" in verse 10 also calls for something other than hair. Regardless of whether ἐξουσία ἐπὶ τῆς κεφαλῆς is "author-

GL 457; Vierneisel-Schlörb, B. 1979, 490-501, no. 44, figs. 237-41. http://www.perseus.tufts.edu/

[17] See Thompson, "Hairstyles," 112.

[18] Livy does mention women in Rome, who had their hair unbound and disheveled at a Bacchic cult celebration (39.13). But, as Livy himself notes, this occurred c. 200 years prior to Paul's ministry and was subsequently outlawed by the Roman Senate (39.19)

[19] *The Cambridge Ancient History*, edited by S.A. Cook, F.E. Adcock, M.P. Charlesworth, vol. of plates IV (Cambridge: University Press, 1934) 164-171. Compare, Gill, "Roman Portraiture," pp. 251-252.

[20] Κομή is the hair of the human head; θρίξ is the hair either of a person or of an animal (Louw & Nida, *Semantic Domains*, 8.12-14).

ity upon" or "power over" her head, there is nothing in the literature of the day to connect hair with either one.[21]

There is much, however, to connect κατὰ κεφαλῆς ἔχων (vv. 4-5) and γυνὴ ἐξουσίαν ἔχειν ἐπὶ τῆς κεφαλῆς (v. 10) with the conventional toga. Socio-historical research has shown that both Roman clergy and laity covered (not veiled) their head with their toga, while performing liturgical functions.[22] Roman portraiture confirms that this was the case for both genders.[23] The protocol for religious and state functions was to pull up the toga to the middle of the ear (e.g., δύσφημον ἄχρι τῶν ὤτων ἀνελάμβανον το ἱμάτιον; Plutarch, *Roman Questions* 266D).[24] A first century statue of Augustus making a sac-

---

[21] The interpretations of ὀφείλει ἡ γυνὴ ἐξουσίαν ἔχειν ἐπὶ τῆς κεφαλῆς διὰ τοὺς ἀγγέλους. though many and varied, can be grouped around the meanings, "power," "freedom," and "authority." The wearing of a head covering symbolizes a woman's (1) subjection [to men], (2) power [to ward off the attacks of evil spirits or angels]), (3) need for protection as the weaker sex or during spiritually vulnerable moments (e.g., during ecstatic experiences), or (4) rightful claim to influence and honor. See, for example, Robert, "Power on the Head," *Expositor* 4th series, 10 [1894] 139-149; Leon Morris, *1 Corinthians*, (Grand Rapids: Eerdmans, [2]1985) 154. Usage of ἐξουσία elsewhere in 1 Corinthians encourages us to consider "freedom" over her head" (e.g., Thomas Shoemaker "Unveiling of Equality: 1 Corinthians 11:2-16," *Biblical Theology Bulletin* 17 [1987] 60-63), "power" to do with her head as she wishes (e.g., David Hall, "A Problem of Authority," *The Expository Times* 102 [1990] 39-42) or "equality of status in Christ" (e.g., Sheila McGinn, "ἐξουσίαν ἔχειν ἐπὶ τῆς κεφαλῆς: 1 Cor 11:10 and the Ecclesial Authority of Women," *Listening*, 31 [1996] 91-104). Compare βλέπετε δὲ μή πως ἡ ἐξουσία ὑμῶν αὕτη πρόσκομμα γένηται τοῖς ἀσθενέσιν. (1 Cor 8:9); οὐκ ἐχρησάμεθα τῇ ἐξουσίᾳ ταύτῃ (1 Cor 9:12). The traditional suggestion is that women wore a head covering to symbolize their subjection to men. Greek syntax indicates just the opposite. To have ἐξουσία is not to be in subjection, but to possess "authority" or "freedom." See Hooker, "Authority," 415.

[22] Veiling was not a Roman style of clothing and limited in Paul's day to frontier posts along the eastern border of the Empire. See Matthews, "Roman Life and Society," 743-44; compare Thompson, "Hairstyles," 112-113. An appeal is sometimes made to Greek and Jewish customs of hair or dress. But this overlooks the fact that Corinth was a Roman colony and provincial capital. Moreover, the trend setting elites of the day were Roman. David Gill rightly calls into question the relevance of such an appeal ("Roman Portraiture," pp. 245-46).

[23] For a discussion of the first century custom of using the toga as a head covering, see Richard Oster, "When Men Wore Veils to Worship: The Historical Context of 1 Corinthians 11.4," *New Testament Studies* 34 (1988) 495; Mark Black, "1 Cor. 11:2-16-A Re-investigation," in *Essays on Women in Earliest Christianity*, edited by Carroll Osborn, vol. 1 (Joplin, MS: College Press, 1993) 201-02; Thompson "Hairstyles," 112; Gill, "Roman Portraiture," 246-253.

[24] This would indicate that Roman men and women typically left their head uncovered in public. Greco-Roman statuary confirms this. http://www.perseus.tufts.edu/ It is also important to keep in mind the inseparability of Roman reli-

rifice has his toga framing the face with a fringe of curled locks combed forward on the forehead.[25] This is the same for Empress Livia.[26] It is an image that is also found on statuary and coins for subsequent emperors.[27]

The connection of the toga and the phrase κατὰ κεφαλῆς ἔχων is readily found. Caesar is said to have "pulled his toga down over his head" (ἐφειλκύσατο κατὰ κεφαλῆς τὸ ἱμάτιον) after being stabbed (Plutarch, *Caes* 66.12.4) Scipio did the same, while walking down the streets of Alexandria (ἐβάδιζε κατὰ κεφαλῆς ἔχων τὸ ἱμάτιον; Plutarch *Moralia* 200F). In a cultic context, the gesture was clearly a religious one. A statue at Pompeii of the priestess Polyaena with her toga pulled up over her head has the following inscription:[28]

> To Polyaena, daughter of Marcus, priestess of Victory. The high priest [Publius] Licinius Priscus Junventianus, [while still living, (set up this monument)] with the official sanction of the city council to (this) excellent woman

This matches Paul's language in 1 Corinthians 11:4-16. Church protocol for women was κατακαλύπτεσθαι τὴν κεφαλὴν (vv. 4-7). The fact that the outer garment draped the head at about the same point as long hair explains how it is that Paul can argue that κωμᾶ ("long hair") is nature's *equivalent* to a head covering (ἡ κόμη ἀντὶ περιβολαίου δέδοται, v. 15).[29] Once the toga (τὸ ἱμάτιον) is pulled up, it is said to be ἐπὶ τῆς κεφαλῆς ἔχοντες (Plutarch *The Roman*

---

gion and the Roman state. Civic life was essentially religious in nature and function. Each city had its patron deities, sacrifice and prayer accompanied civic meetings, tax dollars supported the cults, and the civic calendar was thoroughly religious in observance. See Linda Belleville, *Women Leaders in the Church* (Grand Rapids, MI: Baker Books, 2000) 32.

[25] Ara Pacis Augustae, Rome (13-9 B.C.) in *The Cambridge Ancient History*, S.A. Cook, F.E. Adcock, M.P. Charlesworth, eds., vol. of plates IV (Cambridge: Cambridge University Press, 1934) 146-149. Thompson ("Hairstyles," p. 101), Oster ("When Men Wore Veils," p. 495 n. 6) and Gill ("Roman Portraiture," p. 247) note that the religious symbolism of Augustus' covered head would have been unmistakable.

[26] *The Cambridge Ancient History*, vol. of plates IV, 169.

[27] Ibid., 153 (Tiberius); Thompson, "Hairstyles," 103 (Nero).

[28] The toga was also pulled up over the head during liturgical prayers. See, for example, Plutarch, *Roman Questions* 266D.

[29] For ἀντὶ + the genitive to denote equivalency, see *BAGD s.v.* Περιβόλαιον is anything that "covers around" such as clothing, a bedcover, a chariot-cover, a covering for the feet, and a dressing-gown—and not a veil per se. See *LSJ s.v.* and *Moulton-Milligan s.v.*

Questions 266C; identical to Paul's γυνὴ ἐξουσίαν ἔχειν ἐπὶ τῆς κεφαλῆς, v. 10).[30]

Given this socio-religious practice, the truly surprising aspect is not Paul's directive that female liturgists cover their heads but his dictum that the uncovered head of a male liturgists is "shameful" (v. 4). Even within Paul's own Judaic-priestly circles, a head covering was the norm. Mosaic Law stipulated a linen turban (Exod 28:4; 28:37-39; 29:6; 39:28, 31; Lev 8:9; 16:4), a practice that continued well into exilic times and beyond (Ezek 44:18; *m. Yoma* 7.5). Some attempt to deal with the cultural discrepancy by positing a Pauline interpolation.[31] Others try to reconcile the discrepancy by defining the concern as marital, rather than liturgical. "Every man who prays and prophesies" becomes "every *husband*" and "every woman who prays and prophesies" becomes "every *wife*."[32] Head covering then is construed as a wife's public act of submission to her husband's "headship" (κεφαλὴ δὲ γυναικὸς ὁ ἀνήρ, 1 Cor 11:3) and authority (διὰ τοῦτο ὀφείλει ἡ γυνὴ ἐξουσίαν ἔχειν ἐπὶ τῆς κεφαλῆς διὰ τοὺς ἀγγέλους (1 Cor 11:10). The net effect is to bring these verses under the umbrella of the NT Haustafeln pericopes (Eph 5:21-6:9; Col 3:18-4:1; Tit 2:1-9; 1 Pet 2:18-3:7).

---

[30] Jerome Murphy-O'Connor is, therefore, wrong in saying that ἔχειν ἐπὶ + the genitive τῆς κεφαλῆς demands a hairdo piled up on the head, as opposed to clothing that covers the head ("Sex and Logic," 485-486). Compare Plutarch, *Quaest.Rom.* 266C-267B, where the preposition ἐπι appears six times. The root idea of "rest upon" fits either hair piled "upon" the head or clothing "over" the head. See Murray Harris, "Prepositions and Theology in the Greek New Testament" in *The New International Dictionary of New Testament Theology*, edited by Colin Brown, 3 vols. (Grand Rapids, Michigan: Zondervan, 1975) 3:1193.

[31] See, for example, W.O. Walker, "1 Corinthians 11:2-16 and Paul's View Regarding Women," *JBL* 94 (1975) 94-110; L. Cope, "1 Cor. 11:2-16: One Step Further," *JBL* 97 (1978) 435-36; G.W. Trompf, "On Attitudes Toward Women in Paul and Paulinist Literature: 1 Corinthians 11:3-16 and Its Context," *CBQ* 42 (1980) 196-215. Alan Padgett suggests reading verses 3-7b as the Corinthians' beliefs and verses 7c-16 as Paul's critique and opposition ("Paul on Women in the Church. The Contradictions of Coiffure in 1 Corinthians 11.2-16," *JSNT* 20 [1984] 69-86). The difficulty is that Paul introduces vv. 3ff with a stereotypical phrase signaling the impartation of new information: Θέλω δὲ ὑμας εἰδέναι ὅτι. Also, there is nothing in the text that signals Paul's citation of a contrary opinion.

[32] See, for example, Corrington, "The 'Headless Woman'," 225; James A. Walther, *1 Corinthians* (*Anchor* 32; New York: Doubleday, 1976) 259; J. Duncan M. Derrett, "Miscellanea: A Pauline Pun and Judas' Punishment," *ZNW* 72 (1981) 131-133; Craig Blomberg, *1 Corinthians* (*NIVAC*; Grand Rapids, Michigan: Zondervan, 1994) 209-210; Gill, "Roman Portraiture," 251-56. Jason BeDuhn maintains that Paul begins with husband and wife but broadens it to men and women by verse 7 ("Paul's Anthropology in 1 Corinthians 11," *JBL* 118 [1999] 300-301).

To be sure γυνη and ἀνήρ can mean "wife" and "husband" (as well as "woman" and "man"; *BAGD s.v.*). But Paul normally adds a possessive or reflexive pronoun or adjective for clarity. He is precise about this elsewhere in 1 Corinthians: "A man is to have τὴν ἑαυτοῦ γυναῖκα" (1 Cor 7:2; cf Eph 5:25, 33); a woman is to have τὸν ἴδιον ἄνδρα" and they are to consult with τοὺς ἰδίους ἄνδρας (1 Cor 7:2; 14:34; cf Eph 5:22; 1 Pet 3:1). Also, the context does not support "husband" and "wife." Praise is given for holding to the transmitted *ecclesial* traditions and there is a command to follow "*church practice*" (not marital; vv. 2, 16). The focus of the pericope is theological. Prayer is *to God*, the churches are *God's*, and everything is *from God* (10:32; 11:11, 16), and the topics are liturgical (prayer, prophecy, and the Lord's supper), not marital (11:2-34). Paul's appeal throughout is to the creation of humankind as male and female (not as husband and wife). "The two shall become one flesh" and "a husband shall leave his father and mother and cleave to his wife" (Gen 2:24), which figure so prominently in the NT Haustafeln, are conspicuously absent here. Instead, Paul appeals to God's intent for gendered humankind as male and female created in his image (v. 7; cf Gen 1:27) and for mutual dependence: πλὴν οὔτε γυνὴ χωρὶς ἀνδρὸς οὔτε ἀνὴρ χωρὶς γυναικὸς ἐν κυρίῳ (v. 11). The basis for the latter is a symbiotic relationship: ὥσπερ γὰρ ἡ γυνὴ ἐκ τοῦ ἀνδρός, οὕτως καὶ ὁ ἀνὴρ διὰ τῆς γυναικός· τὰ δὲ πάντα ἐκ τοῦ θεοῦ (v. 12). It is sometimes argued that virtually all women were married in the first century so that ὁ ἀνήρ can readily be understood as "her husband." But this overlooks the many women in the early church who were virgins, widowed or divorced at the time of writing. It also discounts Paul's statement four chapters earlier that these women do well to remain unmarried (7:8, 11, 25, 40).[33]

The key issue, therefore, becomes the ecclesial relationship between male and female that requires women to cover their heads and men not to do so. Some focus on Paul's citation of Genesis 2:18 (אֶעֱשֶׂה-לּוֹ עֵזֶר כְּנֶגְדּוֹ). and read the relationship along hierarchical

---

[33] Although the Roman government made every effort to encourage —and even legislate remarriage (and so increase the critical mass of adult males), *univira* was the popular ideal. It cut across rank and social standing. The tombstones of an upper-class woman named Cornelia, a slave named Tabia, and a freedwoman named Aurelia equally extol the fact that they were once-married. See M. Lightman and W. Ziesel, "Univira: An Example of Continuity and Change in Roman Society," *Church History* 46 (1977) 21-25. Paul, of course, went even further and encouraged 'never-married' for the sake of expanding the Kingdom.

lines (1 Cor 11:9). Creation διὰ τὸν ἄνδρα is thought to be a statement about female subordination with head covering as a symbol
of subjection.[34] Yet, this misrepresents both Genesis 2:18 and Paul's
use of it. It assumes that the idea of subordination is implicit in
אֶעֱשֶׂה-לּוֹ עֵזֶר כְּנֶגְדּוֹ (e.g., NIV, NASB, NKJV, RSV, GW, YLT, JB
"helper") Recent scholarship has pointed to the fatal flaw in this line
of thinking. All of the other nineteen occurrences of עֵזֶר in the OT
have to do with the assistance that one of strength offers to one in
need (i.e., help from God, the king, an ally, or an army). More, fifteen
of these nineteen references speak of the help that God alone can
provide (Exod. 18:4; Deut. 33:7,26,29; Pss. 20:2; 33:20; 70:5; 115:9-
11 (3x); 121:1-2 (2x); 124:8; 146:5; Hos. 13:9). Help given to one in
need fits Genesis 2:18 quite well. The male's situation was לְבַדּוֹ; and
God's evaluation was לֹא-טוֹב (Gen. 2:18; 20). Therefore, a strong
"partner" (NEB, REB, CEV)—and not an "assistant" or "helper"—
accurately captures the sense of the Hebrew. This also fits with the
woman's creation כְּנֶגְדּוֹ—"in correspondence to" and not "suitable"
(NASU, TEV, CEV, NIV, JB), "fit" (RSV) or "right" (GW). She is
created as a personal counterpart—"equal and adequate to himself"
(*BDB* 14.55.2.a).

The question then is why a head covering is proper for a woman
but shameful for a man. First, it is important to notice what Paul
does not say. He does not say that the presence of a head covering
stigmatized a male in the eyes of society. What he does say is that
such an action shames *Christ* τὴν κεφαλὴν αὐτοῦ (v. 4) and that a
woman's uncovered head shames *the male* τὴν κεφαλὴν αὐτῆς· (vv.
5, 7).[35] This indicates that the concern is primarily theological, rather
than sociological; it is when a woman *prays to God* that a head covering is called for (v. 13). Paul's appeal to creation suggests the same.
A woman ought to cover her head because of her origin ἐξ ἀνδρός·

---

[34] For a classic statement of this position, see Bruce Waltke, "1 Corinthians
11:2-16: An Interpretation," *BibSac* 135 (1978) 46-57. William Martin goes so far
as to argue that long hair is a woman's "visually distinctive mark of womanhood"
and "a gesture of subordination" ("I Corinthians 11:2-16: An Interpretation," in
Apostolic History and the Gospel, edited by Ralph Martin and Ward Gasque [Grand
Rapids, Michigan: Eerdmans, 1970] 239). Joseph Fitzmyer states unequivocally
that 1 Corinthians 11:2-16 treats "woman's subordination to man according to
the Genesis account of creation" ("A Feature of Qumran Angelology and the Angels
of 1 Cor. XI.10," *NTS* 84 [1957-58] 51).

[35] Even those who take τὴν κεφαλὴν literally, acknowledge a secondary anaphoric
use of the article.

(vv. 7-9) and because ἡ φύσις αὐτὴ διδάσκει ὑμᾶς that women and men are to coiffure themselves differently: ὅτι ἀνὴρ μὲν ἐὰν κομᾷ ἀτιμία αὐτῷ ἐστιν, γυνὴ δὲ ἐὰν κομᾷ δόξα αὐτῇ ἐστιν; (v. 14).

Ἡ φύσις αὐτὴ and ἐξ ἀνδρός suggest that a blurring of creation-based gender distinctions is at issue. One thing is clear, however. There is nothing in the pericope to indicate that these distinctions are functional in nature. Paul decidedly approves of both women and men praying and prophesying (vv. 4-5). What they have (or do not have) over their heads as they engage in these liturgical activities is the concern. This means that the mention of woman coming ἐξ ἀνδρός and created διὰ τὸν ἄνδρα is not an attempt to subjugate women. Paul is equally at pains to show from creation that male liturgists should not cover their heads. Creation in the εἰκὼν καὶ δόξα of God excludes it (v. 7) and ἡ φύσις countermands it (v. 14).

The distinction between male and female is rooted in the term δόξα. It appears twice in Paul's rationale for a woman's head covering and the lack thereof for a man: The parallelism is important (vv. 7-9):

> ἀνὴρ μὲν γὰρ . . . εἰκὼν καὶ _δόξα θεοῦ_ ὑπάρχων·
> _οὐ_ γάρ ἐστιν ἀνὴρ _ἐκ γυναικὸς_
> καὶ γὰρ _οὐκ_ ἐκτίσθη ἀνὴρ _διὰ τὴν γυναῖκα_
>
> _ἡ γυνὴ_ δὲ _δόξα ἀνδρός_ ἐστιν
> ἀλλὰ γυνὴ _ἐξ ἀνδρός_
> ἀλλὰ γυνὴ (ἐκτίσθη) _διὰ τὸν ἄνδρα._

The male, by virtue of formation from the stuff of creation, reflects the δόξα of God (Gen 2:7 וַיִּיצֶר יְהוָה אֱלֹהִים אֶת-הָאָדָם עָפָר מִן- הָאֲדָמָה); the female, by virtue of creation ἐξ ἀνδρός and διὰ τὸν ἄνδρα, reflects the δόξα of the male (vv. 7-9). This idea is clearly present in Jewish theology. Men were fashioned to glorify God: וְלִכְבוֹדִי בְּרָאתִיו יְצַרְתִּיו אַף-עֲשִׂיתִיו (Isa 43:7); and women bring glory to men: καὶ αὗται ποιοῦσιν δόξαν τοῖς ἀνθρώποις καὶ οὐ δύνανται οἱ ἄνθρωποι εἶναι χωρὶς τῶν γυναικῶν (1 Esdr. 4:17).

The thrice repeated _dis_honor in verses 4-6 (καταισχύνει 2x; αἰσχρὸν) shows that δόξα in verses 7-8 has the vernacular meaning of "praise" or "honor," (_BAGD_ s.v.). The woman brings honor to τὴν κεφαλὴν αὐτῆς (ὁ ἀνήρ) by virtue of her creation ἐξ ἀνδρός and διὰ τὸν ἄνδρα. The difficulty in public worship, though, is that all honor and praise is to go to God. Commentators too often lose sight of Paul's theological focus. The object of worship is God, not man.

Paul underlines this point five times. "Whatever is done, is to be done so as to *glorify God*" (10:31), "a man who prays or prophesies with his head uncovered *glorifies God*" (11:7), "everything comes *from God* (v. 12), and every act of worship is to be directed *to God* (v. 13). If a woman uncovers her physical head, in-so-doing she draws attention to her creation ἐξ ἀνδρός. And this is wholly inappropriate in *God's churches* (v. 16). She must cover herself so that all attention is focused on God.

Διὰ τοὺς ἀγγέλους also points to a theological (versus sociological) concern (v. 10). 1 Corinthians highlights the place of angels in the affairs of the world and the church. "We have become a spectacle *to the world, both to angels and to human beings*" (1 Cor 4:9); "Do you not know that *we will judge angels?* (1 Cor 6:3); "If I speak in the *tongues of mortals and of angels*" (1 Cor 13:1). This accords with Jewish tradition, which places angels at the creation of humankind (e.g., Philo, *De OpifMundi* 24 [#72-75]; *De ConfLing* 35 [#179]) and at community worship. In LXX Psalm 137:1 David sings praises to God ἐναντίον ἀγγέλων and God's people. A similar idea is found in 1QSa 2.3-11, where "the Angels of Holiness are [with] their [congregation]" (compare 1QSb 4.26 "May you attend upon the service in the Temple of the Kingdom and decree destiny in company with the Angels of the Presence in common council [with the Holy Ones] for everlasting ages).[36] This same thought is present in early-church tradition. According to 1 Timothy 5:21, the angels function to provide witness and accountability: "I solemnly charge you in the presence of God and of Christ Jesus and of [His] chosen angels , to maintain these [principles] without bias" (1 Tim 5:21). The Church, in turn, reveals "God's manifold wisdom to [angelic] principalities and powers" (Eph 3:10).

It is within this context of gender-distinct worship that κεφαλὴ δὲ γυναικὸς ὁ ἀνήρ is to be understood. Although some are quick to assume that κεφαλή means "authority over," it is a conclusion drawn more from English usage and a Western mindset than from Greek linguistics and exegesis. Virtually all English translations render κεφαλή as "head." Yet, it is difficult to translate it this way without suggesting the idea of dominance.

---

[36] See Fitzmyer, "Qumran Angelology" pp. 48-58. See also, Beduhn's novel interpretation of διὰ τοὺς ἀγγέλους as Paul attributing gendered humanity to the flawed, creative act of angels ("Because of the Angels," 308-313.)

The simple fact is that κεφαλή rarely means anything other than the physical head of a body (human or otherwise).[37] In the case of non-literal, first-century uses (and earlier) of κεφαλή, the vast majority have to do with *prominence*—such as the top of a mountain (e.g., Gen. 8:5), pride of place (e.g., Deut. 28:13; Jer. 38:7; Isa 7:8-9), the foremost position in a column or formation (e.g., Job 1:17), the capstone of a building (Ps. 117:22), or the end of a pole (e.g., 2 Chron. 5:9). Κεφαλή is also used to denote "beginning," "source," or "origin"—such as the *progenitor* of a clan (e.g., Philo, *De Congress* 61 κεφαλὴ δὲ ὡς ζῴου πάντων τῶν λεχθέντων μερῶν ὁ γενάρχης ἐστὶν Ἠσαῦ,), the *beginning* (Orphica *Fragmenta* 6.13-14 Ζεὺς κεφαλή, Ζεὺς μέσσα, Διὸς δ᾽ ἐκ πάντα τέτυκταὶ), the *source* of evil (*Life of Adam and Eve* 19:3 ἐπιθυμία γάρ ἐστιν κεφαλὴ πάσης ἁμαρτίας.) and the *starting point* or origin of a river (Callimachus *Aetia* 43.44 [3rd B.C.] οἶδα Γέλα ποταμοῦ κεφαλῇ ἔπι κείμενον ᾄστυ Λίνδοθεν ἀρχαίη [σ]κιμπ [τόμενο]ν γενε[ῇ; Heroditus, *Hist.* 4.91.2 Τεάρου ποταμοῦ κεφαλαὶ ὕδωρ ἄριστόν τε καὶ κάλλιστον παρέχονται πάντων ποταμῶν·). There are also a few passages where κεφαλή appears to mean "leader" (e.g., Plutarch, *Cicero* 14.6-7 τί γάρ" ἔφη "πράττω δεινόν, εἰ δυοῖν σωμάτων ὄντων, τοῦ μὲν ἰσχνοῦ καὶ κατεφθινηκότος, ἐχοντος δὲ κεφαλήν, τοῦ δ᾽ ἀκεφάλου μέν, ἰσχυροῦ δὲ καὶ μεγάλου, τούτῳ κεφαλὴν αὐτὸς ἐπιτίθημι;).[38]

There is no evidence in first century (and earlier) extra-biblical Greek literature or papyri of κεφαλή with the meaning "master" or "ruler." Neither Liddell-Scott-Jones' *Greek-English Lexicon* nor Moulton and Milligan's *The Vocabulary of the Greek Testament Illustrated from the Papyri and Other Non-Literary Sources* give examples of κεφαλή with this meaning.[39] The LXX appears to use κεφαλή to mean "master," but

---

[37] In some instances, κεφαλή can stand for the whole person (e.g., Judg. 5:30) or for the "self" (e.g., Isa. 4:34). In Luke 21:28 ἐπάρατε τὰς κεφαλὰς ὑμῶν (literally "raise up the head") is an idiom for demonstrating courage in the face of danger or adversity. The phrase can also mean "to be proud" or "to try to take precedence over others." In Acts 18:6 τὸ αἷμα ὑμῶν ἐπὶ τὴν κεφαλὴν ὑμῶν· is an idiom for accepting responsibility for wrongdoing. In Romans 12:20 ἄνθρακας πυρὸς σωρεύσεις ἐπὶ τὴν κεφαλὴν αὐτοῦ. (literally "heap coals of fire on the head") is an idiom for causing someone to be ashamed or embarrassed. See Louw and Nida, *Semantic Domains* 25.160, 199; 37.102.

[38] See Judges 11:11, where Jephthah is chosen to be the leader of the people of Gilead; 2 Samuel 22:44 and Psalm 18:43, where David is said to be the leader of the nations (cf. Jeremiah 52:31).

[39] There are also no examples of κεφαλή with the meaning "ruler" in F. Preisigke's *Wörterbuch der griechischen Papyrusurkunden* (4 vols. and suppl.; Berlin: Gelbstverlag der Erben, 1925).

not in a positive sense. Israel's κεφαλαί are her foes (Lam. 1:5 ἐγένοντο οἱ θλίβοντες αὐτὴν εἰς κεφαλήν καὶ οἱ ἐχθροὶ αὐτῆς εὐθηνοῦσαν).

Four New Testament texts speak of Christ as the κεφαλή of the Church. In each case, the primary idea is source. The language throughout is physiological. As κεφαλή τῆς ἐκκλησίας· (no article) Christ is the *source* of the church's existence and αὐτὸς σωτὴρ τοῦ σώματος· (no article; Eph 5:23). The absence of an article with the nouns κεφαλή and σωτήρ indicates a descriptive, not titular use. Christ brings forth the church from himself as his "fullness" (Col. 2:10) and his body (μέλη ἐσμὲν τοῦ σώματος αὐτου; Eph. 5:23, 30-31).[40] The language is more than analogical. It is a "mystery." Where there had been "two" there is now "one" (οἱ δύο εἰς σάρκα μίαν [citing Gen. 2:24]). Christ is also the *source* of the church's health and growth. He feeds and care for the church (ἐκτρέφει καὶ θάλπει αὐτήν; Eph 5:29).[41] It is ἐξ οὗ that the whole body, is supported and held together by its ligaments and sinews and grows as God causes it to grow (Eph 4:15; Col. 2:19).

Two texts have Christ as the κεφαλή vis-à-vis the powers that be: The Colossians have been given fullness in Christ, who is ἡ κεφαλὴ πάσης ἀρχῆς καὶ ἐξουσίας (Col. 2:10). God placed all things under Christ's feet and appointed him to be κεφαλὴν ὑπὲρ πάντα τῇ ἐκκλησίᾳ, which is his body, the fullness of him τοῦ τὰ πάντα ἐν πᾶσιν πληρουμένου (Eph. 1:22). Despite the lack of linguistic support, it is often assumed that κεφαλή in these pericopes refers to "rule." Christ as Lord of the Church certainly has a place in the Pauline tradition. It is explicit in Paul's standard greeting, "the grace of our *Lord* Jesus Christ." But that lordship is what is meant by the term κεφαλή is dubious given the lack of linguistic evidence for this usage.

Stephen Bedale in his 1954 study is undoubtedly correct in assigning κεφαλὴ its most common non-literal meaning of "pre-eminent" or "foremost."[42] Christ as the pre-eminent member of the

---

[40] The nominative case of both phrases makes it clear that κεφαλὴ τῆς ἐκκλησίας and αὐτὸς σωτὴρ τοῦ σώματος are in apposition and, hence, parallel ideas.

[41] See Ceslas Spicq, *Theological Lexicon of the New Testament*, translated by James D. Ernest (Peabody, Mass.: Hendrickson, 1994) 2:184.

[42] Stephen Bedale, "The Meaning of Κεφαλή in the Pauline Epistles," *JTS* 5 (1954) 211-215. See also Andrew C. Perriman, "The Head of a Woman: the Meaning of Κεφαλή in 1 Cor. 11:3," *JTS* 45 (1994) 602-622.

relationship fits quite nicely. He is the beginning, the first-born from the dead in order that he might be *pre-eminent* in everything (Col. 1:18). God seated Christ ὑπεράνω πάσης ἀρχῆς καὶ ἐξουσίας καὶ δυνάμεως καὶ κυριότητος and placed all things ὑπὸ τοὺς πόδας αὐτου (Eph. 1:21-22) so that he is κεφαλή or "preeminent, supreme."

The *theo*-logical focus of 1 Corinthians 10:31-11:16 encourages us to understand κεφαλη in verse 3 as "pre-eminent part" as well. When a woman uncovers her head in the worship service, she draws inappropriate attention to her "foremost" part—the man. But when a man uncovers himself, he draws attention appropriate to his "foremost" part—God. Is this not, after all, what Paul means when he says that the man is the δόξα of God (v. 7)? Perhaps comparison with the top or "head" of a mountain is not far afield. All attention is draw to the highest of its snow-covered peaks. Κεφαλὴ and δόξα then are really two sides of the same coin:

κεφαλὴ δὲ γυναικὸς ὁ ἀνήρ
ἡ γυνὴ δὲ δόξα ἀνδρός ἐστιν

The female is the glory of the male by virtue of her creation ἐξ ἀνδρός and διὰ τὸν ἄνδρα (verses 7-9)—not by virtue of an act or gesture of subordination (such as covering the head). And the male has "pride of place" by virtue of the female coming ἐξ ἀνδρός and being created διὰ τὸν ἄνδρα—not by virtue of having authority over the female. A woman therefore must cover the male's glory, so that all worship and praise go to God, the Creator, and not to the male, the creature. Paul makes a similar point in Romans 1:21-25:

διότι γνόντες τὸν θεὸν οὐχ ὡς θεὸν ἐδόξασαν ἢ ηὐχαρίστησαν, ἀλλ᾽ . . . ἤλλαξαν τὴν δόξαν τοῦ ἀφθάρτου θεοῦ ἐν ὁμοιώματι εἰκόνος φθαρτοῦ ἀνθρώπου καὶ πετεινῶν καὶ τετραπόδων καὶ ἑρπετῶν. . . . οἵτινες μετήλλαξαν τὴν ἀλήθειαν τοῦ θεοῦ ἐν τῷ ψεύδει καὶ ἐσεβάσθ-ησαν καὶ ἐλάτρευσαν τῇ κτίσει παρὰ τὸν κτίσαντα.

It is commonly assumed that κεφαλὴ δὲ γυναικὸς ὁ ἀνήρ denotes hierarchy. Too often a Western understanding of "head" as "the person in charge" has been uncritically read into the biblical texts, despite the lack of first century supportive examples. Plus, the order in verse 3 does not really support it. Instead of God→ Christ→man→woman, we have Christ→man→woman→God. There is also the difficulty of explaining how exactly God rules over Christ. Further, there lacks any notion of male rule or authority in the verses that follow. Indeed, nowhere in Scripture is the male commanded to "rule over" the female.

The male as the *source* of the woman has a better claim. The idea is present in verse 8: γυνὴ ἐξ ἀνδρός. But the connection is not one of identity. While man as κεφαλή results from being the physical source of the woman, one is hard pressed to say the same of Christ as the κεφαλη of the man. Neither in this nor in any other New Testament letter is Christ κεφαλή as a result of being the literal and physical source of the male. This actually is the relationship between Christ and the Church (Eph 1:22; 4:15; Col 1:18; 2:19). The Church is "bone of his bones and flesh of his flesh" (Eph. 5:30).[43]

Part of the difficulty stems from the interrelatedness of the notions of "prominence," "origin," and "leader." For instance, privileges often accompany being the first or origin of something. And stature can easily follow from being the progenitor of a clan. This interrelatedness explains why scholars have reached different conclusions about the non-literal uses of κεφαλὴ in various NT texts.

It should finally be noted that κεφαλὴ δὲ γυναικὸς ὁ ἀνήρ is a new idea (v. 3). The opening phrase Θέλω δὲ ὑμᾶς εἰδέναι ὅτι is a stereotypical formula for introducing new information. It is wrong, therefore, to connect (as some do) κεφαλὴ δὲ γυναικὸς ὁ ἀνήρ with the apostolic tradition passed on to all the churches (v. 2).

Conclusion

To treat such matters at length—as Paul does here—leads one to think that some sort of sexual identity confusion lurks in the background. It may be that the Corinthians took "in Christ there is not male and female" (οὐκ ἔνι ἄρσεν καὶ θῆλυ·) to mean that they should seek to do away with gender distinctions (Gal. 3:28). In a culture where dress signalled maleness and femaleness, cross dressing would certainly be a step in that direction. Mosaic law prohibited it: "A woman must not wear men's clothing, nor a man wear women's clothing, for the Lord your God detests anyone who does this" (Deut 22:5). Cross-dressing in Greco-Roman culture was equally offensive.

---

[43] Ephesians 5:30 in the Western and Byzantine families of manuscripts, versions and Fathers from the second century on reads, "For we are members of his body, of his flesh and of his bones." Even if this is not original, it nonetheless reflects a post-apostolic theological understanding of μέλη ἐσμὲν τοῦ σώματος αὐτοῦ.

This may well be what Paul has in mind five chapters earlier with the vice μαλακοί. A papyrus text dating around 245 B.C. seems to use the Greek term in this way: "Send me also Zenobius the effeminate (τὸν μαλακόν) with a drum and cymbals and castanets, for he is wanted by the women for the sacrifice; and let him wear as fine clothes as possible" (P. Hib. I. 54).

Jerome Murphy-O'Connor may not be far off the mark when he supposes that Paul is concerned that the Corinthians' actions would be read by outsiders in a homosexual light.[44] It may be that Paul felt Roman religious practice blurred the sexual distinctions implicit in the creation order of Genesis 1-2. It is significant that what carried a stigma was a woman who cut her hair short or shaved her head (1 Cor. 11:6), a woman praying with her head uncovered (v. 14), a man praying with his head covered (v. 4), and long hair on a man (v. 14).

Whatever meaning we attach to Paul's statement, the context rules out male superiority—be it personal or functional. The female may be δόξα of the man by virtue of her creation ἐξ αὐτοῦ, but she is also the image of God (vv. 7-8). And she may have been created ἐκ the male but all men have come διά her from that point on (v. 12).

---

[44] "Sex and Logic," pp. 485-486.

FROM GOD'S FAITHFULNESS TO OURS
Another Look at 2 Corinthians 1:17–24

Morna D. Hooker

In an earlier article, I suggested that 2 Cor. 1:17–22 lent some support to the view that the phrase πίστις Χριστοῦ referred primarily to the faithfulness of Christ.[1] I argued that Paul's defence in this passage against the charge of vacillation is based on an appeal to the faithfulness of God himself (v.18), a faithfulness that is embodied in the person of Christ, who is the 'Yes' to all God's promises (v.19). Since Christians have been 'made firm' (v.21), and this verb is qualified by the phrase εἰς Χριστὸν, Paul is clearly claiming that he shares in this faithfulness through his incorporation into Christ. The logic of his argument is that he is reliable because God himself is reliable. '[H]e is not guilty of vacillating—of faithlessness—because he shares in the faithfulness of God himself; and he shares in that faithfulness by his incorporation into Christ, who is the embodiment of God's faithfulness'.[2] Since some, at least, of those involved in the ongoing debate about the meaning of πίστις Χριστοῦ have failed to understand my point,[3] it seems worth exploring this suggestion in greater depth.

The situation which Paul addresses in this passage is some kind of misunderstanding between the Corinthians and himself. He has changed his original plans about revisiting them (vv.15–16), and they have accused him of fickleness. He has behaved, they suggest, 'in a

---

[1] 'ΠΙΣΤΙΣ ΧΡΙΣΤΟΥ', Presidential Address to SNTS, 1988, *NTS* 35, 1989, 321–42, reprinted in M.D. Hooker, *From Adam to Christ*, Cambridge: CUP, 1990, 165–86.

[2] 'ΠΙΣΤΙΣ ΧΡΙΣΤΟΥ', 334–5/178.

[3] E.g. James D.G. Dunn, in "Once More, ΠΙΣΤΙΣ ΧΡΙΣΤΟΥ", in Elizabeth Johnson and David M. Hay, eds., *Pauline Theology* 4 (Atlanta: Scholars, 1997), 61–81, reprinted as Appendix 1 in Richard H. Hays, *The Faith of Jesus Christ*, Grand Rapids MI/Cambridge UK: Eerdmans, 2002², 231–48. Dunn's comment, 77/267, n.69, is puzzling. He writes: 'The same is true of 2 Cor 1:17–22—a reference to *God's* faithfulness, not Christ's (*pace* Hooker, "πίστις Χριστου,'" 177-78), though we might speak of God's faithfulness incarnated in Christ'. This, of course, is precisely what I myself had said!

worldly fashion'[4] (v.17), and so clearly cannot be relied on. We might
perhaps have expected Paul to respond immediately to these accusations with the explanation he gives for his actions in v.23: it had
been to spare them that he had decided not to visit them again. The
truth of what he says there is affirmed by the introductory oath:
'I call on God as witness against me'. Although this explanation is
enigmatic—since Paul thought it unnecessary to tell the Corinthians
what they were being spared by his absence—it does at least offer
some kind of reason for his change of plan. Vv.18–22 offer no such
explanation. Rather they maintain that the charge of fickleness is
clearly inappropriate, since what Paul is and does is determined by
the faithfulness of God himself.

Paul's argument begins with an appeal to the faithfulness of God:
πιστὸς δὲ ὁ Θεός. Some commentators suggest that this should be
understood as an oath-formula.[5] Others point out that the various
forms of Paul's oath-formulae are quite different from this.[6] One of
these formulae is, of course, used a few verses later, to introduce the
argument in v.23. Those who argue that the clause is not an oath-
formula suggest, instead, that it should be interpreted as a statement
from which the rest of the argument will be developed.[7] The two
interpretations are not, however, mutually exclusive. Thus Furnish,
who concludes that '[i]t should be interpreted ... as an oath formula',
nevertheless argues that Paul 'is saying, in effect, "Trust God! His
promises have been fulfilled in Christ, and our own faithfulness in
dealing with you has been assured by our preaching of Christ to you."'[8]

If this is indeed an 'oath-formula', then the question we should
be asking is why Paul has chosen to use *this* particular formula, rather
than make his usual appeal to God as his witness (as he does a few
verses later, in 2 Cor. 1:23), or employ, as he does elsewhere, the
phrase 'God knows' (2 Cor. 11:11, 31) or 'before God' (Rom. 9:1;
Gal. 1:20). The relevance of the theme of God's own faithfulness to

[4] Thrall's translation. See Margaret E. Thrall, *A Critical and Exegetical Commentary on the Second Epistle to the Corinthians*, ICC, Vol. 1, Edinburgh: T. & T. Clark,
1994, in loc.
[5] Among them, '[w]ith some hesitation', Thrall, *2 Corinthians*, 144.
[6] E.g. Alfred Plummer, *A Critical and Exegetical Commentary on the Second Epistle of
St. Paul to the Corinthians*, ICC, Edinburgh: T. & T. Clark, 1915, 34–5. See Rom.
1:9; 2 Cor. 11:11, 31; Gal. 1:20 for examples.
[7] E.g. Plummer, *2 Corinthians*, 34–5, quoting Chrysostom in support.
[8] Victor Paul Furnish, *II Corinthians*, Anchor Bible, New York: Doubleday, 1984,
135 and 145.

the argument that follows is sufficient explanation of its occurrence here. In other words, whether or not the clause is in fact an oath-formula, its significance lies in the integral relationship between God's faithfulness and Paul's own trustworthiness.

A comparison with other occurrences of the statement that 'God is faithful' reveals that they, too, link God's faithfulness with the implications for believers' own steadfastness. In 1 Cor. 1:9, Paul reminds the Corinthians that 'God is faithful; by him you were called into the fellowship of his Son, Jesus Christ our Lord'. And because it is God who called them, he will, as Paul has already explained in v.8, 'strengthen you to the end, so that you may be blameless on the day of our Lord Jesus Christ.' Similarly, in 1 Cor. 10:13, he assures them that 'God is faithful, and he will not let you be tested beyond your strength, but with the testing he will also provide the way out so that you may be able to endure it.' A similar link is seen in 1 Thess. 5:23–24. Because God is faithful, he can be relied on to keep the Thessalonians whole and blameless. It is found again in 2 Thess. 3:3: those who have faith (unlike those who have none) rely upon God (v.2), for 'the Lord is faithful; he will strengthen you and guard you from evil.' It is hardly surprising, then, that the same statement is the basis here for an argument about the character of Paul's behaviour: if God is faithful, he can be relied upon to make Paul himself firm.[9]

The accusation brought against Paul is that his word cannot be relied upon: he says both 'yes' and 'no', and the Corinthians do not know what to believe.[10] Paul insists that the accusation is unfounded: his word cannot be inconsistent, since God himself is faithful. But how does he argue from what *God* is to what *he himself* is and to his own actions? The answer, as always for Paul, is *through his relationship to Christ*. Here, the link is provided by the word λόγος, which appears to have a double meaning, since 'our word to you' is not just his own proposal to visit the Corinthians, but the 'word' which 'we'— i.e. 'Silvanus and Timothy and I'—proclaimed among them, and that word was 'the Son of God, Jesus Christ' (v.19). The reliability

---

[9] God's faithfulness—together with his righteousness and his truth—are seen as the guarantee that his purpose will be accomplished in Rom. 3:3-7. See also Rom. 1:17a, where ἐκ πίστεως may refer to God's faithfulness, now revealed in the gospel.

[10] The most likely meaning of v.17b is that Paul is charged with inconsistency. For a discussion of the possibilities, see Thrall, *2 Corinthians*, in loc.

of *this* word—the word of the gospel—is supported by the number
of witnesses: it was proclaimed by Silvanus and Timothy, as well as
by Paul. Its true guarantee, however, lies in its content, for what was
proclaimed among the Corinthians was Christ.

Christ himself is clearly reliable, for he is *the Son of God*, and so
shares God's faithfulness. There can be no suspicion of ambiguity
here, no suggestion that *this* word is both 'yes' and 'no'; on the contrary,
in him there is only a 'Yes'. That means that in him there is a 'Yes'
to all the promises of God.

But what has that 'Yes' to do with Paul and his co-workers? What
is the logical link between his statement concerning Christ—οὐκ
ἐγένετο ναὶ καὶ οὔ—and himself—οὐκ ἔστιν ναὶ καὶ οὔ? Paul's words
about Christ in v.19 deliberately echo the charge laid against himself in v.18. Moreover, the gospel of the Son of God was preached
through Paul and his companions—δι' ἡμῶν ... δι' ἐμοῦ (v.19)—and
their preaching was thus the 'Amen' to God's 'Yes'(v.20). Commentators interpret this 'Amen' in various ways, but the repetition of
δι' ἡμῶν links it with v.19. The 'Amen' is pronounced by those who
preach the gospel—δι' ἡμῶν—but they are enabled to do so through
the agency of Christ—δι' αὐτοῦ. The argument assumes, as Thrall
points out, that Paul is 'Christ's ambassador through whom God
himself speaks (5.20) and Christ speaks (13.3)'.[11]

The reliability of Paul's word, then, is guaranteed because it is
the 'Amen' to God's 'Yes'. This link is clearly set out in v.20:

> ἐν αὐτῷ τὸ ναί.
> διὸ καὶ δι' αὐτοῦ
> τὸ ἀμὴν τῷ Θεῷ πρὸς δόξαν
> δι' ἡμῶν.

The proclamation and acceptance of the gospel are the 'Amen' to
what God has done, in Christ, and redound to God's glory. But this
Amen, too, is pronounced δι' αὐτοῦ.

'The proclamation *and acceptance* of the gospel'. Although the
'through us' refers to what God is doing through the missionaries,
the 'Amen' is clearly *echoed* by those who accept their message. Not
surprisingly, then, Paul includes them in his next words: 'For God
confirms us, with you, into Christ' (v.21). Though the word was proclaimed *among* the Corinthians *by* Paul (v.19), those who accepted it
are also 'in Christ', as he himself is. The significance of the parti-

---

[11] Thrall, *2 Corinthians*, 147–8.

ciples used in vv. 21–22 has been much debated. Is the language baptismal? Are βεβαιῶν, σφραγισάμενος and δοὺς τὸν ἀρραβῶνα all legal terms?[12] The language may well be taken from the world of legal transactions, since that provided appropriate metaphors, and it may well have been used in connection with baptism, since that signified the relationship of the believer to Christ, but it is with this relationship itself that Paul is primarily concerned here, not with baptism. The unexpected use of the phrase εἰς Χριστὸν with βεβαιῶν reminds us that *it is only by being transferred 'into' Christ that believers are 'confirmed' or 'guaranteed'*. The use of the present tense suggests that God *continues* to keep Christians firm,[13] and so takes us back to the accusation made against Paul.

The remaining participles in vv. 21-22 are aorists. They refer to something that has been done and cannot be undone. Most interesting is the first, χρίσας. Following closely on the phrase εἰς Χριστὸν, it is clearly intended as a play on words. Those who have been put 'into Christ' share what he is, and have therefore been 'anointed', as he was. Paul, ever conscious of the true meaning of the term 'Christ', is probably thinking here of Christians being made members of the messianic community. As Messiah, Jesus embodies the qualities that should belong to the whole community. The fact that Christians have been sealed and given the Holy Spirit as a 'deposit', guaranteeing more to come, is yet further proof of the faithfulness of God, for it is he who has done and is doing all these things.

The accusation brought against Paul was that he had changed his travel plans. His use of the word λόγος has enabled him to argue that his word is reliable, since the word he proclaimed to them was Christ himself. If the Corinthians were still feeling contentious, they might well have accused Paul at this point of using a verbal form of sleight of hand! How, they may have wondered, can he equate the word of the gospel with his message about his movements—especially when his plans were in fact changed? The answer is found in his conviction that he, like the Corinthians, is continually 'confirmed into Christ'. Paul's 'Amen' to the gospel is spoken διὰ Χριστοῦ. But *everything* he does or says is now experienced in and through Christ. Even if his plans were changed, he himself is faithful.

---

[12] See the discussion in Thrall, *2 Corinthians*, in loc., and in C.K. Barrett, *The Second Epistle to the Corinthians*, Black's New Testament Commentaries, London: A. & C. Black, 1973, in loc.

[13] So Thrall, op. cit., 159.

Paul's conviction that his whole life is lived 'in Christ', and that
his mission is part of God's purpose for the spread of the gospel,
dominates the early chapters of 2 Corinthians. Paul has already used
this argument that all he does is experienced through Christ in the
opening verses of 2 Corinthians, where he has explained that, because he has shared in the sufferings of Christ, he has also experienced consolation διὰ τοῦ Χριστοῦ (v.5)—sufferings and consolation
which are, in turn, experienced by the Corinthians (v.7). He will use
it again in spelling out how he understands his ministry (2 Cor. 3:1—
6:13). It is set out most clearly in 5:16–21, where he speaks of the
new creation that takes place in Christ, through whom God has
reconciled the world to himself, and has entrusted Paul with the λόγος
of reconciliation. Just as Paul shares in the consolation of God through
Christ in 1:3–7, the life of God through Christ in 1:8–11, the glory
of God through Christ in 3:1—4:6, and the righteousness of God
through Christ in 5:16–21, so in 1:17–24, Paul shares in the *faithfulness* of God through Christ.

It is because Paul understands Christian life to be lived in and
through Christ, that he commonly appeals to statements of the gospel
and to theological principles when offering advice about Christian
behaviour;[14] here he does the same in justifying his own behaviour.
His first, and theological, defence against the accusation of vacillating is to appeal to the faithfulness of God himself—a faithfulness which
was manifested in Christ, and which is now shared by those who
are in him. In vv. 23–4, however, he deals with the accusation in a
much more down-to-earth manner.

He begins, nevertheless, by calling God to be his witness—the God
already declared to be faithful—so affirming the truth of his own
testimony. He changed his plans, he tells the Corinthians, in order
to spare them: whether he wished to spare them further discipline
or sorrow (the two would presumably have been linked) he does not
explain: perhaps sorrow (or pain) is primarily in his mind, since that
contrasts with 'joy' in v.24, and λύπη is in fact the subject of 2:1.
His intention, he says, is not to control their faith (a comment probably occasioned by another Corinthian accusation!), for his concern
is their joy.[15] 'For you', he says, 'stand firm in faith'. The two ref-

---

[14] See, e.g., Rom. 14:9; 15:3; 1 Cor. 8:11-12; 2 Cor. 8:9.
[15] The phrase συνεργοί ἐσμεν τῆς χαρᾶς ὑμῶν is ambiguous. Does it mean
'fellow-workers with you for your joy' or 'fellow-workers with Silvanus and Timo-

erences to πίστις in this verse echo the theme of the previous section. Is this final πίστει in v.24 instrumental?[16] But why, it is asked, should the Corinthians be reminded that the basis of the Christian existence is faith? Is it local?[17] But why, others ask, should the Corinthians be told here that they are standing firm in their faith? The answer to both these questions points us in the right direction. What Paul is affirming is that it is faith—or faithfulness—that makes the Corinthians stand firm, just as he himself does.

In the previous section, vv.17–22, Paul has argued that God himself is faithful, and that he has demonstrated his faithfulness by saying 'Yes' to all his promises in Christ. The apostle and his fellow-preachers said 'Amen' to that by proclaiming Christ, and God 'confirmed' the Corinthians, with them, into Christ. If they stand firm 'in faith' it is because they are in Christ. Paul is not dominating the Corinthians, but enabling them to say the same 'Amen' as he himself has given to the gospel. Christian faith is the response to God's faithfulness, but it is also a sharing in Christ's faithfulness. Believers share in Christ's faithfulness because, like him, they trust in God, and because they trust in God, who is faithfulness, they themselves stand firm.

Paul's defence against the accusation that he is fickle is that he cannot be, since God himself is not fickle. If he shares in God's faithfulness it is because he, like all Christians, has been transferred 'into Christ' and now lives in him. It is *through Christ* that he shares the faithfulness of God, and it is *in Christ* that he 'stands firm in faith', trusting in God to confirm him. 2 Cor. 1:17–24 spells out one aspect of what Paul means when he says that God acts ἐκ πίστεως εἰς πίστιν (Rom. 1:17).[18] It supports the view that the phrase πίστις Χριστοῦ refers primarily to the faithfulness of Christ—the embodiment of God's own faithfulness—and *consequently*, to the faith or faithfulness of those who are 'in Christ' as well.

---

thy for your joy'? The fact that the words follow the plural κυριεύομεν supports this second interpretation. Whichever we choose, Paul's own concern is clear.

[16] So Barrett, *Corinthians*, in loc.

[17] So Furnish, *II Corinthians*, in loc.

[18] The phrase ἐκ πίστεως in Rom. 1:17a has been variously interpreted as referring to (1) God's faithfulness (2) Christ's faithfulness and (3) the faith of believers. Since Paul is speaking of the way in which God's righteousness is revealed in the gospel, however, (3) is excluded. On the meaning of this phrase, see the discussion in Douglas A. Campbell, "Romans 1:17—A *Crux Interpretum* for the Πίστις Χριστοῦ Debate", *JBL* 113, 1994, 265–85, and literature cited there.

TIME OF RECEIPT OF THE RESURRECTION BODY— A PAULINE INCONSISTENCY?

Paul Woodbridge

I am delighted to have been invited to contribute to this book of essays for Dr. Margaret Thrall. I had the privilege of having Margaret as my PhD supervisor in the late 1970s and early 1980s, as well as being taught by her while I was doing a BA in Biblical Studies at the University College of North Wales (as it was called then), Bangor. I found her to be an inspirational teacher while an undergraduate, and students recognised her thorough scholarship and attention to detail. She was also someone who laid great emphasis on the importance of good exegesis. I recall her saying something like 'You should feel free to disagree with commentators, whoever they are, if you think, on the basis of good exegesis, that they are wrong!'. As a student, I benefited from her wise comments on numerous occasions, as she gave freely of her time and guided me through all the rigours of research. Her two volumes on 2 Corinthians in the ICC series are models of precise, discerning exegesis, and evidence of the sort of detailed, conscientious work that characterised her teaching and supervisions. She is a notable scholar and a Festschrift is a fitting tribute to her life as an academic teacher and writer.

1. *Introduction*

When did the apostle Paul believe that a Christian believer would receive their resurrection body? Two passages which appear to give information on this question are said by some scholars to be inconsistent. Thus it seems clear from 1 Cor. 15 that the believer does not receive the resurrection body until the Parousia—see verse 22-26 (the order for the resurrection of the dead taking place is first Christ, then *at his coming*, ἐν τῇ παρουσίᾳ αὐτοῦ, those who belong to Christ, v.23), 50-52 (it is at the last trumpet, at the coming of Christ, that the resurrection body will be given). From v.50 in particular, it would seem that the material elements of the two bodies are not identical; therefore the passage from one to the next requires that special act of God which is associated with the Parousia. According to this argument, Christians who die before the Parousia have not yet been resurrected, and in this chapter this resurrection of all believers takes place at the same moment, at the Parousia. Compare also 1 Thess. 4:15-17—it is at the Parousia that the dead in Christ will rise and then would take place the transformation of the living.

However in 2 Corinthians 5 there seems to be a different answer to this question.[1] Verse 1 is said to show that it is at the moment of death that the heavenly body is received—there is no gap between death and the Parousia during which the believer is disembodied—when the believer's earthly tent is destroyed, and one has (note the present tense—ἔχομεν) a building from God. It is only by receiving the resurrection body at death that this state of nakedness will be avoided (v.3). The believer longs to receive this clothing so that what is mortal may be swallowed up by life without any interval of being unclothed (v.4). So the 'clothing upon' (ἐπενδύσασθαι) with 'our heavenly habitation' (v.2, τὸ οἰκητήριον ἡμῶν τὸ ἐξ οὐρανοῦ) is something that follows immediately upon the dissolution of 'the earthly house of our tabernacle' (v.1 ἡ ἐπίγειος ἡμῶν οἰκία τοῦ σκήνους). So for individual believers, it is at death that they will receive the building that God has provided as soon as their present physical body is destroyed. On this understanding, there is no interval between death and resurrection, as there appears to be in 1 Cor. 15.

Thus Paul appears to give quite different answers to the question: When does the believer receive their resurrection body? According to 1 Cor. 15 no believers receive their resurrection body until the Parousia. Individual Christians dying at different times do not each experience resurrection as soon as they die. But in 2 Cor. 5:1, the believer is clothed with the resurrection body, 'the building that God has provided', οἰκοδομὴν ἐκ θεοῦ, as soon as the 'earthly frame' in which they are now 'housed', that is, their present physical body, is

---

[1] For a survey of the history of exegesis of 2 Cor. 5:1-10, see especially F.G. Lang, *2 Korinther 5,1-10 in der neueren Forschung* (Tübingen: J.C.B. Mohr, 1973), 9-161; P. Hoffmann, *Die Toten in Christus* (Münster: Aschendorff, 1966), 254-267; M.J. Harris, *The Interpretation of 2 Corinthians 5:1-10 and its Place in Pauline Eschatology* (unpublished PhD thesis, Manchester: 1970); C.M. Pate, *Adam Christology as the Exegetical and Theological Substructure of 2 Cor. 4:7-5:21* (New York: University Press of America, 1991), 1-21 (cited by M.E. Thrall, *2 Corinthians* I, (Edinburgh: T. & T. Clark, 1994), 357, n.1150).

destroyed, that is, immediately after death. So on this interpretation there is no interval between death and resurrection, as there appears to be in 1 Cor. 15 and 1 Thess. 4.[2]

A variety of ways of understanding this apparent inconsistency have been put forward, but we will confine ourselves to examining two of the main suggestions, that Paul developed[3] in his thinking between the writing of 1 Cor. 15 and 2 Cor. 5—the exegetical basis for this and possible objections to it will be briefly considered—, and an alternative exegesis which argues that it is possible to understand 2 Cor. 5 not in terms of change or development in Paul's thinking when compared with 1 Cor. 15, but rather in terms of fitting in with Paul's overall teaching on the time a believer receives the resurrection body, which was at the Parousia.

2. *Development Solution*

A number of scholars consider that the apparent inconsistency is resolved by arguing that Paul's thinking developed[4] concerning the

---

[2] Amongst those who note this apparent inconsistency, compare W.D. Davies, *Paul and Rabbinic Judaism* (London: SPCK, 1955, 311); J.A. Schep, *The Nature of the Resurrection Body* (Grand Rapids: Eerdmans, 1964), 206; M.E. Thrall, *The First and Second Letters of Paul to the Corinthians* (Cambridge: University Press, 1965), 144; H.M. Shires, *The Eschatology of Paul in the Light of Modern Scholarship* (Philadelphia: Fortress, 1966), 86-88; H. Ridderbos, *Paul—An Outline of his Theology* (London: SPCK, 1977), 500f., esp. n.33; F.F. Bruce, *Paul: Apostle of the Free Spirit* (Exeter: Paternoster, 1977), 312; D.E. Garland, *2 Corinthians* (Nashville: Broadman and Holman, 1999), 253-5; J. Lambrecht, *2 Corinthians* (Minnesota: The Liturgical Press, 1999), 88-9.

[3] On the matter of hypotheses of development in Pauline theology, particularly his eschatology, see especially J. Lowe, "An Examination of Attempts to Detect Development in St Paul's Theology", *JTS* 42 (1941), 129-142; C.H. Dodd, "The Mind of Paul: I" and "The Mind of Paul: II" in *New Testament Studies* (Manchester: University Press, 1953), 67-82 and 83-128; M.J. Harris, *Interpretation*, 227-260; W. Baird, "Pauline Eschatology in Hermeneutical Perspective", *NTS* 17 (1971), 314-327; W. Mearns, "Early Eschatological Development in Paul: The Evidence of I and II Thessalonians", *NTS* 27 (1981), 137-157; idem, "Early Eschatological Development in Paul: the Evidence of 1 Corinthians", *NTS* 22 (1984), 19-35; B.F. Meyer, "Did Paul's View of the Resurrection of the Dead Undergo Development?", *TS* 47 (1986), 363-387, especially 364-374; L.J. Kreitzer, *Jesus and God in Paul's Eschatology*, (Sheffield: JSOT, 1987), 177-9; I.H. Marshall, "A New Understanding of the Present and the Future: Paul and Eschatology" in R.N. Longenecker (Ed.), *The Road from Damascus*, (Cambridge: Eerdmans, 1997), 51-2.

[4] The theory of development argues that Paul at one stage in his life held a particular view, but at a later stage modified or expanded his thinking so as to hold a different view. Thus his thinking developed and his ideas progressed. Some

time a believer is to receive the resurrection body and that in 2 Cor. 5:1-10, in contrast to 1 Cor. 15, Paul taught that the believer was invested with the resurrection body at the moment of death.

2.1 *Ways of Accounting for Development in Paul's Thinking*

One question probably worth asking is *why* Paul's thinking might have developed concerning the time believers receives their spiritual bodies. Probably the most frequently suggested reason is the influence of the incident described in 2 Cor. 1:8ff. The hard trial Paul endured in Asia showed him that death was lying in wait for him and could overtake him at any moment. The perils that Paul experienced brought about a crisis of thought as he came face to face with death. Such events constrained him to give more thought than he had previously done to what happened to the Christian at death and he was thus led to state his newly formed belief that the Christian at death was not left naked (2 Cor. 5:3—οὐ γυμνοὶ εὑρεθησόμεθα) but immediately received the heavenly body.

So while in 1 Cor. 15 Paul believed that the Christian received the spiritual body at the Parousia, as a result of the experience described in 2 Cor. 1:8ff. which had a deep effect on Paul's eschatological thinking, he brought forward this event to the moment of death (2 Cor. 5:1ff.).[5]

However, many would raise critical comments on the significance of this incident as being a major influence in making Paul change his thinking on this matter. Such criticisms may be summarised thus: a) the danger of death referred to in 2 Cor. 1:8f. was not the first time Paul had become aware of the possibility of dying before the Parousia—cf. 1 Cor. 15:30-32; 2 Cor. 11:23-33. b) Paul's 'solution' to the 'problem' of death before the Parousia was *always* hope of

who argue that Paul developed his eschatological thinking put forward a case for saying that the apostle's later ideas do not necessarily contradict his earlier ones, whereas other scholars appear to think that Paul developed his thinking in the sense that he changed his mind on various issues, so that at a later stage he held to beliefs which contradicted his earlier ones on these topics. This is an important distinction to bear in mind when considering different development theories.

[5] Those who take this line include R.F. Hettlinger, "2 Corinthians 5:1-10", *SJT* 10 (1957), 183, 186f.; K. Hanhart, *The Intermediate State in the NT* (Gronigen: Wever, 1966), 160f.; C. Buck and G. Taylor, *Saint Paul—A Study of the Development of his Thought* (New York: Scribner's, 1969), 54-60; M.J. Harris, *Interpretation*, 41f.; idem, "2 Corinthians 5:1-10: Watershed in Paul's Eschatology?", *TynB* 22 (1971), 56f.; F.F. Bruce, *Free Spirit*, 295, 300, 310.

resurrection—cf. Phil.3:10f., 20f.; Rom.8:17f. c) Paul orientates himself according to his situation rather than changing his views when it seemed likely that his death was near. d) Death was always a real question in the apostle's mind—see 1 Thess. 4:13-18; also 1 Cor. 15 was written partly to answer problems about the dead. e) It is unlikely that Paul would have changed his mind on various matters simply because it was his *own* death that might be in prospect. f) It is doubtful that the apostle would substantially modify his thinking in the short space of time between the writing of 1 and 2 Corinthians. g) The argument that the Asian situation has given rise to particular eschatological ideas being expressed is not the same as saying that this situation also explains the origin of these ideas.[6]

2.2 *Exegetical Basis for Suggesting Development in Paul's Thinking*

We turn now to consider the exegetical basis that has been put forward for suggesting development in Paul's thinking in 2 Cor. 5:1-10. In doing so, we will note particularly the work of M.J. Harris, who has written in considerable detail and provided a strong basis for this view[7].

Clearly the precise identification of οἰκοδομὴ in 5:1 is important. Thrall notes nine proposals for its meaning[8] and Harris argues that as ἐπίγειος οἰκία (5:1a) refers specifically to the physical body (cf. 4:16a), 'it would destroy the parallelism and opposition of the two parts of 2 Cor. 5:1 if the second, antithetical οἰκία were referred to anything other than some form of embodiment'.[9]

Positively in favour of identifying οἰκοδομὴ with the spiritual body (σῶμα πνευματικόν) is the correspondence between Paul's description of the 'building' in 2 Cor. 5:1 and this spiritual body in 1 Cor. 15. Thus both are of divine origin ('from God', ἐκ θεοῦ, 5:1; 'from heaven', ἐξ οὐρανοῦ, 5:2, cf. 1 Cor. 15:38—'but God gives it a body as he has chosen', referring to the naked grain of v.37); both are

---

[6] On these points, see R. Berry, "Death and Life in Christ" *SJT* 14 (1961), 60f.; Hoffmann, *Toten*, 259, 327-329; W.G. Kümmel, *The Theology of the NT* (London: SCM, 1974), 239; B.F. Meyer, "Did Paul's View of the Resurrection of the Dead undergo Development?" *TS* 47 (1986), 384ff.; D.E Garland, *2 Corinthians*, 254f.

[7] See M.J. Harris, *Interpretation*; '2 Corinthians 5:1-10', 32-57; *Raised Immortal. Resurrection and Immortality in the New Testament*, (London: Marshall, Morgan and Scott, 1983).

[8] M.E. Thrall, *2 Corinthians*, I, 363-8.

[9] M.J. Harris, "2 Corinthians 5:1-10", 39.

spiritual ('not made with hands', ἀχειροποίητον 5:1, cf. 1 Cor. 15:44, 46—'spiritual'); both are permanent and indestructible ('eternal', αἰώνιον 5:1, cf. 1 Cor. 15:42, 52-54—'imperishable'); both are heavenly ('in the heavens', ἐν τοῖς οὐρανοῖς 5:1, cf. 1 Cor. 15:40—'celestial bodies' 15:48—'those who are of heaven').[10] This seems to be clear evidence that in 2 Cor. 5:1ff. we are dealing with the believer's receipt of the resurrection body. Further in 5:2 Paul speaks of believers groaning (στενάζομεν) as they long to put on the 'heavenly dwelling'. We may note that in Rom.8:23 Paul also speaks of believers 'groaning' as they wait for the redemption of their bodies; it seems not unreasonable to say that 'heavenly dwelling' refers to the heavenly body. Further when Paul says in 2 Cor. 5:4 that 'mortality is swallowed up by life' and speaks in vv. 2,3,4 of being 'clothed upon', this may well recall 1 Cor. 15:53 where he speaks of being clothed with the resurrection body; also, the term 'swallow' (καταπίνω) appears in both passages (2 Cor. 5:4 and 1 Cor. 15:54). Also the term 'clothe' (ἐνδύω), which is used in 2 Cor. 5:3, occurs four times in 1 Cor. 15:53-54. It would seem that the case for identifying οἰκία and οἰκοδομή has considerable strength.

Another crucial exegetical question is the sense of ἔχομεν. Those who favour development in 2 Cor. 5 usually argue that this signifies a future acquisition of a spiritual body rather than a present possession.[11] The key issue is whether this occurs at the Parousia or at death. Someone like Harris in favouring development in Paul's thinking at this point argues that it is highly unlikely that it refers to the Parousia as the time for receipt of the new body (i.e. the present tense of the verb pointing to an assured, future possession), for two reasons: what sort of consolation would be afforded at the point of death if all Paul is assuring the believer is of something that would happen at the Parousia?

'The moment when the consolation is needed must be the moment when the consolation is given; and the consolation received at death cannot simply be identical with that assurance of the fu-

---

[10] M.J. Harris, "2 Corinthians 5:1-10", 39-40; R. Gundry, σωμα in Biblical Theology, (Cambridge: Cambridge University Press, 1976), p,150; J. Osei-Bonsu, "Does 2 Cor. 5:1-10 teach the reception of the resurrection body at the moment of death?" JSNT 28 (1986), 97, n.24; P. Barnett, 2 Corinthians, (Grand Rapids: Eerdmans, 1997), 259-60.

[11] This is also true of those who want to argue that Paul is consistent in what he teaches on the time of receipt of the resurrection body, i.e. at the Parousia.

ture acquisition of the resurrection body which is already possessed during life'.[12]

One possible response to this might be that in both 1 Cor. 15 and 1 Thess. 4 Paul uses precisely these same terms to comfort those who are worried about believers who have died before Christ's return. It should not be thought that it would be different in his own case.[13]

Harris' proposal is that ἔχομεν is a clear indication that the σῶμα πνευματικόν is received at the point of death, i.e. at the moment when the earthly tent-dwelling is destroyed. Once one state ends, immediately the other state takes over. 'When(ever) our earthly tent-dwelling is taken down, we (immediately) become possessors of a building from God'.[14]

Harris and others who favour development in 2 Cor. 5 also suggest that the use of the verb ἐπενδύεσθαι (vv.2,4) = 'to put on in addition' is a further indication that the spiritual body is to be received at the point of death. Why did Paul use this double compound verb here when in 1 Cor. 15, in a similar context, he uses ἐνδύεσθαι?[15] Some would claim this indicates a difference in meaning: 'those who have been temporarily stripped of their corporeality by death, at the resurrection are *reclothed* by the spiritual body, while those who survive to witness the Parousia are *overclothed* by the resurrection body'.[16] If this is so, then in 2 Cor. 5:2,4 Paul is describing a strong desire to be alive at the Parousia so there will be no unwanted period of nakedness; this would imply that the spiritual body is *not* received at death which would fit in with what Paul wrote in 1 Cor. 15. But this would not fit the interpretation of 5:1 by those who favour development.

Harris cites M. Zerwick, who suggests that in Hellenistic Greek the compound may mean the same as the simple form—in general, Hellenistic Greek preferred a compound in place of simple forms.[17]

---

[12] M.J. Harris, "Corinthians 5:1-10", 41, noted also by M.E. Thrall, *2 Corinthians* I, 368.

[13] This point is made by J. Osei-Bonsu, "2 Cor. 5:1-10", 87.

[14] M.J. Harris, *Raised Immortal*, 99.

[15] See also the discussion on this point in C.K. Barrett, *2 Corinthians*, (London: A and C Black, 1973), 152-3; V. Furnish, *2 Corinthians*, (Garden City: Doubleday, 1984), 267; M.E. Thrall, *2 Corinthians* I, 371-2; P. Barnett, *2 Corinthians*, 259-60; D.E. Garland, *2 Corinthians*, 258.

[16] M.J. Harris, '2 Corinthians 5:1-10', 43.

[17] M. Zerwick, *Biblical Greek*, (Rome: Pontifical Institute, 1963), 162 sec.484, cited by M.J. Harris, *Interpretation*, 88, n.3. See also his comment that there was a

He then goes on to suggest that Paul selected ἐπενδύειν rather than
ἐνδύειν to demonstrate that the 'continuity between the successive
forms of corporeality—the natural body and the spiritual body—
was such that the ἐνδύσις presupposes no ἐκδύσις and was therefore more accurately an ἐπενδύσις, the physical body being the χιτών
over which the ἐπενδύτης of the resurrection body was cast'.[18] It
also demonstrates the immediate succession between the two forms
of embodiment. Thus Paul saw himself as gaining the resurrection
body without first having to take off the earthly body—'it was to be
a case of addition without prior subtraction, a case not of investi-
ture succeeding divestiture, but of "superinvestiture" without any divestiture'.[19] There was to be no time gap between death and the
reception of the new body—the moment of death was the precise
moment when that body was given.

   Those who favour development in Paul in this matter would also
suggest that his use of the word γυμνός supports the view of the resurrection body being received at death.[20] Paul indicates in v.3 (following on from v.2) that while in the present body the believer groans
because of a wish to be clothed with a heavenly dwelling while still
alive, knowing that once it is put on there will never be a state of
nakedness. In v.4 he indicates that while in this earthly body, the
believer does groan because of a desire to be overclothed (i.e. to put
on an overgarment) rather than putting off the present clothing (i.e.
this earthly body). Development scholars would translate v.3 thus:
'On the assumption, of course, that being clothed with a heavenly
habitation at death we shall not be found naked' and v.4 would be
understood as 'We groan, while burdened with the physical body,
as we look forward to the deliverance that comes through death and
the immediate over-clothing with the heavenly garment'. It is some-

---

tendency in Hellenistic Greek to use double compounds by way of reinforcing the
sense (88). So we have δύω ('put on'), from which there comes ἐνδύω with the
same sense, followed by ἐπενδύω ('to put on over')—cf. M.E. Thrall, *2 Corinthians*
I, 372 n.1266.
   [18] M.J. Harris, "2 Corinthians 5:1-10", 44; *Interpretation*, 98.
   [19] M.J. Harris, "2 Corinthians 5:1-10", 44; *Interpretation*, 100; cf. also *Raised
Immortal*, 99.
   [20] For full discussion of the possible meanings of γυμνός, see V. Furnish, *2
Corinthians*, 268, 298; J. Gillman, "A Thematic Comparison: 1 Cor. 15:50-57 and
2 Cor. 5:1-5" *JBL* 107 (1988), 447 n.25; M.E. Thrall, *2 Corinthians* I, 374-380;
D.E. Garland, *2 Corinthians*, 259-260. See also the bibliography in W.L. Craig,
"Paul's Dilemma in 2 Corinthians 5:1-10: A 'Catch-22'?", *NTS* 34 (1988), 147,
n.2; J. Gillman, "Thematic Comparison", 447, n.25.

times suggested that Paul is counteracting the views of those who argue that the disembodied state was the ideal to look forward to and denied a bodily resurrection. Paul is saying that a disembodied immortality, a naked soul, is not the final state and not the Christian hope.[21]

We may note that Harris indicates two other points of contrast relevant to this alleged inconsistency: in 2 Cor. 5:4 we read that 'immortal life' swallows up those who are mortal at death, whereas in 1 Cor. 15:35f. those who are mortal put on immortality at the Parousia. Also κατεπόθη ὁ θάνατος εἰς νῖκος (1 Cor. 15:54) differs from ἵνα καταποθῇ τὸ θνητὸν ὑπὸ τῆς ζωῆς (2 Cor. 5:4) in that in the former, victory over death takes place at the Parousia, while in the latter what is mortal is swallowed up by life at the point of death.[22]

Thus to summarise the case for arguing that in 2 Cor. 5:1-10 Paul is asserting that he (and other believers) will receive their resurrection (spiritual) body at the moment of death:

1) In v.1 ἐὰν effectively has the same meaning as ὅταν: 'whenever the taking down, the dismantling, of the earthly body, the tent, occurred, that would be the point at which the possession of the heavenly dwelling, the spiritual body, would begin'.

2) The present tense ἔχομεν indicates that between the destruction of the 'earthly body/tenthouse' and provision of 'a building not made with hands', there would not be an interval of nakedness, homelessness. In other words death was the moment when the spiritual body was received.

3) Paul uses ἐπενδύεσθαι rather than ἐνδύεσθαι in vv.2,4 not to underline a difference between the transformation of the living and the resurrection of the dead at the Parousia but rather to suggest 'immediate succession between two types of embodiment'. Before the putting on of the spiritual body there was no putting off of the natural body; thus ἐπενδύεσθαι was the more apt term as the dissolution of the natural, earthly body.[23]

---

[21] See on this matter, F.F. Bruce, *1 & 2 Corinthians* (London: Marshall, Morgan and Scott, 1971), 203; R. Bultmann, *The Second Letter to the Corinthians* (Minneapolis: Augsburg: 1976), 135-9; M. Harris, *Raised Immortal*, 223-4; J. Osei-Bonsu, "2 Cor. 5:1-10", 90-91; T.F. Glasson, "2 Corinthians v.1-10 versus Platonism" *SJT* 43 (1990), 145-155; M.E. Thrall, ibid.

[22] M.J. Harris, *Interpretation*, 115.

[23] M.J. Harris, *Interpretation*, 222f.

3. *Alternative Exegesis Solution*

We will now consider an exegesis of 2 Cor. 5:1-10 which seeks to show its consistency with 1 Cor. 15.[24]

It seems reasonable to say that in 2 Cor. 5:1 as in 1 Cor. 15, Paul shows that the consummation of heavenly existence will involve a new bodily form. It may be argued that οἰκία in both parts of v.1 refers to a body, and that this consideration, together with the parallel to 1 Cor. 15:47-49 (where earthly and heavenly bodily existence are also compared), indicate that it is the heavenly resurrection body that Paul has in mind when οἰκία occurs a second time in v.1.[25]

Thus it may be argued that Paul is talking in v.1 of earthly and heavenly bodily existence. The conclusion of the process of dying (4:10-12) and decay (4:16) is the body's demise in death. At death the earthly tent-dwelling is taken down. This sort of description fits only the death of a believer prior to Christ's return. It does not aptly describe what occurs to those who survive and are still alive at the Parousia. The sort of language Paul uses for that is of transformation which will involve a 'putting on' without having first to 'take off' (cf. vv.2-4; 1 Cor. 15:51-2). Those still alive at the Parousia must have their earthly bodies changed, but not destroyed. [26]

Since this clause refers to death before Christ's return, this would support interpreting ἐάν as conditional ('if') rather than as temporal ('when'). Perhaps Paul is considering more specifically the possibility of his own death before Christ's return, but there is still some uncertainty and it could well be argued that here as in 1 Thess. 4:13ff. and 1 Cor. 15:51ff. the apostle is still considering the twofold possibility of death or Christ's prior return which would mean transformation for him. It seems reasonable to say that Paul here in 2 Cor. 5 is more personally involved in the dilemma of death before the

---

[24] See especially on this R. Berry, "Death and Life in Christ. The Meaning of 2 Corinthians 5:1-10", *SJT* 14 (1961), 60-76; A.T Lincoln, *Paradise Now and Not Yet* (Cambridge: University Press, 1981), 59-71; J. Osei-Bonsu, "2 Cor. 5:1-10", 81-101; R.H. Gundry, σῶμα, 146-154; B.F. Meyer, "Paul's View of the Resurrection", 368ff.; J. Gillman, "Thematic Comparison", 439ff.; P. Barnett, *2 Corinthians*, 255ff.; D.E. Garland, *2 Corinthians*, 253ff.

[25] See also the points on pp. 245-6 above; also see appropriate places in commentaries already mentioned, notably C.K. Barrett, *2 Corinthians*, 150-2; J. Osei-Bonsu, "2 Cor. 5:1-10", 85-6; M.E. Thrall, *2 Corinthians*, 363-8; P. Barnett, *2 Corinthians*, 256-8; J. Lambrecht, *2 Corinthians*, 82, 87-9; D.E. Garland, *2 Corinthians*, 252-3.

[26] See on this, J.Osei-Bonsu, "2 Cor. 5:1-10", 82f.

Parousia than in previous passages, but even so he is still convinced as in 1 Cor. 15 that if he does die, he has a spiritual, resurrection body from God.[27]

In the light of this it may well be argued that the present tense ἔχομεν emphasises Paul's assurance and further should be understood as indicating a future possession of the spiritual body. To those who say that ἔχομεν points to an *immediate* succession between the earthly and heavenly bodies, it might be responded, 'it is precisely the element of immediacy which is missing from the text and which has to be read into it'.[28] So it may well be preferable to interpret ἔχομεν as a futuristic present expressing such a firm hope, a confident certainty of possessing the new body at the Parousia that it could be spoken of as present.[29]

To the objection that this interpretation takes away any sense of conditionality in 2 Cor. 5:1 (as receipt of the heavenly body *at Christ's return* was a certainty whether or not death had previously taken place[30]) a response might be that it is more a question of where the emphasis is taken to be. The first alternative would be, '*If* we die we *do* have the spiritual body at the Parousia'. In this case the conditionality would have to be disregarded, since *all* believers, Paul supposed, would receive the resurrection body (not *only* those who died). But the second alternative might be 'If we should *die* we (shall still) have the spiritual body at the Parousia'. In view of the preceding verses, this would make quite good sense. The point would then be to offer the assurance that the prior death does not wipe out receipt of the resurrection body.[31]

Another sort of objection relates to how 2 Cor. 5:1-10 fits into

---

[27] See on this, A.T. Lincoln, *Paradise*, 62-3; A.C. Perriman, "Paul and the Parousia. 1 Cor. 15:50-57and 2 Cor. 5:1-5" *NTS* 35 (1989), 519f.; J. Lambrecht, *2 Corinthians*, 88-9; D.E. Garland, *2 Corinthians*, 246-252

[28] A.T. Lincoln, *Paradise*, 63-4.This point is also made by G. Vos, *The Pauline Eschatology* (Grand Rapids: Eerdmans, 1972), 187-8; H. Ridderbos, *Paul*, 501.

[29] R. Gundry comments that one should expect ἔχομεν to be a futuristic present with reference to the resurrection after Paul's predominant use of the futuristic present with reference to the resurrection in 1 Cor. 15—see vv.12, 15f., 29, 32, 35, 42f., 50 (*Soma*, 151). R.P Martin also notes that this interpretation is 'consistent with the tone of 2 Cor. 4:16-18; there is hope, but it is for something yet to be grasped. See Rom.8:24-5 for this dimension of hope in Pauline thought', similar to his argument in 1 Cor. 15 and 1 Thess.4 (R.P Martin, *2 Corinthians* (Waco: Word, 1986), 104.

[30] See M.J. Harris, "2 Corinthians 5:1-10", 41-2.

[31] See on this, A.T. Lincoln, *Paradise*, 64; J. Osei-Bonsu, "2 Cor. 5:1-10", 87.

the context of the preceding verses. The likelihood of the decline of
the physical body to the point of complete dissolution (4:16) raises
the issue of Paul's personal future. So he recalls both for himself as
well as the Corinthians that in comparison with the temporary,
present affliction, the invisible hope being prepared is one of 'vast
and transcendent glory' (4:16-18). 'For if we die, which now seems
likely', he says in 5:1—what? According to this exegesis 'we shall
receive a building from God *at the Parousia*'! This it is argued is surely
something of an anticlimax. Having considered the problems raised
by the fact that he may *not* now survive to the Parousia, Paul is apparently expressing his assurance of something that will happen only
if he *does* survive to the Parousia.[32]

However it might be said that Paul's assurance in 2 Cor. 5 is of
something which is already a reality 'in the heavens' and will mean
the giving of the new body at the Parousia whether he remains alive
to that day or not. It is noteworthy that in 1 Thess. 4:15 the apostle
states that those who are alive at Christ's return will not be at an
advantage over those who have died, and it may be argued that in
2 Cor. 5 Paul is applying that assertion to his own possible death.[33]

We may further note some other points concerning the interpretation of ἔχομεν. If it true that Paul has had a radical change of
mind concerning the time of receipt of the resurrection body, it might
be said that the present tense is rather inadequate evidence for this.
Indeed, 'contradiction' would seem a better word to describe such
a change than 'development'. It would mean that the specific order
of events in 1 Cor. 15:23-26 would now be incorrect and what is
stated in 1 Cor. 15:51-53 that the dead would be raised imperishable at the last trumpet would now be untrue (and thus Paul would
be contradicting what he had said about a year earlier to the same
Corinthian church). This change of mind 'would not only involve a
question of chronology but also a quite different idea of the continuity between earthly and heavenly bodies than is suggested in 1
Cor. 15'.[34] Such a considerable departure from what he had previously taught when the apostle mentions the resurrection of the dead
in 2 Cor. 1:9 and 4:14 is hard to see. It is also difficult to see Paul's
apparent new teaching when in letters subsequent to 2 Corinthians

---

[32] See on this, R.F. Hettlinger, "2 Corinthians 5:1-10" *SJT* 10 (1957), 184.
[33] See R. Berry, "Death and Life in Christ", 62f.
[34] A.T. Lincoln, *Paradise*, 64; V. Furnish, *2 Corinthians*, 292-3; J. Osei-Bonsu,
"2 Cor. 5:1-10", 87-8; D.E Garland, *2 Corinthians*, 254-5.

he discusses resurrection (cf. Rom. 8:22-4; Phil. 3:20-1).

It may also be argued that the interpretation which sees the receipt of the resurrection body at death includes seeing Paul as looking forward to death. Against this it might be said that such a desire for death does not tie in with what Paul says elsewhere about death which is that it is something foreign, an enemy, bound up with sin (cf. 1 Cor. 15:26). It is also worth noting that in 2 Cor. 1:10 Paul not only gives thanks for past deliverance from death but also indicates his positive hope of deliverance in the future. It would be strange for him to say in the same epistle that he hopes to be spared death and also that he desires it.[35]

Thus it seems fair to conclude that in 2 Cor. 5:1 Paul is looking forward to participating in heavenly glory and expressing his certainty of possessing the spiritual body in the future which, as everywhere else in his writings, he believes will actually become his at the Parousia.

Concerning the reason for the groaning in vv.2 and 4, it might be said positively that Paul groans because of his desire to put on the heavenly dwelling over his earthly, physical body. Two further indications may be seen from the words in vv.2-4 that Paul's desire will come to pass at Christ's return rather than at death:

1) The distinctive use of ἐπενδύσασθαι in vv.2 and 4. The force of the prefix ἐπί is to give the idea not simply of putting on a garment, but of putting one garment over the top of what is already being worn. Verse 4 brings this out specifically: '…because we wish not to be unclothed, but to be further clothed' (NRSV).[36] Paul would prefer not to have to undergo an interval of being unclothed, disembodied, rather that he should simply be able to put on over the top of his earthly body his future spiritual body.[37] Such imagery seems most apt for those who

---

[35] See on this R. Berry, "Death and Life", 67.

[36] Compare also similarly ESV ('…but that we would be further clothed'), JB ('…not that we want to be stripped of our covering, but because we want to be covered with a second garment on top', REB ('…we do not want to have the old body stripped off. Rather our desire is to have the new body put on over it').

[37] This is argued, among others, by P.E. Hughes, *Paul's Second Epistle to the Corinthians* (Grand Rapids: Eerdmans, 1962), 168-171; C.F.D. Moule, "St. Paul and Dualism: The Pauline Conception of Resurrection" *NTS* 12 (1965-6), 118-9; C.K. Barrett, *2 Corinthians*, 152-3; R. Gundry, *Soma*, 152; A.T. Lincoln, *Paradise*, 66; B.F. Meyer, "Development", 380-1; J. Osei-Bonsu, "2 Cor. 5:1-10", 88-9; M.E. Thrall, *2 Corinthians* I, 370-73; P. Barnett, *2 Corinthians*, 261; J. Lambrecht, *2 Corinthians*, 82-3, 86-7; *Pace* T.F. Glasson, "Platonism", 149-50; A.C Perriman, "Paul

are alive at Christ's coming, rather less so for those whose earthly body has already been taken off at death.[38] It seems clear that this cannot be applied to the same event Paul thinks of when he describes the earthly tent being taken down. When he is thinking of the change that both dead believers and those alive at the Parousia will experience, he uses the image expressed by ἐνδύσασθαι (as in 1 Cor. 15:53-4), but when he is considering specifically those who will be alive, the special import of ἐπενδύσασθαι becomes applicable (i.e. to receive the new body without having first to put off the old).

2) A further pointer to when Paul's desire will take place is in the idea in v.4 that when the heavenly body is put on, then 'what is mortal may be swallowed up by life' (NRSV). This is reminiscent of 1 Cor. 15:54 where there is little doubt that Paul is referring to the Parousia as the time when this takes place. It seems reasonable to conclude that this also will be the case here in the absence of specific pointers to the contrary.[39]

Concerning the meaning of γυμνός, it seems reasonable to argue that this word is the opposite to the notion of being clothed in v.3, and identical with that represented by ἐκδύσασθαι in v.4. Where this clothing is understood as portraying embodiment, then γυμνός would seem to refer consequently to a state of disembodiment, which believers encounter at death.[40] As we have already noted,[41] to those in the church who had a general disdain for embodiment, this may well have been seen as an expedient state, and Paul wishes to make clear that this is not the goal of the believer's yearning. He argues that a new type of heavenly embodiment is the object of the believer's existence.

However, the prospect of being disembodied also brings a nega-

---

and the Parousia", 519-20; D.E. Garland, *2 Corinthians*, 258, 262 n.692.

[38] See on this point, R. Berry, "Death and Life", 63 n.1; C.K. Barrett, *2 Corinthians*, 152-3; J. Osei-Bonsu, "2 Cor. 5:1-10", 89.

[39] See C.K. Barrett, *2 Corinthians*, 256; A.T. Lincoln, *Paradise*, 66; R. Martin, *2 Corinthians*, 107; B. Witherington III, *Conflict and Community in Corinth* (Carlisle: Paternoster, 1995), 391; M.E. Thrall, *2 Corinthians* I, 382; J. Lambrecht, *2 Corinthians*, 84.

[40] See, in addition to those mentioned in footnote 20, J.N. Sevenster, "Some Remarks on the *yumnos* in 2 Cor. 5:3", in *Studia Paulina* (Haarlem: Bohm, 1953), 202-214. This influential essay is mentioned by many scholars, and its contribution noted particularly by B.F. Meyer, "Development", 380-1.

[41] See p. 249 and footnote 21.

tive feature into the tension of groaning because the Christian essentially recoils from a state of not being clothed (v.4). In v.4 in contrast to verse 2, the groaning is connected with great agony, and this is (NRSV) 'because we do not wish (ἐφ' ᾧ[42] οὐ θέλομεν) to be unclothed, but to be further clothed' (clothed upon). Paul underlines that the basis for this groaning is, on the one hand, an aversion and antipathy of a 'putting off', and on the other hand, a positive yearning for a 'putting on over'. He is burdened because he does not wish for the disembodiment which he realises his death prior to the Parousia would entail. As Barrett succinctly comments,

'Paul is not in the ordinary sense afraid of death; he dreads it precisely for the reason he proceeds to give—because it would be a much happier thing to survive till the Parousia, that is, not to die, be buried, pass some time naked, and then be raised up, but to be transformed immediately by the substitution of a spiritual for the natural body...'.[43]

So the apostle did not particularly desire a state of nakedness (disembodiment), but considered it a possibility.

Yet Paul is confident even in considering the possibility of a time of nakedness through dying before the Parousia, because God had given a guarantee in the form of the Spirit that he will receive the new body (v.5). In vv.6-8 Paul gives further reasons for confidence. He knows that if he is at home in the body, he is away from the Lord, i.e. absent from the Lord's immediate presence, these states being coincident, so that also when one stops being at home in the body, one also stops being absent from the Lord. Thus in v.8 Paul says that in the face of possible death, he is confident that to be absent from the body (ἐκδημῆσαι ἐκ τοῦ σώματος) means to be present (ἐνδημῆσαι) with the Lord. So while dying might mean a time of being disembodied (nakedness), it would nevertheless mean closer fellowship with the Lord.[44]

---

[42] For discussion of the meaning of ἐφ' ᾧ see C.K. Barrett, *2 Corinthians*, 155-6; V. Furnish, *2 Corinthians*, 269-70.

[43] C.K Barrett, *2 Corinthians*, 156. Cf. also A.T. Lincoln, *Paradise*, 67; R P Martin, *2 Corinthians*, 106-8; B.F. Meyer, "Paul's View of the Resurrection", 380-2; J. Osei-Bonsu, "2 Cor. 5:1-10", 91; P. Barnett, *2 Corinthians*, 264-5.

[44] See on this line of interpretation of 5:6-8, among others, G. Vos, *Eschatology*, 193-4; C.K. Barrett, *2 Corinthians*, 157-9; M.J. Harris, *Raised Immortal*, 136-7; R. Martin, *2 Corinthians*, 109-113; V. Furnish, *2 Corinthians*, 301-3; P. Barnett, *2 Corinthians*, 268-272; M.E. Thrall, *2 Corinthians* I, 389-392 (who while accepting that 'being at home with the Lord follows immediately upon 'being away from

It is not easy to see that the expression ἐνδημῆσαι πρὸς τὸν κύριον indicates the possession of a spiritual body and that Paul is merely continuing the comparison between two stages of embodiment.[45] The phrase itself only indicates being with the Lord, which could be either in the body or not. But it is perhaps noteworthy that Paul does not say 'away from *this* body', rather 'away from *the* body', which could well imply he is not thinking of two successive stages of embodiment.[46]

So, as Lincoln sums this up: 'Death before the Parousia will bring a fuller enjoyment of heavenly existence than believers can experience in this life, yet their enjoyment will not be complete until they possess the heavenly body for which God has prepared them'.[47]

A possible objection to this line of interpretation is that it involves Paul in two contradictory attitudes towards death within the same passage. So initially, he recoils from death and its nakedness (5:3), but a few verses later (v.8), he says he would prefer to die given a choice between life and death, as this would mean being in the Lord's immediate presence. Surely this would be an 'intolerable contradiction', Paul changing his mind in a very short space![48]

However, G.E. Ladd helpfully comments, is this not 'precisely the kind of psychologically sound tension a man could express when caught in the grasp of strong ambivalent feelings? Death is an enemy; disembodiment is to be abhorred … But meanwhile, if he must die, … it will be all right, indeed far better, for it means to be with the Lord even without resurrection'.[49]

---

the body', nevertheless thinks that this is in some form of interim body which anticipates the final resurrection body given at the Parousia); L.L. Belleville, *2 Corinthians* (Leicester: IVP, 1996), 138-140; J. Lambrecht, *2 Corinthians*, 85,87-8; D.E. Garland, *2 Corinthians*, 264-5.

[45] As is argued, for example, by R.F. Hettlinger, "2 Cor. 5:1-10", 177-8; Hoffmann, *Toten*, 284; M.J. Harris, *Raised Immortal*, 99-100.

[46] On this point, see G. Vos, *Eschatology*, 194, who says, 'the state in … a new body would hardly be describable as the state of one absent from the body'; R. Berry, "Death and Life in Christ", 65: 'Here the phrases ἐνδημοῦντες ἐν τῷ σώματι, ἐκδημῆσαι ἐκ τοῦ σώματος are much more natural as descriptions of present "physical" clothing and future "nakedness" in death than they would be as descriptions of present physical "clothing" and future spiritual "clothing"'; R. Hoekema, *The Bible and the Future* (Grand Rapids: Eerdmans, 1979), 107; A.T. Lincoln, *Paradise*, 69; J. Osei-Bonsu, "2 Cor. 5:1-10", 93.

[47] A.T. Lincoln, *Paradise*, 69.

[48] See especially on this, R.F. Hettlinger, "2 Cor. 5:1-10", 176, 180; K. Hanhart, *Intermediate State*, 154, cited by J. Osei-Bonsu, "2 Cor. 5:1-10", 93, notes 64 & 65.

[49] G.E. Ladd, *The Pattern of NT Truth* (Grand Rapids: Eerdmans, 1968, 106, cited by J. Osei-Bonsu, "2 Cor. 5:1-10", 94.

Thus, as Berry comments, 'Paul was in two minds about death. A man may dislike one aspect of an experience intensely and yet be prepared to undergo that experience because of its other aspects'. So in a sense, Paul is demonstrating two reconcilable aspects in the thinking of one mind. Thus 'death has its attractive side for the Christian' and indeed has 'two faces' for Paul as he sees life in the flesh in two ways: The body is

1) 'a means of security by virtue of which we live in the solidarity of human life, and

2) it is that which ties us to sinful "Adam" and denies us sight... To leave the body at death is therefore to be stripped of its security and to be delivered from its encumbrances'—both desirable and undesirable.[50]

Thus to summarise the main points for arguing that what Paul says in 2 Cor. 5:1-10 is consistent with what he writes elsewhere on the matter of the time of receipt of the resurrection body—at the Parousia (1 Cor. 15 and I Thess.4):

1) In v.1, Paul is referring to the death of a believer before Christ's return. Thus ἐὰν should be interpreted conditionally.

2) ἔχομεν should be taken as designating a future possession of the spiritual body at the Parousia, indicating a firm assurance on the part of Paul that he would gain his resurrection body at that time. Thus it is to be seen as a futuristic present, expressing a certainty and confidence.

3) The force of the prefix ἐπί in ἐπενδύσασθαι (vv.2,4) should not be diminished. It indicates the putting on of one garment over another, imagery which seems most appropriate for those who are alive at Christ's coming who will then put on their new bodies over their earthly bodies without the need to first put off the old.

4) Paul sees death as a paradox. On the one hand, it would mean a state of disembodiment (nakedness), which, while at one level undesirable, would nevertheless mean closer fellowship with the Lord. Yet embodiment is needed for total enjoyment of existence in heaven, which will occur at the Parousia.

---

[50] See on these points, R. Berry, "Death and Life in Christ", 65-7.

4. *Conclusion*

Overall it would seem that there is strength in both methods of interpreting 2 Cor. 5:1-10. Yet it may well be argued that the alternative exegesis has greater cogency and in the light also of some general arguments objecting to the apparent major difference between 2 Cor. 5 and Paul's earlier letters concerning the time of receipt of the spiritual body on the development theory,[51] it may be argued that the alleged inconsistency (as outlined on pp. 241-3) is best resolved by an alternative exegesis of 2 Cor. 5:1-10 which interprets these verses in terms of the resurrection body being bestowed at the Parousia, not at the moment of death.[52]

---

[51] These objections may be summarised as: the fact that 2 Cor. 5 is prefaced by 'we know' (οἴδαμεν) hardly suggests new teaching is about to follow, which had been made clear to Paul only recently; the time gap between 1 & 2 Corinthians was too brief to permit any major change in Paul's eschatological thinking; to place the giving of the new body at death 'is to rob the Parousia of its temporal significance, do less than justice to the corporate emphases of Pauline eschatology, and remove the tension between the "already" and the "not yet"' characteristic of the time between Christ's first and second comings; lack of parallels to this idea of receipt of the new body at death. See on this, M.J. Harris, *Raised Immortal*, 255, n.4. It should be said that Harris makes a response to these objections, in *Interpretation*, 177-182. See also 3 above. Note also the comments of W.L. Craig, "The Bodily Resurrection of Jesus" in *Gospel Perspectives—Studies of History and Tradition in the Four Gospels* (Sheffield: JSOT, 1983), 62-4.

[52] See also on this, W.L Craig, "Paul's Dilemma", 145-7, where he argues that Paul was in a sort of 'Catch-22' situation, and the appearance of inconsistency 'arises out of the paradoxical situation in which Paul was placed and the Catch-22 decision with which he was confronted'; B. Witherington, *Jesus, Paul and the End* (Exeter: Paternoster, 1992), 152-231.

BRIEF ANTHROPOLOGICAL REFLECTIONS
ON 2 CORINTHIANS 4:6-5:10

Jan Lambrecht

In her discussion of the phrases the 'outward self' and the 'inward self' in 2 Cor 4:16 Margaret E. Thrall distinguishes two lines of approach, one reflecting a dualistic way of thinking, the other holding that each phrase refers to the human person as a whole.[1] As elsewhere in her commentary, the discussion is nuanced in an exemplary way. In the process Thrall manifests her preference: "At least it seems probable that Paul at times made more of a distinction between body and spirit than is sometimes allowed".[2] On page 351 she remarks: "The first alternative is not as un-Pauline as it is said to be, and it is without doubt the simpler. Furthermore it fits the context". A few lines further on the same page she then concludes: "At the deepest level, in his inmost self, he [Paul] is subject not to decay but to renewal. Whether or not this is 'dualism', it makes good sense, and it is the preferable interpretation".

Hans Dieter Betz's presidential lecture at the 54th General Meeting of the Studiorum Novi Testamenti Societas at Pretoria, South Africa (1999), entitled 'The Concept of the "Inner Human Being" ('Ο ἔσω ἄνθρωπος) in the Anthropology of Paul', is now published.[3] In his comment on 2 Cor 4:16 Betz assumes that "Paul accepts the concepts of 'outer' and 'inner' human being" from the Middle-Platonic dualism present in Corinth. "Accordingly, the human being is a composite entity".[4] But "the apostle interprets the concepts in ways

---

[1] M.E. Thrall, *The Second Epistle to the Corinthians. I*, (ICC; Edinburgh: T. & T. Clark, 1994) 347-351.

[2] Ibid., 349. Just before the quotation Thrall comments: "There are, in fact, several occasions where the more natural interpretation might well be 'dualistic' in a general sense: Rom 7.22-25; 1 Cor 5.5; 7.34; 2 Cor 7.1". Cf. A.J. Malherbe, *The Letters to the Thessalonians*, (AB 32B; New York: Doubleday 2000) 338: "Paul's use of anthropological terms is neither original, systematic, nor consistent".

[3] H.D. Betz, "The Concept of the 'Inner Human Being' ('Ο ἔσω ἄνθρωπος) in the Anthropology of Paul", *NTS* 46 (2000) 315-341. See idem, "Der Mensch in seinen Antagonismen aus der Sicht des Paulus", in J. Beutler (ed.), *Der neue Mensch in Christus. Hellenstische Anthropologie und Ethik im Neuen Testament*, (QD 109, Freiburg-Basel-Wien: Herder 2001) 39-56.

[4] Betz, "The Inner Human Being", 334.

characteristically different from the Platonic tradition". The outer
human being and the inner human being must not be distinguished
as body and soul; they "are the two aspects of the same ἄνθρωπος".[5]
In his exegesis of 1 Cor 15 Betz had already emphasized that "the
identity of the Christian as ἄνθρωπος is associated with the σῶμα,
rather than with the σάρξ. While the σάρξ is regarded as mere
perishability, the σῶμα is a 'spiritual' entity destined for imperish-
ability".[6]

The question may be asked: does 2 Cor 4:7-5:10 justify the view
of the body as a 'spiritual' entity? How does Paul, in this passage,
see the connection between the outer self and the body? What are
the differing nuances between Thrall and Betz? The second part of
this brief contribution will deal with 'outer' and 'inner' in 4:7-18,
the third with death and life in 5:1-10. However, because of the
broader context and the interpretations of Thrall and Betz, a first
reflection precedes; it brings together the reasons for a 'missionary'
interpretation of 4:6.

Illumination

In the phrase πρὸς φωτισμόν of 4:6 Thrall is not inclined to see a
reference to Paul's evangelistic work ("that he might bring to others
the enlightenment") since "the subject of this activity is more naturally the same as the subject of the verb ἔλαμψεν", i.e. God.[7] The
literal translation of the whole verse reads as follows: "For (it is) the
(same) God who said, 'Let light shine out of darkness', who has caused
his light to shine in our hearts to spread the light of the knowledge
of God's glory in the face of Jesus Christ".[8] Verse 6 grounds (cf. 'for')

---

[5] Ibid.

[6] Ibid., 328. In his interesting study Betz does not refer to the monograph by
R.H. Gundry, *Sôma in Biblical Theology with Emphasis on Pauline Anthropology*, (SNTS
MS 29; Cambridge: Cambridge University Press 1976). Probably as a consequence,
Gundry's distinctive use of the term 'duality' is also absent. The book of Gundry
is likewise omitted in the bibliography of D.B. Martin, *The Corinthian Body*, (New
Haven-London: Yale University Press 1995) (moreover, one misses a reference to
2 Cor 4:6-5:10, the discussion of which certainly would qualify Martin's views of
Paul's anthropology).

[7] *2 Corinthians*, 318.

[8] Cf. Thrall, *2 Corinthians*, 297-298: "... [God] is the one who shone in our hearts,
to effect the enlightenment of the knowledge..."; Betz, "Inner Human Being", 331:
"... [God] who has caused a light to shine in our hearts, to provide the enlight-

verse 5. Paul is not proclaiming himself but Jesus Christ as Lord; he himself is but a servant, a servant for Jesus' sake. To prove verse 5 Paul reminds his readers of the event of his conversion and call to apostleship, the Christophany given him by God Creator. It would seem that the second λάμπω in v. 6 has a causative meaning ("has caused his light to shine") and that φωτισμός retains its original active sense of 'enlightenment, illumination'.[9]

The reasons which favor a missionary understanding of πρὸς φωτισμόν are numerous, at least five. (1) It is probable that a grounding of the missionary verse 5 equally refers to Paul's evangelistic task. (2) Through the mention of God verse 6 contrasts with verse 4 which speaks of 'the god of the present age'. The two verses, however, are very similar in wording and structure. Verse 4 deals with unbelief and refusal to see the light of the gospel. This suggests, it would seem, a positive, missionary sense for verse 6. (3) The same applies to the whole of 4:1-6, a passage which itself corresponds with 2:14–3:6, especially 2:14-17: Paul presents himself as a minister of the new covenant, sent by God and made competent by God. (4) In 4:7-15, the passage which immediately follows 4:6, Paul demonstrates the antithetical character of his apostolic existence. (5) The fifth and last reason depends on the most probable answer to the alternative questions: does the last part of verse 6 only repeat and explain the inner result of the Damascus event (the conversion)[10] or, rather, does it not point to the missionary task which flows from that event: "in order that Paul may make the knowledge of God's glory in the face of Jesus Christ illuminate the others", i.e., that he may spread the gospel?[11]

The missionary interpretation presumes that Paul is the implied

---

enment which comes from the knowledge..."; NRSV: "... [God] who has shone in our hearts to give the light of the knowledge...".

[9] In 4:4 the term could mean 'light', the equivalent of φῶς which is present in v. 6a: "let light shine...". Cf. LXX Ps 26:1 and, perhaps, 138:11; see also Liddell-Scott, *sub voce*.

[10] Cf. Betz, "The Inner Human Being", 331-331, who limits the content of 4:6 to an occurrence of enlightening of the human heart which results in the renewal of the inner self.

[11] Cf. R. Bultmann, *The Second Letter to the Corinthians*, (Minneapolis: Augsburg Publishing House, 1985) 108-109: "... so that (through our preaching) we bring to light" the very knowledge ... (108); M. Winter φωτισμός in *EDNT*, III, 450: "Paul is not referring here to his own enlightenment ..., but rather to the purpose of his proclamation ...".

subject of the action of enlightening[12] and that the direct object itself
(the others, the Gentiles), not expresssed, can be mentally supplied.
These two hypotheses within the same clause of verse 6 are perhaps
too much for a sound exegesis. A clear-cut decision, i.e., a palat-
able choice between the purely autobiographical and the missionary explanations, does not appear possible. With regard to the difficult
verse 6 we may, at the end of our first reflection, quote Betz and
agree with his statement: "Untying this verbal package is not easily
done".[13]

Outer and Inner

Although 2 Cor 4:7-5:10 can be divided into two passages, 4:7-15
and 4:16-5:10,[14] for this analysis we must take 4:16-18 together with
what precedes. In verse 16 one encounters the seemingly anthropological opposition of 'outer' and 'inner' in the phrases ὁ ἔξω ἡμῶν
ἄνθρωπος and ὁ ἔσω ἡμῶν ἄνθρωπος.

Notwithstanding the various shifts within 4:7-18, that same opposition is focused upon in the entire text unit. One can take the
first person plural as pointing primarily to Paul. By means of 'in our
hearts' in verse 6 the inner center of Paul himself is indicated. In
verse 7 the 'treasure', contrasted with 'clay jars', probably refers both
to the enlightenment of his heart and the ensuing ministry; at the
end of the same verse, the opposition between Paul and God appears. Verses 8-9 depict the antitheses of, on the one hand, outer
hardships, nearness to death and, on the other, through God's power,
perseverance and salvation. In verses 10 and 11 Paul explains that
opposition in the minister's existence christologically: the presence
of Jesus' death and simultaneously the manifestation of Jesus' life.
The shift in verse 12 is remarkable: in the apostle (only) death is at
work, in the Corinthians life. Verse 13 adds a comparison with Israel's
past (the same faith in the apostle as that of the psalmist) and in verse
14 Paul connects his future resurrection with the past resurrection
of the Lord Jesus. God is the one who raises. Then in the summa-

---

[12] Note that 'knowledge' probably is not an objective genitive (so Bultmann)
but a subjective genitive or one of origin.
[13] "The Inner Human Being", 331.
[14] Cf. my *Second Corinthians*, (Sacra Pagina 8, Collegeville: Liturgical Press 1998)
76.

rizing verse 15 Paul states that his entire apostolic existence is meant for the sake of the Corinthians in order that the thanksgiving may increase and 'abound to the glory of God'. The beginning of verse 16 is an anacalouthon; in the rest of the verse one meets the contrast between the outward self (ὁ ἔξω ἄνθρωπος) who is wasting away and the inward self (ὁ ἔσω ἄνθρωπος) who is renewed day by day. This contrast is extended, in verse 17, by a temporal one ('momentary' and 'eternal') and by one of weight ('light' and exceedingly 'heavy'), furthermore, in verse 18 by the opposition between 'what is seen' and 'what is unseen' and by that between 'transitory' and 'eternal'.

We can say that in the whole of this passage Paul, by means of a variety of concepts and terms, clearly distinguishes between two 'men' in himself, his outer ἄνθρωπος and his inner ἄνθρωπος (v. 16). But is this distinction purely anthropological and completely balanced? Almost certainly not.

True, the outer self is the clay jar (v. 7), the suffering body (v. 10), the mortal flesh (v. 11). It is visible, wasting away, transitory. In this context the term 'flesh' is employed in a neutral anthropological sense, not 'hamartiologically', thus without a reference to its proneness to sin (so typical of Paul). Therefore, the outer self (v. 16) is not ὁ παλαιὸς ἄνθρωπος of Rom 6:6; it is the body (cf. v. 10) but not τὸ σῶμα τῆς ἁμαρτίας of that same verse from Romans.[15]

But the opposite concept, the inner self in verse 16, is not merely anthropological.[16] The center of Paul, his heart, is indwelled by God's power. It is regenerate; it is being renewed day by day (cf. 3:18). It is able to endure the hardships and carry Jesus' death and thus to manifest the life of Jesus. Paul himself realizes in his inner self that his tribulation is producing eternal glory, already now, though it remains invisible. Thus the inner self is not the inner side as such, only human. No, it is the inner self of a regenerate human being, a Christian, rescued by God, redeemed by Jesus Christ, living in the Spirit.[17]

---

[15] Cf. Gundry, *Sôma*, 136: "The outer man is not the old man of sin, then, but the physical body subject to hardship, decay, and death".

[16] Otherwise Gundry, *Sôma*, 136-137: "The inner man is the human spirit, the center of psychological feelings. We cannot evade anthropological duality in 2 Cor 4:16" (137).

[17] In Rom 7:22-23, on the contrary, the distinction within the unregenerate 'I' appears to be solely anthropological. Cf. C. Markschies, "Innerer Mensch", *RAC* 18 (1998) 266-312, esp. 280-282: the human being as intended by God, but

Death and Life

Is it correct to state that for Paul in 2 Corinthians the outer and inner are aspects of the human person,[18] that the outer self as well as the inner self are the whole person—be it considered differently—and that therefore a human being does not 'have' a body but 'is' a body? A careful reading of 5:1-10 does not justify a positive answer to these questions.

Paul can look to what is unseen and eternal since he knows that the destruction of the earthly house or tent, concretely speaking his death, is not fatal. Another body is ready in heaven: a building from God, an eternal house not made with hands (v. 1).[19] While still alive in this suffering and mortal body Paul groans; as a matter of fact, he desires to put on his heavenly body as an over-garment over his earthly body (v. 2). A new idea is expressed here: future possession of the eternal body after death (resurrection) becomes 'putting on over', i.e., transformation of the body before death. From verse 3 we learn indirectly that Paul does not want to be found 'naked'; he apparently fears a disembodied state. In verse 4 he seems to indicate two reasons for his sighing and groaning: first, he is weighed down by the burdensome body which suffers pain and hardship; second, he wishes not to die but to be transformed, not to take off but to put on over. From verse 4c ("in order that what is mortal may be swallowed up by life") arises the impression that the very thing which immortal and glorious 'life' accomplishes is not the destruction of Paul's body (v. 1) but the radical transformation of his body still alive at the parousia. For this future event God has prepared Paul through the gift of the Spirit (v. 5).

A surprising shift then occurs in verses 6-10. Paul knows that being in the earthly body means being away from the Lord (v. 6). Faith is

---

in fact sold under sin; J. Lambrecht, *The Wretched 'I' and Its Liberation. Paul in Romans 7 and 8*, (Louv. Theol. & Past. Monogr. 14; Louvain: Peeters Press 1992). In the 'I' Paul appears to distinguish the ἔσω ἄνθρωπος (and the 'mind') from the 'body' (and the 'members'). The 'I' is sold into slavery under sin; so the 'I' is 'of the flesh' (cf. v. 14). Through the inner self the 'I' delights in the law of God; however, the law of sin is at war with the law of the mind and dwells in the members of the 'I'. Its body is destined to death (cf. vv. 22-24).

[18] Cf. Betz, "Inner Human Being", 334.

[19] Most probably Paul envisions that this body will be given at the parousia, not at the moment of death. Otherwise, as far as 2 Cor 5:1-10 is concerned, Thrall, *Second Corinthians*, 370, 373, 392 and 399.

not yet sight, not yet face to face vision (v. 7). Therefore, Paul now says, he would rather go away from the body, that is, die before the parousia, and get home to the Lord immediately (v. 8). Fear of death seems to have disappeared. What remains, however, is his profound aspiration to please the Lord since he realizes that he will be 'manifested' before the tribunal of Christ and judged according to what he has done through his earthly body (vv. 9-10).

In 5:1-10 Paul speaks of the earthly body in an objective way, as if it were a substance, an entity of its own. It is a house to dwell in; it is a garment to put on; it is the opposite of the heavenly body. Paul even refers to the possibility of a 'naked', disembodied state. Paul is at home in the body, now, but he would prefer to go away from this body. He fully realizes, however, that what he has done he did through his body. Moreover, he is convinced that in the eschaton eternal life supposes a risen and transformed body. Finally, though what is mortal will be annihilated, both resurrection and transformation point to a continuity between the two bodies: body is more than flesh and corruption.

The reality of the 'outer self' of 4:16 is taken up in 5:1-10 by several terms and concepts: the nouns house, tent and garment; the adjectives earthly and mortal; the verbs to be destroyed, to take off and to be at home in; but above all, the term 'body' in verses 6, 8 and 10. Given this vocabulary and given the fact that in verse 1 regarding the heavenly body the verb ἔχομεν is used, one can hardly deny that Paul as it were claims 'to have and possess' a body. It must strike the reader that within 5:1-10 the 'inner self' of 4:16 is no longer explicitly distinguished. Paul employs the first person plural and thus points to himself, whether 'in the body' or 'out of the body'. But this 'we' seems to be the incorporeal self.[20] That in verses 6-10 the fear of death and a disembodied state has disappeared may probably be explained by Paul's increasing conviction that his union with Christ in the life of faith, already on earth, cannot be destroyed by death. He must have thought that leaving the earthly body at death would bring him "closer to the full, immediate presence and the face to face vision".[21]

The way Paul speaks both of himself and his earthly body in 5:1-10 does not indicate a dualistic view of the human person accord-

---

[20] Cf. Gundry, *Sôma*, 149: "Paul writes quite dichotomously here".
[21] Lambrecht, *Second Corinthians*, 89.

ing to which the body is inherently evil. Yet, assuming in 4:7–5:10 only an external influence of hellenistic terms and categories of thought does not go far enough.[22] The term 'duality' seems appropriate, although we saw that in 2 Corinthians the duality of 'outer self' and 'inner self' or that of 'we' (Paul) and 'body' is not completely balanced. Paul is in Christ; but the Christian Paul is still in the mortal flesh and the earthly body. His reflection is not purely anthropological.

To round off our three reflections: it would seem that for Paul 'body' is not just an aspect of the person. In 5:1-10, as in 4:7-18, there is no radically holistic use of the term σῶμα.[23] Because the human being constitutes a living unity, the 'body' (as e.g. the 'heart') is representative of the whole. Of course, in order to stress the unity of this dually composed human being, one can say that Paul is his body; but he is more than his body. Therefore, one can also say that Paul has an earthly body. Moreover, in the eschaton Paul and all Christians expect a glorified, 'spiritual' body, which implies a somatic existence.

---

[22] Cf., e.g., Thrall, *Second Corinthians*, 347: Paul "uses, though in modified form, hellenistic categories of thought which might appeal to some of his readers"; and, of course, the publications by Betz.

[23] Cf. Gundry, *Sôma*, passim.

2 CORINTHIANS 5:14—A KEY TO PAUL'S SOTERIOLOGY?

A.J.M. Wedderburn

'For Christ's love controls us, because we made this judgement, that one died for all, therefore they all died' (tr. M.E. Thrall)[1]—a curious piece of logic, since one would normally expect that, if one died for all, then that meant precisely the opposite, that the rest did not need to die. Certainly one would expect that if one describes Christ's death as 'vicarious' or 'substitutionary', and there are many New Testament texts that have been and can be understood in that way. But this one resists that interpretation, despite those exegetes who argue that only by translating ὑπέρ as 'instead of' can one make sense of the 'therefore they all died'.[2] Rightly, Dr Thrall sees that logic would then rather demand 'therefore all escaped death'.[3] The importance of this distinction is underlined further by Reimund Bieringer, who shows how scholarship has become aware that one must hold apart two senses of 'Stellvertretung', an exclusive and an inclusive, although some maintain that the one shades over into the other.[4] Windisch achieves a similar precision by referring to the latter

---

[1] M.E. Thrall, *The Second Epistle to the Corinthians* I (ICC; Edinburgh: T. & T. Clark, 1994) 400.

[2] Thrall, *2 Cor*, 409 n. 1527, cites P.E. Hughes, *Paul's Second Epistle to the Corinthians* (NICNT; London/Edinburgh: Marshall, Morgan & Scott/Grand Rapids MI: Eerdmans, 1962) 193–5 (Hughes cites a number of other, earlier examples of this interpretation, from Athanasius on); R.P. Martin, *2 Corinthians* (WBC; Waco TX: Word, 1986) 129–30; G. Delling, "Der Tod Jesu in der Verkündigung des Paulus", *Apophoreta* (FS E. Haenchen; ed. W. Eltester, F.H. Kettler; BZNW 30; Berlin: de Gruyter, 1964) 85–96, 87; cf. also idem, *Der Kreuzestod Jesu in der urchristlichen Verkündigung* (Göttingen: Vandenhoeck & Ruprecht, 1972) 24–5—but he then interprets this as meaning that Jesus' death included all humanity in itself (27–8; cf. 'Tod Jesu', 91). Cf. also R. Bultmann, *The Second Letter to the Corinthians* (Minneapolis: Augsburg, 1985) 151.

[3] *2 Cor*, 409. Cf. H. Windisch, *Der zweite Korintherbrief* (MeyerK; Göttingen: Vandenhoeck & Ruprecht, 9th ed. 1924) 182.

[4] "Traditionsgeschichtlicher Ursprung und theologische Bedeutung der ΥΠΕΡ-Aussagen im Neuen Testament,", *The Four Gospels 1992* (FS F. Neirynck; ed. F. van Segbroek; BETL 100; Leuven: Univ./Peeters, 1992) 1.219–48, here 238–47; cf. also O. Hofius, "Sühne und Versöhnung: Zum paulinischen Verständnis des Kreuzestodes Jesu," *Versuche, das Leiden und Sterben Jesu zu verstehen* (ed. W. Maas;

as 'Repräsentation' and reserving 'Stellvertretung' for the former.[5] Failure to distinguish these two senses can lead to a certain conceptual looseness or imprecision in the discussion of the interpretation of the death of Christ.[6] For in the one instance only the *Stellvertreter* dies and thereby rescues the many; in the other the *Stellvertreter* embodies the destiny of the many, and it is this latter sense which 2 Cor 5.14 seems to imply. Bieringer also documents how several scholars have argued that it is preferable if the use of ὑπέρ in this verse is also similar to that in the phrase τῷ ὑπὲρ αὐτῶν ... ἐγερθέντι in v. 15, and there 'instead of' is hardly a likely meaning.[7] In v. 21, too, ὑπέρ does not mean 'instead of'; it may be that we are not made sin with Christ, but do we need to be? God has identified him with the state in which we already are, in order that we may share in that state which he has gained, God's righteousness.[8]

Yet how is the text which we in fact have to be understood? Here I want to take as my starting-point Dr Thrall's careful exposition of this verse (I), so characteristic both of her own work and of this series to which she has contributed her commentary, an exposition and analysis with which I find myself in agreement at many, if not all, points. After that I note some of the religio-historical dimensions of this statement (II), before adding certain hermeneutical reflections on how Paul is to be understood (III) and finally a very brief summary of my own conclusions (IV).

Schriftenreihe der Kath. Akad. der Erzdiözese Freiburg; München/Zürich: Schnell & Steiner, 1983) 25–46=idem, *Paulusstudien* (WUNT 51; Tübingen: Mohr–Siebeck, 1989) 33–49, esp. 41 (citing H. Gese, "Die Sühne," idem, *Zur biblischen Theologie: Alttestamentliche Vorträge* [BEvTh 78; München: Kaiser, 1977] 85–106, here 97, 99).

[5] *2 Kor*, 182.

[6] Cf., e.g., Delling and Bultmann in n. 2 above and in subsequent nn. below.

[7] Cf. Bieringer, "Ursprung," esp. 238–9, citing P. Bachmann, *Der zweite Brief des Paulus an die Korinther* (KNT 8; Leipzig: Scholl, 3rd ed. 1918) 254. On the other hand Delling, *Kreuzestod*, 119 argues for two different meanings in 14 and 15c (cf. G. Barth, *Der Tod Jesu Christi im Verständnis des Neuen Testaments* [Neukirchen-Vluyn: Neukirchener, 1992] 42). Or is the ὑπὲρ αὐτῶν linked only to the ἀποθανόντι and not to the ἐγερθέντι? (Although Windisch [*2 Kor*, 183] dismisses this question as an idle one it can nevertheless legitimately be posed; at any rate he rightly compares Rom 4.25b.)

[8] Delling, "Tod Jesu" 87 translates ὑπὲρ ἡμῶν here and in Gal 3:13 as "an unserer Statt", but is that appropriate if we are in fact sinful and accursed?

I.

Thrall herself distinguishes six possibilities which have been suggested, but which may at times overlap with one another, and her analysis of these and comments upon them help to stake out the ground for her own tentative solution of the problems of the verse:[9]

(1) Because of Christ's representative function all are, juridically, regarded by God as having died,[10] as if they had died, even though that 'as if' adds something to the text which we have before us.[11]

(2) In the death of Christ as the 'second Adam' all 'did really undergo the death of their sinful selves' as 'an objective reality'.[12] Thrall's objection to this solution is that, whereas all are automatically 'in Adam', it is only through faith and baptism that one can be in Christ (Gal 3:26–8). However, this is not a distinction which Paul consistently maintains, for, especially in 1 Cor 15:22, one finds precisely the same sort of seemingly comprehensive 'all' on both the Adam and the Christ side of the comparison.[13] What distinguishes

---

[9] *2 Cor*, 409–11. To these one may add the suggestion of J. Murphy-O'Connor, *The Theology of the Second Letter to the Corinthians* (NT Theology; Cambridge: CUP, 1991) that Paul means that all were seen to be "dead"—Paul wished to shock the Corinthians who would here have expected something very different along the lines of 1 Cor 15:22. But Paul does say ἀπέθανον, not that they were νεκροί or τεθνήκασιν. R.G. Hamerton–Kelly's argument that Paul means 'that all have died in the sense that all are now victims, and if all are victims, then none is a victim' (*Sacred Violence: Paul's Hermeneutic of the Cross* [Minneapolis: Fortress, 1992] 70) may make sense within the framework of his Pauline hermeneutic, but those who do not share that presupposition will remain unconvinced.

[10] H. Lietzmann, *An die Korinther I/II* (HNT 9; Tübingen: Mohr–Siebeck, 4th ed. revised by W.G. Kümmel 1949) 124; F.F. Bruce, *1 and 2 Corinthians* (NCB; London: Marshall, Morgan & Scott/Grand Rapids MI: Eerdmans, 1971) 207; E.-B. Allo, *The Second Epistle of Saint Paul to the Corinthians* (EBib; Paris: Gabalda, 1937, 2nd ed. 1956) 166.

[11] C.K. Barrett, *A Commentary on the Second Epistle to the Corinthians* (BNTC; London: Black, 1973) 168. Bultmann in fact wishes to interpret ὑπέρ as "instead of" in the sense of "a juridical idea of substitution" which means that those so represented 'are regarded as also having performed' the deed of their representative (*2 Cor*, 151).

[12] Thrall, *2 Cor*, 410, citing Windisch, *2 Kor*, 182–3; cf. also Bachmann, *2 Kor*, 254.

[13] It is in the treatment of the comparison in Rom 5:12–21 that Paul qualifies this apparent universalism; he breaks the parallelism between the Adam side and the Christ side by saying that in the case of the latter it is those who receive the gift of righteousness who shall reign in life through Christ (5:17); cf. my "The Theological Structure of Romans v.12," *NTS* 19 (1972/3) 339–54, here 353.

2 Cor 5:14 and 1 Cor 15:22 is that in the latter the death of all is linked to the death of Adam and it is the life of all which is linked to Christ.[14]

(3) All are 'potentially dead' in that Christ's death has made it possible for them to die to themselves.[15] With considerable restraint, Thrall observes that this 'seems to be rather less than what Paul is saying' (410). It is true that such ethical consequences or at least their corollary in a living for Christ are stated as the purpose (a ἵνα-clause) of the death of Christ for all in 2 Cor 5:14, but if one compares Rom 6 one finds there (a) a death with Christ which believers make their own in baptism (vv. 3–6, 8), (b) an admonition to the Christians to regard themselves as, like Christ, dead to sin, to realize that they are dead to sin (v. 11)—not just to regard themselves as if they were dead, for here there is no ὡσεί or the like as in v. 13—, and (c) exhortations to live out that death in a new obedience (vv. 12–19). The death with Christ should not simply be merged with the ethical consequences which flow from that death; that is to confuse cause and effect.

(4) The individual believer has (in baptism) died with Christ.[16] Rightly, Thrall objects that the 'all' should be as comprehensive as the 'all' for whom the 'one' has died,[17] and that the time designated by the ἀπέθανον should be the same as that of the ἀπέθανεν. That is an argument that could be supported by F.F. Bruce's observation

---

[14] *Pace* V.P. Furnish, *II Corinthians* (AB 32A; New York: Doubleday, 1984) 326. Instructive, however, is his appeal to 2 Cor 5:17, 'everything old has come to an end'; does the neuter τὰ ἀρχαῖα imply that it is not just all humanity that is caught up in Christ's death, but all creation; Gal 6:14 also suggests that that is the case.

[15] Barrett, *2 Cor*, 168–9; Bultmann, *2 Cor*, 152–3. J. Lambrecht interprets 5:14–15 in the light of Christ's role as a corporate figure, the new Adam ("'Reconcile Yourselves ...': A Reading of 2 Corinthians 5,11–21", in: L. de Lorenzi [ed.], *The Diakonia of the Spirit [2 Cor 4:7–7:4]* [Benedictina 10; Rome: 'Benedictina', 1989] 161–209=R. Bieringer and idem, *Studies on 2 Corinthians* [BETL 112; Leuven: Univ./Peeters, 1994] 363–412, here 376), but then goes on to give the death of believers (not 'all' in the fullest sense) the metaphorical sense of a death to sin (378 n. 31).

[16] R.C. Tannehill, *Dying and Rising with Christ: A Study in Pauline Theology* (BZNW 32; Berlin: de Gruyter, 1966) 66; Martin, *2 Cor*, 131 is also mentioned here—his formulation is that the reference is to 'the "symbolic" death that Christians die to self based on Christ's death to sin'.

[17] So too, emphatically, F. Hahn, "'Siehe, jetzt ist der Tag des Heils': Neuschöpfung und Versöhnung nach 2. Korinther 5,14–6,2,' *EvT* 33 (1973) 244–53, here 248, against any 'restricted, introvertedly ecclesiastical interpretation': the whole of humanity is the sphere of Christ's saving work (similarly Windisch, *2 Kor*, 182). But cf. W.G. Kümmel, in: Lietzmann–Kümmel, *1–2 Kor*, 204.

that the use of the definite article indicates that 'the reference is to the all for whom one has died'.[18]

(5) So strong was the sense of Christ's 'representative function' that 'the whole of humanity was really included in his death'.[19] (Yet can this interpretation be satisfactorily distinguished from the second one mentioned above?)

(6) All have the opportunity to identify themselves with Christ and to die his death or may fail to do so and therefore die their own death.[20] Again, Thrall points out that (a) the ἀπέθανον is a past tense and that (b) the text does not warrant dividing the 'all' into two camps in this way (nor, for that matter, dividing the death which they die into two sorts). It is, however, important to distinguish again at this point between the death of all in Adam (1 Cor 15:22) and the death of all in and with Christ, as here, and also to insist that, whatever Paul sees as the ethical corollary of this latter death, this death of all for him is in the first instance something which rests on the decision of God and of Christ, not upon the decision of believers to identify themselves with Christ.

Thrall herself finds it plausible, at any rate, that the idea of Christ as the second Adam is in the background here, and she argues that, if 'all' participated in Adam's original act of sin,[21] then it was fitting

---

[18] *1–2 Cor*, 207.

[19] So Delling, "Tod Jesu" 91–2, 94, despite his interpretation of ὑπέρ (see n. 2 above); cf. also C. Wolff, *Der zweite Brief des Paulus an die Korinther* (THKNT 8; Berlin: Evangelische Verlagsanstalt, 1989) 121, who speaks of Christ dying *coram Deo* that death of humanity which it had brought upon itself by its sin, and F. Lang, *Die Briefe an die Korinther* (NTD 7; Göttingen: Vandenhoeck & Ruprecht, 1986, 2nd ed. 1994) 295, who refers to the representative death of Jesus the son of man.

[20] J.D.G. Dunn, "Paul's Understanding of the Death of Christ," *Reconciliation and Hope* (FS L. Morris; ed. R. Banks; Exeter: Paternoster, 1974) 125–141, esp. 130, 141; what puzzles me here is Dunn's assertion that 'only those who identify themselves with him in his death are identified with him in his life. Hence it is a mistake to confine the "all" of 5:14 to believers' (130–1)—despite that "Hence" it would seem that a limitation to believers follows from the first sentence. In his *The Theology of Paul the Apostle* (Grand Rapids MI/Cambridge: Eerdmans/Edinburgh: T. & T. Clark, 1998) 210–11 Dunn's argument seems to be rather different: if Christ, who doubles for the dying Adam, had to die, then no one can escape death (cf. 'Paul's Understanding', 130). But if death is the gateway to life for Christ and for all, then no one should want to escape it.

[21] This reading of Rom 5:12d is, however, less compelling, because Paul has not written that Adam ἥμαρτεν; in other words, there is no parallel formulation which constrains us to say that the ἥμαρτον of all took place simultaneously with Adam's sin; for a different interpretation of the significance and function of the ἐφ' ᾧ clause see my "Structure," 349–53.

that they also participated 'collectively in the initial event whereby the power of sin was destroyed' (411).

II.

It is incumbent upon any exegete of an ancient text to offer an exposition which is consistent with what the author of that text could conceivably have meant. It is a further bonus if that exposition would also have been intelligible to the presumed original readers and hearers of the text, but that is not an indispensable condition for its plausibility. A writer's meaning could be misunderstood by his readers and hearers and 1 Cor 5:9–11 shows that Paul was not immune to that danger. Paul's meaning should therefore be one that is consistent with either Paul's Jewish background or with his upbringing in the Graeco–Roman world or with both. To be intelligible to his Corinthian readers his thought would have to have had points of contact with ideas current in the Graeco–Roman world.

Both these cultural worlds, the Jewish and the Graeco–Roman, do indeed offer points of contact with Paul's statement here, but at the same time differ markedly from what this verse seems to be saying, so that one can say that Paul's concept is a novel one, but by no means without its points of contact with both worlds—and if it had points of contact with the one, it is to be expected that they would be echoed in the other, too, so much was the Jewish world part of the Graeco–Roman world then. One can say that in both worlds the ideas of one dying for many and of many sharing the fortunes or misfortunes of one can be paralleled, but the logic of this statement of Paul's seems to suggest that he has put these two motifs together and therein lies the novelty of his position.[22]

In Jewish traditions the sense of the bond between an individual and a collective entity was a strong and developed one, both as a synchronic relationship and as a diachronic. Whether or not one uses the expression 'corporate personality' at this point, the phenomenon expressed by it remains: synchronically many are caught up, usu-

---

[22] K. Kertelge, "Das Verständnis des Todes Jesu bei Paulus," *Der Tod Jesu: Deutungen im Neuen Testament* (ed. K. Kertelge; QD 74; Freiburg: Herder, 1976) 114–36=idem, *Grundthemen paulinischer Theologie* (Freiburg: Herder, 1991) 62–80, here 68–9 (121–2), speaks of the linking of the idea of atonement by a representative with the idea of "corporate personality," so that atonement occurs through the union between the destiny of all and that of Christ, the one who represents all.

ally in the misfortunes rather than the good fortune, of the one, and
diachronically many subsequent generations are regarded as sharing the experiences of one generation in the past. The synchronic
relationship is reflected in many ways, but perhaps nowhere more
vividly than in the sin of Achan and its punishment in Josh 7. For
there we have a twofold manifestation of this relationship: the individual Achan took as spoil what had been placed under the ban and
God therefore caused Israel's attack on Ai to fail. If God's fury was
directed against the whole people and not just the individual who
sinned, the people's punishment of the individual was then directed,
not just against the individual sinner, but against his family. The sin
of the individual acted like an infection, a contamination of the whole
people, and the individual's family was treated as the source of the
contamination. The other, beneficial side of such a relationship
between the one and the many is occasionally indicated by the idea
that the prosperity of the land and the people and even of all peoples
is bound up with God's blessing on the king or by the idea that God's
servant may even be a blessing to other nations.[23] Diachronically a
similar relationship is expressed in the idea, so important for Paul's
thought, of the future blessing of the nations in Abraham (Gen 12:2–
3; 18:18; similarly Jacob in 28:14), even if the sense of the relationship envisaged here is disputed.[24] We also see later generations
addressed as if they themselves had been brought out of slavery in
Egypt at the Exodus (e.g. Exod 20:2; Amos 3:1), a way of speaking
that found its way into the annual celebration of the Passover (e.g.
m.Pes. 10:5).[25] In these latter examples, however, we see a nation
addressed as if it were a single person; to speak of an individual such
as Christ as a 'corporate personality' seems to reverse the relationship, treating the individual, not the collective, as the 'corporate

---

[23] E.g. Ps 72:15–17 (cf. 144.12–14); Isa 42:1–7; 49:5–6.

[24] Cf. J. Scharbert, Art. *brk*, *TDOT* 2.279–308, here 297.

[25] That holds good, even if one must be cautious about invoking the Passover
Haggadah's "with them" as a possible linguistic parallel to the Pauline "with Christ"
as I did in my *Baptism and Resurrection: Studies in Pauline Theology against Its Graeco-
Roman Background* (WUNT 44, Tübingen: Mohr–Siebeck, 1987) 344, in view of the
fact that this passage of the Haggadah may be later in date: cf. G. Stemberger,
"Pesachhaggada und Abendmahlsberichte des Neuen Testaments," *Kairos* 29 (1987)
147–58=id., *Studien zum rabbinischen Judentum* (Stuttgarter biblische Aufsatzbände
10; Stuttgart: Kath. Bibelwerk, 1990) 357–374, esp. 154=369. The sense of this
commemoration, with its associated OT quotations, nevertheless remains a close
parallel.

personality', and therein lies at least part of the problem of this phrase
as a clue to Paul's Christology.[26]

Martin Hengel and Hans Hübner have both pointed out that
similar ideas were familiar in the Graeco–Roman world.[27] Polluted
by Oedipus' unwitting sin in murdering his father and marrying his
mother the entire city of Thebes must suffer from the pestilence. The
people suffer because of what their king has done. In this case,
though, it is the unwitting sinner whose self-inflicted suffering averts
the wrath of the gods;[28] apart from the suicide of his mother and
wife his children at first emerge unscathed, but then fall under their
father's curse because of their treatment of him. And less spectacular, but nevertheless equally important for our purpose, since Christ's
fate brings blessing for the many, is the belief that the good fortune
of a ruler brought blessing upon the people whom he represented.[29]

Examples of the second motif, the death of an individual for the
sake of the many, a death which rescues the many, abound in the
Graeco–Roman world, as Clement of Rome recognized (*1 Clem.*
55:1). Again it is Hübner who quotes the death of Menoeceus who,
in response to the prophecy of Teiresias, sacrificed himself for the
city of Thebes to rescue it from the assault of the Seven under
Adrastus and Polynices, as well as the Roman P. Decius Mus who
ensured victory over the Latins by his voluntary death. A similar
devotio by his son of the same name is recorded which ensured victory over the Samnites in 295 B.C.E. Hengel adds many other examples, stressing the profoundly religious dimension of such voluntary
deaths for others. Yet the *Neuer Wettstein* cites only one parallel to 2
Cor 5:14: out of Aeneas' company the helmsman Palinurus will be
the only one to die: *unum pro multis dabitur caput.*[30] This is, however,

---

[26] Again, is "corporate personality" something which one is or something which
one has? See my "The Body of Christ and Related Concepts in 1 Corinthians,"
SJT 24 (1971) 74–96, here 83–5, and *Baptism*, 351–6.

[27] M. Hengel, *The Atonement: A Study of the Origins of the Doctrine in the New Testament* (London: SCM, 1981) esp. 1–32; H. Hübner, "Rechtfertigung und Sühne
bei Paulus: Eine hermeneutische und theologische Besinnung," *NTS* 39 (1993) 80–
93, here 90–1.

[28] Hübner, however, tries to force the Oedipus story to yield the same sense
as 2 Cor 5:14: if the one Oedipus atoned for all, then all atoned ("Rechtfertigung,"
90). But would it not be more correct and usual to say that all had atonement
made for them?

[29] Cf. the references from the early principate mentioned in my *Baptism*, 345–
6.

[30] Vergil *Aen.* 5.815 (cf. G. Strecker, U. Schnelle [eds.], *Neuer Wettstein: Texte*

no voluntary self-offering by Palinurus, but rather a concession wrung from Neptune by Venus. But such a self-sacrifice for another was recognized as an act of love in an example like that of Alcestis, although this is only a matter of one dying for one person.[31]

In the Old Testament it is Jephthah's daughter (Judg 11) who perhaps most readily springs to mind as a parallel, but she is again hardly a willing victim, but must instead acquiesce in her father's *devotio* of her. Perhaps nearer in sense is Moses' readiness to perish for the sake of his people (Exod 32:32), a readiness which Paul himself echoes (Rom 9:3), even if God does not take up either of those offers, as well as the suffering of the Servant of the Lord in Isa 53. The last-named passage, however, makes it clear how far the thought of the Old Testament is at this point from a suffering of the one which includes and involves the suffering of the many, for from this vicarious suffering flows healing for the many (53.5b).[32]

Thus, despite the many parallels, particularly to the idea of the one dying for the many, and thus rescuing them from death, in the case of the Graeco–Roman parallels which Hengel in particular has brought together, and also to the idea of the solidarity of the many both synchronically and diachronically, which is especially pronounced in Jewish traditions, a true parallel to Paul's argument in 2 Cor 5:14 has not been found. For Paul, I have suggested, at this point joins two motifs in a remarkable way: the death of the one is coupled with the death of the many, but that death means salvation; the death of the one for the many means, accordingly, not that the many thereby escape death, but that they are drawn into that death, for that is the only route to salvation. And in making this change Paul may have been helped by the figurative use of the idea of 'death' in the Graeco–Roman world. For not only was there the idea of physical death as a liberation from the prison of the body in dualistic traditions of Greek thought,[33] but a metaphorical use of 'death' also played its part in Graeco–Roman ethical thought as well, and particularly in the writings of Philo of Alexandria. On the one

---

zum Neuen Testament aus Griechentum und Hellenismus 2: Texte zur Briefliteratur und zur Johannesapokalypse [Berlin/New York: de Gruyter, 1996] 450).

[31] Plato *Symp.* 179B; Epict. 3.24.64–5 describes Diogenes as ready to suffer for the sake of the good of his fellow human beings.

[32] The same applies to 4 Macc 17:22.

[33] See the reff. in my *Baptism*, 119 n. 17.

hand the life of the wicked may there be regarded as death,[34] but more relevant here is the idea that the virtuous may regard their life as already ended,[35] or, drawing on the idea of physical death as liberating the soul, may see their physical death as no true death,[36] but as the gateway to life.[37] Nevertheless, this usage only goes part of the way to explaining Paul's thought, for the apostle takes the further step of declaring those who are Christ's to have died, to have been crucified, to sin, the world and the law (Rom 6:2, 10–11; Gal 2:19; 6:14). That use of dying (and also living) with datives which blend elements of the dative of reference or relation and of the dative of (dis)advantage are a further novelty in Paul's usage.[38] Also distinctive in Paul's usage is the fact that he connects this ethical death with the physical death of another person with which Christians have been joined in the rite of baptism (above all Rom 6:3–5). To that extent the Graeco–Roman *commentatio mortis* theme which David Aune compares with Paul's usage is at best a partial analogy.[39] It is one

---

[34] E.g. Philo *Deus imm.* 89; *Fug.* 55; *Congr.* 57; *Som.* 1.151; 2.66; *Quaest. in Gen* 1.16; 4.173 (this Philo describes as the death of the soul: e.g. *Leg. all.* 1.76 etc.); also the Pythagorean maxim in *Fragmenta philosophorum Græcorum* (ed. Mullach; Paris: Didot, 1875) 1.495 §125.

That we are "dead" in our sinfulness is an idea that is not alien to Paul (cf. Rom 6:13), but here (and elsewhere in Rom 6), the act of dying that is meant is saving and rescues us from our deadness, although Paul does not exploit to the full that paradox, a paradox made possible by the fluidity or versatility of these terms; cf. Wedderburn, *Baptism*, 45.

[35] Philo *Vit. cont.* 13.

[36] It is but a seeming death: Philo *Det. pot. ins.* 49, 70.

[37] E.g. Philo *Fug.* 59; *Praem.* 110; *Quaest. in Gen* 1.16; 4.152. Also Epict. 4.1.165 (Socrates ἀποθνήσκων σώζεται); Plut., Frg. 178 (LCL)—the soul that has (seemingly) perished (ὀλωλέναι) has attained to a complete (εἰς τὸ ὅλον) change and conversion; here, too, he compares the mysteries, with a a similar word-play on τελευτᾶν and τελεῖσθαι. Hengel, *Atonement*, 5 remarks that Proteus Peregrinus, whom Lucian so mocks, was in his self-immolation following "the example of Heracles, the Indian Brahmans and the strict Cynic doctrine that death is on no account to be feared because it brings the liberation of the soul.".

[38] See the discussion in my *Baptism*, 43 n.1. The reference to Plut. *Agis et Cleomenes* 31.5 in BDAG s.v. ἀποθνήσκω 2 is no real exception since the dat. there is a pure dative of advantage: 'For it is disgraceful both to live and to die for oneself alone.' In other words there is lacking that sense of the break with, and separation from, that to which one dies which Col 2:20 expresses by using this verb with ἀπό and the genitive instead of the dative alone. (Comparable with Paul's usage is also 1 Pet 2:24, which uses ἀπογίνομαι with the dative—a parallel surprisingly not mentioned in J. Herzer's *Petrus oder Paulus? Studien über das Verhältnis des Ersten Petrusbriefes zur paulinischen Tradition* [WUNT 103; Tübingen: Mohr–Siebeck, 1998].)

[39] D.E. Aune, "Human Nature and Ethics in Hellenistic Philosophical Traditions and Paul: Some Issues and Problems," *Paul in His Hellenistic Context* (ed. T.

thing to practise dying in this life in that one prepares for one's eventual and still future death by already separating oneself from the lower nature and its cravings and values,[40] another to recognize as the basis of an ethical life the fact that one has already been caught up in the death of another, whose death was both physical and ethical, a death to sin leading to a life to and for God (Rom 6:10). It is, in other words, not just a 'metaphor of death' which is 'the basis for the transformed life', as Aune asserts (311), but Christ's death, which is very far from just a metaphor. In the ethical out-working of that death with Christ, however, there may well be parallels in that for the Stoic Seneca the one who has learnt so to die has unlearnt that slavery in which he formerly was and is subject to no power (*Ep.* 26.10); Paul differs, however, in paradoxically speaking also of the service of righteousness as a bondage (Rom 6:16, 18–19, 22).

Moreover the 'death' which is a present reality in the lives of Christians, or at least in the lives of apostles like Paul, is not just a matter of ethics and what Christians do, but of physical suffering too and what Christians have done to them by others: it is the persecuted apostle who not only dies daily (1 Cor 15:31),[41] but bears about in his body 'the putting to death of Jesus' (2 Cor 4:10), just as he speaks of bearing in his body the marks of Jesus (Gal 6:17). Aune recognizes that the 'possible ethical implications' of such language are not developed here (310): Paul's 'mortal dangers ... are construed as analogous to those experienced by Christ', an *imitatio Christi* or, more accurately, an *imitatio Christi* which is rooted in a union with Christ and which results in Christ's life-through-death being manifested in the existence of his followers (2 Cor 4:10–12).

Engberg-Pedersen; Minneapolis: Fortress, 1995) 291–312, here 305–12 (2 Cor 5:14 is set in this context on p. 310). Misleading, too, is his claim (312) that the use of 'cognitive' language of knowing and believing and having one's mind set on something (Rom 6:6, 8–9, 11; 8:5–6; cf. also the reckoning of 6:11) in itself means that no automatic transformation of the person is meant: one may simply recognize and be aware of what one is, willy-nilly. To make that point one needs rather to refer to the imperatives which Paul uses in 6:12–19.

[40] Cf., e.g., *Ep. Diogenes* 39.1; *Ep. Socrates* 14.8 (ed. Malherbe, pp. 164, 256, 258); Iambl. *Protrepticus* 3.

[41] This death is a sign of the true follower of Christ in contrast to that which the guilty Flaccus must die daily in anticipation (προαποθνήσκω) of the retribution for his crimes which he has committed (Philo *Flacc.* 175).

Or, noting the sacramental context in which this language of dying
is set, at least in Rom 6 if not expressly elsewhere,[42] should one seek
a clue in the understanding of Paul's theology as 'liminal' and as
drawing on a sense of a Christian rite like baptism as meaning that
the baptized enter, and remain in, a state that may be likened to
death?[43] Yet seeking an explanation in such a feature of rites of
passage is made more difficult by the fact that the Christian initiation rite of baptism is, unlike most other such rites, no imitation or
re-enactment of the destiny of the redeemer.[44] That is a serious
difficulty, since a similarity between the rite and the saving events
of the past is so central to many accounts of sacramental ritual. So,
for instance, Gerd Theißen speaks of the transforming power of
sacramental acts when the correspondence between the redeemer
and the redeemed is displayed in vivid form, but that correspondence
is absent from the Christian initiation-rite.[45] And if 1 Cor 7:29–31
with its repeated ὡς μή might also be regarded as an example of
liminal existence,[46] then it is to be noted that 6 Ezra 16:41–5 is
frequently treated as a parallel to this passage.[47] Does that not then
suggest that apocalyptic-eschatological hopes provide another pos-

---

[42] Caution is necessary here in case one assumes too readily that all such language in Paul stems from a sacramental context, even when that is not expressly
mentioned. The other possibility is that such language is based on Paul's inclusive and corporate Christology and used in Rom 6 to interpret the significance
and implications of the sacrament. (Cf. my *Baptism*, 49–50 and n. 2.)

[43] C. Strecker, *Die liminale Theologie des Paulus: Zugänge zur paulinischen Theologie
aus kulturanthropologischer Perspektive* (FRLANT 185; Göttingen: Vandenhoeck &
Ruprecht, 1999).

[44] Equally problematic is David Seeley's description of our dying with Christ
as a re-enactment of Christ's death (*The Noble Death: Graeco-Roman Martyrology and
Paul's Concept of Salvation* [JSNTSup 28; Sheffield: JSOT, 1990] 101).

[45] G. Theißen, "Soteriologische Symbolik in den paulinischen Schriften: Ein
strukturalistischer Beitrag," *KuD* 20 (1974) 282–304, here 294. The difference
between other such rites and the 'aniconic abstraction' of the early Christian rite
of baptism (and the eucharist) is emphasized in his *A Theory of Primitive Christian
Religion* (London: SCM, 1999) 131–2.

[46] Yet Strecker, *Theologie*, does not mention this possibility—perhaps because
it so manifestly does not fit into the pattern of rites of passage. In part the problem is that 'liminality' for Strecker (and also for Victor Turner on whom he draws
so heavily) occurs in two essentially separate contexts, in a ritual one ('rites of
passage') and in the context of "liminal movements," whose liminality or anti-struc-
ture is not ritually based, but nevertheless shares many features in common with
the liminality of those in the middle phase of the ritual passage.

[47] E.g. W. Schrage, "Die Stellung zur Welt bei Paulus, Epiktet und in der
Apokalyptik: Ein Beitrag zu 1 Kor 7,29–31," *ZTK* 61 (1964) 125–54.

sible path to a way of life which can be described as 'liminal'? It arises from the coexistence of two worlds, the old and the new: even if the new world is not yet fully realized—far from it—, its structure and its values already affect and shape the lives of those still living in the old world, and Christian believers have, so to speak, a foot in both worlds. That is more likely than that sharing Christ's death explains why Christian existence could be seen as liminal. For Christ's death was followed by his entry into a life to and for God (Rom 6:10b), and that life is shared by those who are his, at least ethically, if not yet physically (6:4, 11). In other words, seen from that angle, those united with Christ are regarded and are to regard themselves as having already passed over the *limen*, the threshold, as ὡσεὶ ἐκ νεκρῶν ζῶντας (Rom 6:13). And yet all such considerations are not an insuperable obstacle to such a ritual dimension if baptism is viewed as an eschatological rite, e.g. in the sense that it declares the end of the old age and the old humanity and the beginning of the new and the integration of the baptized into the new humanity. At the same time this must be regarded as a peculiarity of the Christian rite, and not a factor common to all eschatological sacraments, let alone to all sacramental rites or rites of passage: if one looks at the closest analogy, John's baptism,[48] then it is clear that it is anticipatory and lacks the twofold focus of the Christian rite, which also looks back to the past in the belief that the decisive change and the beginning of the new are already to be found there. In other words, this feature of early Christian ritual and thought is indissolubly linked with this characteristically Christian eschatological perspective.

In short, the way in which the death of Christ is regarded as involving many others in it and at the same time as entailing their salvific death with Christ has at best partial analogies in the thought-world of Paul's day, but no complete ones.

III.

'Death' was in itself a fluid concept: Philo recognizes, for instance, that there is a death of the body and also a death of the soul.[49] The

---

[48] For A. Schweitzer recognizes that this, too, was an eschatological sacrament: *The Mysticism of Paul the Apostle* (London: Black, 2nd ed. 1953) 230.

[49] See, e.g., n. 34 above and n. 52 below.

latter can occur when the body is still very much alive. Paul, too, can speak of himself and other Christians as having already died when, on the face of it, they were still alive. But this use of the metaphor of 'death', unlike that in Graeco–Roman ethical teaching mentioned above, does not treat it as something reprehensible; on the contrary, it is a death to sin and is the way to life.

Christ's death was, however, whatever else it was, a very physical one and no mere metaphor. But it is clear that its meaning for Paul does not end there, with the fact of the violent ending of Jesus' earthly life. It is, for Christ too, a death to sin whose counterpart and corollary is a life to and for God (Rom 6:10). For Christ it means a break with the old order and birth into a new one, just as it does for Paul who shares in Christ's fate (Gal 2:19–20; 6:14). It leads those who are Christ's into a life for Christ (2 Cor 5:15) as well as a life for God. But for Christ, too, the death which leads to this is a death under judgement, even if is not a judgement which Christ himself, in his own person, has deserved (cf. 2 Cor 5:21). For in his assimilation to human sinfulness Christ has become, in Paul's eyes, the vehicle of God's word of condemnation on that sinfulness (Rom 8:3)—and not just a word of condemnation, for the law could and did utter that too, but the carrying out of the sentence as well.[50] In other words, one must reckon with the dimension of Christ's death as an expression of God's judgement, a judgement that is at the same time creative of new life.

Is it then perhaps significant, too, that Paul does not just speak of Christ becoming accursed for our sakes, but of his becoming a 'curse' (Gal 3:13), even though the whole logic of Gal 3:10, 13 would rather lead one to expect the adjective here? Some may regard the distinction as of no consequence,[51] but the one is more active in sense, the other passive. Does that mean, not just that Christ bears the consequences of humanity's sins, but is at the same time the declaration of God's verdict upon them? What Christ has become has implications for others too and involves and includes them in his destiny.[52]

---

[50] So, rightly, C.E.B. Cranfield, *A Critical and Exegetical Commentary on the Epistle to the Romans* 1 (ICC; Edinburgh: T. & T. Clark, 1975) 382–3.

[51] So, e.g., E. de W. Burton, *A Critical and Exegetical Commentary on the Epistle to the Galatians* (ICC; Edinburgh: T. & T. Clark, 1921) 171 (metonymy); F. Mußner, *Der Galaterbrief* (HTKNT 9; Freiburg, etc.: Herder, 5th ed. 1988) 233 (abstractum per concreto; cf. F. Büchsel, in *TDNT* 1.450).

[52] Heinrich Schlier, at least, sees a point in Paul's use of the abstract "curse"

Underlying this way of speaking of death is thus again the sense that it is God's judgement. This dimension of human death has been implicit from the day that God declared to Adam that on the day that he ate from the tree of the knowledge of good and evil he would die; Adam ate, but lived for 930 years (Gen 2:17; 5:5). He was, it is true, banished from the garden and the presence of God, and that could be interpreted as a death: for Philo any fleeing from God is death (*Fug.* 78).[53] In the original context of the Genesis text, however, with its repeated curses (3:13, 17), the idea of dying as God's curse is pronounced lies nearer to hand.

Accordingly, to speak thus of death as God's judgement invites us to think of it as a speech-act (in the sense of an act which speaks, says something, communicates something), and, if Christ's death for us and our death with Christ can be viewed from the perspective of speech-acts, then that may help to answer the troublesome question of when we died with Christ. For, on the one hand, if God's verdict on us was uttered at the moment when Christ, our representative, died, it is also the case that this verdict can be repeated and heard anew, afresh for each individual. Rightly, Thrall resists here the temptation to force a decision in favour of the one or the other alternative: the 'all' participate collectively in that event in which Christ destroyed the power of sin *and* they appropriate its results in baptism.[54] For Paul that repeating and our hearing takes place when the preaching of the crucified Christ is heard, but also when the rite of baptism joins the baptized to the crucified Christ, but that rite has also the nature of a speech-act, a semantic function, a proclamation, in that it declares to the baptized the destruction of sin and the old life and promises new life now and in the future.

IV.

The logic of this verse in 2 Corinthians is, then, most readily intelligible if, as Gerhard Delling puts it,[55] 'what the representative has

---

here: "Christ so took the curse upon himself for our sake, that he represented the curse that lay upon him" (*Der Brief an die Galater* [MeyerK; Göttingen: Vandenhoeck & Ruprecht, 5th ed. 1971] 138).

[53] Though Philo prefers to explain Gen 2:17 as referring to the death of the soul, the death of the evil man (*Quaest. in Gen.* 1.16).

[54] *2 Cor,* 411.

[55] "Tod Jesu," 91.

experienced also applies fully to the one whom he represents'—as long as the representation is understood in that inclusive sense which is implied by the comparison of Adam and Christ.⁵⁶ In contrast with 1 Cor 15:22, however, where Adam's death and that of all humanity with him is viewed as wholly negative, here it is the death of Christ as the δεύτερος ἄνθρωπος, as Windisch rightly sees,⁵⁷ which is shared by all, and this death is a necessary stage in a change of lordship, the way to a life for and with God, just as Christ, having once died, now lives for and with God. The one death with the one inclusively representative figure is wholly destructive, the other is the first step in God's new creation of humanity.⁵⁸ For, in so dying, Christ submitted to a judgement that God passed in Christ's death upon all humanity, all whom Christ represented; similarly God's raising Jesus from the dead signifies God's acceptance of, and promise to, that same humanity (cf. Rom 3:23–4, 'all ... being justified', together with 4:25, 'raised for our justification'). In other words, although it must be granted that it is an idea which seems out of step with our ways of thinking, Paul speaks very concretely of our involvement and participation in Christ's death and resurrection; at the same time it is hard to make much sense of what he says if he does not at the same time view that death and resurrection here primarily from the perspective of divine declarations about humanity as a whole.

At the start I remarked that the logic of 2 Cor 5:14 seems at first sight strange—not just to us, but perhaps also, as I have tried to show, within the framework of ideas current in Paul's own time. But perhaps this very strangeness is all the more significant because it is strange and novel, laying bare one aspect of Paul's thinking and his way of looking at the saving significance of Jesus' death. However central and fundamental this aspect may be, it should nevertheless not be played off against other features of Pauline soteriology, such as the forensic or cultic categories which he also uses. These should

---

⁵⁶ Whether one describes this as "mystical" (so, e.g., Windisch, *2 Kor*, 182–3) may depend on the definition of that adjective. It reflects, at any rate, a way of thinking which is in many ways alien to us, but the fault may, of course, lie at least in part in our individualism.

⁵⁷ *2 Kor*, 183.

⁵⁸ Whether one is right to describe this constellation of ideas in this particular Pauline context as a "stellvertretende Sühne" (cf. Bieringer, "Ursprung") seems to me questionable, regardless of other uses of the ὑπέρ-terminology in pre-Pauline tradition and in other passages in Paul.

rather be treated as all complementing one another, balancing one another and correcting any one-sided concentration on a single element. Nonetheless it may be claimed that in this surprising logic one underlying presupposition of Pauline soteriology comes to expression with a succinctness not surpassed elsewhere in his writings.

PART FOUR

SECTS, POLEMIC AND THE APOLOGETICS OF PAUL

SECTARIAN DIVERSITY AT CORINTH

C.K. Barrett

I may perhaps be allowed to introduce this paper with a line or two of autobiography. In preparation for the Pauline Colloquium of 1983 I was asked to deal with the references to Adam in Paul's discussion of the resurrection in 1 Corinthians 15. Adam is mentioned twice, in v.22 and again in v.45. The question immediately suggests itself, Why are the two references to Adam so far apart? Do they serve the same purpose or is the figure of Adam adduced for two different purposes? I shall not here repeat or even summarize what I have written elsewhere.[1] It seems that Adam was introduced into Paul's argument for two different reasons. There were Christians in Corinth who believed in the resurrection of Jesus; if they had not done so Paul could not have said, with reference to 15:3–5, So we preach and so you believed (v.11). They did not however draw from the resurrection of Jesus the inference that believers also will rise; on the contrary, they said, There is no resurrection of the dead (meaning, of the dead other than Christ; v.12). Paul replied by invoking the figure of Adam, the universal man. Christ is the new Adam, the new universal man, and his resurrection is the pledge of ours. There was however a second group, who faced the resurrection not with aggression but bewilderment. How are the dead raised? With what kind of body do they come? (15:35). This calls for a different answer, but it too is based on Adam. Adam became a living soul (15:45, εἰς ψυχὴν ζῶσαν, quoting Gen. 2:7); this leads to the affirmation that if there is a ψυχὴ ζῶσα there must also be a πνεῦμα ζωοποιοῦν. This is hardly a logical inference, but the contrast he has stated (with some aid from Daniel 7) enables Paul to answer the question ποίῳ σώματι. So there are two groups who attack belief in the resurrection of Christians, one that flatly denies it, and another that is puzzled and sceptical because it cannot understand.

This observation suggested a theme for a contribution to the

---

[1] See *Résurrection du Christ et des Chrétiens (1 Co 15)*, ed. L. De Lorenzi, Série Monographique de 'Benedictina', Section Biblique-Oecuménique, 8 (Rome: Benedictina, 1985) 99–122.

Festschrift for Archbishop Methodios.² Paul's own answer to the
question whether a Christian might eat εἰδωλόθυτα was that he was
undoubtedly free to do so provided that he did not by thus exercising his freedom offend and hurt a weaker Christian brother who did
not share the other's theologically based freedom. There were, it
seems, in Corinth two groups both of which might seem to have been
Paul's allies. They are dealt with in chapters 8 and 10 respectively.
Those in ch. 8 may be described as gnostics, provided we do not
give the term too rigid and technical a definition. They had γνῶσις;
they knew that there was no god but one, and that in consequence
an idol was nothing (8:4). It followed that to sacrifice an animal to
a nothing did nothing to the animal or to the meat derived from it.
One was therefore free to eat it. True, Paul comments; but what of
your brother who does not have this γνῶσις (8:11,13)? The gnostic
argument is valid on the theological but not on the ethical level. The
position of the second group is not stated so plainly but may be
inferred from ch. 10. They argued: to eat εἰδωλόθυτα cannot harm
us because we have supernatural protection: we have been baptized
and we partake of spiritual food and drink. This claim is presupposed by Paul's reply. You must not rely on such defences. Our
Israelite forebears were baptized into Moses (10:2), yet God was not
pleased with them and they were laid low in the desert (10:5). They
ate spiritual food and drank spiritual drink (10:3,4), but this did not
prevent them from falling into gross sin and suffering condign punishment (10:6–10). Be warned therefore and do not assume a security you do not possess. These persons we may if we wish, and do
not put too large a meaning into the word, call Sacramentarians.
Both Gnostics and Sacramentarians reach the same conclusion as
Paul: there is nothing inherently sinful in eating food sacrificed to
idols. But the latter group reach the conclusion on unsatisfactory
grounds, and neither group shows concern for their fellow Christians. Paul does not seek their support.

Here there are already four distinct groups—for we must not for-
get those, showing perhaps the influence of Jerusalem (Acts 15:29),
who maintained, against Paul, that to eat food sacrificed to idols was
in all circumstances forbidden. There may, of course, have been cross-
membership of groups.

---

² *Aksum—Thyateira*, ed. G.D. Dragas (London: Thyateira House, 1985) 155–8.

We are not far into the epistle when party divisions appear. Paul has heard from members of Chloe's household that there are contentions (ἔριδες) in Corinth, and these could lead to actual divisions (σχίσματα). These were exhibited in the watchwords used by each party. Each member had his own: I belong to Paul; I belong to Apollos; I belong to Cephas; I belong to Christ (1:10–12). Here are four (potential) leaders of divisive groups; perhaps we should say three rather than four.[3] They may not have wished to be leaders; it is certain that Paul did not so wish and this may be taken to imply the possibility of the same conclusion with regard to the others. What the incipient groups stood for we do not know. Paul's people presumably accepted his theology so far as they understood it, but their support may have been personal rather than doctrinal: He was our founder, he is our friend, and we stand by him. Speculations about the Apollos group are usually based on Acts 18:24: he was an Alexandrian and he was learned (or eloquent, λόγιος). We should be cautious; not every Alexandrian Jew was a Philo. But it may be that Apollos had introduced and made popular the theme of wisdom, which Paul, though in the right context (2:6–16) he accepts it, treats with some reserve. Cephas[4] was probably the travelling[5] representative of the great apostles in Jerusalem; he may have stood (or may have been taken to stand) for a Judaizing tendency and have required abstention from εἰδωλόθυτα.[6] Most difficult is the claim 'I belong to Christ', and there is something to be said for the view that the words should be regarded as a marginal gloss or as Paul's own outraged comment on the party cries. See 3:22,23; you do not

---

[3] ἐγὼ δὲ Χριστοῦ seems to be read by all Greek MSS and VSS. There is no reference to a 'Christ party' in 3:22f. (possibly but improbably at 2 Cor. 10:7). 1 Clement 47:3, however, mentions only Paul, Cephas, and Apollos as leaders of parties in Corinth. 1 Clement is our oldest reference to 1 Corinthians. It is not impossible that it bears witness to a text that mentioned only the three. 'I belong to Christ' would then be a pious marginal comment by a very early scribe.

[4] Was Peter the unnamed opponent of Paul in 2 Cor. 10:7? It is an attractive view and I have in the past been inclined to accept it; see however below, p. 300. But what we know of James and Peter subsequent to Gal. 2:9 is hardly such as to win a favourable view of the 'Pillars'. See further M.D. Goulder, *A Tale of Two Missions* (London: SCM Press, 1994). R.P. Martin, *Word Bible Commentary, 2 Corinthians* (Waco: Word, 1986) 307, sees the singular not as an identifiable individual but as the opposition 'personified as a single number (τις) as in Gal. 5:10 and Col. 2:8.' So many other commentators.

[5] See 'Cephas and Corinth', in *Abraham unser Vater, Festschrift für Otto Michel*, ed. O. Betz, M. Hengel, P. Schmidt (Leiden/Köln: Brill, 1963) 1–12.

[6] Cf. however Acts 15:7–11, but also Gal. 2:11–14.

belong to Paul, Apollos, or Cephas; they belong to you. You belong
to Christ. If however there was a 'Christ-party' there is still much to
be said for T.W. Manson's judgement.[7] 'I should be very much inclined
to think that they were groups for whom Christ meant something
like "God, freedom, and immortality", where "God" means a re-
fined philosophical monotheism; "freedom" means emancipation from
the puritanical rigours of Palestinian barbarian authorities into the
wider air of self-realization; and immortality means the sound Greek
doctrine as opposed to the crude Jewish notion of the Resurrection.'
The difficulty with Manson's view is that, as a word, Christ, Messiah, suggests 'crude' Judaism as clearly as any single word could do
(except perhaps Torah). It may be however that the word had become simply a divine name, detached from its origins in Jewish
Messianic expectation.

With these important leading persons may be linked the Corinthian
tendencies described in ch. 4, to which party slogans would make
an effective appeal. The Corinthians, it seems, wish to exercise their
own desire for power by choosing a leader and exalting him above
other potential leaders.[8] This goes with their adoption of a triumphalist
realized eschatology (4:8–10), which accompanies their failure to
recognize that the 'leaders' (at least, Paul and Apollos; is it by chance
and for brevity that Cephas is not mentioned?) are fellow servants
with each other and live in humble circumstances. The Corinthian
church provided good soil for the development of division.

The first four chapters are evidently of great importance for our
theme. We know the names of three (four) party leaders (leaders
perhaps against their own wish) and can form some notion of their
party lines.

Chapter 5 begins with a reference to a gross act of immorality on
the part of two people. Two do not constitute a party, but their action
was applauded by a group so considerable that Paul can address them
simply as *you*. Are you puffed up? Did you not rather go into mourning
that he who had committed this deed might be taken away from
you? *You* is not specified, but can hardly mean the whole community without exception; it therefore represents a party. The church

---

[7] See T.W. Manson, *Studies in the Gospels and Epistles*, ed. M. Black, (Manchester: Manchester University Press, 1962) 207.

[8] For the translation of 1 Cor. 4:6 see my commentary on 1 Corinthians (London: A. & C. Black, 2nd edition, 1972) 105–7; also B.D.R. # 247, n. 10.

should have constituted itself as a court to judge—not outsiders but its own members; the party however prevailed, preferring unbridled freedom, in regard to sexual relations and perhaps other matters also, to discipline.

The church as a whole however was not averse to litigation. Some were involved in suits against fellow Christians and took them for adjudication to the civil, that is, to non-Christian courts (6:1,2). This to Paul was a double offence against Christian principles. It would have been better to accept loss at the hands of a Christian brother than to inflict loss upon him; and if some kind of court had to be involved it should have been a Christian court. A taste for litigation however is hardly the substance of sectarianism, so that though another aspect of Corinthian Christian life displeasing to Paul appears here, it does not belong in our list of divisive groups.

Chapter 7, however, is different. In it Paul replies to a letter (7:1) which evidently contained a number of topics relevant to marriage. The letter itself we do not possess, and therefore cannot tell in what terms, whether purely interrogative or disputatious, it was expressed. Much turns on the punctuation and interpretation of 7:1. Should the words καλὸν ἀνθρώπῳ γυναικὸς μὴ ἅπτεσθαι be placed within quotation marks? If they should, who was being quoted, by whom? The letter writer by Paul? This seems the most probable view. If it is correct there was a group at Corinth which believed that Christians should not marry. Not only (as Paul had said) is intercourse with a prostitute forbidden; so also is marriage if it includes sexual union (see 7:3). If, as appears, there was in Corinth a group that advocated the free use of sexual capabilities and opportunities, there was another that advocated, perhaps required, abstention from marriage. This principle is pursued in ch. 7 in a number of aspects which there is no space here to deal with in detail. It suffices to observe that Paul's reaction to this principle is that it is good advice (for those who can take it) but bad law. The ideal is that everyone should continue in that state in which he or she was at conversion; but in view of human frailty (7:2) marriage is to be commended. The fact that Paul develops his advice to 'stay as you are' in other directions also confirms his own statement that its basis is eschatological (7:26,31). It is enough here to observe that there was a Corinthian group that held that marriage was to be avoided.

Chapter 8 brings us to a theme that has already been mentioned. There was in Corinth a party that we may fairly describe as Gnostic. They had Gnosis; and they had no regard for those who had it not. They come to our notice in relation to the question of food sacrificed to idols, and we cannot doubt that their existence presupposes the existence of another group which maintained, You may not eat food offered to idols. It is unlikely that a gnostic group confined its attention to this one element in Christian life. They had gnosis about God and Christ (8:6), and no doubt they applied it generally.

It is in ch. 10 that Paul deals a second time with the eating of εἰδωλόθυτα. Like the 'Gnostics' the 'Sacramentarians' reach more or less the right conclusion by a fallacious method. What is to be noted here is the existence in Corinth of a group that found a magical protective agency in baptism and the Sacred Meal.

For our present purpose it is convenient to deal with chs. 8 and 10 together, but Paul had good reason for placing ch. 9 where he did.[9] This chapter may seem to have little that bears on our subject, but this is not so, and it points forward to 2 Corinthians. Especially in 9:1–6 we see a picture of the 'great apostle'—the sort of apostle Paul had made up his mind not to be. Apostles (the word is not defined here) have the right (and Paul defends it) to be accompanied on their travels by their wives and to be maintained at the expense of the churches in which they are at work. The right is supported by reason, by Old Testament Scripture, and by the teaching of Jesus himself, but Paul has made no use of it lest it should hinder the work of the Gospel, which to him is more important than any personal considerations. Though free of all men he has enslaved himself to all, that he may win more of them for Christ.

Those who accept the privileges that Paul renounces are described (9:5) as the other apostles, the Lord's brothers, and Cephas. The name Cephas adds nothing to the list; he was an apostle. Specific reference was logically unnecessary. It seems likely[10] that he is mentioned because he and his behaviour were personally known to the Corinthians. This recalls the reference in 1:12 to those who say, 'I belong to Cephas', and suggests that the Petrine group may have had not a doctrinal but a personal motivation. 'Peter, the foundation of the church (contrast 3:10–13), the great apostle, who accepts

---

[9] See my commentary (n. 8) 16f., 200. Paul had good reason for placing ch. 9 where he did.

[10] See the essay mentioned in n. 5.

our service and gives orders that we obey, is the man for us.' This in turn suggests the question, which at this stage it is impossible to answer, how far Peter had backing from Jerusalem. Gal. 2:12 seems to mean that he accepted orders from James (one of the brothers of the Lord, who also enjoyed a privileged life (9:5)).

In 11:2 it seems that we return to the letter sent to Paul from Corinth. The Corinthians give a good account of themselves. 'In all things we remember you, and we observe the traditions as you handed them on to us.' Paul evidently doubts this, and expresses his doubts, focused mainly in chs. 11, 12, 14, in relation to the church's gatherings. Over 11:2–16 we need not linger. The paragraph turns mainly on the difference between men and women and the way the difference should be expressed (and not concealed) in the context of public meetings. Evidently there were women who behaved in a way society would associate with men, and men who would correspondingly behave like women, growing their hair long and wearing a head-covering. It is not clear whether these were the actions of a few individuals or arose out of an organized feminist movement. There is of course no hard and fast line between the two possibilities, and each merges into the other. It will be wise here to keep an open mind.

Paul moves on (11:17–33) to a new situation in which the dividing line between two groups is clear; it is not theological but social. At least it begins on the social level. The gifts brought for the common meal were not shared, so that it is not the Lord's Supper that you eat; each of you eats his own supper, with the result that one goes hungry and another gets drunk (11:18–21). This is a social sin; in it you despise your impecunious brother, for whom nevertheless Christ died. This means however that we are already on the way to a theological as well as social and economic difference. The richer members are not only segregating themselves in order to enjoy their supper. They are denying the universal scope of Christ's death. It may be that there is a further point to note. Chapter 10 suggests that there were those who felt themselves so well guarded by their sacramental immersion and spiritual food and drink that they might safely eat εἰδωλόθυτα; they were supernaturally protected against any evil consequence. The same misplaced confidence probably lies behind 11:27–31. So far from taking up spiritual protection (Paul says), you are incurring spiritual danger; physical danger too, and many are weak and sick and not a few have fallen asleep (v.30). The 'sacramentarians' (see above) appear again. Paul does not depreciate the Christian meal, but attacks its misuse both as an occasion for selfish gluttony and as a supposed protection against divine retribution.

Chapter 12 appropriately follows with an exposition of true Christian unity. The church is like a body in which the several limbs and organs work together in harmony, each performing its own function for the good of the whole. Ch. 13 follows even more appropriately, and need not be discussed here. Ch. 14 turns from the ideal to the actual. Behind the chapter lies a dispute about the relative value of spiritual gifts. It appears that there was in Corinth a group that found the most significant expression of and the weightiest argument for Christianity in visible and especially audible manifestations of the work of the Spirit. Speaking with tongues was particularly important. Paul does not deny that it is or may be a genuine gift of the Spirit; indeed he himself speaks with tongues more than any of them (14:18). But it is something that should be practised between a man and God, an individual phenomenon that does nothing to build up the church as a whole. Hence, in the assembly I would rather speak five words with my mind, that I might instruct others, than tens of thousands of words in a tongue (14:19). This is the principle; practical advice follows in vv.26–40. It probably goes too far to say that there was a charismatic party in Corinth; but there were a good many charismatics, and they had much in common.

Chapter 15 contains important material. The two references to Adam (15:22 and 15:45) were mentioned above. They seem to arise from two groups, of which one reached the sceptical conclusion, ἀνάστασις νεκρῶν οὐκ ἔστιν—it does not happen (they may have preferred the notion of immortality), the other the not necessarily sceptical question, πῶς ἐγείρονται οἱ νεκροί; We can hardly claim that there were two anti-resurrection parties, but there was at least one. Again, there were those who held that Paul was no apostle, or at best a worthless one (15:8,9). Correspondingly, the vital qualification of Cephas, and of his notable Jerusalem colleague James, is given in traditional words at 15:5,7. Not only Cephas but James also precedes Paul in the list of resurrection appearances.

In ch. 16 the reference (v.12) to Apollos may show some sensitivity on Paul's part: he does not wish anyone in Corinth to think that he has in any way prevented Apollos from visiting them. In fact Paul has begged him to go to Corinth. It was his own choice (or perhaps God's will—θέλημα) not to go. There is here nothing solid enough to build on, though it agrees with the suggestion of chs. 1–3, that Apollos was by some looked up to as a leader, and that Paul was on closer terms with Apollos than with Cephas.

It is now time to make a list of the groups and tendencies that we have observed and to attempt an analysis of it, remembering that any such attempt must be conjectural and hypothetical and that members of the church may have belonged to more than one party.

(1) A Paul party—I belong to Paul
(2) An Apollos party—I belong to Apollos
(3) A Cephas party—I belong to Cephas
(4) A Christ party—I belong to Christ. The existence of such a party must be considered doubtful. See above, pp. 289f.
(5) A sexual freedom party—we boast of our freedom (5:2). See also ch. 7.
(6) A celibate party—it is good for a man not to touch a woman (ch. 7).
(7) 'Gnostic' freedom to eat food sacrificed to idols.
(8) 'Sacramentarian' freedom to eat food sacrificed to idols.
(9) Some abstain from eating food sacrificed to idols.
(10) A Cephas, James, and Jerusalem party. Ch. 9.
(11) The rich and the poor.
(12) The charismatics (but it is doubtful whether these constituted a party)
(13) Doubters of the resurrection (possibly of two kinds).

How far is it possible to put together any of these groups and tendencies? Only in a way both conjectural and loose; anything less characteristic of the church in Corinth than a neatly ordered set of party lists is difficult to conceive.

We may begin with the Apollos party, who, we may guess, exaggerated a legitimate element in Apollos' teaching into the stress on *wisdom* that appears in chs. 2 and 3. They are also the most probable defenders of freedom to eat εἰδωλόθυτα on the ground of the knowledge they possessed—γνῶσις was not far from σοφία. Apollos was, according to Acts 18:24, ἀνὴρ λόγιος, and λόγιος may mean *eloquent*. Eloquence was practised in the courts, and there may be a connection with those who were ready—too ready in Paul's view—to take their differences to pagan courts. We may perhaps add some of those who doubted the resurrection, not because they believed that the death of the body was the end of everything but because they preferred to believe in the immortality of an immaterial soul.

This makes a considerable list (2,6,8,14) and it would be wrong to ascribe all the errors involved to Apollos personally; though it is possible that he failed to keep some of his wilder adherents under control. Their errors, moreover, were for the most part exaggerations of virtues. They were right about food sacrificed to idols, wrong so far as they forgot their colleagues who lacked *gnosis*. Eloquence is a useful gift for Christians. And Paul, who believed in the resurrection of the body, thought not of a natural but of a spiritual body (1 Cor. 15:44).

So much for the Apollos party. We will continue with the named leaders. 'I belong to Cephas,' said some—understandably, for he was the church's link not only with its mother, Judaism, but with Jesus himself. 'You are Peter, and on this rock I will build my church.' They knew this saying, and Paul probably thought that they made too much of it (3:11). Cephas is mentioned again, at 9:5, together with the other apostles, Palestinian Jews, no doubt, and with the Lord's brothers, who would of course include James. These were the great apostles, who knew and accepted the deference and privileges to which an apostle was entitled. We should probably take Peter to have been the leader of the party that thought that εἰδωλόθυτα should be forbidden. He is represented in a different light at the Council of Acts 15, but in Acts 10 he declares that he has never touched unclean food, and at Antioch, under pressure from James, he had withdrawn from table fellowship with Gentile Christians (Gal. 2:12).

If 'I belong to Christ' is to be taken as representing a party, and if T.W. Manson's suggestion (above, p. 290) is correct, the party may be taken to include the celibates (7:1; cf. 8:26), also conceivably, by a complicated argument, those who found in prostitutes an outlet, alternative to marriage, for their sexual desires (6:18–20; 5:2,9–13).

Identifications become more doubtful when we have no names to guide us. The sexual freedom party may belong not with the Christ party but with the sacramentarian acceptance of εἰδωλόθυτα. Paul's Old Testament analogy includes not only eating and drinking but also fornication (10:8). He reminds the immoral persons in Corinth that they could not claim that they were protected from punishment for their immorality by the sacraments they had received; remember the 23,000 who died in one day! The rich, who enjoyed their own supper rather than the Lord's, were presumably a group socially rather than theologically defined, though their social approach to the supper had a theological implication: μὴ διακρίνων τὸ σῶμα

(11:29). The greedy and selfish rich man does not perceive that the significance of the meal is to be found in the body of Christ (in the various meanings of this term) rather than in the tasty dishes he has been careful to provide for himself.[11] In the church's fellowship meal he has substituted magic for loving concern. The charismatics do not constitute a party, though there seems to be a possibility that they will swamp the church meeting. They may have been distributed among various groups.

There is nothing like 1 Corinthians in the Pauline corpus, no other letter in which Paul moves from one practical matter to another, sometimes answering questions addressed to him in a letter, sometimes dealing with matters he has heard of in other ways. The Galatians no doubt had other problems, some of which can be detected in their epistle, but it is dominated by the great peril of the demand for circumcision and the observance of the Law. The Philippian church also is threatened from without. The letter contains exhortations to humility and unity, but these relate mainly to a general condition of self-opinionatedness. Ephesians and Colossians, both doubtfully from Paul's hand, both contain sets of household rules, but the husbands, wives, parents, children, masters, slaves, addressed do not constitute parties; nor does the primitive gnosticism that may be detected behind Colossians. 1 and 2 Thessalonians (the latter improbably Paul's work) contain a good deal of incidental information about the church in Thessalonica, and in fact these two letters come in this respect closer to 1 and 2 Corinthians than any others in the Pauline corpus. There is an implicit question about Paul's eschatology (1 Thess. 4:13–18; cf. 2 Thess. 2:1,2). There is advice about marriage which may imply that Paul has heard that all is not well in that area (1 Thess. 4:3–8). Paul recalls that he has put no pressure on the Thessalonians though as an apostle he might legitimately have done so (1 Thess. 2:7). In addition there are general words of comfort and exhortation.

But not even here is there anything quite like 1 Corinthians. Even when we turn to 2 Corinthians[12] the first impression is of difference.

---

[11] Many interpretations of μὴ διακρίνων τὸ σῶμα have been given; for a sketch see my commentary (n. 8) 274ff. I am here broadening somewhat, but not developing, the interpretation given there. See, among many other works, G.D. Fee, *The First Epistle to the Corinthians* (NICNT, Grand Rapids: Eerdmans, 1987) 563f.; H.-J. Klauck, *Herrenmahl und Hellenistischer Kult* (Münster: Aschendorff, 1982) 326f.

[12] Probably two letters, chs. 10–13 being written somewhat later than chs. 1–9.

There is in 2 Corinthians no specific reference to parties under the names of Paul, Apollos, Cephas, and Christ.[13] We hear of no gross case of fornication, or of litigiousness. No problems are raised regarding marriage, or the eating of εἰδωλόθυτα. People are not said to speak with tongues.[14] Rich and poor do not separate on economic or social grounds. Paul can affirm (5:10) that we must all appear before the judgement seat of Christ, and does not have to explain what he means. At a first reading of the epistle it might appear that the problems that underlie 1 Corinthians had disappeared. This seems improbable; at the end of the first century the Corinthians were still a divided church.[15] Had the old problems lost their importance through the emergence of a new and more dangerous problem? This is nearer to the truth. What is to be seen in 2 Corinthians is a violent personal attack on Paul. The party that appears most clearly is an Anti-Paul party. Anti-Pauline activity takes several forms.[16]

(1) In ch. 1 Paul is blamed for changing his travel plans. He is a fickle person whose word cannot be believed. He had expressed the intention of paying a double visit to Corinth, on his way to Macedonia, and again on his way back. He had not done so. But it was precisely in order to spare the Corinthians (1:23) that he had changed his plan. Some however, if not all the Corinthians, had taken the opportunity to accuse him of double talk.

(2) Chapter 2 refers to an unhappy event in Corinth which had elicited from Paul a stern letter, of which no copy has survived.[17] As Paul writes he is able to express the hope that the matter is ended. It was, it seems, not a Corinthian but a visitor to Corinth who had in some way hurt, injured or insulted, Paul; but Paul had forgiven him, and those Corinthians who had failed to take his part, and he evidently now believed that the church as a whole was on his side. The grief he had caused by his letter was a godly grief (7:10), and it had done good.

(3) After his extraordinary but serious assertion (2:17) that the

---

[13] Unless at 10:7 there is a special claim to belong to Christ; see below, p. 300.

[14] Some see in 5:13 (ἐξέστημεν) a reference to Paul's own ability to speak with tongues or see visions.

[15] See 1 Clement 47:5–7.

[16] For many details see my and other commentaries. For a clear statement of a 'pessimistic' view of chs. 10–13 see B. Corsani, *La Seconda Lettera ai Corinzi, Guida alla lettera* (Turin: Claudiana, 2000) 33–5.

[17] Unless, as some think, in 2 Corinthians 10–13. This view is improbable.

majority of preachers water down, adulterate, the word of God, and possibly with the same preachers in mind, Paul observes that, un-like others, he does not come armed with commendatory letters designed to establish his status as a true apostle. He has and needs no such letter. The Corinthians are his letter; that is, his authority as an apostle is established not by commendation from Jerusalem or elsewhere but by the fruit of his evangelistic ministry. It is suggested, though hardly proved, by 3:4–18, that the commended but not commendable preachers are Judaizers.

(4) In the intervening chapters there is much that throws light on the relation between Paul and the Corinthians—he hopes that their own consciences will show them the truth, with no self-commenda-tion on his part (5:11,12), and urges them to be whole-heartedly sincere in their Christian life (6:14–16)—but the unhappy incident at Corinth and the sorrowful letter reappear in ch. 7. It seems, and this is in agreement with ch. 2 (see above), that a visitor to Corinth had at-tacked Paul, and that the Corinthians, impressed by this man's cre-dentials and aggressive, self-assertive, manner, had not defended their own apostle as they should have done. The injured person (7:12) is almost certainly Paul; the injurious one (also 7:12) is not named, and we are left to guess both his identity and the source of his creden-tials. He, and others like him, had not finished with Corinth. There is a short interval between the writing of chs. 1–9 and chs. 10–13; the situation in Corinth has deteriorated.

(5) When Paul resumes there again appears to be an individual at the heart of an anti-Pauline movement. There is certainly a plural-ity of false apostles, evil workers who disguise themselves as apostles of Christ. In fact, though they represent themselves as ministers of righteousness, they are ministers of Satan (11:13,15). They are not themselves the great Jerusalem apostles[18] but appear to be in some relation with them. It may be (though this can be no more than a guess) that they carried commendatory letters (see above) from these men—the Pillars of Gal. 2:9. Certainly in 2 Corinthians Paul treats these 'super-apostles' (11:5; 12:11) with the same irony that he uses in Galatians. What we should note here, however, is a sequence of

---

[18] Opinions on this matter differ, but it still seems to me quite impossible that Paul should describe the same group as servants of Satan (11:15) and servants of Christ (11:23). See p. 302, and especially E. Käsemann in *ZNW* 41 (1942) 33–71, and the reprinted article, *Die Legitimität des Apostels* (Darmstadt: Wissenschaftliche Buchgesellschaft, 1956).

passages in which Paul refers to a single person.

10:7: If anyone is confident with regard to himself that he belongs
to Christ, let him consider again by himself that as he belongs to
Christ, so also do we.

10:10,11 'His letters', he says, 'are weighty and powerful, but his
bodily presence is weak and his speech excites contempt.' Let the
man who says that kind of thing...

11:4: If your visitor proclaims another Jesus, whom we did not proclaim, or you receive a different Spirit, which you did not receive,
or a different Gospel, which you did not accept, then you put up
with him all right!

That an anti-Pauline group had a leader who took a particularly
active line against Paul recalls the groups of 1 Cor. 1:12. Among
those mentioned there the only possible anti-Pauline leader is Cephas.
Cephas is scarcely mentioned by Paul except in disagreement; but
his place is with the Pillars in Jerusalem. He is not the one who
preaches a different Jesus, and we must in the end be content not to
know the name of the man who was.

We may however consider the effect and content of his work and
the outcome of his mission in Corinth. He contributed to the question, Who or what is an apostle? How may one be recognized? It is,
as I have said, most improbable that the Corinthians had no new
questions to ask about marriage, that none of them was fascinated
by questions of wisdom and *gnosis*, that they had unanimously decided to eat (or not to eat) εἰδωλόθυτα, and to keep speaking with
tongues within limits. They may well have been dissatisfied with the
answers they received from Paul. What, they might ask, does the
man, who cannot even make travel plans and stick to them, want us
to do? Are we, for example, to eat εἰδωλόθυτα or not? He tells us
that an idol is nothing, that what is sacrificed to the idol is nothing,
that we do not need to make anxious inquiries in the market place
or at the table of a friend. But then he tells us that we must consider
the conscience of our fellow Christians. What? Go round the church
asking one after another, Will it trouble your conscience if I eat meat
from the temple of Isis? Must I submit a menu to the church meeting? Again, what does he want us to do about marriage? He wishes
all to be like himself, unmarried. But he tells us that because of cases
of fornication we had better be married. He tells us that some men
and women living celibate lives under the same roof should stay as
they are, others that they should marry. He tells us that he speaks

with tongues more than any of us, but would rather speak five rational words than tens of thousands in a tongue. He assumes that
we have been baptized, and thanks God he baptized none of us (or
very few). He speaks to us in solemn words about the Lord's Supper, but assures us that no amount of spiritual bread and wine will
keep us from sin and the consequent destruction.

They could and no doubt did continue in doubt and disputation
on these and other matters, and it would be understandable if they
drew the conclusion, This is no apostle for us. We want one who
knows his own mind and will make up our minds for us. And it would
be well if one should appear to offer himself, or perhaps impose himself,
as the desired authoritative apostle. It is not surprising that this false
apostle should attack Paul on the grounds of his weakness. It is easy
to add the unexpressed supplement to 10:10,11 (quoted above). *He*
(singular), the anti-Pauline leader, says, his letters are weighty and
powerful, but his bodily presence is weak and his speech excites
contempt. It is likely enough that he added, I do not write letters;
I am here in person, and know how to impose myself and my will
on the community. I am not their slave (4:5); they are mine and I
am their lord (1:24). I am Christ's man, for I am from Jerusalem
and bear a commendatory letter from the chief apostles (10:7; 3:1),
the true and authoritative witnesses of the resurrection (1 Cor. 15:5–
9). Paul indeed, driven from pillar to post, may have reached Corinth
before I did, but I have now come to take over and do for you what
he could never do (10:13–18). Moreover, I see visions; I tread the
way of heaven (12:1–5). Over against this Paul will boast but only
of his weakness—his failure to meet the demands of his Corinthian
people, to whom, when they asked for strength and a show of strength,
he could offer only weakness and a show of weakness. It was his way
of following Jesus, who was crucified because of his weakness but
lives because of God's power (13:4). In Corinth, if he visits Corinth
again, he can expect only humiliation (12:21), but this will be the
scene on which Christ's power is revealed. The argument is complicated and difficult, the more complicated because Paul did not know[19]
the extent of the backing that his opponent, and his opponent's
colleagues, were receiving from the Peter, James, John group (the

---

[19] It is clear that Paul believed that the super-apostles (11:5; 12:11) had something to do with the matter; this is why they are mentioned. If he had known that
they were fully supportive of the false apostles (11:13) he would have used stronger language. See n. 4.

Pillars of Gal. 2:9) in Jerusalem. It is impossible to identify 'false apostles, servants of Satan' with 'super-apostles', who are not only Hebrews, Israelites, and seed of Abraham, but also servants of Christ (11:22f.). But if the false apostles were able, whether falsely or with some truth, to claim the support of these Jerusalem authorities, Paul's difficulties in combating them would be greatly increased, and the Corinthians would find it hard to know whom to believe, especially in view of the fact that the false apostles seem to have given them the kind of apostleship that pleased them and could provide authoritative answers to their questions.

It seems that we have an account of Paul's opponent (ὁ ἐρχόμενος, 11:4) that not only satisfies Paul's description of him and fits the account of Paul's dispute with him, including its often confusing references to the Jerusalem apostles, but also accounts for the disappearance of the detailed disputes and directions regarding particular points of Christian belief and behaviour which occupy a great deal of 1 Corinthians. 'We Christians no longer need to think for ourselves and ask questions about marriage, εἰδωλόθυτα, tongues, and the like; it suffices that we take our orders from our great apostle. We know now what apostleship means.' And Paul knew that he was dealing with a church in its death-throes. Could even the authority God had given him for building them up, not for throwing them down, save them (2 Cor. 13:10)?

VISIONS AND REVELATIONS OF THE LORD
(2 CORINTHIANS 12:1–10)

Michael D. Goulder

Margaret is not only the gentlest, most generous and humblest of my friends and colleagues; she is also a formidably learned, careful and balanced exegete. Her ICC commentary on *II Corinthians* has taken more than two decades to write, and it will stand for at least a century. It is a treasure-chest of things old and new; wheat is regularly sifted from chaff; and no one enjoys disagreeing with it. But over the difficult and important passage 2 Cor 12:1–10 she breaks a lance with me, and a response here may be a testimony to the seriousness with which I treat her comments. What is so nice is that her fair-minded criticisms have forced me to reconsider, improve, and now to restate my solution.

Our disagreement here is considerable. Margaret thinks (with almost all critics, alive and dead) that the "man in Christ" who is ravished to heaven is Paul, and I do not. She has discussed the matter in a paper given to the Leuven Colloquium in 1994,[1] and in the second volume of her commentary, pp. 772–832.[2] I will treat the issue in three parts. First I will reproduce Margaret's translation with brief glosses summarizing her own interpretations, taken from her exegesis; and will append a series of questions which are raised by this exposition. Then I will offer my own alternative view, with some responses to Margaret's criticisms. Finally I will try to broaden the discussion, so as to show that my own perspective is the more plausible.

(1) *Margaret's Interpretation*

"Boasting is necessary", in order to counter a further attack on Paul's apostolic authority. "It is not expedient, but I will come to visions

---

[1] "Paul's Journey to Paradise: Some Exegetical Issues in 2 Cor 12, 2–4", in R. Bieringer ed. *The Corinthian Correspondence* (BETL 125; Leuven: Peeters, 1996) 347–363.

[2] *The Second Epistle to the Corinthians* I/II (ICC; Edinburgh: T. & T. Clark, 1994/2000).

and revelations of the Lord"—two words covering the same experiences, visions of Christ, since it has been alleged that he had none. "I know a man in Christ" (a Christian); Paul is speaking of himself, but uses the third person, partly because in such an ecstasy there is a sense of self-transcendence, and partly also to avoid giving the impression of egocentric arrogance. "Fourteen years ago" is specified partly for factuality; but partly perhaps because the vision had been associated with the first coming of the thorn in the flesh.

"Whether in the body I do not know or out of the body I do not know (God knows)": Jewish visionaries sometimes seem ambivalent, e.g. 1 Enoch 71:1–5, and Paul shares this ambivalence. "That such a man was caught up to the third heaven", that is the highest heaven, as we find in the Testament of Levi 2–3 (α-text), before the sevenfold heaven schema became normative. "And I know that such a man— whether in the body or apart from the body I know not (God knows)": the same single experience is described in almost identical words. "That he was caught up to paradise", that is to the third heaven, as in 2 Enoch 8:1. There stood the divine Throne, and Paul will have seen the Glory of God in the form of Christ (cf. 4:6). "And heard unutterable words, which it is not lawful for a man to speak": that is the name of God, perhaps sung repeatedly by the angels, or some such divine mysteries. "On behalf of such a person I will boast, but on my own behalf I will not boast", again distancing himself from the transcendent person of the rapture. "Except of my weaknesses": Paul goes on to speak of "the extraordinary quality of the revelations" he had had, in consequence of which God had given him the thorn, to humble him.

This seems to me as strong a case as can be made for the standard interpretation, but it raises a number of questions: –

(i) Is it plausible that Paul's critics could have said, "And furthermore he has had no visionary experiences of Christ"? Would Paul not have been expected immediately to reply, "No visionary experiences! I have seen the Lord! I was one of the original apostolic witnesses to whom the risen Christ appeared! You have known this from the beginning" (1 Cor 9:2; 15:8). As in fact Paul does not make this reply, he clearly understood ὀπτασίας καὶ ἀποκαλύψεις κυρίου to mean something different.

(ii) The use of modern psychology is appealing, to explain the "man in Christ", but it is flawed in the context. It truly is a skilled business to "boast" without giving the impression of egocentric arrogance;

but if one leans too far to avoiding the second, one will hardly be understood. If his critics said, "Paul has never had a vision of Christ", and he replied, "I know a man who had one fourteen years ago", they would inevitably say, "Just as we said! He has never had one himself"—particularly when he goes on to say that he will boast of such a man, but not of himself! It might be different if Paul on other occasions spoke of himself in this way; but he never does—nor, so far as I know, does anyone else in ancient times, for many have tried to find parallels, and none is cited. Margaret adduces Baruch's remark following his vision, cited by Furnish,[3] "And when I came to myself, I praised God" (3 Apoc. Baruch [Greek] 17:3). But then Baruch has described his experience in the first person throughout, and any one might say after a slight shock, let alone a vision of the Almighty, "When I came to myself..."

(iii) There is something peculiar about the vision as recounted. Margaret gives no real explanation of why the whole "in the body/ out of the body" rigmarole is repeated, or of why the ambivalent nature of the experience is relevant here. We have many accounts of apocalyptic visions, and normally the climax of the experience is the vision of the Merkabah. Also there is commonly an *angelus interpres* who shows the saint the secrets of heaven—the store-houses of snow, or the future of mankind, or the fate of the wicked—and the point of the vision is to pass this information on. The present account is rather bathetic. The man was ravished, to the third heaven, to paradise: but then he saw nothing, and what he heard cannot be told. There must be some reason for this.

(2) *An Alternative View*

Point (i) above seems to dispose of the "visions of Christ" interpretation; but Paul responds to the criticism with what looks like the standard beginning of a vision of the Glory of God on the Throne. We must assume that the response in some measure answered the attack, and this then implies that the critics were speaking about visions and revelations *of God*. It is no use going through Paul's use of the anarthrous genitive κυρίου. He is citing his opponents, and they may well have used κυρίου to mean *of the LORD (God)*, like the LXX ἄγγελος

---

[3] V.P. Furnish, *II Corinthians* (Anchor Bible 32A; New York/ London/ Toronto/ Sydney/ Auckland: Doubleday, 1984) 543.

κυρίου, ὁδὸς κυρίου, which are used or cited in the NT. ἀποκάλυψις is used with an objective genitive ("a revelation of Jesus Christ") in 2 Thess 1:7, 1 Pet 1:7, 13; 4:13; so the Greek of the attack might mesh happily with Paul's response: both refer to visions of God.

But what about the move into the third person? The NT Church tended to send its missionaries in twos and threes. The Jewish Christians of 11:22 are a group, and Paul writes his Second Epistle as from himself and Timothy, while repeatedly associating himself with Titus. In the long apologia of 10:1–12:13 he uses the first person singular when he is speaking of his letters, his policy of working, his sufferings, his revelations; but almost through the whole of ch. 10 and in some other verses, he uses the first person plural. It is at least an open possibility that this "we" is intended as a genuine plural; and that just as Paul speaks genially of his rivals as ministers of Satan, so did they return the compliment. In that case, they might easily have said, "This Paul has never had a vision of the Merkabah, *and nor have any of his Timothys, Tituses and the rest*". Since we do not have direct access to the critics' attack, we are obliged to infer its form, as before, from Paul's response; and this will then give satisfying sense. Paul replies, "Oh yes, we have: a friend of mine had just the experience in A.D 41".

The response is weak, and that is because he is in a situation of embarrassing weakness. The new missionaries are full of their Merkabah-visions, whereas Paul never had such a thing himself, nor have any of his colleagues for more than a decade. Hence in the first place his reluctance to "boast": he has not the least objection to thanking God that he speaks in tongues more than all the Corinthians (1 Cor 14:18), or saying that he worked more effectively than all the apostles (1 Cor 15:10). But visions of God are a competition he cannot win, so he starts off, "It is not expedient", that is, it is unspiritual.

This gambit, of decrying the whole idea, serves his purpose throughout. The repetition of so much in vv. 2–4, with its "I do not know—God knows", sounds bad-tempered; it recalls Gal 2:6, "But from those who were supposed to be something—whatever they were makes no difference to me; God is no respecter of persons". It was unclear what happened in a Throne-vision. The seer was ravished to heaven, but then his companions could see his body with them throughout. However such visionaries might speak of falling on their faces or raising their hands. No doubt such problems were discussed at Corinth, and Paul is happy to exploit this. "Whether in the body

I do not know or out of the body I do not know (God knows)...whether in the body or apart from the body I do not know (God knows)": the whole business is presumptuous and a muddle. These things do not happen very often, and one cannot but suspect either self-deception or fraud.

This then accounts also for the half-hearted (and polemical) way in which the vision is described. Of course Paul's friend was not only ravished to paradise but saw the Throne, and the divine Glory seated thereon; but mentioning all that would only play into the hands of the new missionaries—it would fascinate the congregation and glorify the experience and give them importance. So only enough is said to make a reasonable minimum "boast". Paul knew the man, he was a Christian, it happened at a remembered date. He knows he was really taken to the highest heaven, to paradise, and heard certain secret things. But for the rest he does not know, and nor does anyone else: they are God's secret.

The polemic comes through more clearly in the final clause, "and he heard ἄρρητα ῥήματα, unutterable utterances which it is not permitted for a man to speak". The insistent double prohibition at once suggests that someone else *has* been uttering words which they have heard in a vision, and that this is a dangerous practice. It was in fact a simple way of manipulating church opinion in NT times, and was freely practised by both sides. In the first three chapters of the Apocalypse, John sees a vision of Christ telling him to warn the Asian churches against various Nicolaitans, Jezebels, Balaams, etc. Col 2:18 tries to protect the simple against such fast footwork: "Do not let anyone disqualify you, wanting to do so through asceticism and the worship of angels, taking his stand on what he has seen, vainly puffed up by fleshly thinking". Here the "anyone" is a Jewish Christian who in 2:16 has been "judging" the Pauline congregation over food-laws and the Jewish calendar (festivals, new moon, sabbath). An attempt is being made to drive out ("disqualify") anyone who would not accept Jewish lore, just as John does with Jewish Christians in Apoc 2–3. They try to do this by appealing to their spiritual experiences. They have gone in for fasts and other ascetic practices (ταπεινοφροσύνη), and have witnessed the worship of angels before the divine Throne; they have taken their stand on such visions (ἃ ἑόρακεν), and pronounced angelic judgement on anyone who ventures to dissent—again, just like John the Seer.

Paul is not standing for this sort of moral blackmail, so he makes a virtue of the colourlessness of his friend's experience. Of course he heard important mysteries, or he would never have been carried up there in the first place: but he behaved properly and kept his mouth shut, unlike some other people who blurt out a lot of things they claim to have heard—a practice which is absolutely forbidden.

Paul now seals off his friend's story with the clear distinction which has caused so much embarrassment: "On behalf of such a man I will boast, but on my own behalf I will not boast—except of my weaknesses". I have remarked on the skill it takes to combine boasting with giving the impression of humility, but Paul is a master of the technique, and those who give courses in assertiveness could learn a thing or two from him. He starts from an apparently hopeless position. He is up against a group of hostile critics who have had visions of the divine Glory, an accepted sign of blessing and authority, while Paul has had nothing of the kind. But he makes one telling point after another. The whole business of boasting is unspiritual and disgusting. One of his colleagues has in fact had a vision in the highest heaven. Disputes about whether these things happen in the body or out of the body are vapid: only God knows about such matters. Paul's friend heard divine mysteries, but it is strictly forbidden to mention such things on earth—unlike some who try to use their "revelations" to exclude other Christians. And finally—actually Paul has had a lot of revelations himself (on earth (Gal 1:12, 16; 2:2; 1 Cor 9:1; 14:26) like others during worship), such an *excess* (ὑπερβολή) in fact that he had to be given a thorn in the flesh to stop him from getting above himself. Of course he only mentioned the multitude of revelations in order to say about the thorn.[4]

---

[4] I have made two changes in this exposition, as against the versions in "Vision and Knowledge," *JSNT* 56 (1994) 53–71, and in *Paul and the Competing Mission at Corinth* (Peabody MA: Hendrickson, 2001), both thanks to Margaret's critique. I suggested then that visions and revelations were different things, and that visions implied visions in heaven: they are in fact two sides of the same coin, and what makes them visions in heaven is that they are visions *of the Lord (God)*. I also offered no explanation of why Paul should be attacked for lacking such an experience, and should then reply with a story about someone else: but in fact the response implies an attack on Paul *and his colleagues*.

(3) *Pauline Opposition to Visions*

Even in 1 Corinthians there are signs that other groups are appealing to visions of God, and that Paul is resistant to this. In ch. 2 they claim to have certain knowledge. This seems to be rooted in visionary experience, for he contests such knowledge with a (modified) citation from Isa 64:4, "What eye has not seen and ear has not heard, and has not arisen upon the heart of man". These things, he says, God has revealed to us through the Spirit, even the deep things of God (τὰ βάθη τοῦ θεοῦ). Such "deep things" are sometimes thought to imply the experiences of visionaries,[5] who, in a Jewish technical term, "went down" (*yarad*) for their visions. Paul says that such visions were not the way: God has simply revealed to Christians every profound truth about the Godhead by the Spirit—eye has not seen it.

One could not aspire to a vision of the Throne without ascesis, and I have noted the mention of ταπεινοφροσύνη in Col 2:18. A significant element in this was sexual abstinence. Moses told the people not to go near a woman before the revelation on Sinai (Exod 19:15), and David assured Ahimelech that the young men had kept themselves from women before accepting the shewbread. The requirement of sexual abstinence by Paul's opponents in 1 Cor 7 is all part of their aspiration to be "spiritual", and this again links back to 1 Cor 2: spiritual people do not touch women, and so are ready to know the deep things of God.

We seem to have echoes of the same aspirations in 2 Cor 3:1–4.6. Paul is not content just to contrast the old dispensation on Sinai with the new one in Christ (3:1–11). There is also an extended disputation about the veil which Moses wore on Sinai, and the relative glory of the two covenants. For some reason Paul is blatantly unfair in his account of this. He says, "Moses put a veil on his face that the sons of Israel might not look on the end of what was passing away" (13); in fact Moses put the veil on because his face shone from the reflection of the divine glory, with which he had been communing in the Tent (Exod 34:35). Now Paul concludes the discussion in ch. 3: "But we all with unveiled face reflecting the glory of the Lord are transformed into the same image from glory to glory, as from the Lord the Spirit".

This seems to give us the key to what the chapter is about. The new missionaries have come with their letters (3:1–3), insisting on

---

[5] H. Räisänen, "The Nicolaitans: Apoc. 2; Acta 6," *ANRW* 2.26. 2, pp. 1602–44, here 1617, with a list of supporting scholars.

the observance of the Law; but they also maintain that they have had experiences similar to Moses, in which they have seen the Glory of God; for this is implied in their challenge to which Paul replies in 12:1–5. But the context here suggests more: that they claimed that their faces had been transformed into a glory like his. As in 2 Cor 12:1–10, Paul does his best to cry down the whole business: it was a dispensation of death, of condemnation; Moses only wore the veil to stop people seeing how evanescent the shining was. But then he makes the telling contrast. They claim to have had the special privilege of seeing the Glory, they were transformed, their faces shone, they had to put on a veil, did they? "But we all (ἡμεῖς δὲ πάντες)...", we ordinary Christians can achieve the same as them through the Spirit. Moses spoke face to face with the Lord God: we have the Lord the Spirit. He reflected the divine glory and was transformed physically, with a veil over his face; we reflect the glory of the Lord the Spirit, and are transformed spiritually into the same image as he was. In this we go from glory to glory, and need no veil. The "But we all" only makes sense as a contrast with grandiose claims of Moses-type privilege by Paul's rivals.

This seems then to be confirmed in 4:1–6. Paul has forsworn all trickery of which he has been accused; if, as they say, his version of the gospel is obscure, "veiled", that is because the devil his blinded them, "lest the light of the glory of Christ, who is the image of God, should enlighten them. For we do not proclaim ourselves, but Jesus Christ as Lord, and ourselves your slaves through Jesus".

It is the same polemical background which gives sense to these verses. It is the rival missionaries who say Paul's gospel is veiled; he retorts that they are blinded, and are perishing. The issue is still about the glory and the image of God, as it was in ch. 3.; and now the linking γάρ implies a contrast on another level. Paul and his fellow-missionaries do not proclaim themselves but Jesus Christ as Lord, as opposed (we must presume) to his rivals who do proclaim themselves, and by no means regard themselves as slaves (δοῦλοι) of other Christians—indeed Paul says elsewhere that they enslave them (καταδουλοῖ, 11.20)! It is easy to think that they proclaim themselves as visionaries who have seen the Glory of God, and expect deference. No, says Paul, our authority comes not from special visions of the Throne; it comes from having believed "the gospel of the glory of Christ who is the image of God". The gospel is not about having seen the *kabod*, the Glory of God: it is about the coming of the glory of Christ into our world—he is himself the image of God.

The final mysterious sentence of the section also makes sense in this polemical context: "Because it is God who said, From darkness light will shine, who shone in our hearts for the illumination of the knowledge of the glory of God in the face of Jesus Christ". We are the true evangelists, not these arrogant newcomers; because all depends on God who said (Isa 9:2), "Light will shine"—it is not a matter of some visionary who says with his eyes shut, "Out of darkness light will shine". We ordinary Christians have all received the illumination of the gospel, and that gives us true experience of the Glory of God, which has been made known to us in the face of Jesus Christ. Once more we are having to fill in the other side of a disputation; but the surprising, "It is God who said", implies that someone else has been claiming to say it, and "the Glory of God" suggests who it is who has been doing so.

The Pauline movement is resistant to visionary claims elsewhere in the New Testament, as we may tell from repeated emphatic denials. I will mention only two further authors, the Pastor and John. 1 Tim 6:16 speaks of God as "he who alone has immortality, who dwells in light unapproachable, whom none of humankind has seen, nor can see". Of course the sentiment is a truism, for which parallels are available in Jewish literature: but why is there a triple negative? God dwells in light ἀπρόσιτον, unapproachable; none of men has ever seen him; none can. If we were dealing with a liturgical text, we might feel that this was the amplitude of praise; but 1 Tim is not a liturgical document, it is a polemical tract. The same verse opens with an implied negative, "who *only* has immortality", and a few verses later we have a warning against "the falsely so-called gnosis". One cannot help suspecting that those who enthused over "Jewish myths" (Tit 1:14) spoke of other immortal beings whom they had seen on their progress to the Merkabah. The Pastor, like his master, thinks all that is a fraud, and appeals to the old Hebrew tradition of Exod 33:20, that no one can see God and live.

We find the same insistent denials through John's Gospel, and also his Epistle. Already in the Prologue we are into disputation with "the Jews"—probably the Jewish Christians: "The Law was given through Moses: grace and truth came through Jesus Christ. No one has seen God ever: the only-begotten God who is in the bosom of the Father, he has made him plain" (1:17–18). Grace and truth, the name of

God in Exod 34, took human form in Jesus Christ: he has "declared" the Father in his incarnation—no visions of the Throne have ever taken place. In dispute with Nicodemus, later a half-Christian Jewish ruler, Jesus says, "No one has ascended into heaven, except [to take a later perspective] him who came down from heaven, the Son of Man" (3:13). Only the incarnate Christ has ever gone up to heaven, no one else. "Not that anyone has seen the Father, except him who is from God; he has seen the Father" (6:46). By 6:52 the Jews are disputing, and a few verses later many of his disciples find his words hard. At 14:8 Philip asks Jesus to show him the Father, and the reply is, "He who has seen me has seen the Father". We are back to 2 Cor 4:6, the light of the glory of God in the face of Jesus Christ. 1 Jn 4:12, "No one has beheld God ever. If we love one another, God abides in us". What matters is Christian love, not claims of visions, which are spurious.

The NT thus provides a remarkably consistent picture. From 1 and 2 Corinthians and Colossians through to the Pastorals and the Johannine writings we meet echoes of Jewish Christian claims to have been taken to heaven, and to have seen the glory of God. In some cases it is clear that attempts were made to manipulate churches on the strength of these visions. They were certainly used to boost the authority of their leaders, and in 2 Cor 12 to impugn the authority of the Pauline leadership. Paul himself had never seen the Merkabah, and it is an error to claim such an experience as the basis of his life as a Christian.[6] All he does is to appeal to the rapture of a friend. His unenthusiastic account of the vision arises from this situation. All talk of such visions is beset with boasting, with self-important discussion of matters about which only God knows, and with bogus assertions of angelic commands which in any case are totally forbidden. In time the Pauline movement came simply to exclude all such visions by definition: no one can see God ever.

---

[6] So, for example, A.F. Segal, *Paul the Convert* (New Haven: Yale University Press, 1990).

PAUL, APOLOGIST TO THE CORINTHIANS[1]

Paul Barnett

Paul uses the language of the apologist in each of his extant letters to the Corinthians.[2]

> 1 Cor 9:3
> This is my defence (ἀπολογία)
> to those who would examine me.

> 2 Cor 12:19a
> Have you been thinking all along
> that we have been defending (ἀπολογούμεθα) ourselves before you?

Why was this self-defence necessary? Broadly speaking his apologias were necessary because he spent so little time with the congregations he founded. Paul withdrew from the Corinthian church quite soon after founding it, a strategy mystifying to modern church planters who plan for a much longer period to stabilize new congregations. Due to his brief associations with his churches and the reality that in human relationships misunderstandings become suspicions which easily become criticisms and even opposition. There is evidence in Paul's letters that these very dynamics were operative. His letters and the envoys that bore them must address precisely these problems.[3] Most modern church planters would spend more time with nascent churches before handing them over to more permanent local pastoral leadership.

Yet this 'brevity' factor was no *ad hoc* thing with Paul. First and

---

[1] My working assumptions are: (a) Paul began his year and a half visit to Corinth in early AD 50, writing 1 Cor from Ephesus 54/55 and 2 Cor from Macedonia 55/56, and (b) 2 Cor as we have it was written as one letter (as in P. Barnett, *The Second Epistle to the Corinthians* (NIC, Grand Rapids: Eerdmans, 1997), 17-25 *contra* M.E. Thrall, *II Corinthians* (ICC, Edinburgh: T. & T. Clark, 1994), Volume 1, pages 3-49). For a broad survey of Paul's relationships with the Corinthians see V.P. Furnish, 'Paul and the Corinthians,' *Interpretation* 52 (1998) 229-245.

[2] See also 2 Cor 7:11.

[3] His relationships with the Thessalonians are a case in point. Paul devotes no less than first three of the chapters of First Thessalonians to 're-connecting' with the readers. The same felt need can be sensed in Second Corinthians where 1:8-2:13 is given to explanations and clarification of misunderstandings.

foremost he saw himself as a 'foundation layer' rather than a super-structure 'builder.' In the former capacity he was able to claim that he had 'fulfilled (πεπληρωκέναι[4]) the gospel in an arc' from Jerusalem to Illyricum (Rom 15:19) in key centres of Roman civilization in the northeastern quadrant of the Empire. It appears that Paul 'fulfilled the gospel' by proclaiming its message and gathering a congregation, delivering to it the key 'traditions' that embodied 'the faith,' establishing patterns of worship, ordering the leadership of the new church by appointing *presbyteroi*. This cluster of activities could be summed up as 'foundation laying.' In brief, Paul set about creating a network of new 'synagogues' founded on the conviction that the long-awaited Davidic Messiah was Jesus of Nazareth, crucified and resurrected.

Paul envisaged that from this 'foundation' (θεμέλιος—1 Cor 3:10-12; Rom 15:20) would arise a 'building' (οἰκοδομή—1 Cor 3:9), through the labours of various 'artisans' (1 Cor 3:10; cf. Rom 15:20). In Corinth and Ephesus Paul's longer-than-usual sojourn meant that his 'foundation laying' merged into superstructure 'building.' In other places, however, this 'up-building' was entrusted to the *charismata* of the Spirit-filled members, guided by local *presbyteroi*.[5]

This strategy provided for the rapid spread of the gospel in Syria-Cilicia, Galatia, Macedonia, Achaia and Asia. The stability of these fledgling assemblies, however, was another matter. Inevitably problems arose locally due to the novelty of the new faith in its struggle to remain distinctive in the face of the powerful religious culture of Judaism (as in Galatia) and the politico-religious culture of the Roman Empire (as in Thessalonica).

Instability in the church of Corinth arose from both. It came from the Graeco-Roman quarter (e.g., temple culture—1 Cor 8-11:1; 2 Cor 6:14-7:1), but also—to put it broadly—from Judaism (2 Cor 3:1-18; 11:12-22). To state the obvious, Gentile converts would have been especially susceptible to the former, Jewish converts to the latter and God-fearers to both (depending on where they stood on the God-fearer spectrum).

In sum, then, Paul's very strategy of rapid 'foundation laying' of these faith communities radically different from existing dominant

---

[4] Various translations (e.g., RSV, NIV, NRSV) take a liberty in rendering πεπληρωκέναι as 'fully proclaimed/preached.'

[5] No *presbyteroi* are mentioned in 1 Corinthians, though it is likely that Stephanas fulfilled this role (16:15-18; cf. 1:16).

religious cultures of Greeks and Romans and from Jews almost invited trouble for those new bodies. After all, baptism 'into' a Jewish man, who though poor was supposedly the rightful heir to the throne of Israel through his descent from king David, a man who had been crucified and allegedly resurrected and ascended as *Christos* and *kyrios*, was an extraordinary doctrine!

Nowhere were these problems for Paul more acute than in 'Roman' Corinth. The Achaian capital, however, presented the 'foundation layer' with an additional set of problems not yet encountered in other places. During two 'periods of his absence' from Corinth new preachers came to the city creating havoc within the church.

1. *First Corinthians: Apollos and Cephas*

First Corinthians, was written near the end of Paul's first 'period of absence,' an expanse of at least two and a half years.[6] During that period the Corinthians received visits from Apollos (Acts 18:27; 1 Cor 1-4 *passim*) and Cephas (1 Cor 9:3-7) and, perhaps, Barnabas as well (9:6).

Furthermore, it is evident from the first four chapters of First Corinthians that the Corinthians had become factionalized during the first 'period of absence.' There can be no doubt that the parties in Corinth were connected in some ways with the visits of Apollos and Cephas.[7] The nature of those connections between Apollos and Cephas and those who claimed to belong to them must remain conjectural.

In First Corinthians Paul does not say outright whether the factions in the church were intentionally created by the visitors or were 'unintended consequences' of their ministries. The letter leaves open both interpretative possibilities. It does appear, though, that Paul is rather cool about Cephas' visit (9:5) and less than enthusiastic about the Corinthians' request[8] for a return visit by Apollos

---

[6] The 'first period of absence' was two and a half years if 1 Cor was written in the Spring of A.D. 54 or three and a half years if the letter was written in the Spring of A.D. 55. See further A. Thiselton, *The First Epistle to the Corinthians* (NIGT, Grand Rapids: Eerdmans, 2000) 31-32.

[7] The order of the names most likely corresponds with the sequence of the visits of these leaders. See Thiselton, *First Epistle*, 121-122, 140 for a review of opinion regarding the nature of the groups and relationship with the three men.

[8] Most likely περὶ δὲ in 1 Cor 16:12 signals Paul's answer to the Corinthians'

(16:12). The reference to Barnabas (9:6) is most likely positive.

1.1 *Apollos*

The assertion that Paul was uneasy about Apollos' return to Corinth depends on an accumulation of references in First Corinthians.[9]

First, N.A. Dahl is surely correct in observing that the slogans 'I am of Apollos, I am of Cephas' (1:12) are to be understood as 'declarations of independence from Paul.'[10] Paul's appeal in that context is not so much for unity between these parties (and his own) but for unity under his apostolic leadership.

Second, Paul's reminder that he preached 'Christ crucified' (1:23) but not in the 'wisdom of speech' (σοφία λόγου—1:17; cf. πειθοῖς σοφίας λόγοις—2:4) is most likely a corrective of the Corinthians' appreciation of Apollos' recent ministry among them.[11] It scarcely needs arguing that rhetoric was highly prized in the cities of the Graeco-Roman east.

The precise nature of the Alexandrian Jew's expertise is not known though the fact of its impact (noted in the book of Acts) is not in doubt (18:24, 28—ἀνὴρ λόγιος...δυνατὸς ὢν ἐν ταῖς γραφαῖς... εὐτόνως γὰρ τοῖς Ἰουδαίοις διακατηλέγχετο δημοσίᾳ ἐπιδεικνὺς διὰ τῶν γραφῶν εἶναι τὸν Χριστὸν Ἰησοῦν). From 1 Cor 1-4 it appears that Apollos' ministry had the effect of elevating rhetorical preaching among local Corinthian preachers,[12] perhaps in the direction of 'Alexandrian' exegesis, as in Philo's allegorical style.[13] Lack

request seeking a return visit from Apollos (*contra* M.M. Mitchell, "Concerning ΠΕΡΙ ΔΕ in 1 Corinthians," *NovT* 31, 1989, 229-256.

[9] See Donald P. Ker, "Paul and Apollos—Colleagues or Rivals?" *JSNT* 77, 2000, 75-97.

[10] "Paul and the Church in Corinth According to 1 Corinthians 1-4," in W.R. Farmer et al. (eds.) *Christian History and Interpretation: Studies Presented to John Knox*, (Cambridge: Cambridge University Press, 1967) 322.

[11] According to D. Litfin, *St Paul's Theology of Proclamation: 1 Corinthians 1-4 and Greco-Roman Rhetoric* (SNTMS 79 Cambridge: Cambridge University Press, 1994) the practice of rhetoric was associated with σοφία, which in the first century was largely 'decorative,' drawing attention to the speaker (11, 110-111, 123).

[12] Most likely in 3:10 Paul is referring to local Corinthian preacher(s) rather than Apollos (so D.R. Hall, 'A Disguise for the Wise,' *NTS* 40 1994, 143-149 *contra* Ker, "Paul and Apollos" 88-89, 92 following M.D Hooker, "Beyond the Things that are Written'? An Examination of 1 Corinthians 4:6," *NTS* 10 1963, 127-132.

[13] Ker, "Paul and Apollos" 81 warns against over confidence in identifying too precisely the character of *sophia*-rhetoric or of over-confidence about Apollos' background (page 83). For a list of texts devoted to wisdom, rhetoric, preaching and the cross see Thiselton, *First Corinthians*, page 134.

of further information, however, leaves us unsure of Apollos' approach. At the least it must be pointed out that there were many Jews in Alexandria; Philo was not alone!

From 1 Cor 1-4 it seems that in Paul's mind in recent times the 'substance' of the *kērygma* of the crucified Messiah had been diminished by the 'style' of its presentation. The 'faith' of the Corinthians was now 'rest[ing]...in the wisdom of men' (2:5—ἦ ἐν σοφίᾳ ἀνθρώπων). Equally, it meant that a different 'building' was being erected upon Paul's 'foundation' which was Christ crucified and risen (3:10-11). An immediate consequence was the devaluing in their eyes of the less fluent Paul.[14]

Third, the impact of 1 Cor 3-4 is twofold. On one hand, Paul affirms that Apollos is, with him, both a *sunergos* 'of God' (3:9) and a *diakonos*[15] 'through whom' the Corinthians have believed (3:5). Yet, on the other hand, there is no question that Paul has the priority over Apollos. In the agricultural image Paul planted and Apollos fulfilled the subsidiary role, watering (3:6). In the architectural image Paul is the foundation-layer but no role is attributed to Apollos. More to the point, though they may have 'countless guides' (including Apollos, presumably), Paul is their sole 'father' (4:14-15). In short, Paul is 'the planter', 'the foundation layer' and 'the father' with Apollos playing a lesser role in each case. With great diplomacy Paul manages to relegate a subsidiary role to Apollos while not dis-affirming his ministry and thereby bringing continuing division in Corinth.

Fourth, though less clearly, Apollos' visit may have aroused the Corinthians' exuberance in the exercise of the *charismata* of the Spirit, especially tongues-speaking and prophesying.[16] I am not suggesting that the manifestations of these phenomena following Apollos' arrival in Corinth were unprecedented. Most likely Paul himself was a 'man of the Spirit' (14:6—'I speak in tongues more than you all';

---

[14] This was a continuing problem in Corinth as reflected several years later by Paul in the second canonical letter when he is forced to defend his 'knowledge' as against his 'speech' (11:6—εἰ δὲ καὶ ἰδιώτης τῷ λόγῳ, ἀλλ' οὐ τῇ γνώσει...). True, the context of that remark was his perceived lack of effectiveness in disciplining his opponent during the second visit. Nonetheless, it boiled down to the same thing in their eyes, that is, his unimpressive personal presence and his lack of rhetorical power (10:10).

[15] According to E.E. Ellis, "Paul and His Co-Workers," *NTS* 17 1971 'the *diakonoi* appear to be a special class of co-workers, those who are active in preaching and teaching' (442).

[16] Ker, "Paul and Apollos," raises this possibility, but admits lack of evidence for it (page 78-79).

cf. 1Thess 5:19-20—'Do not quench the Spirit. Do not despise prophesying'). Yet his words, 'Now concerning pneumatic things/ people, I do not want you to be uninformed' (12:1) imply a new teaching (or emphasis) on this subject, suggesting recent 'spiritual' developments in Corinth. At all events, much of First Corinthians is devoted to cooling down their preoccupation with the *pneumatika* and its likely accompaniment, a heightened eschatology.[17] Did Apollos contribute to this new interest in the *pneumatika*? According to Acts 18:25 Apollos was ζέων τῷ πνεύματι.

Fifth, the context and the tone of Paul's final reference to Apollos are rather negative.

1 Corinthians 16:12
Περὶ δὲ Ἀπολλῶ τοῦ ἀδελφοῦ,
πολλὰ παρεκάλεσα αὐτόν, ινα ἔλθη πρὸς ὑμᾶς μετὰ τῶν ἀδελφῶν·
καὶ πάντως οὐκ ἦν θέλημα ἵνα νῦν ἔλθῃ· ἐλεύσεται δὲ ὅταν εὐκαιρήσῃ.

i. The Apollos reference is placed between Paul's strong directions to the Corinthians to welcome and respect Timothy when he comes and to 'be subject to' and to 'recognize' Stephanas in Corinth. The strength of the affirmation of Timothy and Stephanas is in stark contrast with his announcement that Apollos will not be coming to Corinth.

ii. The initial Περὶ δὲ...indicates that Corinthians have requested Paul to allow or send Apollos back to Corinth, a request that will not be fulfilled.

iii. Apollos will not be coming with 'the brothers,' that is, with approved members of the Pauline mission like Timothy. The implication is that Apollos is a freer agent than Paul's more direct associates were.

iv. Paul's assurance that Apollos will come at a convenient later time sounds like a polite but indefinite postponement of the Corinthians' hopes of a return visit.

---

[17] Symptoms of an over-realized eschatology may have included a desire to separate from unbelieving spouses (7:10-16) and an outright insistence for singleness ahead of the parousia (7:25-35) evoking Paul's warnings against the dire peril of *porneia* (7:1-9; cf. 6:18). It is possible that external factors may have contributed to eschatological excitement in Corinth, for example, (a) chronic food shortage arising from the well known protracted famine in the east, with accompanying inflated food prices and health problems, and (b) the (conjectured) decision to create an imperial cult for Claudius at Isthmia (see A.J.S Spawforth, "Corinth, Argos and the Imperial Cult: Pseudo-Julian Letters 198," *Hesperia* 63 1994, 211-232).

In 1 Cor 4:1-5 Paul defends his ministry to the Corinthians, though without the precise forensic vocabulary as in 9:3. In his 'stewardship' he is accountable to the Lord, not to them.[18] At the same time in his oblique remarks he is making a sidelong glance to Apollos for their benefit.

It is not as though Apollos has set out to undermine or compete with Paul. Rather, the problem lies with (some of) the Corinthians who have elevated Apollos above Paul while prompted to move off in unhelpful directions in the prizing of *sophia*-rhetoric and, perhaps, of the *pneumatika*.

The two men were different, both as to their names and their education. Saul of Tarsus is named after the first king of Israel and Apollos after a Greek god! Saul was educated in the strict pharisaic academies in Jerusalem whereas Apollos of Alexandria, who was an *anēr logios* (Acts 18:24), would have been nurtured in an educational culture that we sense was different, despite not knowing how it was different.[19]

Critical to the problem between them, however, was the fact that Apollos had never been subject to Paul's tutelage. Apollos arrived in Ephesus sometime after Paul's brief visit en route from Corinth to Jerusalem (Acts 18:19-20). By the time Paul arrived back in Ephesus Apollos had been 'mentored' by Priscilla and Aquila and had moved on to Corinth with the written commendation of the Ephesians (Acts 19:24, 26-28). Paul called Apollos a 'brother' yet he was not part of Paul's mission. Most likely he had withdrawn from Corinth some time earlier and had by now returned to Ephesus. We sense a continuing ministry for Apollos in Ephesus but parallel with Paul's and not integrated within it (1 Cor 16:12).

---

[18] Litfin, *Proclamation* (page 130) points out that rhetoricians were performers who were 'judged' by their audiences, suggesting that the Corinthians are most likely adjudicated and appraised the performances of Paul and Apollos. One problem with the too-ready identification of Apollos as a *sophia*-rhetor, however, is that he was a Jew whose education and accompanying eloquence were quite different from Graeco-Roman rhetors.

[19] Ker, "Paul and Apollos" (78) follows Litfin in making a connection between 'eloquence' and (rhetorical) 'education.' True as this was for Greeks and Romans it was not true for Jews. Apollos was an educated *Jew*. The assumptions regarding educated/eloquent Gentiles do not obtain for Jews. The education of Apollos the Jew and his 'eloquence' could not have been more distinct from the educated and eloquent Gentile.

1.2 *Cephas*

1 Cor 8-11:1 is devoted to the problem of the Christian interface with Graeco-Roman 'temple' culture whose vocabulary abounds throughout these chapters (*eidōlon*—8:4,7; 10:19; *eidōlothutos*—8:1,4, 7,10; 10:19; *hierothutos*—10:28; *eidōleion*—8:10; *eidōlolatreia*—10:14).[20]

Yet, unexpectedly, Paul digresses or appears to digress in 9:1-18 about his 'right' (ἐξουσία) *not* to exercise his 'right' as an apostle to be supported financially. To be sure, his exposition about 'rights' sprang from the use of the word in the previous chapter (8:9). Yet, this tangential discussion is curious.[21]

Significantly Paul calls this exposition 'my defence (ἡ ἐμὴ ἀπολογία) to those who would examine (ἀνακρίνουσιν) me' (9:3). Both ἀπολογία and ἀνακρινεῖς have forensic associations. Who are these 'examiners'? Not the Corinthians, since to them his apostleship is not in dispute (9:2), at least, not yet! Given Paul's insistence that he has 'seen Jesus our Lord' (9:1) and his specific bracketing of himself with witnesses to the resurrected Christ (15:5-8) it would make sense if these 'examiners' were connected with the 'apostles' whose names Paul supplies. In saying, 'I am no less an apostle than these' he implies their questioning of his status as an apostle.

It is hard to escape the conclusion that Cephas himself raised doubts about Paul's equal apostolic status.

Paul's problem, of course, was that his manner and circumstances of 'seeing' the Lord were so different from the others 'before' him who saw the Lord, in particular the original disciples of Jesus. Whereas Cephas was the first to 'see' the Lord, Paul was 'last of all' (15:5, 8). Worse, Cephas, the Twelve, the 500, James and 'all the apostles' saw the Risen One 'on earth' within a limited number of days (Acts 1:3). Paul, however, saw and heard the Lord 'from heaven' many months after the ascension. Theirs was a seeing of 'bodily' manifestations of the Risen Lord, his a heavenly christophany. To

---

[20] Various opinions have been offered suggesting that circumstances special to Corinth at that time underlay Paul's expositions in 1 Cor 8-11:1. In my view, however, Corinth is unlikely to have been different in principle from other major cities in the east. For a review of various theories and for his own suggestions see unpublished PhD thesis R. Butarbutar, *Resolving a Dispute Past and Present* (1999; South East Asia Graduate School of Theology). In any case, the positing of a supposed historical circumstance to explain trends in a NT church is precarious.

[21] See P.D. Gardner, *The Gifts of God and the Authentication as a Christian*, (Lanham MA: University Press of America, 1994) 67-110.

be sure, he stoutly insists that he and they proclaim the same *kērygma* of the crucified and risen Christ (15:11). But he concedes that his manner of 'seeing' the Lord was as one 'untimely born' (15:8—τῷ ἐκτρώματι) which I take to be a reference to seeing the glorified Lord *ahead* of others at the parousia, 'prematurely,' as it were.

Paul's refusal to act on his 'right' to be provided for, and his stubborn insistence on working' were, in effect, tantamount to removing the badge of apostleship. Paul had his own good reason for doing so. Yet those who regarded Paul's preaching as idiosyncratic easily placed him outside the circle of true apostles and witnesses on this account. In a sense, Paul invited his own marginalization. Yet notwithstanding the evident difficulty for him reflected by his 'defence' in 1 Cor 9 he insisted on continuing this policy, as declared in 2 Cor 11:12, 'what I do (work) I will continue to do...'

2. Second Corinthians: Long Term Consequences of Cephas' Visit to Corinth

It appears that Cephas' coming to Corinth stimulated long term problems for Paul that he must apologetically address in Second Corinthians (as well as problems of more recent origin).

Like First Corinthians, the Second Letter was written to address difficulties that arose during an absence from the city. He speaks of his second visit as 'painful' (ἐν λύπῃ—2:1).

2.1 'Painful' Visit and 'Tearful' Letter

This visit was unscheduled and followed hard on his dispatch of First Corinthians and Timothy's negative report on return to Ephesus about their response to a particular matter in that letter.

But what was it? Opinions differ. Was it an unresolved problem relating to the 'incestuous man' (1 Cor 5:1)[22]? In my view, however, Paul's dispute was related to (some of) the Corinthians' continuing involvement in the 'temple' culture of the city.[23] Civic life centered on the temples. To separate oneself was to be cut off from work, trade, social intercourse and any hope of regional preterment. To

---

[22] For a defence of the 'traditional' view see C. Kruse, "The Offender and the Offence in 2 Corinthians 2:5 and 7:12," *EvQ* 88 1988, 129-39 and for a detailed rebuttal see V.P. Furnish, *II Corinthians*—(Anchor Bible 32A, New York: Doubleday, 1984) 164-166.

[23] See Barnett, *Second Epistle to the Corinthians*, 28-31.

withdraw from the temples was to withdraw from the city, inviting oneself to be treated as a Jew yet without the protections Jews enjoyed as from Augustus' time.

Associated with this conjecture is the likelihood that Paul engaged in a power struggle with one man in particular (7:12; 2:5-8). This appears to have been marked by public quarreling (12:20-3:2). It is clear enough from the Second Letter that many local people saw Paul's second visit as inconclusive, at best, evidence of his lack of 'presence' and force of personality (10:1, 10). Worse, his failure to return directly as promised (1:15-17) and his dispatch instead of Titus bearing yet another letter, and a harshly worded one at that (7:8), raised serious questions about his probity and sense of balance. In reply Paul must insist that his ministry in Corinth during that visit was truly effective because divinely empowered (10:3-7) as he assures them it will be in his third and final visit (10:2, 8; 12:21-13:4).

2.2 *Money Matters*

Prior to the writing of First Corinthians Paul's envoy Titus had initiated the Corinthians' 'contribution (λογεία) for the saints' in Jerusalem (1 Cor 16:1; 2 Cor 8:6,10). Their letter to Paul sought clarification, which he provided (περὶ δέ...1 Cor 16:1; cf. 7:1). The problems demanding his second visit and its corollary, the 'severe' letter have, so it appears, halted the Corinthians 'contributions,' necessitating Paul's pastoral sermon in 2 Cor 8-9.

But now Paul must deal with doubts and suspicions about his motives and integrity. Hints of 'deceit' and 'craftiness' are in the air (12:16-19; cf. 2:17; 4:2; 7:2). 'We know he works and refuses a stipend,' they say. 'But what about the money we give to Titus? Perhaps Titus passes that on to Paul. He takes the high moral ground, but maybe he is not what he appears.'

2.3 *'Superior Apostles'*

The greatest problem Paul must address in Second Corinthians, however, is the recent arrival of Jewish missionaries (11:4, 22).[24] These are 'ministers of Christ' (11:23; cf. 11:12) who preach 'another Jesus' and a 'different gospel' from that taught by Paul. This 'gospel' as-

---

[24] For discussion and review of this major subject see Barnett, *Second Corinthians* 32-40.

serted that the old covenant remained current and un-eclipsed and that 'righteousness' with God was fulfilled through the continuing observation of its tenets (in Paul's 'shorthand,' 'Moses'—11:19; cf. 3:9; 5:21).

To whom were these missioners directing their teachings? Since 'circumcision' finds no mention in the letter it seems that their target audience were those Jews who had become Christian believers and who were becoming lax in their observances of Jewish practices.[25] If circumcision and such like matters were merely 'cultural,' matters of relative indifference (as implied by Paul—1 Cor 9:19-23), might these not begin to slip (cf. Acts 21:21). It was difficult being a Jew in the diaspora! Paul's emphasis on a circumcision-free, Law-free Gospel doubtless had its attractions not only for God-fearers, but also for Jews.

Intentionally or otherwise, Cephas' mission to Corinth may have paved the way for the coming of these missioners bent on re-confirming Jewish believers in their Judaism. Cephas' visit to Antioch some years earlier appears to have been followed by the arrival of sterner brothers from Jerusalem, sparking a crisis in Antioch (Gal 2:11-17; Acts 15:1-2, 5). Cephas' very distinction as the leading disciple of Jesus, the prime witness to the resurrection and the apostle to the Land of Israel (Gal 2:7-8) inevitably put Paul down a peg or two. As well, Cephas' separation from table fellowship with Gentile believers in Antioch demonstrated significant differences of emphasis from Paul's. Perhaps Cephas' uncertainty about the integration of Gentiles and Jews in Christ in Corinth prompted him to voice concern elsewhere, issuing in the arrival of counter-missionaries determining on overturning the impact of Paul's mission on Jews.

These newcomers apparently sought to authenticate themselves by 'visions and revelations of the Lord' (12:1) and paranormal speech (5:13). They presented themselves as 'apostles,' indeed as 'superior apostles' (ὑπερλίαν ἀπόστολοι—11:5; 12:11),[26] far 'superior' to Paul. This is not their self-description but Paul's sarcastic tag. Paul responds to their claims with his ironic 'Fool's Speech' accepting but subverting such claims (10-12). By contrast, they say that Paul is 'weak' and inglorious, an assessment readily agreed to in Corinth in view of his

---

[25] So P. Barnett, "Opposition in Corinth," *JSNT* 22 1984, 3-17.

[26] Scholars debate whether or not the 'False Apostles' and the 'Superior Apostles' were one and the same. See Barnett, *Second Corinthians*, 33.

recent 'painful' visit and harsh follow-up letter. How can this man
be an apostle of a glorious Christ (whom he claims to have 'seen'
going to Damascus) when he is such a pitiful bearer of his message?

Paul counters by accusing these men of 'deceit' and 'falsity,' deceit as 'workmen' of the Lord and falsity in their masquerade as
'apostles of Christ' (11:13). In truth they have trespassed into the
'field' (κάνων) that God had marked out for Paul's missionary labours
(10:13, 15-16).

Their claim to 'power' is matched by their allegations of his 'weakness.' In response Paul mostly 'defends' rather than attacks. This he
does by a remarkably sustained argument throughout the length of
the letter. That argument seizes the core teaching of the gospel,
Christ's death (his 'weakness') and Christ's resurrection (his 'power').
Thus God leads his *doomed* captive Paul in *triumph* (2:14). His genuineness is seen not in a display of 'power' but in his fidelity to the
message about Christ but also in faithfully replicating Christ's cru-
ciform-resurrection shaped life (2:15-16). As God by his 'power' raised
the Lord Jesus from the dead so God delivers Paul from various tight
corners in ministry (1:8-11; 12:7-10). An earthen vessel bearing the
light of God's word, yes, but not crushed by adversities (4:7-11). No
stranger himself to 'visions and revelations of the Lord' Paul identifies true 'power' from God resting on him in the 'weakness' of
helplessness in ministry sufferings. He is impaled on a 'stake'
(σκόλοψ—12:7) which is un-removed despite prayer but he finds
'power' to endure through Christ's 'grace.'

Against their assertions of 'power' demonstrated in expressions of
religious or paranormal phenomena, Paul accepts the reality of
'weakness' seen in the pioneer preacher's *thlipseis* that arise from and
continue Christ's 'weakness' in crucifixion. At the same time, however, Paul knows God's resurrection 'power' in deliverance from dire
circumstances (1:8-11; 4:7-11; 12:7-10; 13:4).

2.4 *Apologia*

As Paul concludes his letter he is conscious that it is, in effect, from
first to last an 'apologia' for him and his ministry (12:19). But it is
for their 'up-building' (οἰκοδομή), the completion of the spiritual
superstructure whose 'foundation' he laid some years earlier. Although not using the *typos/mimētēs* vocabulary favoured by him in
the First Letter (4:16; 10:6; 11:1), it is most likely implied. In that

case, Paul's 'apologia' of himself is not ultimately for self-defence, but for their imitation, as Paul in turn modelled his life on Christ's ministry in 'meekness and gentleness' (10:1), his servant mind in crucifixion and resurrection (1 Cor 11:1; 2 Cor 4:5). Thus Paul is exercising his apostolic 'authority' (ἐξουσία) given him by the Lord for the 'up-building' of the churches and not their 'tearing down' (10:8; 13:10).

The Corinthians are able to validate or otherwise Paul's genuineness as an apostle. Let them test themselves. Are they 'in the faith' (13:5—ἐν τῇ πίστει)? If so, as the grammar implies, then this is the divine stamp upon him. Certainly he is confident that he is a true apostle (13:5-7; cf. 12:12).

3. *Conclusion*

In both extant letters to the Corinthians Paul employs the terminology of 'apology' or self-defence. Although the precise need for the 'apologia' differs from letter to letter, there are several continuing issues that prompt his ongoing defence to them.

Due to his tactic of rapid 'foundation laying' then moving on Paul's churches were prone to re-absorption into their cultural environment, whether Graeco-Roman or Jewish, or both.

As well, the assembly of believers in Corinth was affected by visits from very significant persons, the powerful Alexandrian Jew Apollos and Cephas, leading disciple, prime witness to the resurrected Lord and apostle to Eretz Israel. In differing ways these men created uncertainty about Paul that were to affect his relationships with the Corinthians for the next few years.

Apollos' rhetorical abilities raised the profile of 'the wisdom of speech' among unnamed Corinthian preachers. The people in Corinth may have wondered, 'Who, then, is this man Paul whose speech and presence are so unremarkable?' Questions like this may have provoked his sustained pastoral sermon in 1 Cor 1-4.

Paul's second visit necessitated by a local crisis did little to reassure the Corinthians about his effectiveness and leadership. A harsh letter instead of a promised return visit shook the Corinthian confidence in his integrity and capacity. In a sense these problems were a legacy of Apollos' brilliant ministry in Corinth. Perhaps, too, an apparently deepened interest in the *pneumatika* was aroused by Apollos, a man 'fervent in the Spirit.'

Cephas' visit called into question Paul's place among the inner circle of apostles; his vision of the risen Lord was much later and of a different order. They may have asked, 'Is this man truly an apostle, as he claims? Why, then, does he refuse our money, which apostles like Cephas are pleased to receive?' As well, the arrival of this pre-eminent Jewish apostle may have validated further Jewish missioning in the Achaian capital by the shadowy newcomers who appear in the Second Letter. Their intention may have been to retrieve Jewish believers back into a more conservative expression of Judaism.

Paul's self-defence in these two letters is, of course, time-bound by the specific circumstances that necessitated their writing. Yet those apologias are also timeless in their appeal and application.

Against the 'wisdom of words' Paul argued for the centrality of the message of Christ crucified and risen delivered in plain language as the only true 'foundation' and 'building' of the Christian church.

Against the eschatological excitement and attendant world denial and asceticism of the moment Paul steered a middle course urging a realized eschatology consistent with the identity of the Risen One. Against the triumphalist Jewish missioners Paul gives all subsequent sufferers the comfort that the power of God is made perfect in weakness. In opposition to their (likely) under-realized eschatology that confined Jesus to an extant, as yet unfulfilled covenant Paul insisted that the day of salvation had indeed dawned and that it is high time to be reconciled to God, through Christ in whom those who belong to him are already 'the righteousness of God' (2 Cor 5:18-6:2).

In short, Paul's apologetic against his various critics and opponents in Corinth is intrinsic to the theological argument of both letters. The two are inseparable.

THE LEGACY OF 2 CORINTHIANS 12:2-4
IN THE *APOCALYPSE OF PAUL*

Vernon K. Robbins

Biblical interpreters have investigated with great energy and skill Paul's assertions in 2 Corinthians 12:2-4 about a man who was 'caught up into Paradise.'[1] Dr. Margaret E. Thrall, whom it is a privilege to honour with this essay, has contributed substantively to this activity.[2] Paul's comments reach deeply into Jewish and Hellenistic-Roman traditions about journeying into the heavens, and they exhibit many presuppositions in the Mediterranean world about the nature of a person in relation to the heavens.

Rather than focus directly on 2 Cor 12:2-4, this essay will explore the manner in which the third or fourth century author of the *Apocalypse of Paul* created an entire Apocalypse out of these verses.[3] Overall, the essay is an exploration of the manner in which early Christians developed a first century apocalyptic rhetorolect into multiple literary apocalypses from the end of the first century through the fourth centuries C.E.[4] More specifically, the essay investigates the resources

---

[1] The research has been so extensive that it is necessary to be highly selective in the notes. I am grateful to Robert von Thaden for his bibliographical assistance for this essay.

[2] Margaret E. Thrall, "Paul's Journey to Paradise: Some Exegetical Issues in 2 Cor 12,2-4", in *The Corinthian Correspondence* (BETL 125; ed. R. Bieringer; Leuven: University Press, 1996), 345-363; idem, *A Critical and Exegetical Commentary on the Second Epistle to the Corinthians* (2 vols., ICC; Edinburgh: T. & T. Clark, 1994-2000), 2: 772-799.

[3] In recognition of J.K. Elliott's contribution to NT scholarship and this honorary volume, this essay will use the translation of the Latin manuscript of *Apoc. Paul* in J.K. Elliott, *The Apocryphal New Testament: A Collection of Apocryphal Christian Literature in an English Translation based on M.R. James* (Oxford: Clarendon Press, 1993), 616-644. Cf. Martha Himmelfarb, *Tours of Hell: An Apocalyptic Form in Jewish and Christian Literature* (Philadelphia: University of Pennsylvania Press, 1983), 16-19. For an alternative English translation of the Latin text, which includes variants from other manuscript traditions, see H. Duensing, "Apocalypse of Paul", in Hennecke-Schneemelcher (1965), 2:755-798.

[4] For rhetorolect, see Vernon K. Robbins, "The Dialectical Nature of Early Christian Discourse", *Scriptura* 59 (1996) 359-361. Online: http://www.emory.edu/ COLLEGE/RELIGION/faculty/robbins/dialect/dialect353.html; idem, "The Intertexture of Apocalyptic Discourse in the Gospel of Mark", in D.F. Watson

328   VERNON K. ROBBINS

of invention early Christians used to elaborate basic apocalyptic *topoi* through amplificatory description.[5] In addition, the essay explores the creation of a Christian cosmos that inspired Dante's *Inferno*.[6]

Only occasionally do commentaries on 2 Corinthians refer to the *Apocalypse of Paul*. Including this later literature can enrich our insights both into the NT and into early Christian discourse beyond the first century. First, the essay focuses on 'visions and revelations of the Lord' in 2 Cor 12:1. Second, it focuses on 'hearing unutterable words' in 2 Cor 12:4. Third, it focuses on Paul's body and on the journey of souls when they leave the body. The overall goal of the essay is to contribute to an environment for interpreting NT texts that moves down at least to the fourth century c.e.

Visions and Revelations of the Lord

Paul's reference to 'visions and revelations of the Lord' in 2 Cor 12:1 invites many questions. First, does 'the Lord' refer to God or to Christ? Second, if it refers to Christ, is the genitive subjective or objective? Third, if 'the Lord' has, in any sense, an objective function, does it mean that Christ appears directly to Paul? Victor P. Furnish asserts that the reference to the Lord 'is certainly to Christ, as in vv. 7-8.' Christ, and not God, is the originator of the experience, but Christ does not actually appear to Paul.[7] Margaret E. Thrall agrees that 'these could be revelations originating with Christ (with *kuriou* as a genitive of origin), visions bestowed by Christ.' She suggests in addition, following A.T. Lincoln,[8] that we should consider it possible that Paul's statements 'imply a visionary experience of Christ.'[9]

(ed.), *The Intertexture of Apocalyptic Discourse* (Symposium; Leiden: E.J. Brill, 2002) forthcoming.
   [5] Robbins, "The Intertexture of Apocalyptic", forthcoming. There is not space here to investigate the manner in which *Apoc. Paul* elaborates apocalyptic *topoi* by means of argumentative enthymemes.
   [6] Cf. Elliott, Apocryphal New Testament, 616; A. Hilhorst, "A Visit to Paradise: Apocalypse of Paul 45 and Its Background," in *Paradise Interpreted: Representations of Biblical Paradise in Judaism and Christianity* (*Themes in Biblical Narrative, Jewish and Christian Traditions* 2; ed. Gerhard P. Luttikhuizen; Boston: Brill, 1999), 129.
   [7] Victor Paul Furnish, *II Corinthians: Translated with Introduction, Notes, and Commentary* (AB 32A; Garden City, NY: Doubleday, 1984), 524.
   [8] Andrew T. Lincoln, "'Paul the Visionary': The Setting and Significance of the Rapture to Paradise in II Corinthians XII.1-10", *NTS* 25 (1979): 218.
   [9] Thrall, "Paul's Journey", 359; cf. *idem, Commentary*, 774-775.

One might suppose, on the basis of a near consensus in NT scholarship that 'the Lord' in 2 Cor 12:1 refers to Christ, that second through fourth century Christian apocalypses would feature Christ centrally in their writings and this central function would create a context in which 'the Lord' would almost always refer to Christ. Christ is important in *Apoc. Paul*, as we will see below, but it is not the case that the role of Christ produces a predominant use of 'the Lord' for Christ. Rather, most usually in *Apoc. Paul* 'the Lord' refers to the Lord God who made the earth and the heavens and all that is in it.

Apoc. Paul 3 begins with Paul asserting, 'While I was in the body in which I was snatched up to the third heaven, the word of the Lord came to me saying, "Speak to the people,…".' This is a prophetic commissioning that is not unusual in an apocalypse.[10] As in Paul's writings, so here 'the Lord' could refer either to God or to Christ. The introduction refers to 'the shoes in which he [Paul] walked teaching the word of God' (2). Thus, 'the Lord' in 'the word of the Lord' could refer to God. Perhaps the phrase 'the word of the Lord' in *Apoc. Paul* 3 is an intentional merger of 'word of God' with 'word of Christ.' In this case, the Lord God could be the source and the Lord Jesus Christ could be the agent of the word, like Rev 1:1: 'The revelation of Jesus Christ, which God gave him to show to his servants ….'

'The word of the Lord' extends throughout *Apoc. Paul* 3-10.[11] 'The word' opens by commanding Paul to 'Speak to the people' (3) and continues by stating information he is to tell them. At the beginning the word warns against tempting 'the Lord who made you,' calls humans 'sons of God,' accuses people of doing works of the devil in the 'faith of Christ,' and asserts that humans sin against God while all other creatures serve God (3). This means that the only other use of 'the Lord' in the opening context refers to God. As *Apoc. Paul* 4-7 continues, four times the narration refers to 'the Lord' in contexts where the subsequent speech or narration indicates that the reference is to 'the Lord God Almighty.' In *Apoc. Paul* 9, the voice of God explains to the angels who oversee righteous people who hunger and

---

[10] Cf. 1 Enoch 14:24: And the Lord called me with his own mouth and said to me, 'Come near to me, Enoch, and to my holy Word'. See G.W.E. Nickelsburg, *1 Enoch 1* (Hermeneia; Minneapolis: Fortress Press, 2001), 254-256.

[11] There is a shift in narration at 8, but 'the word' ends with the final sentence in 10.

thirst because of God's name that God's grace is appointed to them
(the angels), and God's help, who is God's well-beloved Son, 'shall
be present with them [the suffering righteous], guiding them every
hour; ministering also to them, never deserting them, since their place
is his [the Son's] habitation.' When the discourse refers to Christ, it
uses the term God's Son, rather than 'the Lord'. In the context of
the opening 'word', then, when the discourse refers to Christ, it uses
the term 'Son' rather than Lord.[12]

The cosmic interests of *Apoc. Paul*, like the cosmic interests of the
Revelation to John, keep 'the Lord God' in a place of prominence.
The Lord Jesus Christ is a highly important personage, but he functions in the context of the power of the Lord God Almighty who
created all things. In other words, this apocalyptic discourse does
not emphasize the role of the Lord Jesus Christ as the agent of
creation, in the manner of precreation discourse.[13] Rather, God is
the source of creation, and Christ is a primary agent of its redemption through the grace of God which has brought forth the suffering, death, and resurrection of the beloved Son.[14] 'The Lord' in 2
Cor 12:1 probably refers to Christ, since it follows the statement about
'the God and Father of the Lord Jesus' in 2 Cor 11:31. In *Apoc. Paul*
3, in contrast, the originator of 'the word of the Lord' probably is
the Lord God Almighty. As we will see, the Lord Jesus Christ remains at a distance from Paul throughout the composition, never
appearing directly to Paul or speaking directly to him. It is possible,
of course, that Christ still could be perceived by the reader to be
the transmitter of God's word to Paul in *Apoc. Paul 3*. One cannot
automatically presume, however, that 'the Lord' refers to Christ
rather than to the Lord God.

As the narration proceeds, the term Lord occurs in the phrase 'the
Lord Jesus Christ' in *Apoc. Paul* 21. While moving down from the
third heaven to the great ocean, the angel tells Paul that 'the Lord
Jesus Christ, the King Eternal' will come to reign over his saints for
a thousand years in the land of promise, which will appear when

---

[12] *Apoc. Paul* 11, 12 use 'the Lord' when referring to the potential helper for
the wicked souls, which one would expect from 9 to refer to Christ.

[13] Vernon K. Robbins, "Argumentative Textures in Socio-Rhetorical Interpretation", in *Rhetorical Argumentation in Biblical Texts: Essays from the 2000 Lund Conference* (ed. A. Eriksson, T.H. Olbricht, and W. Übelacker; *Emory Studies in Early
Christianity*; Harrisburg: Trinity Press International, 2002), 54-63; cf. idem, "The
Dialectical Nature", 359-361.

[14] *Apoc. Paul* 44.

the first earth is dissolved. This differs from Rev 20:4-6; 21:2, where the thousand years of Christ's reign occurs before the first earth passes away (Rev 21:1).

In *Apoc. Paul*, 'the land of promise' exists outside of heaven, beyond the great ocean; and it is the realm of 'the light of heaven which lightens all the earth' (21). Prior to the appearance of the land of promise, souls of the just are dismissed to this place for a while when they have gone out of the body. References to 'the meek who shall inherit the earth' (Matt 5:5) and to 'those who hunger and thirst after righteousness' (Matt 5:6) in *Apoc. Paul* 21-22 suggest that Matthean conceptions of 'the kingdom prepared for you from the foundation of the world' (Matt 25:34) play a role in the function of the land of promise in *Apoc. Paul*.

As a result of a primary focus on the third heaven (2 Cor 12:2) and Paradise (2 Cor 12:3) in some scholarship on *Apoc. Paul*, there is not always a clear focus on the land of promise.[15] In *Apoc. Paul* 21, Paul explains that 'the beginning of the foundation' of the land of promise is 'on the river which waters all the earth,' which is the great ocean. One gets there by going down from the third heaven through the second heaven to the firmament and over the gates of heaven to the great ocean, where one sees the foundation of the land of promise (21). From the perspective of *Apoc. Paul*, this land would have been created on 'the face of the waters' when God said, 'Let there be light' (Gen 1:2-3). In other words, the light God created and separated from darkness (Gen 1:3-4) is a realm of light with its foundation on the great ocean. This realm was created before God created the heavens and the earth in the midst of the great ocean, with the ocean surrounding all of the heavens and earth (Gen 1:7-10). The realm of light with its foundation on the great ocean constitutes 'the land of promise' that will appear only when the present earth passes away (*Apoc. Paul* 21).[16] In *Apoc. Paul*, this land is the special kingdom God has given to Christ (Luke 22:29), which the righteous inherit through Christ (Matt 25:34).[17]

---

[15] Cf. Hilhorst, "*Apocalypse of Paul* 15", 138.

[16] For the relation of this description of the cosmos in *Apoc. Paul* to Babylonian and early Greek cosmographies, see Nickelsburg, *1 Enoch 1*, 282-283. *Apoc. Paul* envisions the land of promise as one of regions beyond the river Oceanus.

[17] It appears that the land of promise in *Apoc. Paul* is an insertion of the Matthean 'kingdom prepared for you' (Matt 25:34) into traditional apocalyptic cosmographies. This accounts for much of the overlap and confusion about the relation of the land of promise to Paradise in *Apoc. Paul*.

References to Christ become frequent when the angel takes Paul
to 'the City of Christ,' which is by the Acherusian Lake in the land
of promise (*Apoc. Paul* 22-30).[18] The angel explains to Paul that a
journey into this city leads to God, so not everyone is permitted to
enter it (22).[19] If a person is a fornicator and impious, but has converted and is repentant, when the person first goes out of the body,
that person is taken to worship God. After the person worships God,
by 'command of the Lord' (read 'God') the person is delivered to
the angel Michael, who baptizes the person in the Acherusian Lake.
Then Michael leads the person into the City of Christ alongside
people who have never sinned (22).

During Paul's journey through the City of Christ, he does not see
Christ. The reason is that 'Christ the Son of God sits at the right
hand of his Father' in the seventh heaven (29), and the City of Christ
is in the land of promise outside of heaven. After the angel takes
Paul throughout all the land of promise, including the City of Christ
within it, he leads Paul outside this region, over 'the ocean which
supports the foundations of heaven' toward the outer limit in the
direction of the setting sun (31). There Paul sees the place of darkness, which existed before God created light (Gen 1:2) and which
God separated from the light after creating the light (Gen 1:4). All
kinds of sinners dwell in the place where all is darkness, sorrow and
sadness, and the angel takes Paul to see all of them (*Apoc. Paul* 31-
43). This is the outer darkness where the unrighteous 'weep and gnash
their teeth' (16, 42).[20] Paul weeps and cries out at various times when
he sees the punishments the sinners are enduring (33, 39, 40, 42).

Finally, when Paul is fully in the north he looks to the west and
sees men and women in extreme cold and snow 'who say that Christ
did not rise from the dead and that this flesh will not rise again' (42).
When Paul stretches out his hands, weeps, and sighs, 'It were bet-

---

[18] For the Acherusian Lake, see Nickelsburg, *1 Enoch 1*, 283. For *Apoc. Paul*,
the kingdom over which Christ is in charge (Matt 25:34) is currently a 'land' located beyond the river Oceanus in which the subterranean Acherusian Lake flows
to the surface.

[19] There is a direct mode of access between the seventh heaven, where God is,
and the City of Christ, which is perceived to be in a region 'below' the heavens.
Thus, the angel explains to Paul: David sings psalms before him [God] in the seventh
heaven, and as it is done in the heavens so also below [in the land of promise] ...
as it is performed in heaven, so also on earth [the new earth, which is the land of
promise].

[20] Cf. Matt 8:12; 13:42, 50; 22:13; 25:30.

ter for us if we had not been born, all of us who are sinners,' the people see Paul weeping with the angel, and they cry out, 'Lord God have mercy upon us!' (43). At this point, Paul sees the heavens open and the archangel Michael descend with 'the whole army of angels.' Michael tells the sinners that he prays unceasingly for the entire human race, and he asks them to weep with him, and he will weep with them, the angels and 'the well-beloved Paul.' When the people weep and cry out, 'Have pity on us, Son of God!', Paul prays, 'O Lord God! Have pity on your creation, have pity on the sons of men, have pity on your own image' (43).

When Paul prays to God, he sees the heaven move 'like a tree shaken by the wind,' which allows him to see the throne room of God (44). In addition to seeing twenty-four elders and the four beasts,[21] Paul hears a voice that asks why God's angels and ministers intercede for humans. When the angels answer that they see God's many kindnesses to the human race, Paul sees 'the Son of God descending from heaven' with a diadem on his head (44). When all the people in punishment cry out to the 'Son of the High God' to have pity on them, a voice goes out from the Son of God telling the people of his suffering on the cross. Then the voice of Christ tells them that for the sake of Michael the archangel, Paul the well-beloved, their brethren in the world, their sons, and for the sake of his own kindness, he gives all people in punishment 'a night and a day of refreshment forever,' i.e., a 'sabbath' rest every seventh day (44).[22] After the sinners cry out, 'We bless you, Son of God …,' the evil angels assert that the sinners received this great grace simply 'for the sake of Paul the well-beloved of God who descended to you' (44). After this episode, Christ does not appear again in *Apoc. Paul.*

In sum, Christ does not appear directly to Paul in *Apoc. Paul.* Paul is not taken before the throne of God, nor does he see a vision of Christ seated at God's right hand.[23] Paul sees the throne of God at a distance, and he sees Christ at a distance, observes the gracious-

---

[21] Cf. Rev. 4:4-6.

[22] There are strong arguments that the source of this concept of 'sabbath' rest is rabbinic tradition: I. Lévi, "Le repos sabbatique des âmes damnées", *Revue des études juives* 25 (1892), 1-13; T. Silverstein, *Visio Sancti Pauli: The History of the Apocalypse in Latin together with Nine Texts* (Studies and Documents 4; London, 1935), 79, 124, n. 96); cf. Himmelfarb, *Tours of Hell*, 17.

[23] Contrast J.D. Tabor, *Things Unutterable: Paul's Ascent to Paradise in its Greco-Roman, Judaic, and Early Christian Contexts* (Studies in Judaism; Lanham, MD: University Press of America, 1986), 123-124; cf. Thrall, "Paul's Journey", 359.

ness of Christ's approach to sinners, and evokes a response of mercy
from Christ for sinners. Paul does not see Christ in the third heaven,
and he does not see Christ in the land of promise, which is the place
of light in which the City of Christ is located. However, when Paul
visits the place of darkness, sees all the suffering there, and responds
to it with weeping and prayer to God, the heavens open and he sees
the descent of the archangel Michael with a multitude of angels and,
after a while, the descent of the Son of God with a diadem on his
head. The function both of Michael and of Christ are redemptive,
relieving the suffering of sinners in the place of darkness. Paul's
weeping, sighing, stretching out of his hands, and praying to God
plays a role in calling forth the actions of kindness by God, by
Michael and by Christ.

Utterances Forbidden to Express

It has already become clear that *Apoc. Paul* features Paul seeing many
things as well as hearing many things. According to Paul in 2 Cor
12:4, the experience of the journey into the third heaven was auditory, but Thrall and others observe that Paul's experience had to
be visual as well as auditory.[24] It is interesting that the opening
paragraphs of *Apoc.Paul* (3-10) focus on Paul's hearing 'the word of
the Lord.' 'The word of the Lord' instructs Paul to ask the people
how long they will continue with their transgressions, their sins and
their tempting of God. Paul is to tell them that they are sons of God,
but they are doing the works of the devil in the faith of Christ. Every
creature serves God, but humans sin against God 'more than all
nature' (3). 'The word' continues by recounting instances where
creation has pleaded with God to do something to deal with the
impieties and injustices of the human race. The sun often addressed
God about it (4); so did the moon and stars (5), and the sea and the
earth (6).[25] God responded to all of them that his eye sees and his
ear hears, but his 'patience bears with them until they be converted
and repent' (4, 5, 6 [2]). After this sequence, the section explains
the special arrangement in the cosmos for humans, since they are

---

[24] Thrall, "Paul's Journey", 359; but see her comment that 'He focuses exclusively on the "word character" of the event' in *idem, Commentary*, 545.

[25] Cf. 1 Enoch 5:6, where the earth complains about the lawless ones in the
universe.

the only ones in the world who sin. Every evening when the sun sets
and twelve hours later when morning begins, all the angels go to
God, worship God, and recount all the deeds of humans to God.
'The word' reaches an initial conclusion with: 'To you, therefore,
I say, you sons of men, bless the Lord God without fail all the days
of your life' (7).

Up to *Apoc. Paul 7*, Paul has only heard things. But these are not
unutterable things. They are things he is commanded to speak to
the people. This 'word' introduces all the events in *Apoc. Paul*, for
the overall text deals with the sins of humans and the manner in
which God deals with humans who sin and those who do not. *Apoc.
Paul* 8-10 appears to be a continuation of 'the word of the Lord,'
but it is transitional. The description of action by 'the word' moves
into narration that seems to describe things Paul actually sees. At
the appointed hour, all the angels come to God, worship God, and
report the deeds of the humans to which they have been appointed.
Thus, when 'the word' ends with 'Know therefore, sons of men, that
whatever things are wrought by you, these angels report to God,
whether it is good or evil' (10), the narration has already moved
beyond 'hearing alone' to both hearing and seeing.

While *Apoc. Paul* begins with direct command to Paul to speak
things to the people, there is a context in which Paul encounters
'unutterable things.' The geography of the heavens appears to be
the controlling factor for the presentation, for it is only when Paul
is in Paradise that he hears things 'it is not lawful for a person to
speak' (21). According to *Apoc. Paul* 3, Paul had been 'snatched up
to the third heaven' when the word of the Lord came to him. This,
however, is not Paradise. In 11, the angel leads Paul 'into heaven,'[26]
where he is able both to look back upon the firmament and to look
on high (11-12). Only in 19 does the angel lead Paul to the gate of
Paradise in the third heaven. When Paul enters, Enoch meets him
and hails him as 'Paul, beloved of God,' then Elijah meets him and
expresses a wish that Paul receive great rewards for his labours on
behalf of the human race (20). At this point the angel tells Paul he
is to 'tell no one on earth' both what he sees and what he hears.
Paul reports that he 'heard words which it is not lawful to speak'
(2 Cor 12:4), then the narrative continues with the angel telling him

---

[26] Presumably Paul was simply at the opening of the third heaven, rather than
actually 'in it.'

he will show him what he 'ought to report in public and relate' (21).
The scene is similar in some respects to the angel's command to John
in Rev 10:4 not to write down the content of the seven thunders.
John does not write the content of the thunders, but continues with
a description of the unfolding events, just as he has been told to write
them down in Rev 1:11.

In summary, there is no hint in *Apoc. Paul* concerning the content
of the 'unutterable things' Paul heard in Paradise. Furnish's suggestion that he may have heard the utterance of the divine name,[27] while
interesting in relation to Merkabah visions,[28] receives no support from
Apoc. Paul, since there is no emphasis on God or mysteries of God
in relation to Paradise. Some say there would be a vision of God or
Christ in Paradise, but there is no support for this in *Apoc. Paul*. God
and Christ are in the seventh heaven, and not in Paradise.

In the Body or Outside the Body

It is fascinating that 2 Cor 12:2 exhibits Paul raising the issue whether
he was 'in the body or outside the body'. Furnish might well be
correct to suppose 'that a bodiless journey would have been inconceivable to Paul'.[29] Paul's initial statement in *Apoc. Paul* skillfully
avoids the issue by referring to 'the body in which I was snatched
up to the third heaven' (3).[30] There is no indication in *Apoc. Paul*
that Paul has an unusual body on his journey. He follows the angel, speaks to the angel, looks all around, weeps, sighs and prays.
Enoch recognizes, embraces and kisses Paul when he comes into
Paradise, and Elijah recognizes him as well (20). But *Apoc. Paul*
describes similar actions on behalf of souls that have come out of
the body when the body has died. For *Apoc. Paul*, earthly people taken
into heaven and souls that leave the body at the point of death
function in basically the same ways in heaven, namely, like normal
bodies.

The topic of being 'outside the body' emerges in *Apoc. Paul* 13,

---

[27] Furnish, *II Corinthians*, 545; cf. Thrall, *Commentary*, 795.
[28] J.W. Bowker, "'Merkabah' Visions and the Visions of Paul", *Journal of Semitic Studies* 16 (1971): 157-173.
[29] Furnish, *II Corinthians*, 545.
[30] Based on the Latin manuscript translated in Elliott, *Apocryphal New Testament*, 620, but different from the wording translated by Duensing, 'Apocalypse', 760 (but see n. 2).

when Paul tells the angel he would like to see 'the souls of the just
and of sinners going out of the world'. When the angel tells Paul
simply to look down on the earth, Paul explains that he would like
to see the manner in which the souls of the just and of sinners 'go
out of the body' (14). Just at that moment a just man was about to
die, so Paul watches the process. First, all the works the man did
for the sake of God, and all his remembered and unremembered
desires, stand in the man's sight in the hour of his need. Both holy
and impious angels approach the soul, but the impious angels can
find 'no place of habitation in it', since it is the soul of a just man.
Holy angels guide the soul out of the body and rouse it by instructing it to remember the body it is leaving, because it must return to
the same body on the day of resurrection to receive the things promised to the just. The angels kiss the soul, as if it were familiar to them
and tell it to be of good courage, since it has done the will of God
while on earth. Also, 'the spirit' meets the soul and tells it not to be
afraid or disturbed, because 'I found in you a place of refreshment
in the time when I dwelt in you, while I was on earth'. The spirit
strengthens the soul, and 'his angel' receives it and leads it into
heaven.

While another angel taunts the soul for daring to enter heaven,
the angel and the spirit of the soul lead it to worship in the sight of
God. When it ceases worshipping, Michael and all the army of angels
worship God and tell the soul, 'This is your God of all things, who
made you in his own image and likeness'. Both the angel and the
spirit run ahead to God and remind God about the good works of
the soul which they have reported daily. The voice of God tells
Michael, the angel of the Covenant, to lead the soul into 'the Paradise of Joy', that it may become co-heir with all the saints. This brings
forth hymns and glorifying of God (the Lord) from all the angels and
archangels, the cherubim, and the twenty-four elders. At this point,
the angel asks Paul if he has 'believed and known that whatever each
man of you has done he sees in the hour of need,' and Paul answers,
'Yes, sir' (14). When an unjust man dies, the soul experiences rejec-
tion in the midst of a reminder of all the things that happen daily
with God, and finally it is sent into outer darkness for 'weeping and
gnashing of teeth' (15-16). When another unjust man dies, the angel is told that if he had repented five years before it died, he would
have indulgence and remission of sins. When none of this happens,
this man also is sent to outer darkness (17-18).

In summary, a major difference in *Apoc. Paul* between being in the body and outside the body seems to lie in the function of the person's enlivening spirit. When a person is 'in the body', the spirit finds rest in the body. This means that only the angel who is assigned to the person, and not his spirit, confronts the person while he is in the body. Once the person is out of the body, if the person is just, both his angel and his spirit confront him, encourage him, lead him, care for him and plead his case before God. If a person is evil, his spirit rejects the soul, because it did not follow the spirit's will (16).[31]

Conclusion

The major players in *Apoc. Paul* are humans and angels. They are the 'workers' in the world. The task of humans on a daily basis is to produce good deeds, but, in overwhelming proportions, they produce evil deeds. The task of angels is to observe the deeds of humans and report them every evening and morning to God. A significant amount of God's work lies in the past when God created the universe and all that is in it. But God also has very special daily tasks: (1) to be present on the throne to be worshipped; (2) to listen to the morning and evening reports by the angels of the activities of individual humans; (3) to make decisions whether a soul who has been brought to the throne after leaving the body should be delivered to Michael (14), who will take it to Paradise, or to Tartaruchus (16) or Tartarus (18), who will take it to the outer darkness.

The archangel Michael, as we have seen, also is busy. He must be present whenever a soul comes to God, in case this is a person who should be taken into Paradise. In addition, he says he prays unceasingly for all humans (43). At certain times he descends from heaven to perform special tasks for the benefit of humans (43).

Christ performed very special work in the past for humans (44). Christ responded to special intercessory prayer by Paul for sinful human beings (43-44). Christ regularly sits at the right hand of God in the seventh heaven (29). Perhaps especially in this role God calls him 'my helper' (9).[32] In the future when the earth dissolves, Christ

---

[31] Thus, 'the spirit is willing but the flesh is weak', i.e., not willing to do what the spirit wills.

[32] References throughout to 'the helper' of people do not always appear to refer to Christ, but perhaps they do.

will come with all his saints to the land of promise and reign over his saints for a thousand years in it (21).

The weeping and mourning of the angels and Paul, in the sight of the suffering and weeping of the unrighteous, are special features in *Apoc. Paul*. In some ways, the entire apocalypse is a lamentation over the sins of humans in the world. There are, however, extended moments of joy, in particular in the City of Christ when noteworthy people within the history of Israel greet Paul and bless him (25-27).[33] There is special emphasis on the manner in which Paul empathizes with the sinfulness of humans, and his identification of himself as a sinner plays a key role in causing both Michael and Christ to respond with mercy to the suffering of sinners (42).

Apoc. Paul does not express rebellion or disobedience beyond the human race that threatens the order of the universe, in contrast to phenomena of disobedience or disruption of order as described in 1 Enoch 18-21 or 80:2-8. Rather, the universe appears to function in *Apoc. Paul* as it should, in accordance with 1 Enoch 2:1-5:3 or 72-82. Evil desires in humans produce unrighteousness without any help from Satan or Satan's helpers. Evil, fierce angels do what they are supposed to do, namely, torment and punish the souls of unrighteous people when they come out of the body. In this apocalypse, then, focus on desires and disobedience within humans consumes the focus in many earlier apocalypses on dramatic acts of God that would end one age and begin a new one. It appears that the principalities and powers in the universe have truly become subservient to God and Christ (Col 2:15), overseeing the deeds of humans every moment of their lives both in the body and outside the body. How appropriate for Paul, then, knowing the man who was caught up to the third heaven, and into Paradise, to boast of nothing but his weaknesses (2 Cor 12:5). In later tradition, as exhibited in *Apoc. Paul*, Paul's awareness of his own weaknesses allows him to identify with the sinfulness of humans throughout the world and intercede on their behalf with God and Christ.

---

[33] Also in the second visit to Paradise in 45-51, which is only in the longer Latin recension.

INDEX OF THEMES

INDEX OF SCRIPTURAL REFERENCES

OLD TESTAMENT

NEW TESTAMENT

SUPPLEMENTS TO NOVUM TESTAMENTUM

ISSN 0167-9732

69. Newman, C.C. *Paul's Glory-Christology*. Tradition and Rhetoric. 1992. ISBN 90 04 09463 6
70. Ireland, D.J. *Stewardship and the Kingdom of God*. An Historical, Exegetical, and Contextual Study of the Parable of the Unjust Steward in Luke 16: 1-13. 1992. ISBN 90 04 09600 0
71. Elliott, J.K. *The Language and Style of the Gospel of Mark*. An Edition of C.H. Turner's "Notes on Marcan Usage" together with other comparable studies. 1993. ISBN 90 04 09767 8
72. Chilton, B. *A Feast of Meanings*. Eucharistic Theologies from Jesus through Johannine Circles. 1994. ISBN 90 04 09949 2
73. Guthrie, G.H. *The Structure of Hebrews*. A Text-Linguistic Analysis. 1994. ISBN 90 04 09866 6
74. Bormann, L., K. Del Tredici & A. Standhartinger (eds.) *Religious Propaganda and Missionary Competition in the New Testament World*. Essays Honoring Dieter Georgi. 1994. ISBN 90 04 10049 0
75. Piper, R.A. (ed.) *The Gospel Behind the Gospels*. Current Studies on Q. 1995. ISBN 90 04 09737 6
76. Pedersen, S. (ed.) *New Directions in Biblical Theology*. Papers of the Aarhus Conference, 16-19 September 1992. 1994. ISBN 90 04 10120 9
77. Jefford, C.N. (ed.) *The* Didache *in Context*. Essays on Its Text, History and Transmission. 1995. ISBN 90 04 10045 8
78. Bormann, L. *Philippi – Stadt und Christengemeinde zur Zeit des Paulus*. 1995. ISBN 90 04 10232 9
79. Peterlin, D. *Paul's Letter to the Philippians in the Light of Disunity in the Church*. 1995. ISBN 90 04 10305 8
80. Jones, I.H. *The Matthean Parables*. A Literary and Historical Commentary. 1995. ISBN 90 04 10181 0
81. Glad, C.E. *Paul and Philodemus*. Adaptability in Epicurean and Early Christian Psychagogy. 1995. ISBN 90 04 10067 9
82. Fitzgerald, J.T. (ed.) *Friendship, Flattery, and Frankness of Speech*. Studies on Friend-ship in the New Testament World. 1996. ISBN 90 04 10454 2
83. Tilborg, S. van. *Reading John in Ephesus*. 1996. 90 04 10530 1
84. Holleman, J. *Resurrection and Parousia*. A Traditio-Historical Study of Paul's Eschatology in 1 Corinthians 15. 1996. ISBN 90 04 10597 2
85. Moritz, T. *A Profound Mystery*. The Use of the Old Testament in Ephesians. 1996. ISBN 90 04 10556 5
86. Borgen, P. *Philo of Alexandria - An Exegete for His Time*. 1997. ISBN 90 04 10388 0
87. Zwiep, A.W *The Ascension of the Messiah in Lukan Christology*. 1997. ISBN 90 04 10897 1
88. Wilson, W.T. *The Hope of Glory*. Education and Exhortation in the Epistle to the Colossians. 1997. ISBN 90 04 10937 4
89. Peterson, W.L., J.S. Vos & H.J. de Jonge (eds.) *Sayings of Jesus: Canonical and Non-Canonical*. Essays in Honour of Tjitze Baarda. 1997. ISBN 90 04 10380 5

90. Malherbe, A.J., F.W. Norris & J.W. Thompson (eds.). *The Early Church in Its Context*. Essays in Honor of Everett Ferguson. 1998. ISBN 90 04 10832 7

91. Kirk, A. *The Composition of the Sayings Source*. Genre, Synchrony, and Wisdom Redaction in Q. 1998. ISBN 90 04 11085 2

92. Vorster, W.S. *Speaking of Jesus*. Essays on Biblical Language, Gospel Narrative and the Historical Jesus. Edited by J. E. Botha. 1999. ISBN 90 04 10779 7

93. Bauckham, R. *The Fate of Dead*. Studies on the Jewish and Christian Apocalypses. 1998. ISBN 90 04 11203 0

94. Standhartinger, A. *Studien zur Entstehungsgeschichte und Intention des Kolosserbriefs*. ISBN 90 04 11286 3

95. Oegema, G.S. *Für Israel und die Völker*. Studien zum alttestamentlich-jüdischen Hintergrund der paulinischen Theologie. 1999. ISBN 90 04 11297 9

96. Albl, M.C. *"And Scripture Cannot Be Broken"*. The Form and Function of the Early Christian *Testimonia* Collections. 1999. ISBN 90 04 11417 3

97. Ellis, E.E. *Christ and the Future in New Testament History*. 1999. ISBN 90 04 11533 1

98. Chilton, B. & C.A. Evans, (eds.) *James the Just and Christian Origins*. 1999. ISBN 90 04 11550 1

99. Horrell, D.G. & C.M. Tuckett (eds.) *Christology, Controversy and Community*. New Testament Essays in Honour of David R. Catchpole. 2000. ISBN 90 04 11679 6

100. Jackson-McCabe, M.A. *Logos and Law in the Letter of James*. The Law of Nature, the Law of Moses and the Law of Freedom. 2001. ISBN 90 04 11994 9

101. Wagner, J.R. *Heralds of the Good News*. Isaiah and Paul "In Concert" in the Letter to the Romans 2002. ISBN 90 04 11691 5

102. Cousland, J.R.C. *The Crowds in the Gospel of Matthew*. 2002. ISBN 90 04 12177 3

103. Dunderberg, I., C. Tuckett and K. Syreeni. *Fair Play: Diversity and Conflicts in Early Christianity*. Essays in Honour of Heikki Räisänen. 2002. ISBN 90 04 12359 8

104. Mount, C. *Pauline Christianity*. Luke-Acts and the Legacy of Paul. 2002. ISBN 90 04 12472 1

105. Matthews, C.R. *Philip: Apostle and Evangelist*. Configurations of a Tradition. 2002. ISBN 90 04 12054 8

106. Aune, D.E., T. Seland, J.H. Ulrichsen (eds.) *Neotestamentica et Philonica*. Studies in Honor of Peder Borgen. 2002. ISBN 90 04 126104

107. Talbert, C.H. *Reading Luke-Acts in its Mediterranean Milieu*. 2003. ISBN 90 04 12964 2

108. Klijn, A.F.J. *The Acts of Thomas*. Introduction, Text, and Commentary. Second revised edition. 2003. ISBN 90 04 12937 5

109. Burke, T.J. & J.K. Elliott (eds.). *Paul and the Corinthians*. Studies on a Community in Conflict. Essays in Honour of Margaret Thrall. 2003. ISBN 90 04 12920 0

110. Fitzgerald, J.T. *Early Christianity and Classical Culture*. Comparative Studies in Honor of Abraham J. Malherbe. 2003. ISBN 90 04 13022 5